Parenting for Primates

Parenting
for Primates

HARRIET J. SMITH

HARVARD UNIVERSITY PRESS

CAMBRIDGE, MASSACHUSETTS, AND LONDON, ENGLAND   2005

Library of Congress Cataloging-in-Publication Data

Smith, Harriet J.
Parenting for primates / Harriet J. Smith.
  p. cm.
Includes bibliographical references (p.).
ISBN 0-674-01938-5 (hardcover : alk. paper)
1. Parenting.   2. Primates—Behavior.
3. Parental behavior in animals.   I. Title.
HQ755.8.S6328 2005
306.874—dc22   2005050235

Designed by Gwen Nefsky Frankfeldt

FOR RACHEL AND JUSTINE

two wonderful primate kids

Contents

Illustrations

Parenting for Primates

Prologue

IT was a steamy night in Tucson, Arizona, in July 1976. I was soundly asleep in my two-room graduate student apartment when I was awakened by bloodcurdling screams. I ran into the living room and turned on the light. An adult pair of monkeys were careering frantically around their cage making ear-piercing distress calls. I also heard a very high-pitched whine and saw one tiny baby monkey, smaller and lighter than an egg, clutching the wire on the bottom of the cage. The other new baby, its twin, was hanging on for dear life to the back of its mother, Cassie. Cassie acted as though she was terrified of the infant and did not recognize that it was her baby. The father appeared similarly panicked and clung screaming to the side of the cage. Desperate to get the baby off her back, Cassie finally succeeded in flinging it to the bottom of the cage. Heart pounding, I reached into the cage and plucked the two infants to safety. This was the first of many times over the next 7 years that I would rescue and raise cottontop tamarin infants born into my colony.

How can something so *natural* as parenting feel so unnatural? And shouldn't we expect that a species of monkey whose brain weighs less than a third of an ounce would instinctively know how to parent? In my interactions with my clients in my practice as a clinical psychologist, I have become aware that many people feel that they should somehow automatically know how to parent—that maternal (or paternal) instincts lurk within us, waiting for the right opportunity to emerge. Then our first child arrives and we discover to our chagrin that knowing how to care for an infant is neither automatic nor obvious.

Over the last 30 years, I have trained as a primatologist and clinical psychologist, raised 2 daughters and over 50 monkeys, and treated hundreds of patients in my counseling practice. All these experiences have shaped my ideas about parenting.

I grew up in the 1950s, the youngest of three sisters in what was then considered to be a traditional family. Dad was the breadwinner and Mom was in charge of the house and kids. My parents never questioned this division of labor and it worked well for them. Rather than helping around the house, my sisters and I were simply expected to do well in school and stay out of trouble. Our parents assumed that we would grow up to be responsible, upstanding citizens, although like most parents, they offered little in the way of formal training.

As a little girl, my ambition was to be a mommy, but as a college freshman, I was no longer sure what I wanted to be. A friend convinced me to take an introductory anthropology course with her to satisfy a science requirement, assuring me that we wouldn't even have to listen from the back row of the 900-seat auditorium if we didn't feel like it. Midway through the semester, the instructor showed us a movie on baboon behavior. I was suddenly transfixed—utterly fascinated by the complex social world of baboons. I immediately decided that a career in primatology was the only acceptable option for me.

As a graduate student I remained fascinated with the behavior of nonhuman primates. I earned a Ph.D. in comparative psychology, which allowed me to work with many different species of nonhuman primates. Most fortuitously, I had the opportunity to work with cottontop tamarins, a tiny, high-strung species of New World monkey. My major professor at the University of Arizona, Dr. James King, was studying reflex development in a variety of primates when I joined his laboratory, and he put me in charge of data collection for a set of newborn cottontop tamarin triplets. Each baby weighed only a little over an ounce and fit snugly into the palm of my hand. I brought home these tiny creatures with the Mr. Spock ears to live on my parents' kitchen table for the next few months, since I needed to collect data on them every day.

The baby cottontops initially needed to be bottle-fed every two hours during the day and night. I left them in a small cage by my bed and set my alarm to make sure I didn't miss a feeding. When I realized that I naturally awoke to their soft cries, I discarded the alarm and fed them on demand. As I ministered to these three little monkeys, I began to learn a lot about raising babies and the meaning of the term "unconditional love."

Soon though it became clear that cottontops made poor subjects for learning studies, and our laboratory was at a loss as to what to do with them. This was before cottontops were declared an endangered species, and there were literally no rules about how to dispose of un-wanted research subjects. I had already decided to keep the triplets I had raised and reasoned that a few more monkeys wouldn't measur-ably increase the chaos at home. By that time I was no longer living in my parents' house, to my mother's considerable relief. By 1975, I had a colony of 6 adult tamarins. I paired the males and females and they (and their descendants) have produced more than 50 babies over the last 30 years. These monkeys taught me many lessons about parenting, some of which I share in this book. They also taught me that monkeys, like other wild creatures, should not be kept as pets. Cute baby primates mature into aggressive, unpredictable adults and are extremely difficult to care for properly in captivity.

As a graduate student, I thought that nonhuman and human pri-mates couldn't be more different, and I was far more interested in learning about the former than the latter. Over time, however, I be-came more intrigued with the similarities between human and non-human primates than the differences. I returned to school in 1982 and earned a post-graduate degree in clinical psychology from George Washington University. I became a clinical psychologist with a colony of monkeys in her back yard, who thought about her cases from a different perspective than that adopted by most of her col-leagues. I found myself becoming an observer of human behavior, delighting in those occasions when my understanding of nonhuman primates enriched my ability to understand my human clients.

In examining my clinical cases over the last 8 years, I have found that although some clients come to see me about parenting issues, many are unaware of or initially reluctant to discuss difficulties they are having with childrearing. During the first session, most adult clients focus on a problem they are having with their partner or themselves. Only when asked about their children do clients begin to reveal the parenting problems that may be connected to or even the source of the marital discord. Parenting issues often become a significant focus of treatment, and their resolution may be crucial to achieving a successful outcome.

How often does this scenario occur? In about 50 percent of adult patients I see that have children under the age of 18 living at home, parenting issues emerge and are added to the treatment agenda. In addition, adults with dependent children, in single- and two-parent homes, are almost twice as likely to seek my services as are individuals or couples without children. In families with young children, there are simply more people jockeying to get their needs met, which paves the way for increased conflict and emotional distress. It is also not unusual for parents with grown children to seek help with parenting issues, whether their children continue to live in the family home or elsewhere. Although we hope for good relationships with our adult children, this outcome is far from automatic.

In therapy, my clients and I often find that exploring the past helps us understand the present. For example, if a client tells me that regular whippings are the best way to keep his children in line, I will ask him where that belief came from. He often tells me that he is repeating the tried-and-true formula that his parents used with him. Even when we promise ourselves as children never to make the same mistakes our parents did, we often find ourselves unconsciously repeating destructive behaviors with our own children. We can't help learning from our parents how to interact with our children, because our parents are our first and most important teachers. And our parents couldn't help learning from *their* parents, and so on, throughout our family history. In this way, both healthy and problem behaviors pass from generation to generation.

Psychologists seek to uncover and help clients to understand these generational patterns, but seldom look beyond a generation or two. What I hope to do in this book is to look back even further, to the parenting behavior of our closest living relatives, the nonhuman primates. Are there any basic primate parenting patterns? Do characteristics of different living environments, the type of societies in which a primate lives, and age of offspring affect parenting behavior? And are all primate parents of the same species alike or do different parents have their own unique parenting style? Individual differences in parental behavior reveal the influence of temperament, environment, and early experience on the kind of parents we become. Yet whatever our background or temperament, we can learn to parent better.

WHY focus on primates, rather than other mammals, birds, or even insects? I compare parenting in humans with that of nonhuman primates because of our close biological link to other primates. Humans, the only primates that regularly walk on two legs instead of four, shared a common ancestor with the great apes as recently as 6 million years ago and evolved in similar habitats. Most intriguing, genetic analyses have revealed that humans share more than 98 percent of their genetic material with two species of ape, chimpanzees and bonobos. As interesting as other species are, especially other intelligent species such as elephants, whales, and dolphins, the absence of a common genetic pathway makes a comparison with these creatures less compelling.

In addition to our genetic relatedness, monkeys and apes are like us in many ways. You simply have to spend a few moments with the monkeys or apes at the zoo to notice how much their looks and behavior resemble our own. People line up three-deep to watch the

orangutan mother and her new baby, or the group of juvenile baboons cavorting around their grassy enclosure. There is something
about primates that makes us pause, and stay a little longer.

The physical similarities between human and nonhuman primates
are startling. It is intriguing to look at the hand or foot of a monkey
and see the long, slim fingers and toes finished off with nails rather
than claws. Many monkeys and all apes have opposable thumbs similar to those of humans, which provide them with a powerful grasp as
well as the ability to pick up and manipulate small objects. Possession of an opposable thumb is considered crucial to the ability to use
tools, and thus is associated with the evolution of intelligence in humans. And although all nonhuman primates walk on four legs, a
number of them adopt a two-legged stance on a regular basis.

Most compelling, though, are the faces of nonhuman primates. As
in humans, the eyes are set in front of the face and are very expres-
sive. The faces of nonhuman primates are pliable, and their moods,
transparent. Even an untrained human observer can easily discriminate a monkey in a playful mood from one who is frightened or
ready for a fight.

Nonhuman primates, like their human cousins, are relatively intelligent and curious creatures. Human intelligence has accompanied a
significant increase in brain size (particularly in the neocortex, the
part of the brain that allows us to think abstractly, use language, plan
for the future, create, imagine, and reflect on our experiences). Although the human brain is about three times larger than the average
ape brain, primates generally have larger brains, relative to their body
size, than other mammals (the brains of most newborn mammals
account for about 6 percent of their body mass, whereas the brains of
newborn primates constitute about 12 percent of body mass).[1]

Nowhere is the intelligence of nonhuman primates more evident
than in their ability to understand social relationships, and human

and nonhuman primates are perhaps most alike in their need to interact with others. Unlike most mammals, which are typically solitary, primates usually live in family groups, although family composition varies among different species. Nonhuman primate families can consist of a mother, father, and offspring of various ages (monogamy), a father, his multiple mates, and their youngsters (polygyny), a mother, her multiple mates, and their young (polyandry—exceedingly rare among primates), or a mother and her dependent offspring, either living alone (solitary) or within a larger community (multimale multifemale). Only a handful of primate species are solitary, and all but one of these (the orangutan) belong to the most primitive group of primates, the prosimians.

Like humans, most nonhuman primates give birth to one infant at a time. Nonhuman primates are relatively helpless at birth, are carried about by their parents, and grow up slowly relative to other mammals, requiring extensive and prolonged caretaking by their parents. In all primate families, the bond is strong between parents and their dependent offspring. In many nonhuman primate species, relationships between parents and young persist well past the period of infant dependence, and, in some species, for life.

ALTHOUGH about 350 species are included in the order Primates, I have chosen to concentrate primarily on monkeys, apes, and humans. I rely heavily on field studies, but occasionally use examples from research on captive nonhuman primates because some of the most intriguing examples of abnormal parenting come from this literature. Most of the species I describe have been studied for many years by the same investigator. Long-term research ensures that primatologists not only know the basic ecology, social structure, and behavioral repertoire of their species, but intimately know the life history of individuals in their study populations. Knowing who is related to whom, who is friendly with whom, and the significant events in the life of each individual gives us a better framework for understanding behavior.

As you can imagine, studying primates in their natural habitat is no easy task. Not only do primatologists have to be able to locate and track their animals through inhospitable terrain, but they also have to habituate the animals to their presence—the animals must become so used to the investigator's presence that they behave naturally in front of her and allow her to follow them. Jane Goodall, who pioneered the habituation technique, and other primatologists have found that this process can take weeks, months, even years.

In 1980, I had the opportunity to spend a few months observing wild squirrel monkeys in the Manú National Biosphere Reserve in Peru, at the Cocha Cashu biological station created by the ecologist John Terborgh and his students. Observing monkeys, giant otters, capybara, anteaters, and countless species of flamboyant birds, bats, insects, and plants in the wild was an excellent motivator for enduring the unpleasant parts of fieldwork—dodging poisonous snakes, tripping over vine tangles, walking face first into gigantic spider webs, bathing in a lake that was home to 200 caimans, eating piranha for dinner, and itching from head to foot from chigger and mosquito bites. I developed a sincere appreciation for the tenacity, bravery, and fierce independence of the primatologists who have devoted a large portion of their lives to their primate research subjects.

Primatologists come to know individual animals intimately, and the anecdotes they tell about them are sprinkled throughout this book. Some primatologists, such as Jane Goodall, Dian Fossey, and Birute Galdikas, name their animals, but most do not. I have invented names whenever I felt that would facilitate storytelling. If, as you read of this monkey or that ape, you would like more information about a particular species or are curious about where it is found on the primate family tree, you may refer to "Who's Who among Nonhuman Primates," located near the end of the book.

THIS book has emerged from the marriage of my early training in primate behavior and comparative psychology with my current career in clinical psychology. My focus is on learning to parent. Biologically speaking, parenting is perhaps the most important of our life endeavors. Adequate parenting increases our chances of ensuring our own "immortality": when our offspring grow up and reproduce, they pass on our genes to future generations. And yet, the fascinating and complex ways in which primate parenting behavior varies with characteristics of the environment, the social context, and individual experience shows us that parenting behavior is not totally determined by our genes. The flexibility and malleability of primate parenting behavior reveal that we have the ability not only to change our behavior but to make conscious choices about the kinds of parents we wish to be.

Although my approach is primarily descriptive, my training in experimental and clinical psychology and in evolutionary biology influences my perspective on parenting. I will describe normal and abnormal parenting behaviors in human and nonhuman primates, and how a psychologist or evolutionary biologist might understand these behaviors. Since the questions that psychologists and biologists ask about behavior are different, it is no surprise that their perspectives and theories about behavior differ as well. The psychologist wants to understand what stimuli provoke a certain response (why is Jenny having a temper tantrum *now*), whereas the biologist is more interested in the evolutionary "value" of temper tantrums, why they have become a consistent part of a species' behavioral repertoire. I will present these contrasting perspectives because they help us understand the impact of both immediate and long-term consequences on our behavior.

In my discussions of human parenting, I rely on current parenting literature, research in cultural anthropology, and case histories from over 20 years of clinical practice. The examples I cite of hunter-gatherers and other traditional peoples come from ethnographies published many years ago. Quite a few of these societies today are in the midst of a transition to industrialization and are undergoing massive social changes. When I describe these societies, such as the !Kung San, it is as they *were* when anthropologists first studied them. In each chapter I contrast the behavior of human and nonhuman primates, examining the similarities as well as the differences.

The clinical cases I discuss are complex. I emphasize the part of the case relevant to the subject at hand, but I do not mean to imply that it is the only, or even the major, issue for my client. What I hope these case examples demonstrate is that discussions of parenting by primates are clearly relevant to twenty-first-century humans. I have protected the confidentiality of the clients whose stories I have shared in this book by changing their names and certain details of their histories, such as gender, numbers and ages of children, and so on. In some cases, I have combined details from several clients for the sake of both efficiency and confidentiality.

IN my discussion of both human and nonhuman primates, my goal is to paint a vivid picture of primate parenting across the life span and explore the many factors that influence something as "natural" as parenting. My message is not that humans "should" behave more like monkeys or apes, or vice versa. If we can understand the key components of primate parenting and recognize that much of our parental behavior varies greatly with environmental demands, we will see that we are not alone in our struggles to become good parents, and that the natural history of primate parenting reflects our adaptability and openness to learning and change. And now I begin our voyage through primate parenthood where my journey began, attempting to understand why my breeding pairs of cottontop tamarins adamantly refused to care for their young.

CHAPTER 1

Learning to Parent

CHARTIER AND JOE were expecting again, and I was dreading the birth of their twins. It was always the same scenario. I would be awakened at around midnight by the screams of terrified baby monkeys being forcefully rejected by their parents. I would leap out of bed and race into the monkey room. Reaching into the cage, I would carefully pry the babies' fingers from the cage wire, which they were desperately clutching, or gingerly lift out the bodies of infants who had been killed during the struggle. When infants survived the rejection (which to my surprise, they did more often than not), I rescued them; first I warmed and cleaned them, and then I fed them, wrapped them in a soft, furry cloth, and placed them on a heating pad. After the immediate crisis was over, the realization would hit—I had once again committed myself to a couple of months of intensive caretaking of two feisty infant cottontop tamarins. For the next few weeks, I would be sleep-deprived and grumpy, with virtually no time to myself. I would be unable to go out for more than a couple of hours unless I hired a monkey sitter or took the babies with me. What, I thought, can I do, to teach Chartier and Joe how to parent their own young?

W<small>HEN</small> I brought home 2-week-old cottontop tamarin triplets on a seemingly ordinary May day in 1972, it never occurred to me what an impact they would have on my life. At first, my goal was simply to ensure that they would survive. I kept them together, so they had continual contact with other cottontops, but I was clearly their "mother"; I was the one with the doll bottle of infant formula, the one who kept them clean, carried them, and made sure they were out of harm's way. They grew up playing with one another, but attached to me. They rode around on my shoulder and had the run of my apartment. When friends came for dinner, they had to put up with the sights, sounds, and smells of monkeys in the living room.

Time passed and the triplets reached puberty. I had two males and one female, and when the female died, I placed two other hand-raised females with my two males, each pair in a separate cage. Suddenly the two males discovered their sexuality, and that was the first indication that hand-rearing the tamarins had serious consequences for their adult social behavior. The males had erections, but didn't seem to know what to do with them. The females stood close to the males, but the males often mounted them from the wrong direc-

Cottontop tamarins *(Saguinus oedipus)*; photo by Noel Rowe

tion—sometimes broadside, sometimes from the front, and sometimes from the back—but neither male seemed to know that the goal was to insert his penis into his mate's vagina. On occasion I reached into the cage and repositioned the male so that he was at least oriented correctly. Over time, however, both males mastered the challenge of copulation.

When the first set of babies arrived and were fiercely rejected, I was taken aback. How could it be that these monkeys not only refused to take care of their own babies, but appeared terrified by them? I initially thought that perhaps it was normal to refuse to care for the first litter, and that the monkeys would improve with time. I would raise the first set of twins produced by my hand-raised pair, Arthur and Cassie, since I knew exactly what to do. I kept the babies in the monkey room most of the day, hoping that Arthur and Cassie would watch and learn as I took care of them. But when I held the babies close to the cage mesh, both Arthur and Cassie made threat faces and aggressively attempted to grab the twins. My efforts to be a role model for appropriate parenting were not going well.

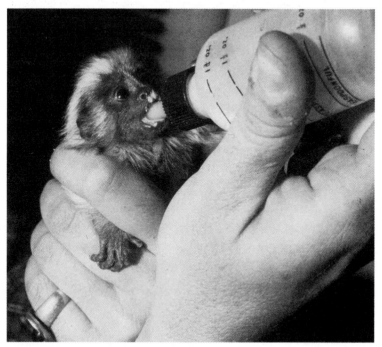

The author bottle-feeding a cottontop tamarin infant; photo by Stephen Alden

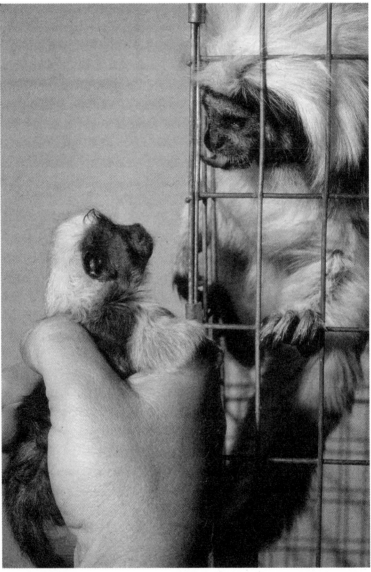

The author introducing a cottontop tamarin infant to its foster mother; photo by Stephen Alden

I soon noticed, however, that my wild-caught monkey, named Rachel, was fascinated by the twins. Rachel had been captured in Colombia as an adult and had therefore been reared in a normal family group. I did not know how old she was, but she was clearly elderly and had spent much of her adult life alone in a cage. I began to hold the babies close to Rachel after I fed them; she gently reached for them, licked their faces clean, and sniffed them. Although Rachel had avoided me in the past, she tolerated my presence when I was holding the twins in order to be close to them. When I approached her with the babies, she made eye contact with them, shook her head gently, and rapidly flicked her tongue at them. When a cottontop flicks its tongue up toward its nose, it is signaling an aggressive intent, but when the tongue is extended outward, as it was by Rachel, it is an invitation to approach.

I realized that even though the twins' parents were not interested in raising them, Rachel was willing to be their foster mother. Over the next 2 months, I prepared the infants for moving in with Rachel. I taught them to drink from a drip water bottle so that they could get their milk on their own. I taught them to feed from a dish instead of hand-feeding them, figuring that eventually Rachel would take responsibility for cleaning them up. When they were old enough to begin climbing, I put them in Rachel's cage while she was locked outside, so they could learn their way around in her absence; I understood that once I allowed contact between them, it might be very difficult to retrieve the twins from Rachel. I built a tiny tunnel between the two cages (too small for Rachel to enter) in case the twins needed a fast getaway. And then, on one memorable afternoon, I opened the door to Rachel's cage and put the youngsters inside.

I will never forget the thrill of that introduction. Rachel was clearly excited to be with them, and yet she was extraordinarily calm and patient. She cautiously approached and presented her side to them, as if inviting them to climb on. They initially refused. Obviously frightened, they clutched each other, clinging together in a little ball, completely immobile. Rachel sniffed them, moved away, and then returned. Eventually the twins let go of each other and began to explore the cage. They found their milk bottle and fed from their dishes. Rachel remained close by, intently watching them, but did not push for contact. When I approached the cage, however, she charged forward and threatened me with an impressive frown, the hair in her topknot standing straight up in a threat display. Her message was clear: I was not welcome.

By the evening, the twins were relaxed and unafraid when Rachel approached them. She jumped into her nest box and signaled for the twins to enter. By nightfall, all three were sleeping in a contented pile, a tamarin family at last.

Rachel continued to adopt infants that were rejected by their parents and hand-raised by me, when they were mature enough to feed on their own. I couldn't place newborns with her because she was unable to nurse them. As new tamarins joined Rachel's family, older youngsters helped with the care of the newest additions, learning to tolerate the feel of an infant on their backs as early as 6 months of age. In this captive environment, Rachel's adopted offspring were exposed to the type of experience they would need to competently raise their own young later on.

Then Rachel died and I was back to square one. At that point, my two breeding pairs had observed Rachel care for their infants for a couple of years, but apparently had not learned enough to stop rejecting their babies. It was time to institute a parent-training program. Training tamarins who are frightened of their young to be competent parents, however, turned out to be no easy task. Just like working with human patients in a clinical setting, it required patience and a firm belief that, with a little bit of help, they could improve. The case histories of three different cottontop families illustrate the process of learning to parent in this species.

My original tamarins, Joe and Arthur, were paired with two hand-raised females, Chartier and Benita, during most of the time they were reproductively active. Arthur was curious, energetic, and fairly aggressive, while Joe was laid back and easy-going. Benita was active and aggressive like Arthur, and Chartier was calmer, like Joe. How did parent training affect the performance of Joe and Chartier, and Arthur and Benita?

Joe and Chartier produced their fourth set of twins shortly after the death of the foster mother, Rachel. Rosie and Ira were rejected upon their midnight arrival, just as the three previous sets of twins had been. One infant's tail was injured in two places, and the other had a swollen foot, but all injuries quickly healed. I placed the twins in a small cage beside that of their parents, and from the beginning attempted to involve Joe and Chartier in their care. Although the parents still could not tolerate carrying infants on their backs, they seemed less afraid of and more curious about them than before. Perhaps that was due to the opportunity they'd had to watch Rachel interact with youngsters, or perhaps it was simply an effect of the passage of time, but now when I held the twins up to their cage after I fed them, Joe often approached to gently sniff them or lick the milk off their faces. Although Joe and Chartier occasionally made threat faces at the infants, they no longer aggressively grabbed at them. And they were interested observers when the infants began to hop around their cage and play with each other.

By the time they were a month old, Rosie and Ira occasionally reached out for Joe or Chartier through the cage mesh. When Rosie reached for Chartier on one occasion, Chartier allowed the contact, gazed at Rosie, and made the same type of tongue flick that Rachel had used to invite youngsters to approach. When Rosie and Ira were 6 weeks old and able to feed themselves, I locked Joe and Chartier out of their cage and put the twins inside, so that the youngsters could become familiar with what I hoped would eventually be their new home. Joe and Chartier huddled together by the entrance, eyes riveted on the babies. They chose to stay inside and watch rather than exit through a chihuahua-sized doggy door to their outdoor cage. Their demeanor indicated curiosity, not aggression. Although Chartier occasionally wandered outside, Joe remained in place the entire time and appeared mesmerized by the sight of the infants in his cage. It was time to attempt to introduce the twins to their parents.

When Rosie and Ira were contentedly climbing around their parents' cage, all was well. But on a couple of occasions, one of the infants became frightened and hopped onto Chartier's back. The first time this happened, Chartier literally froze, with a terrified expression on her face. I intervened and pulled Ira off her back. The second time it was Rosie who jumped on board; Chartier moved around the cage in some distress, twisting her body from side to side, and attempted to dislodge Rosie with her hands. Again I removed the baby, but noted with some satisfaction that Chartier had neither panicked nor injured the infant. Progress was definitely being made.

It was not only the parents who appeared to be anxious—the twins too showed signs of being afraid. During the first few encounters, Rosie and Ira entered their parents' cage with tiny topknots erected and frowns on their faces (displays of aggression), and screamed at their parents. Joe and Chartier did not respond in kind; instead, they slowly approached, gently sniffed the youngsters, and moved away. But tension was high. When Joe and Chartier began to frown at each other, I removed the twins so that they would not be caught in the middle of a parental quarrel.

Over the next 2 weeks, I continued to place Rosie and Ira with their parents for longer and longer periods. The twins alternated between playing together, following their father or mother around, or threatening or screaming at their parents. Joe and Chartier never responded negatively to the threat gestures made by their youngsters, and seemed to grow more comfortable around them every day. Joe appeared particularly interested in the babies; he approached them often, made contact calls, and tongue-flicked in their direction. One day, Rosie jumped into the nest box and Joe followed her inside. She lay down next to him and fell asleep. He stayed beside her, immobile but alert. Chartier entered shortly thereafter, and her attempts to settle in beside father and daughter without touching or stepping on Rosie were hilarious. Joe rested his chin on Rosie's head and closed his eyes.

After the group nap, Joe became even more attentive to his youngsters. When they went outside, he followed them and stayed close by. The twins quickly learned to accommodate to their parents' refusal to carry them—they simply clung to each other when they were frightened. Joe stood close to the twins when they clung to each other, until they recovered from their fright and scampered off. Joe and Chartier continued to appear uncomfortable when the infants jumped on their backs during the day, but no longer forcibly rejected them. Instead, they froze in place until their offspring hopped off.

When the twins entered Joe and Chartier's nest box at the end of the first entire day without mishap (about 4 weeks after their introduction to their parents), it was time to let them stay. Joe and Chartier joined the twins in the nest box and drifted off to sleep. By morning, the four tamarins were a family. Joe and Chartier eventually learned to tolerate the sensation of the twins crawling around on their backs or clinging to them at night, while they were sleeping. They still weren't perfect parents but, finally, they were good enough.

Joe and Chartier's next offspring was a singleton, Amy, whom they rejected as usual. From the beginning, however, they showed great interest in her, and when it was time to place her with them at the age of 2 months, the introduction was rapid, smooth, and successful. I fully expected that the next set of twins would be accepted from the moment of birth.

Wrong again. When Joe and Chartier's sixth pregnancy produced twins, Chartier once again rejected them, although much less violently than before. One of the twins was injured during the struggle and died soon afterward. The other, a lively female I named Natasha, was healthy and strong. Since newborns rely on contact with their parents' bodies to stay warm, I placed Natasha on a heating pad in front of Joe and Chartier's nest box and waited to see what would happen. Joe immediately came out to investigate, but did not attempt to make contact with the infant. Chartier hopped out, nipped at Natasha, and returned to the nest box. Joe lay down next to Natasha on the heating pad, and Amy, now about 8 months old, snuggled next to him. In the morning, Chartier again approached and nipped at Natasha, causing her to cry, but not drawing blood. I removed the infant for safety's sake, but was still hopeful that she would eventually be accepted by her parents.

During the entire first day after Natasha's birth, Joe appeared to be captivated by her; he made contact calls and attempted to gently reach for her through the wire mesh. At the end of the day, I fed Natasha and placed her back in her parent's cage, on a heating pad in front of the nest box. Ira, now almost 2 years old, approached Natasha and attempted to pull her onto his back. She grasped his fur, and they settled down to sleep on the heating pad. Joe joined them and huddled next to Ira. Natasha began to squirm and then climbed across Ira onto Joe's back. Ira returned to the nest box and Joe followed, with Natasha clinging tightly to his back. By morning, Natasha was attached to her mother's breast, nursing. Chartier and

Natasha quickly became the center of the family's attention—Rosie, Ira, Amy, and Joe all wanted to closely examine and touch the infant.

The last remaining obstacle between Joe and Chartier and successful parenting was learning how to transfer Natasha smoothly from the back of one caretaker to that of another. All family members wanted a turn carrying the infant, but no one (understandably) wanted the job full-time. Initially, after Chartier nursed Natasha, she continued to carry the infant for hours at a stretch. After many hours with full responsibility for the baby, however, Chartier became distressed; she began to twist her body and scratch at herself and Natasha. Her inexperienced family members were initially oblivious to her signals and did not respond. As her distress increased, she behaved more aggressively toward Natasha. She began to nip at the baby, although she never injured her. When bitten by her mother, Natasha cried out, alerting other family members to the problem. They quickly approached the unhappy pair, but initially did not know what to do. Over time, however, they learned to respond quickly to Chartier's signal that she was ready to be relieved of her domestic duties, and would confidently scoop Natasha onto their own backs. In the end, Joe and the two oldest offspring, Rosie and Ira, shouldered most of the responsibility for Natasha's care and transportation, and Chartier supplied the milk. After her first 24 tumultuous hours of life, Natasha was raised competently by her entire family and lived happily ever after.

WHEN Arthur's first mate died, I placed him with another hand-raised female cottontop named Benita. By that time Rachel had also died, so there would be no willing foster mother waiting in the wings in the event that Arthur and Benita rejected their offspring. Since Arthur had shown no inclination to parent the two litters he and his previous mate had produced, Benita was a first-time mother, and both monkeys had relatively irritable temperaments, I expected the worst. Arthur and Benita fiercely rejected their first set of twins, as predicted. One baby died of its injuries, but the other was a healthy, uninjured female. It was time to put the parent-training program into action with a second breeding pair of cottontops.

As I had done for Joe and Chartier, I raised Arthur and Benita's first infant, Jessie, in a small cage beside their large one. I held her up to her parents to be touched and inspected as often as possible, especially after feedings. They were curious about her and often reached out to gently touch her or lick her face. By the age of 1 month, Jessie was happily exploring her parents' cage while they watched her through the mesh door that separated them. They made contact calls and gazed at her with apparent interest. Just as Joe had taken the lead interacting with his offspring, Arthur appeared most interested in observing and interacting with Jessie.

When Jessie was a little over a month old, I allowed the family to come together for the first time. Arthur and Benita appeared stiff and nervous. They uttered soft contact calls from a distance, occasionally approached and sniffed Jessie, and then quickly scampered off. Although they did not respond when Jessie playfully attempted to grab their tails or topknots in passing, they did not behave aggressively toward her. The first time Jessie hopped on her mother's back, Benita panicked and raced away with Jessie on board. While Benita neither bit nor attempted to hurt her daughter, it was, no doubt, a scary ride for the infant. Benita panicked on another occasion when Jessie jumped on her back; this time Benita lost her footing, and mother and daughter tumbled 5 feet to the floor of their cage. It wasn't long before Jessie no longer attempted to hitch a ride on her mother.

Over the next month, I continued to place Jessie with Arthur and Benita for increasingly longer outings during the day. Perhaps in response to her parent's anxious behavior, Jessie often acted as if on guard with them. She frequently frowned at them, erected her topknot, and charged them with all the ferocity she could muster. Arthur and Benita ignored Jessie's provocative behavior and quietly observed her displays. They gradually grew more relaxed and appeared better able to tolerate the shenanigans of an active infant racing around their cage, getting into their food, and threatening them. It seemed as though the only thing that really disturbed them was Jessie's attempts to cling to one of them. Being grasped by their daughter continued to elicit desperate, fearful behavior.

By the time Jessie was 6 weeks old, Arthur was allowing her to eat some banana, his favorite food, out of his hand. Benita, in turn, was responding positively to Jessie's attempts to play with her. During one play session, Jessie slipped and ended up clinging to the underside of Benita's neck. For the first time, Benita did not panic; she stood still, patiently waiting until Jessie calmed down and scampered off. That evening, Jessie jumped into the nest box with her parents and climbed onto Arthur's back. He tolerated the contact for about 30 seconds and then gently pushed her off. He still was uncomfortable, but he was no longer terrified.

Three days later—less than 3 weeks after their introduction—Jessie was living with her parents full-time. She cuddled with them in their nest box at night and played with them during the day. Arthur and Benita shared their favorite foods with her and no longer reacted with fear to her touch. But they never really got used to her clinging to them when they were awake, so Jessie accommodated by traveling on her own during the day and enjoying the warmth of contact comfort at night.

Although Arthur and Benita fully accepted their daughter back into their lives 2 months after they had initially rejected her, they continued to abandon their next three litters immediately after birth (but were successfully reunited with all of their offspring when the youngsters were 2 months old, after painstaking training). The fear of being grasped by a newborn seemed to be something they could not overcome. But a fortuitous event that occurred shortly before the birth of Arthur and Benita's fifth infant may have helped them to finally surmount the last hurdle to adequate parenting. Three weeks before Maggie was born, Chartier had given birth to Natasha. Every day, Joe, Chartier, Amy, Ira, and Rosie ministered to Natasha, in full view of Arthur, Benita, Jessie, and their other offspring. Benita observed as Chartier nursed Natasha and passed her to the next eager caretaker.

For the next few weeks, Arthur, Benita, and their offspring intently watched the family next door, following them inside and outside to keep them in view. When Benita gave birth to Maggie, I was blissfully unaware until the morning after. For the first time in the 8 years since my tamarins had begun to reproduce, parturition was disconnected from terror in the middle of the night. When I entered the monkey's quarters, I discovered a calm, contented family, huddled next to Benita as she nursed her new baby. I wondered if Benita's observations of the care bestowed on Natasha had spawned a monkey insight—"Aha! That's how it's done!"

Once again, the greatest obstacle to stress-free caretaking was that other family members initially did not understand Benita's signals that she was ready to be relieved of infant care. But a few gentle nips, followed by Maggie's petulant cries, resulted in immediate, if awkward, infant transfers. Over the next few weeks, every family member took turns carrying Maggie, and all appeared comfortable and unafraid when Maggie was on board.

THESE two cottontop families no longer needed my help in raising their young, to my considerable relief. When I placed one adult child from each family together to form a new breeding pair a year later, I wondered how they would perform as parents. Jessie and Ira both had been raised by their parents from the age of 2 months, after initially being rejected by them. In addition, they had both helped to raise younger siblings—some after the age of 2 months, and some from birth. How would this young pair parent their own first litter?

Jessie and Ira's first infant was stillborn, but its twin was healthy. Jessie immediately rejected the healthy infant, but did not injure it. I cleaned the birth fluids off the baby and put it back inside Jessie and Ira's cage. Ira immediately approached and confidently scooped it onto his back. When the baby cried, Jessie retrieved it, but soon began to nip at it. Ira immediately reclaimed it and carried it almost continuously during its first day of life. Despite Jessie's obvious discomfort, she nursed her baby several times that day. On the following day, I found the infant, dead, on the floor of the cage. The lack of obvious injuries and the absence of noise left open the possibility that the baby had not been forcibly rejected, and may have died of natural causes. The stress of firsst-time parenting, however, also may have played a role in the poor outcome. In other colonies of captive cottontop tamarins, less than 10 percent of first-time parents successfully rear their young.[1]

Jessie and Ira competently raised all of their subsequent infants, without human intervention, from the moment of birth. They cared for their second youngster, Sylvia, with no other family members to help them. Although Sylvia transferred relatively smoothly from the back of one parent to the other, Ira appeared more eager for his turn to carry than Jessie was for hers. Just as in the other two families, it was the father that was most devoted to carrying and caring for the offspring, a finding that has been noted frequently in published studies of parenting in cottontops.[2] The fact that Ira and Jessie had both handled and carried their infant siblings as they grew up was probably the key factor in the success of this pair. Babysitting experience before adulthood appears to be mandatory preparation for good parenting in species, such as the cottontop tamarin, in which parents share infant care from the moment of birth.

As Jessie and Ira's family grew larger, everyone helped care for each new set of twins. Jessie devoted the least time to infant care of all family members except young juveniles; the only time she was reliably in charge was when the babies were hungry.

WE have seen that cottontop tamarins need hands-on experience and a few helpers to adequately care for their young. We will explore the caregiving behavior of parents and their helpers—grandparents, older offspring, and other babysitters—in a variety of primate species and human cultures, and how parental behavior changes as youngsters grow up. We will also look at how different kinds of families and living environments affect primate parenting. Finally, we will delve into parenting's dark side—abuse and neglect—and look at the ways in which primate parents can get the experience or training they need to be good-enough parents.

We start with an in-depth look at mothers, indispensable among nonhuman primates and typically the primary caretakers of infants and young children in humans.

CHAPTER 2

The Primate Recipe for Mothering

MOZU, a female Japanese macaque described by the primatologist Frans de Waal in his book *Good Natured,* has raised five youngsters in the 18 years she has lived in Jigokudoni Park in the Japanese Alps.[1] What is remarkable about her story is that Mozu has a congenital abnormality—she has no hands or feet. While other macaque monkeys travel in the trees to avoid the ice and snow in winter, Mozu has slogged through shoulder-high snow on the forest floor for years, carrying one infant after another.

Most first-time muriqui monkey mothers seem to have no trouble caring properly for their infants, but some of them appear quite befuddled with their new responsibility. "It is as if they have no idea what to do with this thing that is grabbing onto their leg and sliding down their abdomen into their groin," says Karen Strier, a primatologist who studies muriqui monkeys in Brazil. Strier shared a story with me about a new young mother named Blacky who was less than adept at navigating through the trees with her baby in tow. "We could always find Blacky when she was traveling with her baby. When she moved into a tree, we typically heard a loud scream—her baby smashing into the tree."[2] Strier added that Blacky was actually a good mother and that her infant grew up normally, with no ill effects from its early experience. Blacky was less awkward with her second infant, and her location was no longer given away by the screams of her baby.

ONE mother is not the same as another. Mothers take center stage in this chapter for two reasons: first, because in most nonhuman primate species and in virtually all human societies, mothers are the primary caregivers of infants, and second, because we simply know more about primate mothers than fathers.

Why *is* one mother unlike another? Nature and nurture both contribute to who we are and how we behave, whether we are early twenty-first-century humans, chimpanzees, or cottontop tamarins. The most interesting questions concern *how* nature (biological factors) and nurture (psychosocial and cultural factors) affect what kind of mothers we turn out to be. What influences our readiness for motherhood and how we attach to our infants? Do anxious or shy mothers parent differently than calm or extroverted ones? What effect does experience in our family of origin have on our parenting behavior, and are we different mothers with our first babies than our last? And how do our cultural beliefs affect how we care for our babies?

ARE mothers primary caretakers because the cocktail of hormones produced by females (estrogen, progesterone, and prolactin) helps them instinctively "know" how to parent their young?

Certainly the breasts of female mammals give them a great advantage. But motherhood is more than turning on a milk spigot. What are the ingredients in the primate recipe for mothering?

Mothers in good health are most likely to be successful parents. A wild monkey mother who has lost a great deal of weight during a drought, for example, might not have enough stored body fat both to provide milk for her infant and to adequately maintain herself. Nature often takes care of this lack of readiness by terminating the pregnancy via resorption of the fetus—miscarriage. When the pregnancy of a mother in poor condition does not terminate naturally, however, she may provide less care to her baby than healthy mothers. For example, mother vervets in the Amboseli National Park in Kenya who live in areas with less available food wean their babies earlier and are less responsive to their distress cries than those who live in areas with more abundant food.[3]

Working with captive vervet monkeys, the primatologist Lynn Fairbanks and her colleagues looked at the effects of a mother's physical condition on how well she cared for her baby. "Marginal condition" was defined as being significantly younger or older and/or of lower body weight than the average reproducing female. Mothers in marginal physical condition routinely rejected their infants more and were more likely to neglect them than mothers in adequate condition.[4] For example, vervet mothers commonly allow other females to babysit their young. Mothers in good physical condition stay close to and keep an eye on babysitters, ready to retrieve their infant at the first sign of distress. In contrast, mothers in marginal condition abdicate parental responsibility to babysitters for much longer periods and respond less rapidly (if at all) to their infant's distress cries. Although babysitters are eager to care for their charges and usually do a good job, they cannot nurse them. Undernourished, many of these infants die.

Similarly in humans, mothers who are malnourished or ill are more likely to die in childbirth than are healthy mothers.[5] Mothers who have malaria, are anemic or malnourished, or perform heavy labor are also more likely to have low-birth-weight babies, a circumstance that is associated with higher infant mortality.[6]

Nonhuman primate mothers are most effective when they are neither too young nor too old, and the same is true in humans. Human mothers under the age of 20 or older than 35 are more likely to die during childbirth (and their infants are more likely to die during their first 11 months) than mothers of intermediate age.[7] Older nonhuman primate mothers are more likely to die before their offspring become independent. Older bodies are less able to withstand the rigors of lactation and infant care, and because older mothers are more likely to be in poor condition, they may be less able to protect their youngsters from other members of the social group or from predators.

Being too young also has its disadvantages. First-born infants (who usually have younger mothers) are more likely to die during their first year than infants of mothers in their reproductive prime, perhaps because of competition between mother and infant for nutrients, lack of maternal experience, or emotional immaturity.[8] Dian Fossey, who studied mountain gorillas in Rwanda in the 1970s and early 1980s, described a young adult female named Pantsey who gave birth to her first baby at the age of 9, which is relatively young for gorillas. Fossey said that Pantsey initially "seemed both dejected and disturbed by her newly acquired responsibility."[9] Although Pantsey embarked on motherhood reluctantly and in a fairly incompetent manner, by the time her baby was about 6 months old, she had become a capable mother. And she was a good mother to her subsequent young.

If young adult vervet and gorilla mothers are less competent than more mature mothers, what happens when even younger females, such as adolescents, become mothers? Interestingly enough, adolescent female nonhuman primates rarely become pregnant, thanks to two built-in biological mechanisms.

First, the unavailability of high-fat fast food in the treetops combined with an active lifestyle prevents adolescent females from accumulating enough fat to signal to their bodies that they are ready to reproduce. Puberty is delayed in nonhuman primates until females have completed most if not all of their physical and psychological growth. Second, adolescent females enjoy a period of sterility or subfertility for several reproductive cycles (or for apes, years) after menarche, so that although they are sexually active, they rarely become pregnant.[10] By the time most nonhuman primate females are fertile, they are fully grown, have observed their own mothers with younger siblings and helped care for them, have learned where choice foods are found, and so on, all of which has prepared them for adult life and parenthood.

Adolescent pregnancy is so unusual among wild nonhuman primates that we have no natural primate model with which to compare adolescent human mothers. Until this century, adolescent pregnancy was rare in virtually all human societies as well, and is still uncommon today among human hunter-gatherers. Similar to adolescent female nonhuman primates, adolescent girls who live in hunter-gatherer societies put on body weight slowly, owing to their naturally low-fat diet and active lifestyle.[11] Physical and psychological growth proceed in tandem, and girls in hunter-gatherer societies reach puberty in their mid to late teens. Although many are sexually active, they also, like nonhuman primate females, enjoy a period of subfertility for a few years after the onset of menarche. By the time they are fertile, they are fully grown and ready to marry and take their place in adult society.

Adolescent pregnancy is far more common in developed countries such as the United States than among nonhuman primates or human foraging societies, because our typical diet is high in simple carbohydrates and fats and daily life requires little expenditure of energy. Young girls put on fat earlier, which signals to their bodies that it is time to for puberty to begin. American girls may enter puberty by the age of 11 or 12, and sometimes as early as 9 or 10 (well-nourished nonhuman primate females in captivity also reach menarche earlier than their wild peers, and give birth to their first infants at a younger age).[12] Even after a period of subfertility, these girls will be capable of becoming pregnant by early to middle adolescence. But physically and psychologically, they are still children.

Even when a mother is in good condition and old enough to provide reliable care, she may still perform poorly without support from her social environment. Most nonhuman primates are relatively long-lived and are members of families or communities. In family-living species, babies may be at significant risk of neglect or abandonment when no other family members are available to help (helpers usually are older offspring). Lorna Johnson and her colleagues at the New England Regional Primate Research Center studied the breeding success of captive cottontop tamarins for over 22 years, and reported that 57 percent of experienced parents without helpers abandoned their infants—almost five times the rate when helpers were available.[13] When you consider that the cottontops were experienced parents, these statistics are even more remarkable.

In group-living Old World monkeys, young females breed in the community in which they grow up while young males emigrate to other groups to breed. Young females live among close relatives (mothers, sisters, and grandmothers) and other females with whom they are very familiar when they begin to reproduce. Not only is the mother's social life not disrupted after the birth of her infant, but she

Olive baboons *(Papio anubus);* photo by Leanne T. Nash

often becomes the center of attention. Other females vie for the privilege of sitting near or grooming her, to get an opportunity to look at or touch her new baby.

Sixteen years of behavioral observations of wild savannah baboons in Kenya confirmed that sociality is good for primate mothers and their babies. Measures of sociality were being in close proximity to others and grooming or being groomed by others. Researchers found that infants of the most social females had the best chance of survival.[14] Not only is grooming a great stress reducer (it releases endorphins, brain chemicals that create a sense of well-being and relaxation), close relationships with others may protect females from harassment or help them gain access to valuable resources.

Isolate a monkey mother from her social group, however, and the results are very different. When Robert Hinde and Yvette Spencer-Booth housed captive rhesus monkey mothers and their infants separately from other monkeys in the 1960s, they found that mothers interacted less with their infants and were more likely to reject them.[15] There is little need for mothers to restrict infants in the safe, isolated captive environment, which eliminates much of the usual interaction between mothers and babies. Because this isolated environment is so unstimulating (lack of playmates or interactions with other group members), infants pester their mothers for more attention than they do when living in a social group. But as babies become more demanding, isolated mothers become more rejecting. The absence of social companions is hard on mothers too.

Isolation and lack of social support are risk factors for poor parenting in both human and nonhuman primates.[16] Wild primates and human mothers in preindustrial societies remain an integral part of their communities while they continue to do productive work. Stay-at-home mothers in modern industrial societies are at higher risk of becoming socially isolated, and thus are out of sync with the highly social primate way of life.

EVERYONE has heard about bonding. We are fascinated with the puzzle of how a mother "knows" to respond to and love her baby after it is born. For many years researchers believed that there had to be a physiological process, perhaps related to the presence of maternal hormones at birth or to immediate contact with the baby after birth, in order for a mother to bond with her newborn. Because researchers had noted that the mother-infant bond in goats and sheep was cemented by contact immediately after birth, the race was on to find the same phenomenon in primates, human and non-human.

In 1976, two obstetricians, Marshall Klaus and John Kennell, proposed that human mothers and infants must experience skin-to-skin contact shortly after the infant's birth in order to bond.[17] This idea caught fire in the United States and has dramatically altered the way in which babies are delivered. Hospitals used to recommend that mothers be anesthetized (and often, be rendered literally unconscious), and fathers be as far away as possible when babies were born, but today's mothers are painfully awake and fathers are present during delivery. The immediate contact between parents and newborn is widely believed to facilitate bonding.

But much to everyone's surprise, research on nonhuman primates showed that maternal hormones at birth are not the primary determinants of a mother's responsiveness to her infant.[18] And research on both human and nonhuman primates simply did not support the concept of "instant gluing"—that a mother bonds with her baby as a result of immediate skin-to-skin contact.[19] Adoptive mothers bond perfectly well with their infants with neither the hormonal brew of birth nor the early experience of contact immediately afterward.

Mothers who deliver by caesarian section (and thus do not see their babies immediately after birth), and mothers of premature infants (who may not be permitted to hold their infants for hours, days, or even weeks after birth), also adequately bond with their infants.[20] The fact that mothers were unconscious and fathers were absent during delivery in the 1950s did not prevent bonding between parents and their babies. Immediate contact with one's baby after its birth can be delightful, but it isn't crucial for development of sturdy mother-infant bonds. What, then, does affect the attachment between mothers and their babies?

In the 1950s, the British child psychiatrist John Bowlby studied the mental health of institutionalized children who had experienced temporary or permanent separations from their mothers. Bowlby became curious about the nature of the tie between a child and its mother. How is it that some children become securely attached to their mothers, which allows them to confidently explore the world around them, while others cling to their mothers, appearing content to watch as the world goes by? Published in 1969, his book, *Attachment*, became the bible of child-development specialists interested in how the relationship between a baby and its mother develops.

Bowlby's approach to attachment was a radical departure from the Freudian view of mother-infant relationships then currently in vogue. Freud's complex theory was based on interviews with his adult patients and analysis of his own childhood memories. In contrast, Bowlby relied on his work with children and on the observations and experiments of students of animal behavior (ethologists and comparative psychologists) to build his theory of attachment. Bowlby's stimulating discussions with the the British ethologist Robert Hinde were quickly incorporated into his research and teaching. Equally excited by his conversations with Bowlby, Hinde began to study the development of mother-infant attachment in rhesus monkeys.[21] Also influenced by Bowlby's views was the psychologist Harry Harlow, whose intricate studies of mother-infant attachment in rhesus monkeys in turn profoundly influenced Bowlby's thinking. Many of Bowlby's conclusions about attachment in humans stem from the findings of these early primate studies, which remain classics today.

Robert Hinde emphasized that to understand attachment in monkeys one must become familiar with two points of view—the baby's and its mother's. Hinde's studies revealed the reciprocity of the attachment process: the behavior of an infant affects the behavior of its mother, and vice versa.[22] When a baby monkey acts like a baby (clings to its mother, nurses, and cries), its mother is stimulated to respond appropriately. The key behavior that defines monkey babyhood is the tenacious grasp with which an infant clings to its mother. As long as the infant can cling, its mother will care for it, regardless of illness or disability. There are many examples in the primate literature of mothers caring tenderly for mildly handicapped, ill, or wounded infants.[23]

A human mother's responsiveness is stimulated by her baby's behavior. Most helpless of all primate babies, human infants cry to alert us of their distress. A baby's cry is so unpleasant that we try one response after another to make it stop. Mothers hold or rock their babies, offer them food, or change their diapers, and are usually rewarded for their efforts by a quiet baby. After the third month, babies capture our attention in more pleasant ways; they smile, babble endearingly, follow us with their eyes, and seem genuinely happy when we appear. Our ability to comfort and please our babies increases our joy in caring for them.

What happens when a monkey or human infant does not respond to its mother? Harry and Margaret Harlow described a situation in their laboratory when this occurred.[24] A baby monkey who had been separated from its own mother at birth had learned to comfort itself by self-clutching and rocking (autistic, deprived, or institutionalized young children do the same thing). When the Harlows placed this infant with another monkey mother whose infant had been removed, the potential adoptive mother approached and reached for the infant. But the infant rolled itself into a tight ball and screamed when the adoptive mother touched it. After 4 days, the adoptive mother lost interest in the infant.

Less extreme than trauma, but disruptive of attachment nonetheless, are mismatches between the temperaments of mothers and infants. For example, when an infant and its mother both have extremely anxious or irritable temperaments, it may be difficult for the mother to deal with the incessant demands of her baby. Soothing a highly sensitive or irritable infant is challenging for mothers whose own frustration tolerance is low. When babies don't respond to their mother's efforts to soothe them, mothers may become angry with their infants, avoid them, or even abuse them.

And how do mothers influence the development of attachment? The experiments of Harry Harlow and his coworkers with rhesus macaques illuminated the characteristics of monkey mothers that were most strongly associated with infant attachment. Harlow removed baby rhesus monkeys from their mothers at birth and presented them with "surrogate" mothers.[25] One surrogate was a cylinder made of wire-cloth equipped with a nipple and a supply of warm milk. An infant could simultaneously cling to and suckle from this wire mother. Another type of surrogate resembled the wire mother but was covered with a soft furry cloth.

Although the cloth-covered "mothers" offered no nipple or milk, the baby rhesus monkeys preferred them to the wire "mothers." Harlow described how infants leaned over and suckled from the wire mothers while clinging to the cloth-covered mothers. When infants were frightened, clinging to their cloth-covered mother soothed them; but when only wire mothers were available, frightened infants held themselves and rocked, and avoided the wire mother. The wire mothers (with their nipples and milk) did not comfort the infant monkeys, but the soft, warm, cloth-covered mothers did. Harlow concluded that "contact comfort" trumped the provision of food as the key factor in attachment in rhesus monkeys.

Besides being cuddly and warm, a monkey mother must consistently respond to her infant's signals of discomfort or distress for it to securely attach to her. The attachment theorist Mary Ainsworth emphasizes that parental responsiveness is the basis for an infant's development of trust, which is the foundation for attachment.[26] A mother's responsiveness allows her baby to be warm, comfortable, nourished, and safe. She generously offers this maternal responsiveness all through her baby's period of dependence.

Perhaps most important, nonhuman primate mothers are simply always there. As a baby grows up, it uses its mother as a safe base from which to explore the world. At first, it moves a short distance away from her and then returns, each time summoning the courage to move a little farther away. The infant happily embarks on its independence as long as it is neither hurt nor frightened and its mother remains close by.[27] The baby uses its mother's body to regulate its level of arousal; when it is scared or hurt, it clings, and when it is secure and comfortable, it lets go and scampers off to explore.[28] Mothers initially restrict their babies' movements and attempts to explore. To a human observer, this battle between mother and infant over where it is going can be hilarious. The primatologist Leanne Nash, who studies bush babies (large-eyed prosimians), describes a 24-hour period in the life of a baby bush baby in which it is determined to get away from its mother for the first time, and its mother is equally determined that it will not.[29] The baby jumps out of the nest box and its mother drags it back in, with dozens of instant replays.

Northern lesser bush babies *(Galago senegalensis)*; photo by Leanne T. Nash

In some primates, such as apes and Old World monkeys, the attachment between mothers and infants encompasses a rich array of interactive behaviors, such as grooming, cuddling, play, restraint, and retrieval. In other species, however, such as capuchins and squirrel monkeys, attachment is reflected by the most basic behaviors—carrying by the mother and clinging by the infant. Nonhuman primate mothers are aware of their infants' growing capabilities and encourage independent behavior. They do not hover over or dote on their infants; rather, their close proximity allows them to intervene in a squabble or retrieve an infant that has gotten itself into trouble. As the period of infant dependence comes to a close, the responsibility for maintaining proximity falls increasingly on the youngster. At first gently, and then more punitively, a mother rejects her offspring's attempts to suckle or be carried, and the older infant gradually adjusts to being on its own.

Bowlby believed that "learning to distinguish the familiar from the strange is the key process in the development of attachment."[30] As the infant human or nonhuman primate's ability to recognize and respond to its mother increases, the infant selectively prefers her for interaction, especially when it is distressed. The young primate's developing abilities to distinguish the familiar from the strange lead it to fancy the individual whose touch, smell, voice, appearance, and behavior are most familiar to him—his mother.

EFFIE, an adult female mountain gorilla, impressed Dian Fossey as a very skilled mother compared to other gorilla females she had observed. Fossey was struck by Effie's even disposition, affectionate nature, patience, stability, and consistent discipline of her youngsters.[31] The rapport between Effie and her brood was impressive, and Fossey attributed the self-confidence of Effie's offspring to the stable and secure relationship they had with their mother while growing up. Other primatologists have described distinctive differences in maternal style among the primate mothers they have studied.[32]

A mother's maternal style is a blend of her temperament and life experiences. Calm, self-confident, cautious, and anxious mothers each respond to their babies quite differently. It is tempting to look at

Vervets *(Chlorocebus aethiops);* photo by Lynn A. Fairbanks

temperament as the genetic contribution to maternal style, but researchers of human and nonhuman primates have independently found that a mother's temperament and maternal style are at least somewhat influenced by her experiences growing up and by changes in her living environment.

Lynn Fairbanks is intrigued by individual differences in mothering style among nonhuman primate mothers. She and her colleagues have devoted over 20 years to the study of maternal style in vervets, sleek, silvery, peace-loving primates native to Africa.[33] Fairbanks enjoys observing the easy balance of power between male and female vervets, in which females have a slight edge. Although vervets have clear dominance hierarchies in which every monkey is aware of its position, they are able to maintain their ranks without the gratuitous aggression characteristic of many other Old World monkeys. With over 100 captive vervets in her research facility, Fairbanks conducts experiments designed to answer very specific questions about how maternal style develops, and how it affects the personality and behavior of offspring. Fairbank's work with captive vervets offers the best experimental data to date on maternal style in primates.

Fairbanks focuses on two dimensions of maternal style—protectiveness and rejection. She defines "protectiveness" as those behaviors that bring a mother and offspring together, such as grooming, approaching, inspecting, and restraining. "Rejection" is scored when mothers reject, leave, or otherwise break contact with their youngsters. Fairbanks found that there were consistent individual differences in the maternal styles of different monkey mothers.[34] If a mother was protective or rejecting with one baby, she was likely to behave similarly with the next. Carol Berman, who studies semi–free-ranging troops of rhesus monkeys on Cayo Santiago Island in Puerto Rico, has found the same consistency in maternal style with successive infants.[35]

Does the consistency of maternal style reflect a genetic blueprint for the brain chemicals that regulate the sensation of fear or worry (associated with protectiveness) or calm self-confidence (associated with permissiveness and rejection)? Although each vervet mother has her own consistent style of reactivity (or temperament) on these two dimensions, Fairbanks discovered that certain environmental, social, and experiential conditions also influence how protective or rejecting mothers are.

Abundance of food and incidence of predation are just two of many environmental conditions that influence maternal style. Wild vervet mothers who live in both food-rich and food-poor habitats are more rejecting and less protective than those living in habitats intermediate in regard to food availability, but for very different reasons.[36] In high-quality habitats, mothers who reject their infants at an early age give birth yearly (versus every 2 years in poor-quality habitats) without higher risk of infant mortality. The earlier rejection costs the infant little in terms of its survival and eventual reproduction, while it greatly benefits the mother via her increased fecundity, nature's criterion for success. In food-poor habitats, mothers stop responding to their infant's distress calls sooner and wean them earlier than mothers in intermediate habitats because the nutritional cost to themselves, in terms of effort expended, may be too high to justify continued care. Protectiveness is also related to characteristics of habitat; for example, mothers are more protective in habitats perceived to be dangerous. When there are many predators, mothers even respond to the alarm calls of older, weaned offspring, whisking them to safety long after they otherwise would no longer carry them.[37]

Social factors also influence mothering style. Mothers respond to perceived dangers in the social environment, such as the presence of many zealous but inexperienced young females vying for the opportunity to babysit or the absence of their own mothers, who often protect their grandkids.[38] In one experiment, Fairbanks showed that a mother vervet's perception of danger from other group members resulted in greater maternal protectiveness. Adult male vervets are not typically involved with infants and may be perceived by mothers as a threat to their safety. Fairbanks introduced an unfamiliar adult male into a group with mothers and their infants in certain years ("new male years"), but not in others ("resident male years"), and measured how protective mothers were under these two conditions. Although mothers protected their young more when a new male was present, their behavior was not grossly different from their usual modus operandi; maternal style was only moderately influenced by changes in the social environment.[39]

What mothering style works best may differ with a mother's social status. Infants of low-ranking baboon mothers endure regular abuse by other group members, so their mothers protect and restrict them more to ensure their safety. High-ranking baboon mothers restrict and protect their infants less and are both more permissive and more rejecting than lower-status mothers, because their high status affords their infants protection from harassment by other group members.[40] The freedom to explore and interact with others enhances the self-confidence of their infants and facilitates earlier independence.

Experience also affects maternal style. First-time mothers protect their babies more and reject them less than older, more experienced mothers, and a mother is more protective when her previous infant has died. Even more intriguing, Fairbanks learned that an infant's early experience greatly influences its adult maternal style. The best predictor of the average amount of contact between vervet mothers and infants during the first 6 months of the infant's life is the amount of contact that the mother had with her *own* mother when she was a baby.[41] Fairbanks believes that early experience is a better predictor of mothering behavior in vervets than either genetic similarity between mothers and daughters or observational learning.

Carol Berman agrees that maternal style is passed on by nongenetic means to daughters in free-living rhesus monkeys, but her studies show that the best predictor of maternal style in rhesus monkeys is experience after, rather than during, infancy.[42] A rhesus monkey mother's maternal style most closely matches that of her mother with her younger siblings, which suggests that the most profound influence on her adult maternal style is her observation of her mother's maternal behavior, rather than her own experience with her mother.

Individual differences in mothering behavior are passed on to the next generation in monkeys, through individual experience or observation. Fairbanks suggests that the pattern of early mother-infant interaction influences a vervet's "expectations" about and emotional reactions to its environment and future offspring.

Evidence for the effects of experience on temperament and personal style in human children comes from the work of the developmental psychologist Jerome Kagan. Kagan's long-term studies of temperament show that children are born with tendencies to respond in predictable ways to their environment. Some respond to environmental changes fearfully or angrily, while others calmly take changes in stride. Kagan's studies, like those of Fairbanks, also reveal that temperament can be influenced somewhat by the environment in which one is raised.

Kagan measured changes in children's temperament between the ages of 4 months and 7 years.[43] He classified several healthy 4-month-old infants as high reactors (easily excited or fearful) or low reactors (relaxed and unafraid), depending upon their responses to an unfamiliar stimulus. Kagan waved colorful mobiles in front of a baby, played a tape saying, "Hello baby, how are you doing today?" and popped a balloon behind the baby's head. High reactors thrashed around and cried, while low reactors rested or even laughed during the tests. By the time these infants were 4 years old, some of the high reactors were quite shy, subdued, and quiet, while others had moved toward the center of Kagan's "shy-bold" continuum. By the age of 7, only 15 percent of the initially low reactors were ebullient, fearless, and highly sociable kids, and the rest had moved closer to the center. None of the high reactors became fearless, and none of the low reactors became fearful; in other words, environment only moderately affected the final outcome.

Could maternal style also influence a young vervet's temperament? Fairbanks designed clever experiments to tease out the effects of a mother's style on her infant's behavior as it grew up.[44] In one study, she examined the willingness of young vervets to explore a novel environment. To explore a new situation, a monkey must be both curious and unafraid (similar to Kagan's definition of "bold"). Fairbanks discovered that a juvenile vervet's response to a new environment could be predicted by how protective his mother was when he was an infant. Infants with protective mothers were very cautious; they took a much longer time to enter a new enclosure than peers who had been raised by less protective mothers.

The maternal style experienced by vervet infants also predicted their behavior as adolescents.[45] Fairbanks and her coworkers observed the responses of adolescent males to a potentially dangerous situation: the sudden appearance of an unfamiliar adult male in an enclosure close to the adolescent's cage. Adolescence is the time when young vervet males leave their home troop and emigrate into a new troop to breed. A certain amount of boldness is necessary for young males to navigate the transition to adulthood successfully, because they must learn to travel alone, explore new territory, and challenge unfamiliar adult males for the right to breed. Fairbanks tested boldness by observing how adolescent males responded to the unfamiliar adult male. Bold or fearful responses to the male stranger could be predicted from the maternal style the adolescent males had experienced in infancy. Males whose mothers rejected them moderately early were bolder, while males with more protective mothers were more cautious and fearful. The bold adolescents approached the stranger often and aggressively displayed to or threatened him. The fearful adolescents stayed as far away from the stranger as possible.

Although the American ideal is a bold, fearless, highly independent youngster, there are costs to both excessive boldness and timidity. Impulsive, overly confident behavior can be a death sentence. To a vervet, the most serious cost of his mother's permissiveness and early rejection of him (and his subsequent development of boldness), is that he is more likely to die—from ill health due to early weaning, from predation or environmental hazards, or as a result of his mother's lackadaisical response to his distress cries.[46] As juveniles, bold youngsters may be at higher risk than their more cautious peers simply because of the high mortality rates of juvenile nonhuman primates.[47] But when bold youngsters do survive, they become independent earlier and "more enterprising and resourceful" than youngsters whose mothers were more protective.[48] The association of early independence with permissive and rejecting mothers is characteristic of many Old World monkeys, such as rhesus macaques and baboons.[49]

Two clinical case histories demonstrate the problems that may develop when human children experience extremes in parental rejection or protection. Steve is a handsome, muscular 25-year-old whose agenda for therapy was to understand why his relationships with women typically failed. Although he wanted nothing more than to marry and have children, Steve admitted that he had repeatedly cheated on the girlfriend he loved, and his behavior had caused her to leave him. When I asked for his developmental history, I learned that he had instigated many physical fights as an adolescent and had prided himself on his strength and ability to intimidate others. As a small child, he had lived in fear of his father, who beat him severely and unpredictably. Because his mother was also intimidated by his father, she could not protect him. Steve now believes his physical strength protects him from being hurt. He neither trusts nor depends on anyone, avoids his family, and confides in no one. From the outside, Steve appears fiercely independent, bold, and unafraid. His internal reality, however, is that although he longs for connection with others, his expectation that others will hurt him justifies his tenaciousness in pushing them away.

The second case demonstrates how parental overprotection may exacerbate the problems associated with an inhibited, fearful temperament. Faye is a 13-year-old girl who was referred by her physician. She missed school several days a week because she was "sick" with severe head, back, and stomach pain; but the tests her doctor ordered revealed no organic disorder. Faye's parents reported that she had been an excitable child who overreacted negatively to change or novelty. As an older infant, she screamed when babysitters were present. By the age of 4, she was still irritable and easily upset, and refused to leave her mother's side to play with other children. Faye's mother, Gwen, remembered how fearful she herself had been growing up. It had been easier for Gwen to empathize with her daughter's pain than encourage her to confront her fears.

Faye's "illnesses" had made her very powerful at home; her parents allowed her to do whatever she wanted because they were afraid of upsetting her. They brought food to her in her room and allowed her to watch 5 or 6 hours of television a day. They left her alone when she was irritable, so that she would not become ill. Therapy revolved around relabeling the "pain" Faye experienced as anxiety. Faye learned that fear increased her bodily tension, which resulted in headaches and other uncomfortable physical symptoms. Faye did not make up the headaches—her tension and fear of others produced them. A combination of medication, problem-solving skills, and consequences for staying home from school helped Faye to face the challenges of growing up.

There are costs and benefits to protecting and rejecting one's young, and as long as neither behavior is excessive, young primates grow up bold and cautious enough to cope with the demands of life. Although the boundaries of temperament are constrained by the mixture of neurochemicals in our brains, it is clear that our parents' style of responding affects the way our temperament is expressed when we are grown.

J.D. is a retired circus chimpanzee, born in the wild, who now lives at the Stanford Outdoor Primate facility. With the birth of her first baby, nothing went as it should.[50] Normally, chimpanzees give birth at night, like humans. J.D.'s first baby arrived during the day, however, much to the delight of the rest of the chimpanzees in her living group. J.D. was 20 feet above the ground when her baby was born, but she did not reach down and grab it, as experienced mothers do. Her baby fell to the ground, where it was instantly picked up and manhandled by curious juveniles. A more unpleasant introduction to the world is hard to imagine. J.D. handled the births of subsequent young much more appropriately.

First-time mothers, primiparas, behave differently with their young than do experienced mothers (multiparas). Although primiparas protect and restrict their young more than multiparas, their inexperience increases the likelihood that they will make a fatal error. Nancy Nicolson looked at the infant mortality rate of primiparous versus multiparous olive baboon mothers. In their first 6 months of life, 43 percent of the infants of first-time mothers died, compared to 6 percent of the infants of experienced mothers.[51] The rate of infant mortality is higher among primiparous rhesus, howler, and captive squirrel monkeys as well. The behavior of some first-time Japanese macaque mothers shows how maternal inexperience can result in tragedy. The Japanese macaques that live in Jigokudoni Park in Japan enjoy swimming in hot springs and dive for food provided by park officials. But primiparas are no longer permitted to enter the water, because inexperienced mothers may dive for food with their babies on their backs, drowning their infants. Multiparas virtually never make this mistake.[52]

First-time nonhuman primate mothers are more excitable and protective than more relaxed, experienced mothers. They approach and leave their infants more often, react more anxiously to whatever is going on, and handle their babies clumsily or ineptly.[53] Yet primiparous mothers reject their infants less frequently, less vigorously, and at an older age than experienced mothers.

Why are first-time monkey mothers more reactive to their infants than experienced mothers? Maybe it is only partly due to inexperience. Carol Berman believes it also has something to do with the fact that primiparas have only one youngster.[54] Experienced mothers are more rejecting and less protective when they have older offspring to contend with; they offer the breast to their infant less frequently, make the infant more responsible for maintaining proximity, and encourage independence earlier. Human mothers with more than one child can relate—the demands of multiple children reduce the likelihood that mothers will hover over their children.

A mother's behavior with her infant is influenced by a multitude of factors, including maternal condition, age, social support, infant responsiveness, maternal style, and experience, both in her family of origin and as a parent. To this list, we must add the impact of culture, which prescribes the parenting rules believed to produce the behaviors valued by the culture, as well as who is responsible for the routine care of infants.

MOST human mothers want to give their babies the best possible care. But how does one define "best"? Parenting behavior in human societies reflects the values and beliefs of culture, which in turn are influenced by ecology (how we survive in the environment in which we live) and by the economy (how we utilize and manage wealth and resources). The economy, which sets the ground rules for how adults make their living, significantly affects how humans parent their children.[55]

What are some of the parenting behaviors that are affected by cultural values and beliefs? In her book, *Our Babies, Ourselves,* the anthropologist Meredith Small delves deeply into three key parental behaviors with infants that vary greatly with culture: the amount of time spent in contact with one's baby (including holding, carrying, and sleeping with it), nursing, and responsiveness to crying.[56]

How do nonhuman primate mothers perform on these three dimensions of mothering? First of all, most primate mothers are in constant physical contact with their infants. Prosimian mothers, however, are a little different from monkey and ape mothers, especially in nocturnal and solitary species. They regularly "park" their babies on a branch while they go out for an evening of foraging.[57] An infant clings to the spot where its mother left it, quiet and motionless, occasionally for as long as 15 hours. Since the coloring and behavior of infants camouflages them, parking infants is a fairly safe practice. And because the content of prosimian milk is very high in fat and protein, a prosimian baby tolerates long periods without milk without serious nutritional consequences. When a prosimian mother returns from filling up on the insects that will provide the next day's milk, she is as attentive to her baby as monkey and ape mothers.

Nonhuman primate mothers always sleep with their infants. Baby apes sleep with their mothers at least until they are weaned, and sometimes longer. Birute Galdikas, who rehabilitates captive orangutans and reintroduces them into the wild, knows exactly what it is like to sleep with a baby orangutan. The first thing Galdikas discovered while raising orphaned infant orangutans was the strength of the grasp of these tiny orange creatures. A tenacious grasp makes evolutionary sense because an infant separated from its mother will not survive. Galdikas and her husband shared their bed with a series of needy, orphaned orangutan infants, who clung desperately to Galdikas (and urinated on her and her husband during the night for weeks).[58] Attachment in nonhuman primates is a process of nonstop physical intimacy.

Another perk of being their mothers' constant companions is that nonhuman primate infants can suckle on demand. Nonhuman primate infants suckle briefly as frequently as every 10 to 15 minutes, and mothers carry on with many of their normal activities while their babies are nursing.

Infant nonhuman primates rarely cry, perhaps because they are so successful at getting their needs met. When they do cry, however, mothers respond rapidly. Mothers typically are solicitous when infants are sick or injured. Jane Goodall, for example, described a chimpanzee mother named Olly who responded lovingly to her infant, a victim of polio.[59] Olly handled her baby tenderly for the duration of its life.

The nonhuman primate parenting rulebook prescribes that mothers be available and responsive to their babies, sleep with them, and nurse on demand. Mothers may have evolved this strategy to increase the likelihood of infant survival in the face of the many dangers that threaten infants—years of poor food availability, parasites, disease, predators, or even infanticide by other group members.

How do human mothers, who are influenced by culture as well as by experience and temperament, vary from the basic primate pattern? The answer is, until recently, very little. The !Kung San, also known as the Bushmen of the Kalahari Desert in Africa, were studied by the anthropologist Richard Lee (and many others) in the 1960s, during a time when many lived as nomadic hunter-gatherers, the way of life of our earliest human ancestors.[60] Mothering behavior in nomadic !Kung San is remarkably similar to that of nonhuman primates. Mothers are their babies' constant companions for 3 to 4 years; whatever a mother is doing, her baby is along for the ride. Mothers provide two thirds of the food eaten by their community, gathering nuts, berries, and leafy greens, and carrying these foods back to camp. Mothers carry their children on gathering trips until they are 4 years old. Traveling from 2 to 12 miles to gather food, a mother carries up to 35 pounds of food as well as her small child.[61]

Nomadic !Kung mothers tote their infants in a sling on their hip, and their long, pliable breasts dangle free so that older babies can reach out for a breast and nurse whenever they like, as often as every

13 minutes![62] Mothers and babies sleep together, so babies nurse throughout the night. And since mothers are always with their babies, they are immediately aware when their infants are distressed, making rapid responding possible. A mother typically responds to her infant's cry by offering the breast. And since an untended infant is at higher risk of mortality, it is in a mother's best interest to respond to her baby. As in nonhuman primates, the most pressing goal of nomadic !Kung mothers is infant survival.

Many !Kung San today have traded a nomadic, foraging lifestyle for a more sedentary one, based on tending small gardens or a few livestock, or exchanging labor for food. As the mobility of the !Kung has decreased, so has their average interbirth interval. The tolerant, indulgent maternal care that is the trademark of nomadic !Kung whose children are spaced 3 to 5 years apart may have become a casualty of the higher fertility of less mobile populations.[63]

Mothers in preindustrial societies such as the !Kung contribute to family resources *and* simultaneously care for their babies. Mothers in the United States who work outside the home, in contrast, rarely can take their babies along. How does maternal behavior in modern industrial societies differ from that of nonhuman primates and the !Kung San?

The parenting behavior of modern mothers in the United States presents a striking contrast to that of nonhuman primate and !Kung mothers on the three dimensions of maternal behavior described above—breastfeeding on demand, sleeping with infants, and responding to crying. Over the past hundred years or so, mothering has been deemed too difficult for mothers to manage without the intervention of the medical establishment, and doctors and other "experts" have handed mothers a variety of behavioral prescriptions for infant care. Mothers have essentially been advised *not* to behave like nonhuman primates—not to breastfeed on demand (and instead,

feed babies infant formula on a schedule), not to sleep with their infants, and not to rapidly and consistently respond to their baby's
cries (to avoid spoiling them).

How American mothers feed their babies is a prime example of
how the medical establishment has persuaded mothers to deviate
from basic primate patterns. Most primate babies around the world,
human and nonhuman, nurse when they are hungry rather than
according to a schedule prescribed by a physician. But since 1769,
when the London physician William Cadogan penned a widely read
essay on infant care, doctors have instructed mothers about how to
feed their babies.[64] Many aspects of breastfeeding characteristic of
both nonhuman primate mothers and human mothers in preindustrial cultures were questioned; first mothers were told to limit the
number of daily feedings, then to eliminate night feedings, then to
shorten the duration of nursing sessions, then to reduce the number
of months of feeding, and finally to eliminate breastfeeding altogether.[65]

Although babies can learn to eat every few hours rather than
snacking every few minutes, they prefer to be attended to immediately. American mothers don't feed their babies on demand for many
reasons—their doctors have advised them not to, their husbands
don't approve, it is inconvenient, or it is impossible. In the 1990s,
over half of mothers with infants under the age of 1 year were employed full-time, and most working women cannot have their babies
delivered to the office to nurse every few hours, much less feed them
on demand.[66] Half of American babies are bottle-fed, and it is easier
to encourage an infant to take a full bottle every few hours than to
provide a small amount of milk every few minutes. Even breastfeeding stay-at-home mothers rarely have time (or are encouraged) to
nurse every few minutes.

Mothers who want to breastfeed have to carefully plan their itineraries to avoid disapproving stares (or more serious consequences). Breastfeeding in public became legal in Florida and New York only in the early 1990s, and not until 1997 in California.[67] Breastfeeding mothers have been asked to leave museums and department stores, and have even been arrested for indecent exposure![68] Perhaps because breastfeeding is so difficult, the length of time infants are breastfed in the United States differs significantly from the time in other cultures; American mothers nurse their babies on average for about 4 months, compared to the 2 to 3 years that is standard in preindustrial societies.[69]

What is best for babies? Babies have been raised on breast milk for all but the last few decades of our species' history. In the United States, breastfeeding was the standard until the 1930s.[70] With the advent of the first artificial formulas shortly thereafter, women suddenly had a choice about what to feed their babies. Many doctors initially championed formula over breast milk, and companies that manufactured infant formula attempted to persuade mothers that bottled formula was best for their babies.[71] We now know that breastfeeding protects infants in many ways. Breast milk contains substances that provide natural immunities to disease, so breastfed babies are less prone to inner ear infections and respiratory and gastrointestinal disease.[72] In developing countries where the sanitary conditions necessary for properly preparing infant formula are not always available, formula feeding is even less safe. Recent research suggests that breastfed babies are less likely to become obese later in life than bottle-fed infants.[73] Most important, breastfed babies are less likely to die as infants or young children than those who are bottle-fed.[74] There is no denying the advantage to babies who are nurtured with the fluid designed for them by nature.

The medicalization of mothering also has influenced infant sleep patterns in the United States. Doctors first began to warn mothers not to sleep with their babies during the nineteenth century, suggesting that they could inadvertently smother their infants by "overlaying" them. And mothers complied with the doctor's orders—not only do most American babies not sleep next to their mothers at night during their first year or two, they usually sleep alone in a dark, silent room. This certainly isn't the way of nonhuman primate babies, who catch a few winks during the day while clinging to their mother, and snuggle close to her at night, breastfeeding on demand. It is also not the way of !Kung babies, who sleep on their mother during the day and next to her at night. In a study of 186 other preindustrial human cultures, babies under the age of 1 year slept with or in the same room as their mothers, without exception.[75]

When asked why they don't sleep with their babies, some American mothers, who have taken to heart the warnings of experts, say that they might accidentally roll over on and suffocate their babies. The anthropologist James McKenna, who studies the sleep of human infants and their mothers, reassures us that babies around the globe safely sleep with their parents; a piercing wail or a few kicks alert a parent to move over.[76] Unless parents are obese, intoxicated, or drugged, the chance that they will suffocate their infant is negligible.[77] Other mothers feel pressed to quickly resume the sexual relationship with their husband, and think that the marital bed should be private. Marital privacy, however, is a relatively recent concern in the history of our species. The idea that romantic love between spouses (relegated by many couples to the marital bed) is a necessary or even desirable component of marriage first emerged during the seventeenth century in Europe. For millions of years before that, human mothers and their infants were each other's sleeping companions. Expecting our babies to sleep alone, doing without the comfort of the breast and the loving touch of their mother, is a departure from the way evolution has scripted infant care in primates for millions of years.

After mothers were advised not to sleep with their babies, they were then counseled to let their infants cry themselves back to sleep if they awoke during the night, rather than get up and minister to their needs. Doctors and childcare experts then informed mothers that they could actually spoil their babies with too much attention.[78] A study done in the early 1970s revealed that the advice had found its mark—mothers in the United States did not respond to almost half of their infant's crying episodes during their first 3 months of life, believing either that a response was unnecessary or that too quick a response would produce a spoiled child.[79]

Maternal responsiveness was also studied from the baby's perspective—how long must an infant cry before its mother responds? When researchers compared the average amount of crying by infants in different human cultures, they found that the pattern of crying (more in the first 8 weeks than later, more at night than during the day) was pretty similar in most cultures. What was different, however, was the duration of crying; babies from Western industrial countries cry much longer than babies from other cultures. Why are Western infants more prone to long crying bouts? Meredith Small suggests the reason is that their mothers are less likely to quickly respond to them than mothers in other cultures.[80]

Infants carried by their mothers cry less than those contained in other ways—in cribs, playpens, and so on—perhaps because they are soothed by their mother's constant presence, movement, and touch. In an intriguing experiment, Urs Hunziker and Ronald Barr asked one group of mothers to carry their babies for 3 hours (outside of feeding time), and gave no special instructions to a second group of mothers. Mothers in the first group carried their babies about 4.5 hours a day, while the mothers in the second group carried their infants a little over 2.5 hours a day. Although the frequency with which the babies began to cry was similar, the duration of crying was not.

Babies who were carried more cried for much shorter periods—43 percent shorter—than babies who were carried less.[81]

Human hunter-gatherers carry infants on average more than 50 percent of the time (the !Kung San carry infants 80 to 90 percent of the time) during the day in their first few months of life.[82] In the United States in the 1970s, mothers carried their 3-month-old babies only about 33 percent of the time, and their 9-month-olds only 16 percent of the time.[83] And modern mothers who constantly keep their babies close to them in some type of sling may be viewed as providing excessive, rather than essential care. Hunting and gathering (with the baby along for the ride) was our way of life for 99 percent of our history as a species, so we have "suddenly" changed a key component of infant care in the last few decades, a blip on the radar screen of our species' existence.

Are we spoiling our babies when we carry them and respond quickly to their cries? Not according to millions of years of human and nonhuman primate evolutionary history. If crying was not an adaptive way for babies to get their needs met, why would it have evolved in every species in the primate order (and in other mammals and birds, as well)? Crying is a baby's only way to tell us that something is wrong. The crying stops when we respond rapidly and persists when we do not. An unhappy, unattended baby learns that he can not depend on his mother to comfort him. The baby's foundation of trust, which begins with the interactive dance between him and his mother, is a casualty of his mother's unresponsiveness.

OBVIOUSLY, parenting behaviors in nonhuman primates and early human societies evolved in different circumstances than those in which we now live, and were designed by nature to increase the probability that infants would survive. But the primate parenting patterns of breastfeeding, co-sleeping, and rapidly responding to distress are quite agreeable today to those human infants fortunate enough to experience them. An awareness of the evolutionary history of primate parenting may help a mother choose the type of care she wishes to offer her child, rather than simply adhering to the current cultural prescription.

The primate recipe for mothering contains a few basic ingredients—constant body contact, breastfeeding, and consistent, rapid, responsiveness. Although each mother may adjust the amount of each ingredient she adds to the parenting mix in accordance with cultural prescriptions and the demands of her environment, as far as her children are concerned, if a little bit is good, a whole lot is better.

CHAPTER 3

The Diversity of Primate Fathering

On a lazy summer afternoon, Joe, a 10-year-old male cottontop tamarin, stretched out in the shade of the peach tree in his outdoor cage. His 4-month-old daughter, Rosie, toddled down the 30-foot runway to the chihuahua-sized doggy door entrance to her air-conditioned indoor cage. The flap on the doggy door is easy for an adult tamarin to master: lift it up, duck under, and hop inside. Rosie attempted to lift the flap many times, but was not strong enough. The runway was in full sun on a very hot day. Rosie began to utter soft distress cries as she hopped about in front of the doggy door. Joe stood up and stretched, abandoned his shady perch, and ambled down the runway toward Rosie. He lifted the flap, she hopped inside, and he meandered back down the runway to the peach tree.

ALTHOUGH it is fairly simple to describe how primate mothers care for their infants, there are as many different recipes for primate fatherhood as there are for chocolate cake. In fact, the only consistencies are that paternal behavior is enormously variable and that adult male primates are considerably more involved with their young, on average, than are most other mammalian fathers. Fewer than 10 percent of male mammals help raise young, but the figure jumps to nearly 40 percent in nonhuman primates.[1] And among humans, there is no known culture in which fathers (or father-figures) play no role in childrearing.[2]

It may be misleading to call nonhuman primate males "fathers," since paternity is often uncertain. In species that are monogamous or in which only one adult male lives with a group of females, the resident male is probably (but not invariably) the biological father. But many species of nonhuman primates live in communities comprised of many adult males and females who are not bonded to one another. In societies like these, in which both males and females have multiple sexual partners, we can't assume that males are certain which infants are their own. When biological paternity is impossible to infer, I will focus on the behavior of adult males toward youngsters, rather than on the behavior of "fathers."

What type of care do primate fathers offer their young? From our twenty-first-century perspective, we might predict that a father's essential roles revolve around the provision of resources and the offer of paternal care. But we would be missing a key component of primate fatherhood: the protection of infants from unrelated males who wish to kill them (and abscond with their mothers).

PRIMATE fathers (or males who have good reason to believe that they are fathers) offer three types of paternal care: they protect infants from infanticide; they provide care and nurturing, and they provide their families with resources. Nonhuman primate fathers offer only protection and caregiving, while human fathers are capable of all three forms of care.

Protection is probably the type of care most uniformly offered by primate fathers. Infanticide (the intentional murder of unweaned infants) has been documented in five of the six primate radiations (including humans), with tarsiers as the only exception.[3] Adult males who typically kill infants are *not* the infants' biological fathers in any of these species; instead, they are rival males, unrelated to the infants, who either wish to mate with sexually receptive females (nursing primate females typically are not sexually receptive) or do not wish to invest in the care of a new mate's infant by another sire.

The anthropologist Sarah Hrdy, an expert on infanticide, contends that "for a wide variety of primate species, including humans, an incursion of unrelated males who never mated with the mother is potentially bad news for immatures—especially those not yet weaned."[4] In nonhuman primate societies in which one resident male has many female mates (polygynous societies such as those of howler monkeys, Hanuman langurs, and mountain gorillas), when a female joins a male's family or when a new young patriarch takes ownership of another's harem, infanticide is commonly the result. Fourteen percent

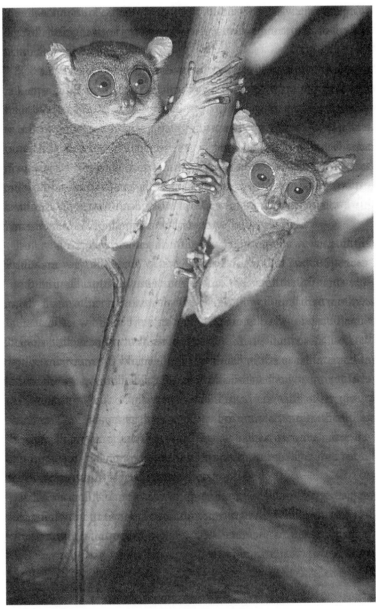

Philippine tarsiers *(Tarsius syrichta)*; photo by Noel Rowe

of mountain gorilla and 12 percent of red howler infants succumb to infanticide.[5] Infanticide also occurs in multimale multifemale societies in which many males and females live together without permanent pair bonds; primatologists have demonstrated that unrelated males attack infants in these species, and actual or "possible" biological fathers (males who mated with the mother during the last period of sexual receptivity before her pregnancy) defend them.[6]

Infanticidal males also lurk in the bushes in human societies today (and undoubtedly did so in our ancient past). Some kidnap women (for mates), killing their infants and sometimes even older children. For example, it has been reported that Yanomamo men raid other communities, stealing women and murdering their children.[7] Among the Paraguayan Áche, a father's mere presence protects his child; when a father dies (or abandons his spouse) soon after his infant's birth, the infant's mother may abandon it, or, more commonly, other members of the group are instructed by elders to kill the infant or bury it alive with its father.[8] And in industrial societies such as those of the United States, Canada, and Great Britain, stepfathers are proportionately much more likely to abuse or even kill the children of their spouses (or girlfriends) than are biological fathers.[9] Sociobiologists would say that men have not been wired to invest in the care of children sired by others. Hrdy says, "I think we can conclude that women have always had a problem with unrelated men behaving savagely toward their children."[10]

The role of devoted caregiver is not one often embraced by primate males, human or nonhuman. Fathers may help out (usually when mothers are unavailable), but rarely act as co-primary caregivers. Male nonhuman primates never are the primary caretakers of unweaned infants, for obvious reasons. In those exceptional instances when fathers take on the role of co-primary caregiver, they typically are reasonably certain that the infants they are caring for are their own. Co-primary caretaking nonhuman primate fathers and their mates are monogamous and usually spend virtually all of their time together, which greatly decreases the chances of infidelity.

There appear to be no human societies in which fathers *typically* act as co-primary caregivers. But in those societies in which fathers are most involved with infants, they are reasonably assured of paternity: monogamy is the rule, and fathers spend most of their time in the vicinity of their mates and children.[11] Aka pygmy fathers in central Africa, for example, invest heavily in their infants, holding them a whopping 20 percent of the time. An Aka pygmy husband can be pretty certain that the children he is investing in are his own—his wife is in view of him during the day about 46 percent of the time.[12] When primate fathers care for their young, however, it is not necessarily easy to discern their true motivation—are they wholeheartedly investing in their children, or are they merely doing whatever is necessary to maintain their relationship (including sexual access) with their mate?[13]

Although nonhuman primate males often allow infants to take food from them, the provisioning offered by human fathers in all cultures is unique among primates.[14] Hunter-gatherer fathers capture and share game, fathers in agrarian societies provide food, shelter, land, and livestock, and fathers in industrial societies provide a home, food, transportation, and college tuition. Many fathers feel that they have done their job well when they provide the resources that their family needs. And society agrees—in the case of divorce, nonresident fathers in the United States who pay child support satisfy society's basic requirements. Divorced fathers may go to jail for not paying child support, but not for failing to visit their children. As Michael Lamb, who has studied fathering behavior for over 20 years, aptly states, "In almost all cultures direct paternal involvement is discretionary, whereas provision is mandatory."[15]

THE paternal behavior of adult male primates with infants runs the gamut from co-primary caregiver to disinterested onlooker. Some fathers specialize in protection; a rare few offer paternal care; and only humans provide resources. Along the spectrum of primate fatherhood, I will look at the roles of protection and provision in four types of primate fathers, who vary greatly on the dimension of paternal care: those who are intensively involved in the daily care of infants; those who have strong, enduring relationships with youngsters but are not responsible for their routine care; those who are occasionally affectionate with or protective of the young; and those who merely tolerate or ignore youngsters.[16]

There are only a few species of nonhuman primates in which fathers embrace the responsibility of full-time parenthood. These devoted fathers are most often found among the small monogamous species of monkeys that inhabit tropical forests in Central and South America. Primary caregiving primate fathers are intriguing to us, perhaps because human males so rarely tackle this role. But a primate male's biological backpack, equipped with testosterone and other androgens rather than estrogen, does not preclude him from becoming a competent caretaker for infants.

Look just above eye level in a tangle of vines in a Peruvian rainforest, and you might be fortunate enough to see what looks like three lumps of reddish-brown clay, glued together. Looking closer, you see three pairs of sparkling brown eyes and identify the three immobile figures as a family of dusky titi monkeys, resting and cuddling together. Below the monkeys hang their thick gray tails, entwined in a single luxuriant braid—a symbol of their mutual devotion.

Bolivian gray titi monkeys *(Callicebus donacophilus)*; photo by Noel Rowe

In the late 1970s, the primatologist Patricia Wright studied the parental behavior of dusky titis in one of the most remote field sites in the world, the Manú Biosphere Reserve, in southeastern Peru. Accessible only by a hair-raising truck journey over a one-way road across the Andes (the direction of travel changes at midnight), followed by several days by motorized canoe down the Alto Madre de Diós and Manú Rivers, this field site was so undisturbed by humans that monkeys quickly accepted the presence of the researchers following them. Wright rapidly earned the respect of her colleagues because of her utter fearlessness in the forest and her uncanny ability to follow her monkeys wherever they went.

Wright chose to study titi monkeys because she wanted to compare the behavior of small, monogamous, primate parents who usually have one infant with those who conceive twins, such as marmosets and tamarins. She found that titi fathers are just as devoted as tamarin fathers. During the first 2 weeks of life, they carry infants constantly, turning them over to mothers primarily for nursing.[17] As babies mature, fathers continue to perform most of the childcare. By 8 weeks of age, infants move around independently almost half of the time, but when they do get a ride, it is usually with their father.

Titi mothers nurse and do the lion's share of infant grooming, but fathers are responsible for everything else. Fathers are more likely than mothers to share food with their infants and act as a secure base for infants learning to travel independently. Wright described how a father sits quietly in a vine tangle, keeping an eye on his youngster, while it learns to maneuver among the vines. Infants rarely venture farther than a foot or two from their fathers and return to them often, "as if tethered."[18] When an infant cries out in distress, it is its father who usually responds.

The bond between titi mothers, fathers, and infants is strong, but the strongest bond of all is between fathers and infants.[19] It is easy to understand why it is essential for fathers to be intensively involved with infants in species which regularly have twins, such as marmosets and tamarins—mothers would have a tough time managing the burden of simultaneously carrying and nursing two relatively large babies. The single titi infant, however, is not nearly as heavy (in proportion to its mother's weight) as tamarin twins, so there is no obvious reason why titi fathers are such dutiful parents. Protection of infants from the murderous intentions of rival males is clearly not the answer, since infanticide has not been observed among the small monogamous South American monkeys that specialize in paternal care.

Although it isn't always clear why adult primate males in some species are more involved in direct infant care than in others, all species in which males help care for babies possess one or more of the following traits: they are small and monogamous (thus males are fairly certain of paternity); males are attracted to infants and actively pursue them; and/or mothers *permit* fathers (or other males) to interact with their babies.

The interdependence between husband and wife is apparently the key to understanding the Aka pygmy father's titi-like devotion to the care of his infant.[20] Aka pygmies are mobile hunter-gatherer-traders who spend their days hunting or gathering vegetable materials for food. But Aka pygmies hunt differently than do most other hunter-gatherers: nuclear families hunt together, and the participation of both spouses is crucial to the success of the hunt. The husband lays out the net and then drives small game forward. The wife hides behind a tree close to the net; when the prey passes, she jumps out, screams (startling the animal into the net), and usually dispatches it before the husband arrives.

Aka pygmies walk 5 to 15 kilometers a day on hunts.[21] The ratio of infant/adult female weight is high by cross-cultural standards, so mothers need help transporting their babies. It is too difficult for older siblings to carry infants over such long distances, so husbands and wives take turns. Husbands are happy to help carry infants on hunting excursions, because if their wives are too tired to actively partake in the hunt, it will not succeed.

The reciprocity and cooperation between husbands and wives is not limited to hunting trips. Fathers babysit in camp when mothers are engaged in preparing food or gathering firewood. Like titis, Aka pygmy spouses are together nearly all the time. In fact, in a 24-hour period (including sleep time, since husbands and wives sleep together in "a remarkably narrow bed"), husband and wife are in view of each other about 72 percent of the time.[22] In this fiercely egalitarian society, in which the work of both husbands and wives is equally respected, devoted fatherhood is part of the Aka's adaptation to their environment.

In the United States today, there are a few titi-like primary caregiving fathers. They manage the home and raise the children while their wives take primary responsibility for the provision of resources. Unlike titi and Aka pygmy fathers, however, they handle their domestic duties (at least, during the work week) in isolation. Rather than cooperatively caring for their infants in a community of like-minded couples, they function more like single parents.

Although these fathers do a good job with house care and childcare, their chosen path puts them at odds with traditional fatherhood, which is focused on provision rather than childcare. The most important predictor of the success of these primary caretaking dads is the support of their wives.[23] But even when wives approve of husbands who mind the kids, the father's (or couple's) friends or community may not.[24] Primary caregiving fathers complain that it is hard to fit in with groups of nonemployed mothers and kids and become "one of the girls." Unlike the Aka pygmy father, primary caregiving fathers in the United States are unlikely to know many (or any) other men embracing the same role and thus may have little in common with traditional fathers. And the economic hardships that often result when fathers don't earn a paycheck send many back to work. For these reasons, only a small minority of two-parent families in the United States put fathers in charge of the kids. And in only a fraction of these do fathers remain in charge over the long haul.[25]

ONE step down from the intensive caretaking of titi fathers are the strong, enduring, relationships that develop between adult males and infants, in which males play a significant role in infants' lives but offer little routine care. Rather than being a primary caregiver (or substitute mother) like a titi father, males in this group behave differently with infants than mothers do. Although they rarely carry infants (the hallmark of primate motherhood), they do cuddle, nuzzle, examine, groom, and protect infants from predators or other group members who might bother them. Males allow infants to feed beside them, so infants can snatch food scraps or beg for the high-quality foods that males often possess. Infants play with adult males far more frequently than they do with their mothers, and males are tolerant of infants scampering around or over them.[26]

A silverback male mountain gorilla, the patriarch of his harem family, not only is affectionate with his youngsters (which are virtually always his biological progeny), but is the individual most likely to adopt and care for immature offspring when they are orphaned. But just as important as, if not more important than, the care the silverback provides, is his role as protector of his biological offspring. The presence of a strong, healthy, biological father is an infant gorilla's best protection against infanticide by unrelated males.

Human fathers often fall into the category of affectionate patriarch because fathers typically are less involved with infants than mothers in most human societies.[27] In a study of 80 preindustrial human cultures, mothers were the primary, if not exclusive caretakers of infants; in only 4 percent of these societies did fathers and infants have regular, close relationships.[28] Similarly, in industrial societies such as that of the United States, fathers interact with children under the age of 5 significantly less frequently than mothers do, but more often when their wives are employed outside the home than when they stay home with the children.[29] As among nonhuman primates, the presence of biological fathers among humans, even when they are not devoted to childcare, protects their wives from the attentions of rival males, a function that indirectly contributes to the safety of their children.

MALES of many primate species don't routinely offer care, but step up to the plate when the situation demands it. Adoption of infants by primate males is one example of this, and protection of infants whose mothers are absent, careless, or inexperienced is another. Prime examples of primate godfathers are the savannah baboons of Amboseli National Park in southern Kenya. On the vast short-grass savannah that baboons share with leopards, lions, hyenas, vervets, elephants, wildebeest, and zebras, the primatologist Jeanne Altmann and her students have made meticulous observations of the behavior of baboons for over 20 years.

Although male baboons are not involved in the direct care of infants, their attention to favored youngsters acts as a buffer against the harsh conditions of savannah life. Infants rest with males, occasionally obtain scraps of meat from them, hitch rides on their backs, and run to them when distressed. Males often retrieve infants when their mothers ignore their cries (or inadvertently move off without them) and protect them from harassment by other group members.[30] For example, adult males may intervene when high-ranking baboon females approach lower-ranking females and wrestle their babies away from them. These "kidnappings" are usually brief, but not always.[31]

Being pulled away from its mother stresses both the infant (who can't nurse and may be handled roughly) and its mother, who appears anxious and frightened. When a low-ranking female has an adult male companion, however, other females are less likely to snatch her baby.

As is the case among vervets one mother in a baboon troop is not like another. Males may offer extra care when mothers reject or withhold care from their young at a relatively early stage in their development. A case in point was the budding friendship between an adult male named High Tail and an immature named Grendel, who was saddled with a relatively punitive and rejecting mother.[32] Although Grendel could no longer persuade his mother to carry him, he usually was able to catch a ride with High Tail, feed beside him, or sit in the shade of his large body on a hot summer's day.

The relationship between Grendel and High Tail is a good example of an adult male–infant relationship, baboon style. Adult males like High Tail, called "godfathers" by Altmann, offer companionship and protection from others in the group to certain mothers and their infants.[33] How do males select mother-infant pairs on whom to shower their attention? In a recent clever study, researchers counted how often adult males intervened on behalf of youngsters involved in a skirmish with another group member. Youngsters were classified into three categories: (1) a male's actual genetic offspring (unambiguously determined by DNA testing); (2) a male's "behavioral" offspring (infants of females with whom the male had repeatedly mated during the previous breeding season, but who were *not* his genetic offspring); and (3) infants that were neither genetic nor behavioral offspring. The lucky recipients of a male's care most often turned out to be his genetic offspring.[34] Because males selectively respond to their own offspring, the care they offer is truly parental, similar to that of dusky titi fathers.

The role of protector is a significant one among primate godfathers, because infanticide occurs in many species in this group. In chacma baboons, for example, an infant is protected from murderous unrelated males by familiar males who *could* be its biological father (males who mated with its mother during the period of sexual receptivity in which it was conceived).[35]

Another type of primate father is one who occasionally is friendly to or protects infants, but most often ignores them. An example of this type of casual, detached relationship between adult males and infants is found among red howler monkeys. During her field study of red howlers in Venezuela, Carolyn Crockett observed an interaction between an adult male and infant that can only be described as disdainful on the part of the adult. After a long bout of group roaring (howlers advertise the ownership of their territories by roaring), a troop of howlers appeared exhausted. Huddling close together, the adults drifted off to sleep. Rest time for adult howlers is the safest and most convenient time for infants to play or explore, and on this day, one infant crept off of his mother and onto an adult male. As the baby crawled across his chest, the huge male displayed his discomfort by pulling his hands back away from the infant as if repelled by its touch.[36]

Since infanticide occurs commonly among howler monkeys, the father's presence (especially in polygynous groups) protects his infants from death at the hands of unrelated males. Although a howler male provides virtually no care, the protection offered by his mere presence is the difference between life and death for his progeny.

Human fathers also commonly fall into the category of casual acquaintances, and these fathers often have more than one wife and many children. Among the polygynous Thonga of South Africa, fathers rarely interact with young children, and in fact, it is taboo for them to handle infants younger than 3 months old.[37] The primary parental role of Thonga fathers is as stern disciplinarian for older children. But like the howler monkey males, they protect their off-spring by blocking the access of male rivals to their mother.

The least paternal nonhuman primate males simply tolerate the presence of infants, rarely interact with them, and do not (directly) protect them. Although most group-living species in which males have essentially no relationship with infants live in relatively large, mixed groups of males and females, fathers in some monogamous and polygynous species fall into this category as well. For species in which infanticide occurs (such as Hanuman langurs), the presence of the resident male in polygynous families deters infanticide by pre-venting a takeover by rival males. In multimale multifemale groups of langurs, males who *could* be an infant's biological father com-monly defend it against rival males.[38] Although these males offer no care, the protection they provide is crucial for infant survival.

Another type of father in this category provides virtually nothing to his offspring beyond fertilization. Although this style is not typical of human fathers in any culture, individual fathers who impreg-nate mothers and then disappear, providing neither protection, care, nor resources, are found in many cultures. South American squirrel monkey males illustrate this type of noninteractive relationship be-tween adult males and infants; adult males rarely interact with in-fants and offer no care, play no role in protecting them, and as far as females are concerned, are persona non grata.

The golden-green squirrel monkeys of the New World tropics race through the forest in groups of 30 to 40 individuals. In my own piti-ful attempts to follow squirrel monkeys in the Manú Biosphere Re-serve in 1980, I was impressed by the speed with which these crea-tures locomote through the forest. After extricating myself from yet another vine tangle, I often looked up to find that, once again, my monkeys had disappeared. Despite the squirrel monkeys' frenetic physical and social activity, it became apparent that adult males

Common squirrel monkeys *(Saimiri sciureus)*; photo by Gustl Anzenberger

were not included in the friendly camaraderie between females and youngsters, who congregated in the troop's central core. Most of the time, males are relegated to the periphery of a large troop or travel together in bachelor groups, apart from females and young.

When the breeding season approaches, however, an adult male transforms into a primate Adonis: he gains weight and appears much larger around his shoulders, arms, and upper body.[39] Exuding virility, he confidently invades the personal space of females. Last year's infants have been weaned by this time, and adult females are sexually receptive. Males and females indulge in an orgy of mating, after which males return to their normal size, and females once again lose interest in them. When mothers give birth, they welcome female relatives and friends as huddling partners, occasionally allowing them to help with infant care. Adult males, no longer part of the "in" group, resume their exile on the troop's periphery.

HUMAN fathers around the globe most commonly enjoy affectionate and enduring relationships with their children without primary responsibility for routine care, but the huge individual differences among human fathers make generalizations about them nearly impossible. At the extremes of human fatherhood are titi-like fathers (albeit very few) who are their children's primary caretakers, and squirrel monkey–like fathers, who play no role in their children's development after conception. Most fathers, however, fall in between these two extremes and comfortably embrace the role of pinch-hitter.

In both preindustrial and industrial societies, the behavior of fathers with their infants is more similar to that of nonhuman primate fathers than it is to that of primate mothers, and fathers are available to their children (present, but not necessarily interacting with or caring for them) about half as often as mothers.[40] Human mothers pick up their babies most often to provide care, while fathers pick up their infants to hold or play with them.[41] Mothers' play is different from that of fathers; mothers choose toys or conventional games like pat-a-cake, while fathers prefer rough-and-tumble, highly stimulating play.[42] Play with Daddy is thus arousing, physical, and unpredictable, and undoubtedly more fun than playing with Mommy.[43] Before long, babies come to prefer their fathers to their mothers as play partners.[44] And since nonhuman primate mothers are not particularly playful, nonhuman primate males, from tamarins to gorillas, play with infants more than mothers do.[45]

In addition to playing with their babies, human fathers carry, babysit, and protect them, just as nonhuman primate fathers do. Human and nonhuman primate fathers are also similar in what they typically don't do—routine daily care of infants.[46] Certainly human fathers "help" with infant care, such as feeding, bathing, and so on, but rarely are they responsible for daily care. In a study of Australian fathers, fathers spent 1 hour per week (compared to 40 hours for mothers) performing routine care of infants, and 60 percent of fathers had never taken sole responsibility for their infants.[47] But although fathers typically don't shoulder the primary responsibility for infant care (and see themselves as helpers rather than as in charge), their interactions with their babies are certainly not negligible. On average, in industrial societies such as the United States and Australia, fathers interact with their children about one third as often as mothers, and are available to their children (present, but not necessarily interacting with or caring for them) about half as often as mothers.[48]

Human fathers, like most other male primates, rarely function as substitute mothers. But despite the fact that fathers behave differently than mothers, infants still form strong attachments to both parents at about the same point during their first year of life, and prefer both parents to other caregivers.[49] Although one parent is often preferred over the other, which parent is preferred may be related to context. For example, infants often prefer their fathers for play and their mothers for comfort.[50] Is this because mothers are naturally more responsive to their infants than fathers?

Ross Parke and his colleagues observed fathers of newborns in maternity wards in the early 1970s to see whether or not the biological makeup of mothers predisposed them to respond to infants differently (and perhaps more effectively) than fathers. For most of the behaviors the researchers measured, fathers and mothers differed little from each other.[51] Fathers spoke to their babies with high-pitched voices, just as mothers did, and responded promptly and sensitively to their infant's cues during feeding. Other researchers measured physiological responsiveness to infants and found that there were no differences between fathers and mothers in heart rate, blood pressure, or skin conductance when handling their babies.[52] But although fathers capably cared for their babies, they deferred to their wives to provide care when their wives were present. The obvious conclusion is that even though fathers are capable of sensitive and responsive caregiving, they do not always offer their services.[53]

Mary Ainsworth believes that babies become securely attached to their parents when parents respond quickly and appropriately to their signals. The strength of attachment of an infant to its parent is more related to parental behavior and familiarity than to gender. For example, when fathers are primary caretakers, infants prefer their fathers to their mothers when they are distressed.[54] Interestingly enough, the parental behavior of fathers who are primary caretakers is more like that of mothers than that of traditional fathers.[55] So although human fathers are typically less involved with their babies than mothers, they are clearly capable of more intense involvement. That infants attach securely to their fathers, despite far fewer interactions with them, suggests that the sheer volume of interaction is not as important as its quality in the development of attachment.[56]

If fathers and infants attach securely to each other and fathers are capable of competent caregiving, why are some fathers much more involved with babies than others? Fathers are influenced by two factors that aren't even an issue for mothers: the certainty that the offspring for whom they are caring are their own, and the "permission" of their spouses or mates to help care for offspring.

Evolutionary biologists and psychologists believe that paternity really matters to fathers, and in most primate species in which males are intensively involved in infant care, paternity is close to a sure thing. If we accept evolutionary theory's premise that an individual's behavior is driven by the ultimate (but unconscious) goal of transmitting genes to subsequent generations, then we must predict that males will behave in ways that will achieve this goal. Mating with many females is one way to reach this goal, and assisting females in caring for infants that are biologically theirs is another. Why should a male sacrifice his time to care for young that aren't his when he could be conceiving or caring for his own progeny?

Evolutionary theory posits that parents should invest more resources to raise biologically related offspring than unrelated young-sters, and three types of evidence support that view. First, monog-amously mated fathers, whose paternity is reasonably certain, offer more infant care than polygynous fathers. This is true in humans as well.[57] Second, a human (and sometimes, a nonhuman primate) mother may conceal evidence regarding the paternity of a child whose biological father is not her husband or mate, for fear he will aban-don her or harm her child. And third, human fathers typically are warmer, more attentive to, and more generous with biological chil-dren than with stepchildren.[58]

And yet the exceptions to the certainty-of-paternity rule merit a closer look. For example, when a langur male takes over a new troop, he frequently kills infants sired by his predecessor. Although the new resident is certain to be the father of subsequent infants that are born, he shows little interest in his progeny. For male gibbons, pater-nity also is fairly certain (although even among monogamous gib-bons, there are opportunities for infidelity), but gibbon fathers rarely interact with their infants and do not participate in their daily care. Thus a high certainty of paternity doesn't always predict paternal caregiving.[59] In some multimale multifemale species in which mating is promiscuous (and paternity is thus uncertain), males interact with and protect infants. There are many examples of adult male non-human primates who are not bonded with any particular female who "adopt" orphans whose mothers have died.[60] If certainty of paternity doesn't perfectly predict the nature of fathering, what other factors might come into play?

The Barbary macaques of Morocco and Gibraltar present an inter-esting exception to the certainty-of-paternity rule. Barbary macaques live in multimale multifemale troops in which sexually receptive fe-males mate repeatedly with most, if not all, adult males. The paternal behavior of male Barbary macaques is puzzling at first glance, because in all other species of macaques, adult males are noted for their lack of interest in young infants. Barbary males, by contrast, actively seek the company of infants. Not only are adult and adolescent males obviously fond of babies, but the care they provide is identical to that of mothers (with the exception of nursing, of course). Barbary males eagerly offer their services to infants without assurance of biological paternity. What about the lifestyle of Barbary macaques could explain the unusual involvement of males in rearing young?

David Taub studied Barbary macaques in the rugged Middle Atlas Mountains of Morocco for about 15 months during the early 1970s.[61] Ranging as high as 2,000 meters, these monkeys live in a harsh environment in which heavy snowfall is common in winter and the bitter needles of cedar trees are the primary source of food. Although Barbary males are not quite as domestic as titi monkey fathers, Taub confirmed the striking findings of others—that they are highly attracted to and intensely involved with infants shortly after their birth, and remain important caretakers for infants throughout most of their first year of life.[62]

Barbary males sit beside new mothers and gaze adoringly at their infants, and from the beginning, mothers permit adult males to touch their babies. And the behavior of Barbary males with infants is extraordinary. In contrast to most other male primates, Barbary males behave like mothers; they nuzzle and groom infants, respond to their distress cries, hold them, and carry them. When infants are old enough to begin spending some time off of their mothers, males zealously pursue them. A male stands in front of an infant and chatters his teeth—an invitation to the youngster to climb aboard. Infants cling contentedly to the backs of males, nestle snugly in their laps, and cavort on their bodies.

Barbary males are most involved with young infants that are becoming independent from their mothers. And infants interact less

Male Barbary macaque with infant *(Macaca sylvanus)*; photo by Noel Rowe

with males as they mature, either because the males' interest declines or because older youngsters would rather play with their peers than interact with the less active males. There are huge differences among male caretakers, with some males having four times as many interactions with infants as other males. Each male devotes himself to only one or two infants. Some infants are the first or second choice of many males, while others are less popular. During his study, Taub saw only one infant that received no care from an adult or adolescent male.

How does a male choose an infant to whom he will offer care? He doesn't necessarily select his own offspring, because the promiscuous mating behavior of both sexes leaves open the possibility that any male in the troop could be the father of any infant. In fact, adolescent males have the fewest opportunities to mate with receptive females, and yet they interact as much as or more with babies than adult males. The choice of an infant does not seem to depend on its size, gender, or its mother's status. Taub wonders if males attend most to younger siblings, but no one really knows.

Why are Barbary macaque males so devoted to babies? Recent research with wild Barbary macaques in Algeria suggests that caretaking males may have an ulterior motive—43 percent of Barbary males who offer their services as an infant's main caretaker become the most frequent mating partner of the infant's mother during the *next* breeding season.[63] Rather than the "mate, then care" strategy that one would expect when paternity is fairly certain, we see a "care, then mate" strategy, in which a male ensures that he remains a player in the game of reproduction. This strategy does not actually increase a Barbary male's chances of fatherhood—main caretakers are not more likely to father young than rare caretakers—but perhaps the males don't know that.

What is the advantage to infants selected to receive male care? The outcome for the one infant that received no male care is instructive—that infant was the only one during Taub's study that did not survive its infancy. Perhaps in the rigorous, harsh, environment that Barbary macaques inhabit, the offer of contact comfort, warmth, and protection by adult (or adolescent) males is the difference between life and death. Because any male *could* be an infant's father, it may be in the best interest of every male that all infants survive.

In other species of macaques in which males do not care for infants, a few dominant males do most of the mating. Paternity is thus physically impossible for some males, rather than simply uncertain, as it is among Barbary macaques. The combination of the extreme environment in which Barbary macaques live plus the possibility of paternity for all males may have created the circumstances in which intensive caretaking of infants by adult males has flourished.

Does being certain of paternity affect the commitment of human fathers to parenting? The answer is yes and no. We have seen that the most devoted primate fathers (titis and Aka pygmies) are monogamously paired with their mates and spend virtually all of their time with their families. The opposite is the case when a father is certainly *not* a child's biological sire. In a study of over 7,000 American men, researchers found that fathers invest more (energetically, financially, and socially) in biological offspring than in stepchildren.[64] And the investment in stepchildren typically lasts only as long as the marriage.

But there also is evidence that fathers are willing to support and care for children they do not perceive to be their own. Male Trobriand Islanders, for example, are very involved in the care of infants, despite their cultural belief that "fathers" have no biological relationship to their children.[65] Western fathers who decide to adopt children invest as wholeheartedly in their children as biological fathers. And some stepfathers are dedicated to their stepchildren (although care offered by stepparents is quite variable, and devoted care is rare).

Perhaps men are most reluctant to care for children who are presented as their own, but whose biological paternity is suspect. If a man chooses to care for an unrelated child, he is more content than when he is betrayed or tricked into doing so. So althoough certainty of paternity may influence human fathering behavior, just as in nonhuman primates, it is an imperfect predictor of paternal care.

We have seen that the most intensive paternal caretaking among nonhuman primates is offered by males in small, monogamous species and by male Barbary macaques, who live in a harsh environment and share the possibility of paternity. Unlike Barbary macaques, other males living in multimale multifemale societies (in which paternity is uncertain) typically are not prominently involved in the care of infants. But is this about uncertainty of paternity or are there other factors involved? Some fascinating laboratory experiments on rhesus monkeys performed during the 1970s suggest that mothers may make or break relationships between adult males and infants.

The rhesus macaques of Asia are the "white rats" of students of primate behavior. The most well studied of all nonhuman primates, in the wild and in captivity, rhesus monkeys range from Afghanistan and India to southeastern China and flourish in a variety of habitats. They breed well in captivity and are one of the few primate species that coexist with humans in their natural habitat and thrive, nonetheless. These beguiling brown bandits take advantage of the bounty of human leftovers, brazenly pilfering food from unsuspecting tourists and children.

Twenty years ago, most of the thinking about primate behavior was based on studies of rhesus monkeys and other macaques. What initially stood out in these group-living multimale multifemale societies were the strict dominance hierarchies adhered to by both sexes

Rhesus macaques *(Macaca mulatta)*; photo by Andrew T. Smith

and the strong, enduring relationships among related females. Females remain in their natal troop throughout their lives, while males emigrate to a new troop to breed. Mothers capably raise their offspring without help, so research on parenting in macaques initially was focused on mother-infant relationships. All that could be said about adult males (whose paternity could not be confirmed) was that they had virtually no interest in babies. In fact, in a study of Indian rhesus monkeys, adult males carried infants only twice in 900 hours of observation.[66] In another study of free-living rhesus monkeys, less than 1 percent of infant interactions were with adult males.[67] When rhesus monkeys were housed in multimale multifemale groups in captivity, the results were the same.[68]

Although free-living adult male rhesus monkeys are usually indifferent to infants, they become more involved with them under certain conditions. Large, dominant males occasionally intervene in squabbles on behalf of infants.[69] Sometimes adult males chase away adult females harassing infants of lower-ranking mothers. In one instance, a male adopted a 6-month-old orphan 1 week after her mother's death, and groomed and huddled with her until she was over a year old. And another adult male often retrieved a crying youngster who had been left behind by an inexperienced, first-time mother.

Curious about why rhesus males are so uninvolved with infants, the primatologist William Redican wondered if there were certain conditions in which male-infant relationships might develop. Redican did a simple but ingenious experiment with captive rhesus monkeys to learn what might occur between infants and adult males if they were housed together without other companions.[70] He created four separate single-parent families, each consisting of a wild-born adult male and an infant, and housed these "father"-infant pairs in separate cages. Two of the infants were male and two were female.

Redican compared the relationships of each adult male and infant pair with normal relationships observed between mothers and infants.

Rhesus males forced into the role of primary caretaker handled and interacted with infants differently than did mothers. Infants typically cling to their mother's chests, but adult males did not hold infants in that way. Males left babies more often than mothers do and interacted more with male than female infants. Another difference was that males remained affectionate with their infants over time, while mothers typically become more rejecting as their babies grew up. Finally, males played a lot more with infants than mothers traditionally do.

The rhesus infants became securely attached to their fathers, despite the fact that their fathers' behavior was different from that typical of mothers. When temporarily separated from their fathers, infants protested just as vociferously as when separated from their mothers. Although awkward at first, fathers rapidly became accomplished caregivers; they carried, groomed, and protected their babies, and as an added bonus, boisterously played with them. Redican proposed that relationships between adult male and infant rhesus monkeys may be short-circuited more by the restrictiveness of an infant's mother than by a male's lack of interest. When mothers were absent, adult males and infants readily attached to one another.

The psychologist Stephen Suomi further explored how mothers influence the development of father-infant relationships in captive rhesus monkeys by housing a male and female jointly with their own biological infant.[71] Suomi observed these highly unnatural nuclear-family threesomes for about 3 years and found that infants raised with both parents interacted with their mothers six times as frequently as their fathers. Although infants were the target of about 60 percent of the social overtures of fathers, babies frequently did not respond to them. The behavior of Suomi's fathers was very different from that of the fathers in Redican's study, in that they did not behave like substitute mothers. Paternal behavior consisted mostly of play, sexual mounting, or aggression. Despite the infrequent behavioral interactions between infants and their fathers when mothers were present, infants could distinguish between their fathers and other adult males by the age of 2 months. They preferred their fathers to other adult males just as strongly as they preferred their mothers to other adult females.[72] Most intriguing, infants only slightly preferred their mothers to their fathers.

The effect of the behavior of mothers on the parenting behavior of rhesus fathers suggests that "cultural" values or expectations influence fatherhood as well as motherhood, even among nonhuman primates. Rhesus monkey males can adequately parent infants—even as primary caretakers—when given the opportunity to do so. Despite the fact that the type of fathering behavior described by Redican is not characteristic of wild rhesus monkeys, we have seen that rhesus males are capable caregivers in a pinch when there is no other alternative. That rhesus males accept the challenge of parenthood when given the opportunity illustrates the plasticity of parental behavior in male primates, and challenges our notion that males lack either interest or competence when they do not participate in the rearing of young.

The cooperation of human mothers crucially influences the behavior of fathers with their offspring, just as it does among nonhuman primates. A study published in 1995 found that most mothers were fairly satisfied with their husband's significantly less-than-equal contribution to childcare, although they did want more help around the house.[73] When asked why they were content with less help from their husbands with the kids, mothers mentioned a variety of reasons; some felt that fathers were less competent or would not handle situations in the same way that they would, while others felt threatened by the idea that they might lose authority in the home, the one arena in which women have been more or less in charge.[74]

BEYOND certainty of paternity and the cooperation of their mates, the three most significant influences on the behavior of fathers are the same as those for mothers: the demands of the environment; individual experiences of fathers while growing up; and cultural beliefs, values, and traditions.

ECOLOGY, or how we make a living within the constraints of our environment, influences the size of the community in which we live, the kind of mating system we practice, how power is distributed within marriages, and to what extent fathers participate in childrearing. In cultures in which husbands and wives typically practice monogamy and both fathers and mothers make equivalent contributions of food or other resources to the family, fathers are more involved in childcare.[75] The contribution of resources by mothers, combined with the higher certainty of paternity that accompanies monogamy, creates an environment in which paternal care is necessary, in harmony with community values, and in a father's own best interest, in terms of investing in his genetic offspring.

The density of human populations also factors into the likelihood that fathers will invest heavily in the care of infants (and older children).[76] When population density is high and men can compete for predictable and defendable resources, a "Cad" reproductive strategy is generally the outcome; the goal of fathers is to acquire multiple wives and invest little effort in childcare. At low population densities (and when resources cannot be accumulated), cooperation trumps competition and a "Dad" strategy, in which fathers heavily invest in childcare, is more likely to prevail.

Fathers in foraging or hunter-gatherer human societies and island communities are more likely to be Dads than Cads. Their population densities are low, and fathers in these societies (for example, the Aka pygmies of Africa, the Batek hunter-gatherers of Malaysia, and the Agta foragers of the Philippines) are likely to offer direct infant care.[77] Contrast these hunter-gatherer fathers with fathers living at a higher population density, who compete with one another for resources and are more likely to be motivated by a Cad reproductive strategy. The goals of polygynous Thonga fathers of South Africa, for example, are to acquire many wives, sire many children, and accumulate great wealth, rather than to personally care for their children. The Thonga are field agriculturalists—husbands herd livestock and manage resources and wives tend the fields.[78] The fact that Thonga mothers contribute to the economy has little impact on paternal care. In societies like that of the Thonga, in which fathers control family finances, husbands typically rule the household and perform little or no childcare.[79]

Industrialization has created yet another kind of father. Living in high-density populations in which there is much competition for resources, fathers have specialized in provision. Fathers in industrialized nations work for a paycheck with the goal of accumulating wealth, rather than many wives and children. In the middle of this century, when most American fathers were their family's sole provider and mothers typically stayed home with the kids, the participation of fathers in childcare was negligible. Fathers retained the ultimate authority, however; they were utilized as disciplinarians of last resort by their wives, whose final recourse when children were misbehaving was, "Wait till your father gets home."

More than 70 percent of married mothers in the United States with children under the age of 18 now work outside the home.[80] As the earning power of mothers has risen, fathers have become more involved in childcare than ever before (although their contribution is by no means equivalent to that of mothers, who still usually assume the role of primary caretaker).[81] Perhaps what has changed most is the authority of fathers at home. The shift from authority figure to partner has been difficult for many fathers, as is evident from the example of my clients, Jerry and Anna.

Jerry and Anna had been married for over 20 years and had three teenagers. Raised in a strict, authoritarian household, Jerry, a naval officer, had expected that he and Anna would raise their children the same way. Jerry's tours of duty took him away from his family for long periods. Each time he returned, he encountered more resistance to his style of parenting. When his wife took a job and began to contribute to the family finances, she became more confident about resisting Jerry's efforts to run the family like an efficient military unit. By the time the kids were teenagers, Jerry no longer was the primary authority figure, to his considerable dismay. The egalitarian parenting style of the parent with the most power, Anna, prevailed.

FATHERS do not automatically know how to care for infants any more than mothers do. In the last chapter, we saw that young female primates learn to care for infants by babysitting those of other females. Are these babysitting "apprenticeships" available to young males too? What is paternal behavior like in those species in which young males learn to care for infants before they become fathers?

Studies of captive saddleback tamarins show that growing up in a family and having the opportunity to babysit for younger siblings is the best predictor of adequate parental care for both fathers and mothers. Tamarins cooperatively parent their young, so like titi fathers, males must act as co-primary caregivers. Among captive saddleback tamarins, 85 percent of the first offspring of socially inexperienced parents (individuals who had not grown up in tamarin families and thus had no babysitting experience) die from neglect or abuse.[82] But when both first-time parents are raised by their families *and* babysit for younger siblings, they adequately care for 80 percent of their infants. Socially experienced parents improve with practice, providing appropriate care to 100 percent of their second or third set of infants.

When a tamarin father is socially experienced but a mother is not, the success rate with infants drops to 30 percent. Eighty percent of pairs are successful, however, when only the mother is experienced. Even though a socially experienced male is a competent caregiver, his good fathering behavior cannot compensate when an inexperienced female rejects their infant or carries it so inappropriately that it cannot nurse.

When neither parent has social experience, the success rate with infants plummets to 15 percent. What behaviors account for the higher success rate of experienced males? When abandoned cotton-top tamarin infants were placed in a cage with either an experienced or an inexperienced adult male, the advantages of early social experience became crystal clear. Both males quickly retrieved infants making distress calls, but only experienced males were willing to continuously carry them. Inexperienced males soon reject their charges, pulling at or biting them until they let go.[83]

The best chance that an infant saddleback tamarin has to survive is having two parents whose social experience has prepared them for parenthood. It definitely takes two parents (who know what an infant is and how to care for it) to successfully raise young, especially when there are no older siblings to act as helpers.

Even when fathers aren't co-primary caregivers, a male's experience with youngsters comes in handy when the mother of a (weaned) infant dies. Since adult females rarely adopt orphans (perhaps because they have sole responsibility for raising their own young), rearing orphans is a task assumed by males. Adult males offer protection, or sometimes even primary caregiving, when infants are orphaned. Male chimpanzees, gorillas, Japanese, Barbary, stumptail, and pigtail macaques, and hamadryas, yellow, and olive baboons have all been observed caring for orphans.

Nonhuman primate males offer care more frequently to older infants or juveniles than to newborns, as is true in humans.[84] And like humans, a male nonhuman primate is more apt to respond to an infant's attempt to socialize with *him*, rather than to actively pursue a baby's attention. Older infants (especially males) in many species are very attracted to adult males, following them about, feeding and playing near them, and initiating physical contact. Experience with older infants prepares adult males for their potential role as substitute caregivers in the event that an infant's mother dies—there may be no point in interacting with unweaned infants, who cannot survive the death of their mother.

Training for parenthood is by apprenticeship for both boys and girls in most preindustrial societies.[85] As children grow up, they are expected to babysit for younger siblings. Many boys and most girls have cared for infants long before they are developmentally ready to have babies of their own, as is generally the case among nonhuman primates. In these cultures, childcare training comes first, and marriage and the formation of a new household follow many years later.

This process of experience first, parenting second, is reversed in contemporary Western culture: we marry and establish our households first, and then get our childcare training on the job. Both mothers and fathers may be in the same boat, if neither have babysat younger siblings or other young children, and both may question their abilities as parents when parenting doesn't come "naturally." Fathers, whose role with infants has long been considered optional, may have little desire at first to become involved. They step aside while their wives become competent mothers by trial and error, with a little advice from family or experts thrown in. The confidence of mothers shifts into drive, while that of fathers remains in neutral. Like nonhuman primates, human fathers are more involved with older offspring than infants, a situation that may be a throwback to the time in our evolutionary history when unweaned infants without mothers simply could not survive.

Some fathers who take the plunge into childcare say they want to emulate their own, nurturing fathers, while others emphatically express their determination to be different from their own, uninvolved fathers.[86] Wanting to become involved is a significant step forward, because it encourages men to acquire the knowledge and experience necessary to build competence and confidence. When fathers start taking care of their babies, the babies' responsiveness increases.[87]

Community programs to educate and reduce the anxiety of fathers-to-be are burgeoning. And they work. For example, Swedish fathers who learn about childcare during their wives' post-partum hospital stay are more involved with their child and their home when their babies are 3 months old than are fathers without this experience.[88] A "boot camp" for Arizona fathers expecting their first child is taught by experienced fathers and their babies at a local hospital.[89] This type of training has the same effect as the apprenticeships for parenting built into childhood in other societies: it increases a father's confidence in himself as he acquires the skills to care for his baby. Programs like these may be most important for the youngest fathers, who lack both skills and maturity.

MODERN fathers in the United States provide a good example of how cultural beliefs and traditions influence fathering. Despite the common belief that fathers are very involved with their children's care, the truth is that although fathers play a greater role in childcare today than they did before mothers were regularly employed, their contribution remains considerably smaller than that of mothers.[90] Fathers are available for care one quarter as often as mothers in two-parent homes in which mothers don't work and about 65 percent as often in two-parent families in which mothers are employed. Most fathers in the United States still assume essentially zero responsibility for their children's care (when responsibility is defined as participating in key decisions, being available on short notice, staying home and caring for sick children, and so on).[91] First and foremost, the most crucial contribution of fathers in the United States to childcare continues to be the provision of resources.[92]

How can we explain that paternal involvement has increased at such a snail's pace? For fathers to actively participate in childrearing, they must have support from their wives, their peers, and the culture in which they live. We have seen that wives often neither expect nor encourage their husbands to be equal co-parents.[93] A father's male friends also must support his involvement (or even better, take a similarly active parenting role in their own families). When it is socially acceptable for fathers and their kids to hang out with other fathers and children, paternal involvement with children is reinforced. In industrial societies, however, it is still uncommon for primary caretaking fathers to be part of a peer group of similarly involved fathers.

Finally, the community (including the father's workplace), must not punish fathers for making their families their top priority.[94] When the workplace supports fathers actively involved in childcare, they are more inclined to assume greater responsibility for childrearing.[95] In Sweden, for example, fathers are offered one month's paid paternal leave when their babies are born, and most of them take it. Groups of fathers pushing strollers down the street is a common sight in Sweden. In the United States, in contrast, there is no paid paternal leave, and flexible time scheduling to accommodate childcare is not an option for most fathers. And a father's livelihood in industrial societies is less compatible with childrearing than it is in preindustrial societies. Most employers still expect mothers to respond when a child needs attention during the work day. Fathers who make childcare a high priority may find themselves on the "mommy" track of career opportunity.[96]

THE key components of primate fatherhood—protecting, providing care, and provisioning resources—are expressed differently among primate males, depending on the demands of the environment, their experiences growing up, cultural traditions, the encouragement of mothers, and certainty about paternity. Individual differences between fathers are huge, but most fathers growing up in normal environments—experiencing neither neglect nor abuse and being raised by their family—provide good-enough care to their offspring. Fathers simply need permission, encouragement, and the opportunity to become more involved with their children.

Plasticity of fathering behavior is the trademark of primate males. Father as pinch-hitter is still the most common role played by both human and nonhuman primate fathers. But the fact that children who have secure, supportive, and sensitive relationships with both their parents are more likely to be psychologically well adjusted than those who don't indicates that the contribution of fathers to childcare, while different from than that of mothers, is nonetheless significant.[97] As fathers become more involved with their children, the care offered by both parents becomes more similar than different. When Dad is cooking dinner and bathing the kids on a regular basis, play will no longer be his primary specialty.

CHAPTER 4

The Babysitters' Club

BARBARA was the fourth infant born to Ira and Jessie, one of my breeding pairs of cottontops. Although all of Barbara's older siblings were fascinated by her, Sylvia (a 2-year-old adolescent) was especially determined to interact with her. One day after Jessie had finished nursing 2-week-old Barbara, she nipped at Barbara and the infant cried out softly. Sylvia dashed over, reached for her infant sister, and pulled her onto her own back. Before long, Sylvia was spending more time with Barbara than were either of her parents. Although Barbara's 6-month-old twin brothers occasionally carried her, they preferred the role of Barbara's playmate to being her caretaker.

Chimpanzee mothers are reluctant to allow others, even close relatives, to handle their infants. Jane Goodall described how an adolescent chimpanzee named Fifi used every trick in the book to get her hands on Flint, her newborn baby brother.[1] Fifi's mother, Flo, initially thwarted Fifi's attempts to handle Flint. When Flint was 14 weeks old, Flo permitted Fifi to pull him away from her for the first time, but only for a few minutes. During the weeks that followed, Flo caved in more often to Fifi's desire to handle her baby brother, but always hovered close by, ready to retrieve him.

MOST mammalian mothers do not allow other members of their species to help care for their infants. In contrast, human mothers regularly rely on the help of others to rear their young. Human babies, having lost the ability to cling, are the most helpless of all young primates, mature the most slowly, and are dependent on their parents for the longest period. Imagine an early hominid mother with a baby in her arms—could she have protected and cared for her infant and still maintained her own physical condition without help? Cooperative caregiving has undoubtedly been part of our species' arsenal of childrearing strategies from the very beginning.[2]

Nonhuman primate mothers, by contrast, rarely depend on the help of others to rear their young. Yes, nonhuman primate infants are helpless and dependent for a relatively long time, but they do have the ability to cling, which frees up their mothers' arms for traveling and foraging. There are some nonhuman primate species in which helpers (called allomothers) are essential for infant survival, but in other species, would-be caregivers are simply interested in infants and pester mothers for opportunities to babysit them.

Babysitting for infant primates includes carrying infants and taking responsibility for them when mothers are absent. Because infant primates tenaciously cling to any fur within reach, providing transportation once a baby is on board isn't difficult. Babysitters also groom infants, share food with them, and, rarely, even nurse them.[3] And like many adult male primates, some females will pitch in to help when infants not their own are in danger.

Who are these babysitters? We have seen that fathers, or other adult or adolescent males, may care for or keep an eye out for infants, especially when mothers are inexperienced, inept, or neglectful. The attentive male could be an infant's older brother, its mother's regular companion, or her recent sexual partner. Primate females of all ages also are fascinated with babies and eager to interact with them, but usually it is the immature females who persistently seek extended bouts of babysitting.[4] Virtually all wild young nonhuman primate females have opportunities for intimate contact with infants before they become mothers themselves, and many are granted babysitting privileges.[5]

Mother nonhuman primates, however, have the final say about who will be allowed contact with their infants. In some species, only close kin (such as the infant's father or siblings) are allowed to babysit, while in others, every eager female is allowed a turn with even the youngest infants. Why do some primate mothers only allow other experienced mothers to handle their babies, while others allow partially grown youngsters, who don't have a clue about proper infant care, to care for them? And finally, why is it that in some species, mothers allow essentially all interested females to handle newborns, while in others, babysitters are permitted to handle only older infants?

A MOTHER'S choice of a babysitter is limited by who is applying for the job. Although most females who have not yet given birth (nulliparas) seek opportunities to handle infants, it is "juvenile" females that most eagerly clamor for a chance to babysit. These youngsters are comparable in age to 6- to 12-year-old girls.[6]

Although very young females are eager applicants, from a mother primate's perspective they are not the most desirable babysitters. Lacking both experience and common sense, young babysitters often have poor judgment. The anthropologist Jane Lancaster, for example, observed a young female vervet lose interest in the infant she had been tending and walk away. When the baby began to cry, its mother scrambled to retrieve it from about a quarter mile away.[7] Fortunately for both mother and infant, a predator did not get there first. Juvenile females may also be quite clumsy with infants. Lancaster hilariously describes how a young female vervet quickly maneuvers a crying baby out of the sight and hearing of its mother: clutching the complaining infant to her chest with both hands, she awkwardly staggers off on two legs as fast as she can.[8] Older infants may actually thwart attempts by juveniles to carry them by refusing to cling. It is similar among humans; preteens are not the first choice of most mothers to babysit their infants, for the same reasons.

After a juvenile nonhuman primate babysitter is granted her prize, she soon learns to soothe her young charge or loses her opportunity to babysit. Since a quiet baby will not arouse its mother's attention, juvenile females learn that babies who are groomed stop crying more quickly than those who are not. Lancaster observed a juvenile female awkwardly pinning a struggling baby down with her foot (to prevent it from running back to its mother) while she intensively groomed it. As clumsy as this looked, it worked. The infant settled down, and the young female was rewarded with more babysitting time.

Adolescent and pregnant females also frequently offer babysitting services. These females typically are more skilled than juveniles because they are older, wiser, and less impulsive or distractable than younger animals, and because they usually have had prior babysitting experience to boot. The females most capable of providing skilled care (multiparous, experienced mothers), however, usually have the least interest in babysitting. They are curious about the troop's (or neighborhood's) newest baby, but after handling it for a few moments, unceremoniously hand it back to its mother. Primate mothers with their own offspring have no desire to take the babies of others home with them.

ALTHOUGH babysitting is more common among primates than other mammals, most primate mothers do not permit others to handle newborns. Exceptions to this rule are two groups of

Eastern black and white colobus *(Colobus guereza)*; photo by Noel Rowe

Northern gray-necked owl monkeys *(Aotus trivirgatus)*; photo by Noel Rowe

nonhuman primates: the leaf-eating colobine monkeys (colobus, langur, and leaf monkeys) of Asia and Africa and the small, monogamous monkeys (marmosets, tamarins, titis, and owl monkeys) of the New World tropics, and some human foraging societies, such as the Efé pygmies of central Africa.

Mara's new infant, a soft ball of tangerine fur, was visible from a half mile away. The striking contrast between the newborn silvered langur's glistening orange coat and the drab gray coloring of its family left primatologists wondering about what nature had in mind. After all, the baby was not camouflaged and could just as easily have attracted the rapacious eye of a hungry eagle as the curiosity of a primatologist. Was this baby flashy to attract its mother's attention and ensure consistent mothering from her? Clearly not, because the coloring of most wild nonhuman primate infants is not drastically different from that of their parents, and yet their mothers unconditionally care for them.[9] Why then are the babies of silvered langurs (and other colobine infants) so flamboyant? Some primatologists believe that it has something to do with attracting babysitters.[10]

Colobine monkey mothers are notorious among primates for allowing almost any interested female in their living group to handle, however ineptly, their newborns. Like a neon sign, the flaming orange infant silvered langur captures the attention of virtually all the young females in the troop. Mothers with older offspring also shadow mothers with newborns, determined to handle the new arrival. Babies in most infant-sharing species of colobines are gorgeous, sporting coats that look nothing like the drab fur of their parents.

Mother langurs allow others to handle their infants only as long as they appear content. When a babysitter tires of her charge, she often handles it rather roughly—pushing it away, nipping at it, or even sit-

Hanuman langurs *(Semnopithecus entellus)*; photo by John R. MacKinnon

ting on it. When the baby cries out, its mother (or another sitter) runs to the rescue. As a signal for the desire to be relieved of baby-sitting duties, the technique of rough handling works well.

Why would colobine mothers permit adult females (who could re-fuse to return the infant) or immature females (who could be inept) to handle their newborns? Perhaps because females living in the same troop are very closely related to one another; they are each others' mothers, grandmothers, aunts, nieces, cousins, siblings, or daughters. The biologist W. D. Hamilton introduced the term "inclusive fitness" to describe how an individual's own biological fitness increases when his or her close kin survive and reproduce, because they share a relatively high percentage of genes.[11] Females in colobine species are especially closely related because these species usually live in harem societies with only one resident adult male. One male breeds with all females, and females remain in their troop of origin throughout their lives. Female Hanuman langurs, for example, share at least one eighth and as many as one half of their genes.[12] It is therefore in the best biological interest of all females for every infant to survive to reproduce.[13] Indeed, primatologists who study infant-sharing colobines have not observed a single instance in which an allomother (or babysitter) purposefully tried to harm her young charge.[14]

Another reason that a colobine mother welcomes help with her baby is that there is essentially no danger that she will be unable to retrieve her infant whenever she likes. Female dominance hierarchies among colobine monkeys confer the greatest status on mothers in the prime of life. Hierarchies are flexible and rank changes with age; the status of both very young *and* very old females is below that of individuals in their reproductive prime. So since mothers occupy the top spots in the hierarchy and are surrounded by close female kin, there is virtually no reason for a mother to fear that her baby will be kidnapped or deliberately harmed by another female.

But just because colobine babysitters don't intentionally harm newborns, it is still puzzling that mothers allow them to babysit, since even inadvertent poor judgment could cost an infant its life. Perhaps the benefits both mother and baby derive from the help of allomothers far outweigh the costs of occasional substandard babysitting.[15] It is easier for mothers to search for food without babies on board, and that improves their physical condition and thus indirectly benefits their babies. Mothers in better condition reproduce at shorter intervals without compromising the health of their babies, which increases their chances of passing genes on to the next generation.

A benefit sometimes reaped by babies from the ministrations of well-intentioned babysitters is faster growth, which enables infants to become independent more quickly than youngsters in species without helpers.[16] As a result of their rapid physical development, colobine infants soon scamper back to their mothers on their own when they tire of a babysitter or are ready to nurse. In the harem societies in which infant-sharing colobines usually live, quickly maturing infants have a huge advantage. Unweaned infants are at the highest risk of being killed by a male stranger who wrests troop ownership from its current patriarch (see Chapter 8). Since the tenure of a patriarch is unpredictable (and often brief), rapidly weaned infants are less likely to end up dead.

Thus being adorable acts as a magnet for baby-craving allomothers. The help offered by a gaggle of closely related babysitters speeds up the maturation of colobine infants, which increases their chance of surviving to adulthood. As colobine infants mature, their eye-catching coats are replaced by the drab brown or gray of their parents, and other females in the troop lose interest in caring for them. Instead of play mothering, juvenile females, once again, just want to play.

Members of the New World primate family Callitrichidae have a serious daycare problem. The diminutive marmosets and tamarins in this monkey family usually give birth to twins, as often as twice a year, when conditions are optimal. But since the combined weight of twins is much greater than that of a single baby, toting them around requires an enormous expenditure of energy. Add to that having to provide enough milk for two, and you have a job that mother marmosets and tamarins cannot accomplish on their own.

Initially, these (mostly) monogamous callitrichid mothers rely on their mates for help. When their first set of twins is born, the stress level of parents shoots up, much as it does for first-time human parents of twins who have no helpers. Fathers typically specialize in transportation and daycare, while mothers focus on manufacturing enough milk for two. In some species (see Chapter 8), a new family is formed by two males and one female; both males mate and share babysitting duties with the female. An extra adult in the nursery relieves a burden that might be too high for two parents. But even three "parents" are often not successful in raising the first set of babies.

Offspring surviving their infancy help with babysitting when the next set of twins arrive, although the age of older siblings influences the quality and type of care they offer.[17] For example, although the small size of juvenile tamarins makes it difficult for them to carry their infant siblings, they make wonderful playmates for older infants, giving parents a much-needed break. By the time the third set of twins has arrived, the oldest siblings are almost fully grown and ready to take on the role of nanny. Adolescent or young adult monkeys appear to relish their babysitting duties and eagerly offer to help, like Sylvia, my cottontop tamarin. They carry, cuddle, and play with the twins, giving (primarily) fathers a reprieve from parenting. Since mothers can't be relieved of nursing duties, it is fathers who reap most of the benefits from the care offered by older offspring.[18]

Perhaps the fact that tamarin siblings share half of their genes (the same proportion shared between parents and young) justifies their investment in each other's care. Still, the costs of babysitting are high. Tamarins carrying infants usually attempt to conceal themselves and are therefore less mobile than they would otherwise be.[19] Their tendency to sit still, probably to avoid attracting a predator's attention, results in less foraging time. Even among captive tamarins (whose provisioning by their human captors guarantees that sufficient food is available), parents without helpers lose up to 10 percent of their body weight.[20] But despite the costs, members of tamarin families actually compete for the privilege of carrying infants.[21]

Beyond their genetic relatedness, environmental factors may further explain the seemingly altruistic behavior of older marmosets and tamarins who care for younger siblings. Tamarin families must find and defend territories large enough to provide for their needs. But acquiring a territory isn't easy. For many species, sufficient habitat isn't available to support all potential breeding pairs. If an adolescent or young adult leaves home too soon, it might not be able to compete successfully for a partner and an adequate territory on which to live, a dilemma not dissimilar to that of young adult humans. If an older sibling can make itself useful at home, it can avoid being thrust out of the nest (so to speak) before the opportunity arises to find a mate and set up housekeeping. Older siblings have found a way to earn their keep in their families while learning about infant care, which makes them better parents when they start families of their own. Even though babysitting diminishes the physical condition of young animals, obtaining permission to stay at home until the time is right to leave may make the effort worthwhile.

Close kinship among group members also characterizes the Efé foragers of Zaire. Communities are made up of several extended families, typically including brothers, their wives and children, unmarried sisters, and parents.[22] In this open society of close relatives, shared childcare is the rule rather than the exception.

The degree of cooperative caregiving among the Efé is extraordinary. A newborn is often nursed by another lactating mother immediately after birth, rather than having to wait until its mother's milk comes in.[23] Infants are frequently carried and cared for by multiple caregivers (including fathers). In one 8-hour observation period, anthropologists counted more than 14 different people who contributed, on average, to a single infant's care.[24]

What factors in addition to genetic relatedness could account for such an exceptional pattern of cooperative childcare? First, the Efé have a history of low fertility: Efé women give birth to an average of 2.6 children in their lifetime, compared to the average of 5.4 for other hunter-gatherers.[25] In a community with twice as many adults as children (and in which almost 50 percent of women have had zero or only one live birth), Efé women are eager to help out with the infants of others.[26] Second, the Efé live in an open camp, in which mothers and infants are in full view of the others in the community. With no walls separating infants from other group members, potential babysitters are both familiar with the community's infants and aware when help is needed. Infant mortality is extremely low (perhaps because of the number of helpers), which is crucial in a population characterized by low fertility.

WE have seen that human and nonhuman primates sometimes allow other, closely related individuals to babysit newborns. But this behavior is actually relatively uncommon among primates. Far more typical are mothers who allow other individuals to handle older infants, which are past the earliest, most helpless stage of development.

The rules for babysitting older infants also have a lot to do with relatedness, for the same reasons mentioned above. When a mother relinquishes care of her baby to another individual, the infant's older sibling is often her first choice. Siblings share on average 50 percent of each other's genes, so when the behavior of one sibling helps to keep another alive long enough for it to reproduce, that is equivalent to contributing a half set of its own genes to the population. Caring for a sibling, therefore, benefits a caretaker as much as caring for her own offspring, genetically speaking. But are nonhuman primates "aware" of their biological relatedness to one another? If not, why are siblings so willing to help one another?

The animal behaviorist Marc Bekoff suggests that the familiarity among siblings, a byproduct of spending much of their time in close proximity, predicts their helpfulness to one another.[27] Primates that are very familiar with one another usually *are* close relatives, because of the slow development of primates and the tendency of virtually all youngsters to stay close to their mothers. Because familiarity is the mechanism by which altruistic behavior toward genetic relatives is reinforced, it may occasionally override the effects of genetic relatedness. Humans who adopt, for example, easily attach to unrelated infants. Nonhuman primates also attach to individuals with whom they spend time, even when these individuals are not related to them. In captivity, individuals in a variety of animal species contentedly foster-rear unrelated infants, sometimes even of a different species. Conversely, if an animal is suddenly introduced to a true biological sibling with whom it is not familiar, its behavior with that sibling will resemble its behavior with strangers.

Older siblings are by far the most common babysitters of older infants among nonhuman primates. Similarly, in many preindustrial societies around the globe, older daughters (and occasionally, sons) also are their mother's primary helpers. Mothers are more willing to release their babies when they can retrieve them at will, so a mother must have some clout with a babysitter before she relinquishes her infant. Since mothers are closely bonded to, larger than, and usually dominant over their juvenile or adolescent daughters, the probability is low that babies on loan to siblings will not be returned.

Some ape mothers, such as chimpanzees and bonobos, will not

surrender their newborns to anyone, period. They are even reluctant to allow others to handle older infants, although ape mothers may relent under pressure from their curious older daughters. Gradually, mothers may allow older daughters to touch, groom, and carry their new sibling for short periods, as the vignette of Fifi and Flo illustrates. But mothers remain close by, ready to intervene at their baby's first whimper. When an older infant tires of its babysitter, it either signals to its mother by crying or simply returns to her on its own.

Like young chimpanzees, immature female rhesus monkeys pester their mothers for opportunities to handle infant siblings, and older siblings groom their younger brothers and sisters even more than their mothers do.[28] Rhesus monkey mothers are very protective of their infants, and because of the real possibility of infant kidnapping by high-ranking females, most mothers do not willingly allow unrelated individuals to handle their babies. And since male rhesus monkeys typically show no interest in babysitting, whatever help rhesus mothers get comes from their daughters. Daughters stay connected to their mothers and siblings even after they are grown, as is true in many other primate species. Daughters thus have ample opportunity to observe their mother's parenting style and become familiar with their younger siblings. This experience comes in handy when daughters reproduce, and sometimes even before that, when an infant is orphaned.

In 1983, Carol Berman observed the adoption of an 11-week-old rhesus monkey infant whose mother had died.[29] The baby initially appeared depressed and agitated, and searched forlornly for his mother. Even when his agitation decreased, his behavior continued to reflect his despair. He sat, motionless, in a hunched posture, and frequently uttered soft, sad "whoo" calls.

In the first week or so after his mother's death, three adult males offered to care for him. One was a dominant male who Berman was certain was not his father. Another was a male who had often associated with the infant's mother (and could have been his father), and the third was the baby's 4-year-old brother. But the infant did not respond to the overtures of any of these males (who, to their credit, offered typical maternal behavior), and they quickly lost interest in him.

The baby's 3-year-old nulliparous sister also pursued the orphan and offered care. After 1 week, she succeeded in adopting him and becoming his primary caretaker. At first, the orphan rejected his sister's efforts to care for him, just as he had done with the adult males. But unlike the males, his sister persisted, and the baby finally relented. Gradually, the orphan and his sister became mutually attached and lived happily ever after.

Berman believes the key to this successful adoption was both the sister's persistence and her possession of female-sized nipples. When the orphan tried to attach himself to the tiny nipples of the adult males, it must have been rather disappointing. It was impressive, nonetheless, that some of the males even tolerated this behavior. When the orphan attached himself to his sister's nipples, he once again became secure. Berman does not know whether or not the orphan's sister ever produced milk—perhaps a pacifier, and the presence of someone who was very familiar to him, was all that he needed.

Siblings offer care to orphans in many primate species. In her study of the chimpanzees of Gombe, for example, Jane Goodall found that six of seven youngsters who lost their mothers were adopted by an older sibling.[30] Human siblings less commonly take over the care of orphaned younger siblings, because human families are not as likely to contain both mature siblings capable of caregiving and dependent infants in need of care.

Older females also make good babysitters. Humans are not the first primates to discover that help offered to mothers by grandmothers is first-rate. A study of five troops of rhesus monkeys showed that elderly females who were no longer reproductive became very involved in the care of the yearlings of their adult daughters, while the mothers busied themselves with their newborns.[31] Another study showed that captive vervet infants were less likely to die when their grandmothers lived in their group.[32] It wasn't that these vervet grandmothers actively participated in routine daily care; rather, their presence protected infants from being manhandled by curious youngsters who wanted to babysit but lacked the skills to do so competently. Mother vervets restricted their babies less when grandmothers offered an extra set of eyes to monitor them, and in this safer environment infants became independent sooner. Grandmothers and older infants developed strong bonds; infants often chose to spend time with their grandmothers, and grandmothers groomed their grandchildren more often than nonkin.

Perhaps the most important contribution of nonhuman primate grandmothers to infant care is their willingness to place themselves at risk to protect their young relatives. Sarah Hrdy shares a tale in her book *Mother Nature* of a true grandmother heroine—a Hanuman langur named Sol.[33] Sol was a 25-year-old arthritic and low-ranking elderly female who had not reproduced for several years. Like other langurs who survive to old age, Sol was relegated to the periphery of the troop, where she engaged in solitary pursuits and minded her own business. But when a male stranger almost twice her size invaded her troop, Sol placed herself between him and the infant he was stalking, while the infant's mother watched from the sidelines. Sol fearlessly pursued the male, even after he had the infant in his jaws, and wrestled the baby away from him. After safely returning the baby to its mother, Sol resumed her position on the troop's periphery.

Evolutionary biologists suggest that one reason some primate females survive for several years after they last reproduce (most female mammals reproduce throughout their lives) is so they will be available to care for their slowly maturing young throughout the long period of dependence.[34] The contributions of human menopausal females are not limited to their own children, and include other kin such as grandchildren.[35] Hrdy calls this the "grandmother's clock hypothesis," to emphasize that there might be an evolutionary reason that women survive long after menopause.[36] In foraging societies such as the Hadza hunter-gatherers, extra food gathered by grandmothers can make a difference in the survival of grandchildren who are old enough to be weaned but too immature to find their own food.[37] The amount of plant food gathered by Hadza mothers is barely sufficient to feed themselves and their babies, so weaned Hadza youngsters learn to go to their grandmothers or great-aunts when they are hungry. Parents greatly value the contributions of grandmothers, who are held in high regard in Hadza communities.

Grandmothers thus earn their keep in human societies by caring for, sharing food with, or protecting young, much as young tamarins and old langurs do in their families. As might be expected from the behavior patterns of primate fathers, the role of grandfathers in the rearing of grandchildren is more typically that of a bit player than that of a star.

Although human grandmothers usually assume a protective role or provide goodies that kids might not otherwise receive from their parents, an increasing number of grandmothers are becoming their grandchildren's primary caregivers. When grandparents in the United States reside with adult children and their offspring, they have the primary responsibility for childcare over 40 percent of the time.[38] Grandmothers often raise grandchildren whose parents are adolescents, have died (AIDS victims), or have abandoned them (substance-abusing parents). Grandmothers whose grandchildren survive to reproduce are winners in the long run, passing on their genes to future generations.

BUT not all babysitters are closely related to their charges. What, then, are the rules for babysitting in primate societies in which not all females are close kin, such as langurs, or part of the same nuclear family, such as marmosets and tamarins? Baboons and macaques, who live in multimale multifemale societies, handle babysitting very differently than do species relying on closely related babysitters.

Some of the differences in babysitting strategy have to do with the type of dominance hierarchy characteristic of a species. Contrast the fluid female hierarchies of infant-sharing colobine monkeys with the rigid hierarchies characteristic of macaques and baboons. The position in the hierarchy of a female macaque or baboon does not change much during her lifetime, and daughters inherit their place in the hierarchy—one notch below that of their mother.[39] Breeding macaque or baboon females are not guaranteed a position at the top of the heap as are breeding females among the harem-living langurs. The difference in the distribution of foods preferred by colobines versus baboons and macaques may explain why strict dominance hierarchies may have evolved in the latter two species.[40] The food that macaques and baboons prefer is neither as plentiful nor as evenly distributed as the mature leaves consumed by colobine monkeys, and a female's position in the dominance hierarchy determines her access to food. But what does this have to do with babysitting?

Although rank probably evolved in baboon and macaque societies to designate, without the need for violence, how choice morsels of food are allocated, rank also significantly affects maternal behavior. In baboon and macaque societies, subordinate mothers do not make their babies available to females of higher rank because if a dominant female chooses not to return an infant to its mother, there is nothing its mother can do. And because female macaques and baboons mate with many males in their troop, females are not as closely related to one another as are cohabiting langur females. The weaker kinship ties among females reduce the benefit to them (in the sense of passing on their own genes) of behaving altruistically toward the infants of others. Infant macaques have starved to death after being kidnapped by high-ranking, nonlactating females. This phenomenon has been vividly termed "aunting to death."[41]

In species with rigid dominance hierarchies, a mother must outrank potential babysitters so that the benefits that she and her infant accrue from the help aren't outweighed by the costs. Dominant females can enjoy babysitting help from subordinates, but not vice versa. In Hrdy's words, "In most species where aunting has been reported, so has maternal supervision of the aunts."[42]

MODERN human mothers have all the same reasons to use babysitters as their nonhuman primate counterparts, and then some. In modern industrial societies, most families have two breadwinners working 8-hour shifts. Unlike nonhuman primates and humans in preindustrial societies, families with young children in the United States today need hours of childcare help every day. Dual wage-earner families don't always have the option of leaving their children with close relatives, who may be employed or otherwise unavailable. Although flexible work schedules, telecommuting from home, more active fathering, and paid parental leave may one day change how we care for our babies, working parents today may have but one choice—to leave their babies with strangers paid to tend their infants. In contrast to nonhuman primate and human mothers in traditional societies, who can work *and* regularly be available to their children, mothers employed full time in industrial societies typically can do only one or the other.

There is no precedent among nonhuman primates—or among humans in preindustrial societies—for sending an infant off to a daycare center for 8 hours, 5 days a week, to be cared for by strangers. In the United States, however, almost 60 percent of married mothers with children under a year old are employed.[43] And the 1997 National Survey of American families revealed that 41 percent of children under the age of 5 spend at least 35 hours a week in daycare.[44]

How does care by nonhuman primate babysitters differ from that offered in human daycare centers? First, nonhuman primate babysitters typically care for one, or at most two, infants at a time, for relatively short periods, usually in view of (or at least within earshot of) the infant's mother. In contrast, mothers in the United States typically are not physically close enough to monitor their childcare providers, who may care for as many as four infants, 8 hours a day, and still meet federal standards for adequate care (standards set by the National Association for the Education of Young Children).[45] Since no babysitter can simultaneously soothe four crying babies, it follows that distressed infants must sometimes go unattended, a situation that nonhuman primate mothers would not tolerate.

Second, nonhuman primate mothers allow only those individuals to babysit who are closely related or subordinate to them. Personally selecting babysitters and paying them wages is a way for human mothers to achieve a higher rank than their babysitters in the human-style dominance hierarchy. A babysitter is motivated to do a good job by a mother who pays well. If a mother does not like how a babysitter cares for her baby, she can seek the services of a different provider or facility. The power a mother wields through her contract with her babysitter is parallel to that of a dominant mother macaque who allows a subordinate female to handle her baby, as long as the infant is properly cared for.

Fairly compensating childcare providers with an adequate salary, benefits, and guaranteed job security increases their incentives to perform well and to stay on the job. And yet, babysitters and daycare workers routinely find themselves at the bottom of the barrel in terms of pay and benefits. Live-in nannies surveyed in the Los Angeles area in the mid 1990s (mostly young immigrant women from Mexico and Central America) were paid on average $242 per week for about 64 hours of care, or around $3.80 per hour.[46] Of almost 500 occupations for which income data were collected during the last U.S. Census, childcare workers were the fifth lowest paid. Almost half a million childcare workers (mostly women) are paid less than workers in 99 percent of occupations in the United States today.[47] The low pay offered to young females who work in daycare centers in the United States sends the message that there is almost no job less important than childcare. The outcome of low pay is stress, dissatisfaction, and high job turnover. Daytime caregivers who are here today and gone tomorrow are less likely to be familiar with their charges and may be poorly motivated to invest in their jobs.

Even when babysitters are adequately compensated for care, mothers may have little say about who will provide care or how that care will be bestowed. For example, welfare mothers who must work in order to receive their benefits may have little choice about the daycare offered to them. A report released in February 1998 by the Office of the Inspector General, Department of Health and Human Services, states, "Difficulty in obtaining affordable and safe child care is widely recognized as a major barrier that prevents families from leaving welfare and entering and remaining in the work force."[48] Because childcare vouchers issued to welfare mothers often cover less than 75 percent of the market rate for childcare, choices of available daycare programs are limited. Low-income families who wish to use high-quality childcare programs (which are often expensive) are faced with higher copayments than they can afford. These families have two options—find less expensive care, perhaps from a license-exempt provider, or refuse to work and lose their benefits entirely. When the contract for childcare is between the government and the daycare facility, rather than between a mother and her babysitter, mothers may find that they have little say in how that care is provided. A mother becomes a subordinate female handing her baby over to a more dominant one, a position that nonhuman primate mothers avoid at all costs.

Offering better incentives to babysitters and daycare workers increases the likelihood that stable, long-term relationships will be formed between babies and their paid caregivers. A baby's best chance for receiving quality care is having a babysitter that knows him, likes him, and wants to please him. As we saw for nonhuman primates, mothers must have clout with those who care for their infants and be willing and able to use it.

Quality daycare given by nonkin babysitters does not have to be a contradiction in terms. Studies have found that high-quality daycare programs may increase childrens' cognitive and language scores, facilitate their social-emotional development, and decrease their behavior problems.[49] But quality daycare programs are hard to find and may be financially out of reach for many, if not most, families.

Do primate mothers benefit from babysitters enough to justify the risks? We have seen that sometimes babies are not returned to their mothers or are inadvertently injured by babysitters. But mothers also have a lot to gain from the help of babysitters; they can search for food unencumbered, suffer less wear and tear on their bodies, give birth more frequently (mother nature's definition of success), and contribute to family income.

Nonhuman primate infants typically aren't permanently harmed by babysitters, and as we saw for langurs, may even benefit from the efforts of multiple caregivers. When a nonhuman primate infant is orphaned, the fact that it has been cared for by an older sibling may be the difference between its life or death. In human preindustrial societies, care by babysitters (including fathers, grandmothers, older siblings, and others within the living group) is common and typically safe for infants. In industrial societies, however, the outcome for infants of babysitting is contingent upon the quality of care provided and the amount of time spent in paid care.[50]

Perhaps it is babysitters who benefit most from babysitting, despite the increased risks they incur while caring for infants. We have seen that tamarins sacrifice valuable foraging time (and thus, physical condition), and sometimes even risk their lives—carrying infants can impair balance in the treetops or prevent a fast getaway from an eagle's sharp talons—to help care for infants. Human babysitters make sacrifices as well: they are paid low wages, work long hours, and often have little job security. But primate babysitters do have the opportunity to learn how to mother before they take on the job, full time, with their own offspring.[51] Just as young male primates prepare themselves for their lives as adult males by competing with other males through play, the play mothering practiced by young females with the troop's (or neighborhood's) newest addition prepares them well for a lifetime of mothering.

Adapting to industrialization has compelled us to drastically modify the babysitting rules derived by our primate relatives over millions of years. Because we need hours (rather than minutes) of childcare, it is no longer possible for most working families to rely on relatives (fathers, grandmothers) or subordinates (older offspring) for care. Sometimes we feel that we have no choice but to settle for caregivers who may have little incentive to provide quality care.

But let's not throw out the babysitter with the bath water. The use of babysitters among nonhuman primates is a common and relatively safe practice under certain conditions; caregivers are supervised by mothers, mothers are related and/or dominant over babysitters, and babysitters are not left in charge of youngsters for extended periods of time.

CHAPTER 5

Weaning Wars

WILD chimpanzee females give birth about every 4 to 5 years, and Flo, a female studied by Jane Goodall, already had 12- and 8-year-old sons and a 4-year-old daughter by the time her son Flint was born.[1] Flo began to wean Flint from her breast when he was 3, early by chimpanzee standards. Much younger than the other weanlings, Flint appeared to be outraged at his mother, as evidenced by his daily temper tantrums.

Flint was 5 when Flo's last offspring, Flame, was born. At first Flint seemed to accept that he was no longer Flo's baby, but soon he reverted to the clingy, dependent behavior which had characterized him in the past.[2] He became listless and lethargic, showing little inclination to play with peers. When Flame died of an illness at the age of 6 months, Flint once again became the happy-go-lucky, playful chimpanzee he was before Flame's birth. But his clingy, dependent behavior actually worsened. Now almost 6 years old, he resumed making nipple contact, again shared Flo's night nest, and even, sometimes, rode on her belly, a spot typically reserved for young infants.

Flo died when Flint was 8 years old. He remained beside her body for many hours. His physical condition rapidly deteriorated, and 3 and a half weeks after Flo died, Flint died too. The loss of Flo's last infant, Flame, combined with Flo's old age and frailty, perhaps explains why she allowed Flint to become her baby once again. The consequences of her failure to withdraw care in this instance, however, were catastrophic.

THE story of Flo and Flint illustrates what can go wrong when the time comes for parents to begin withdrawing care from their offspring, as parents shift their focus to the next child (or themselves), and youngsters start down the road to independence. The journey to self-sufficiency is long and arduous in primates. It begins when a young primate is equivalent in age to a 2- to 5-year-old human being, an age group I loosely call "toddlers." At that point, prosimian, monkey, ape, and human mothers become less attentive and responsive to their youngsters as they approach their next pregnancy or, in the case of human mothers in industrial societies, their return to the world of work. Youngsters are never pleased with the changes in their mother's treatment of them and fight back inventively. The battle between the sexes is nothing compared to what biologists call parent-offspring conflict.[3]

A COMPLEX array of biological, cultural, and psychological factors affect the timing of the withdrawal of parental care. When care is withdrawn too early or abruptly (through neglect, abandonment, or even infanticide), the outcome for the child is obviously poor. Difficulties also arise when parents wait too long to withdraw care. Gradual withdrawal of parental care over the course of development is an inevitable, necessary part of parenting. It sends a message to the child that the parent is confident in the child's ability to handle whatever comes his or her way, and that autonomy is not only acceptable, but expected. Growing children must one day "separate" from their parents in order to become independent adults. But what about a parent's need to separate from a child? Parents are clearly not content to indefinitely give 100 percent to their children. What mechanism tells a parent that it is time to back off?

The evolutionary biologist Robert Trivers tackled some interesting questions about when and why parents withdraw care from their young, and how parents and offspring might "disagree" on the nature of care offered by parents.[4] Trivers theorized that the quality and timing of care offered by parents to young, *and* the vigor with which offspring solicit parental care, are both predictable when judged by the same ultimate goal: striving for maximum lifetime reproductive success (defined as the production of as many surviving offspring as possible over an individual's lifetime). It is essential to remember, however, that the behavioral "strategies" of parents (withdrawing care) and offspring (soliciting care) are *not* conscious, but virtually automatic.

Parents and young clash over the amount and quality of parental care offspring will receive. Youngsters would like their parents to instantly satisfy all of their needs and desires, but parents must limit what they offer in order to ensure their own survival and that of later-born offspring. So parents have to determine what is a sufficient, but not excessive, expenditure of effort on behalf of their offspring. Parents are usually ready to *give* less care before youngsters are ready to *receive* less care, but youngsters have a complete bag of tricks (crying, temper tantrums, and so on) to manipulate their parents into giving them what they want.

Evolutionary biologists and psychologists borrow cost-benefit analyses from the field of economics to predict when parental care will be withdrawn. When does an offspring benefit enough from a parent's behavior (such as nursing) to make it worth the cost to its parent (weight or energy loss, risk of harm, delay of next pregnancy) to perform it, and when is the benefit too small to justify parental effort? For example, the benefit of nursing to a newborn chimpanzee is huge compared to the cost to its mother of producing milk—without milk, the newborn dies, and that wastes the mother's 8-month investment in her pregnancy. What does this analysis look like, however, when the chimpanzee youngster is 4 years old? The cost of milk production to the mother of a 4-year-old chimpanzee is high (it delays her return to sexual cycling and her next pregnancy) compared to the amount of benefit to her 4-year-old, who is now quite capable of feeding himself.

Although Trivers's work on parent-offspring conflict focuses on the ultimate, unconscious goal of maximum lifetime reproductive success, applying his ideas to the conscious choices we all make in our daily lives is illuminating. Tending to a child's needs instead of our own (or those of a younger child) can be difficult and frustrating. Should we work late to finish an important project, or stop early to attend our child's soccer game? In other words, do we satisfy our own needs at the expense of our children's, or do we satisfy our children at the cost of depriving ourselves?

Ideally, mothers gradually withdraw care in response to their awareness of their offspring's increasing maturity and competence. The comparative psychologists Harry and Margaret Harlow called this period in the mother-infant relationship "the stage of ambivalence," as mothers become increasingly indifferent to the needs and wishes of their offspring.[5] As primate young become more capable, mothers become less responsive, and youngsters achieve independence. When youngsters want their mother, it becomes their responsibility to seek her out. If they desire comfort, they approach her for grooming or a hug, and if they are afraid, they stay by her side. Their mother's withdrawal of care sends them the powerful message that they are capable of caring for themselves. The one-step-forward-one-step-back dance of parents and offspring continues until the youngster reaches adulthood.

PRIMATE mothers withdraw care fairly abruptly from their toddlers in three clearly defined circumstances: during weaning from the breast, the back, and the bed. Although weaning is often unpleasant for youngsters, most offspring emerge emotionally unscathed. It is not the withdrawal of care per se but the timing and manner in which care is withdrawn that determine how a youngster adapts.

How does a nonhuman primate mother know that it is time to step back from her older infant? As her youngster matures, he becomes more interested in consuming solid foods. Feeding beside his mother shows him what to eat, how to prepare it, and most important, that he is capable of finding his own food. A youngster at this stage of development is quite mobile and delights in playing with peers when the opportunity arises. He is enticed away from his mother for longer periods and suckles less frequently. When a baby nurses infrequently, its mother's pituitary gland releases less prolactin, the hormone that stimulates milk production and suppresses ovulation in nursing mothers. No longer privy to nature's contraceptive (lacational amenhorrea), mothers decrease milk production and resume sexual cycling. They become interested in (and interesting to) adult males again and now actively discourage their older infants from suckling. Their youngsters adjust to the loss of the breast while simultaneously contending with rivals with whom they can't possibly compete—adult males.

Before the use of wet nurses or the discovery of contraceptives, human and nonhuman primate mothers were on a similar timetable, controlled by the feedback loop between nursing infants and their mothers. Human mothers in most preindustrial societies still finish weaning their toddlers from the breast during their next pregnancy (nursing having already decreased enough to trigger the resumption of sexual cycling). As in nonhuman primates, lactational amenorrhea is the only form of birth control available to nomadic !Kung San mothers—"contraception on the hip"—and babies are born every 3 to 5 years. This interbirth interval is reinforced by cultural values, which are tied to the !Kung economy. A woman could not gather food if she had to simultaneously carry and nurse two children under the age of 4. The !Kung expression "A woman who gives birth like an animal to one offspring after another has a permanent backache" emphasizes the culture's approval of a low fertility rate.

Once a primate female becomes pregnant, she may again become more tolerant of her older infant. She may even extend some or all of the privileges of babyhood. But this is the calm before the storm. As her pregnancy continues, she more consistently rejects her youngster's attempts to suckle and ride on her back. Her focus is to find enough food to sustain her pregnancy, not to provide for her older offspring. Because pregnant mothers are both less agile and more vulnerable to predation than nonpregnant mothers, they no longer can afford to carry their older offspring. By the time the new infant is born, all the rules have changed: mothers attend to their new babies and older offspring must fend for themselves. In some cases, youngsters lose their baby privileges overnight.

The interbirth interval characteristic of each primate species or population reflects the *least* amount of time it takes for youngsters to be able to survive the loss of their mother's *unconditional* care. It isn't that mothers completely refuse to care for older offspring; rather, it is that weaned young—juveniles—can no longer depend on their mother's consistent responsiveness. To be developmentally ready for weaning, older infants must be able to consume solid foods, travel independently from their mother, and be physically capable of exploring their environment and forming emotional bonds with other members of the community.

The interbirth interval is an evolutionary prescription for timing the withdrawal of parental care and is pretty specific for most primates; for example, an interbirth interval of 1 year is standard for squirrel monkeys, 3 years for muriquis, 4 to 5 years for chimpanzees, and as long as 4 or 5 years for some mobile hunter-gatherers. With no competition from a baby brother or sister, the infant nonhuman primate is guaranteed of its mother's undivided attention until it is old enough to essentially care for itself. This is nature's way of diminishing sibling rivalry.

Access to modern birth-control techniques affords some human parents the luxury of planning their families, rather than acceding to the plan embedded in our biology. When we attempt to withdraw care earlier or later than the ideal, however, we may face difficulties, because the child may not be developmentally ready, or may be beyond the age of maximal readiness for the changes we are asking of him.

So what strategies do primate mothers use to wean their young from the breast, the back, and the bed? And how do older infants fight back, manipulating their mothers into prolonging the provision of unconditional care?

Weaning conflict occurs in all species of primates, human and nonhuman.[6] Weaning is a gradual, often conjoined process with a very definite endpoint in most primates: the birth of a new sibling.

Sarji, a 10-month-old red howler monkey, approached his newly pregnant mother to nurse, as usual. But this time his mother ignored him. When he persisted, she crossed her arms over her chest and averted her gaze. Sarji whimpered plaintively but his mother just walked away. Sarji followed her, crying, until she relented and allowed him to nurse. This was the beginning of the end of the maternal comfort and nurturance that Sarji had known from birth.

When nonhuman primate mothers resume sexual cycling, they begin to avoid their offsprings' attempts to suckle. They cross their arms over their breasts, like Sarji's mother, or use a variety of other tactics such as turning, walking away, lying down, or holding their offspring at arm's length.[7] When avoidance doesn't work, nonhuman primate mothers may try to distract their young by grooming them or playing with them. When all else fails, mothers may employ threats or mild aggression. Muriqui mothers, for example, nip or hit especially persistent youngsters.[8] But wild nonhuman primates rarely resort to even moderate aggression, and when they do, reserve it for older infants at a late stage in the weaning process.[9]

Most chimpanzee mothers are gentle and tolerant with their older infants during weaning.[10] Rather than directly threatening their young, they choose the path of least resistance; they distract or gently push their youngsters away, or cover their breasts. Chimpanzee mothers patiently groom their older infants or offer other forms of calming body contact. For example, chimpanzee youngsters are allowed to suck on their mother's lower lip, ear, or skin, or bury their head in her armpit.[11] But this contact is conditional: to receive it, the youngster must keep his head turned away from his mother's breasts.

Human mothers' methods of weaning reflect cultural influences as well as individual differences between mothers, and run the gamut from gentle (like most nonhuman primates) to very harsh. Although mothers in many human societies are inclined to gently wean their toddlers, some human mothers are aggressive enough to make Flo, the chimpanzee mother studied by Jane Goodall, look like a saint.

Cultural prescriptions for indulgent versus harsh treatment may have something to do with fertility.[12] In cultures with low fertility, parents typically are more indulgent or tolerant of their children than in cultures in which families typically contain many closely spaced children. For example, the word for weaning among the very fertile Gusii people of Kenya, "ogotacha," means to stamp or step on, reflecting the view of mothers that weaning should be swift and severe.[13] During the last century in the United States, in contrast, weaning practices became more indulgent as the number of children per family decreased: in the 1980s, women were giving birth to half as many children as women in the 1950s.[14] Mothers in industrial countries are also greatly influenced by the medical establishment, and weaning practices fluctuate with the advice of physicians and childcare experts.

Human mothers employ innovative tactics to discourage their toddlers from suckling. Mothers in foraging and agrarian societies are creative, choosing to smear a variety of foul-tasting or odoriferous substances on their breasts, such as red pepper, bitter chili, goat dung, juice from sour fruits, or bitter medicine.[15] With toddlers that are especially resistant to weaning, mothers from the village of Taira on Okinawa in the South Pacific may pretend that their breasts have been injured.[16] They paste a patch of black paper (normally used to treat toothaches or bruises) onto their breasts, inform their children that their breasts are hurt, and wince in "pain" when a child attempts to suckle. American mothers offer nipple substitutes like bottles or pacifiers, or distract their infants with spouted cups (and praise for using them).

Since mothers in most human cultures sleep with their young children, weaning is most problematic in the middle of the night when youngsters are used to snuggling up to their mothers and nursing on demand. Sometimes mothers cover their chests with clothing, eliminating access to their breasts. Tarong mothers from the Philippines and Mixtecan mothers from Mexico often go away for a day or two, leaving the child in the able hands of an aunt, a grandmother, or the father and older siblings.[17] Although the child misses her mother, she is usually indulged and treated with great sensitivity by her substitute caregivers. Another strategy is sending the child to her aunt's or grandmother's home (or corner of the sleeping room when extended families share the same sleeping quarters) for a few days, until the worst is over. When nuclear families sleep together, the toddler loses her spot next to her mother and is placed between her father and an older sibling to sleep. After 2 nights apart, mothers more firmly and confidently deny their toddlers the breast.

Mothers in most human societies usually wean their children between the ages of 2 and 4, when youngsters have teeth and are used to eating solid foods. Tasty treats like candy, eggs, and fish are offered as bribes by Tarong grandmothers, who use these goodies to distract and comfort their young charges. Sometimes youngsters are simply told that they can no longer nurse. When a 3-year-old !Kung San child comes to her pregnant mother to nurse, she may be told "this milk is no longer for you."[18]

If toddlers persist in demanding the breast, human mothers up the ante and add punishment to their arsenal. As among nonhuman primates, older weanlings are the targets of the most aggressive behavior. Foraging !Kung San mothers use "mild ridicule or social pressure" to wean a 4-year-old. Mothers shame their children, warn them not to cry, scold them, or slap their hands away. A Tarong mother frightens her toddler into compliance by warning him, "Christ will cut out your tongue," or "Wawah [the bogeyman] will come and eat you." Giving up the breast is definitely preferable to the threatened alternative. American mothers also use more severe tactics when older toddlers resist giving up the nipple (or nipple substitutes): they put away bottles, hide pacifiers, and smear nasty-tasting substances on the thumbs of older children.

After primate mothers wean their young from the breast, they may still be willing to share food with them or, at the very least, will allow them to feed close by. Sampling their mother's food and observing her food choices allows youngsters to safely select appropriate items from the broad smorgasbord offered by nature, much of which is unpalatable, nonnutritious, or poisonous. Leanne Nash observed a captive-born juvenile galago, who had refused a tasty cicada she had offered, quickly change its tune when an adult wild-born galago accepted the cicada—the cicada suddenly gained credibility as a food source, and the youngster eagerly grabbed it away from the adult. Weanlings in close proximity to their mothers also are in position to beg for food from the adult most likely to share with them. But as primate youngsters become more capable, mothers become less generous.

Another weaning conflict erupts when primate parents no longer wish to be their infants' primary means of transportation. There is little difference between a 2-year-old child begging to be carried and a 6-month-old baby monkey who would rather ride than walk to the next fig tree. Weaning from riding occurs at about the same time as weaning from the breast in most nonhuman primates and can be every bit as traumatic.[19] Among some nonhuman primates, such as macaques and baboons, the transition from riding to walking may occur literally overnight, after the birth of a new sibling. Baboon mothers simply get up and walk away, with no attempt to signal to or cajole their older youngster to follow.[20] When an older infant attempts to climb on board, her mother pushes or nips at her until she lets go. Even though baboon mothers refuse to carry older infants, youngsters often succeed at hitching a ride with an adult male "friend," as we saw in Chapter 3. The transition to independent travel is least traumatic in those species in which males offer some care to young, since males usually are more willing than mothers to carry older youngsters. Even when mothers are no longer willing to regularly transport their young juveniles, they may run to retrieve them when they cry out in distress, fall, or are trapped, hurt, or in danger of being taken by a predator.[21] Primate youngsters often can count on parental protection far past the end of nutritional dependence.

Nomadic !Kung San mothers carry their children until the age of 4, some months after they are weaned from the breast. At the point when they are left behind in camp under their father's supervision, they lose their perch on their mother's shoulder with its bird's-eye view of the world.[22] This transition is not traumatic because !Kung fathers continue to carry youngsters on their shoulders on long journeys until they are 6 or 7.

But weaning from riding among humans is not always smooth. Weaning from riding is "the unhappiest interval in childhood" for Taira children in Okinawa. Shortly after the birth of a new sibling, Taira toddlers suddenly are ignored or even ridiculed when they ask to be carried. Their mothers, who previously responded rapidly and tenderly to them, now ignore full-fledged tamper tantrums or even scream at them for crying. When older youngsters lag behind defiantly, mothers do not respond and older siblings are responsible for dragging them along. Paraguayan Áche 5-year-olds similarly face unhappiness, and sometimes even danger, as they battle with their parents about being weaned from riding. Parents continue moving when resentful youngsters lag behind, each waiting to see what the other will do. Children are at risk of becoming lost as they and their parents play this "dangerous game of chicken."[23]

Some human parents can keep their children safe *and* unattached to them, an impossibility for most other primates. In the United States, older infants are commonly "cached" in a safe place rather than carried, in the care of babysitters or restraining devices (such as swings, strollers, baby seats, walkers, cribs, and playpens).[24] They typically do not experience the warmth, contact, and continuous motion that is normal for most young primates, whose assigned place is on their mother's hip or back. So rather than being weaned from riding on parents, American toddlers are weaned from their restraining devices, which may be much easier for both mother and child. Young children freed from their tethers are typically raring to go. American toddlers (and their parents) have essentially sidestepped the second of the three weaning conflicts, and in doing so, have lost an opportunity to learn to soothe themselves and tolerate frustration.

Weaning from co-sleeping is the last major hurdle human and nonhuman primate mothers and their older infants must clear as babies make the transition to semi-independence. By the time nonhuman primate young are weaned from the nest, they are no longer nursing or regularly riding on their mother. They experience the final blow to their intimate relationship with their mother when their new sibling arrives: they are not permitted to sleep in Mother's lap or nest. When young nonhuman primates are no longer welcome in their mother's lap, they settle for sleeping next to her, cuddling close.

Among nonhuman primates that build night nests, such chimpanzees, gorillas, orangutans, and bonobos, older youngsters even lose the privilege of sleeping next to their mothers when new infants are born. Birute Galdikas tells how an orangutan mother named Cara encouraged her 8-year-old son, Carl, to stay out of the night nest she shared with her new infant, Cindy.[25] Initially, Carl climbed into the nest with Cara and Cindy. After Carl was settled, Cara got up and moved, making another nest for herself and her infant daughter. After repeatedly being abandoned by Cara, Carl eventually adjusted to sleeping alone, in his own nest. American parents adopt similar tactics. We may allow our children to fall asleep in our beds and then move them to their own, or lie down with them until they fall asleep and then creep back to our own beds. Most primate youngsters do not willingly surrender the comforts of the family bed.

Before a young ape sleeps alone, he has become an expert nest builder. A young chimpanzee constructs its own nest for about a year before actually sleeping in it.[26] Gorillas begin constructing nests at about 18 months of age but do not sleep alone in their nests until they are about 3 years old.[27] And even then, a young gorilla's nest connects with that of its mother for about a year after the birth of a new sibling. Young orangutans also build nests that they don't sleep in, preferring to snuggle with their mothers as long as possible. Bonobo youngsters know better than to enter a night nest uninvited. Mother bonobos need only ignore the plaintive cries of their older youngsters, who will not enter their mother's nest without permission.

Mothers in most human societies sleep next to their young for at least their first year of life, and usually until they are weaned.[28] By this time, a new sibling has usually arrived who takes the coveted place beside mother at night. Although toddlers no longer sleep in their mother's arms, they are not expected to sleep alone; they sleep next to their grandmother, aunt, father, or older sibling.

In the United States, however, a baby sleeping next to her mother is the exception rather than the rule. Mothers (or families) who sleep with their infants, the natural way of primates, often encounter criticism rather than praise. By the age of 3 months, 58 percent of babies sleep in their own beds, outside of their parents' room, and by 6 months, nearly all infants sleep alone.[29] American toddlers make the transition from one type of "nest" (crib) to another (bed), rather than from sleeping with the mother to sleeping with other family members or alone, like most primates. As with other primates, however, the change in sleeping arrangements (from crib to bed) usually occurs around the time of birth of a new sibling, who takes possession of the crib. While parents promote the idea of "a big boy's bed," most toddlers, like young apes, would rather play than sleep in their beds.

Human young don't like being weaned from co-sleeping any more than young primates do. My clients Sam and Terry were struggling to wean their two children, ages 6 and 4, from their bed, and losing the battle. Unlike most American parents, Sam and Terry had always permitted and even encouraged their children to sleep with them. But Sam and Terry had recently been longing to have their bed to themselves again. They carried their children to their own beds every night after they fell asleep, but at some point during the night, both children returned. The nightly battle about where the children would sleep was invariably won by the children.

Perhaps because sharing the "family bed" is so uncommon in America, it was not clear to Sam and Terry how to wean their children from sleeping beside them. There were no older siblings or a live-in grandmother to substitute as sleeping companions, as is common in other societies. Sleeping with parents is a normal part of primate babyhood, but learning to sleep with other companions (or in some species, alone) is part of growing up. Taking into account the comfort their children derived from co-sleeping, Sam and Terry allowed their children to sleep in twin beds that were pushed together, which lessened the impact of their eviction from their parents' bed.

Toilet training is a "weaning" conflict unique to humans, and one that mothers in industrial societies have not been able to avoid. Interestingly enough, the toilet training of American toddlers is often an unpleasant and difficult job, fraught with frustration for both parents and young. What parents want is a 2- or 3-year-old who no longer wears diapers and does not soil her clothing or bedding. What the toddler wants is to continue what she is doing, rather than interrupt her activities to sit on a cold, scary, or boring potty seat. When the parent wins, the outcome is a deposit of urine or feces into the toilet. When the toddler wins, the result is a full diaper.

Our nonhuman primate cousins master bowel and bladder control without training. More mobile than young children, they are soon capable of determining where their urine or feces will go. For example, when cottontop tamarins are only a couple of weeks old, they scoot their rumps backward when they defecate and usually avoid soiling their caretaker. Ape infants are considerably slower than tamarins at developing bowel control because they mature less quickly. Chimpanzee mothers do not enjoy being smeared with their youngster's feces, however, and wipe the soiled area clean with leaves.[30] Since nonhuman primate infants don't wear diapers, they have immediate feedback when urinating or defecating. They rapidly learn to void without soiling themselves, their parents, or their nest. And since nonhuman primates eliminate in public, youngsters can observe exactly how (and where) it is done.

Elimination training in humans reflects cultural beliefs about when infants are physically capable of bowel and bladder control and about the best methods for training them. Perhaps most unusual are the Bantu-speaking Digo people of East Africa, who begin elimination training shortly after birth.[31] Digo mothers and infants are constant companions during the infant's first few months of life, and mothers begin elimination training when their babies are 2 or 3 weeks old. Digo mothers believe that their babies are ready to learn at this age and expect that their infants will be fully trained before their first birthday. They train their infants in the middle of whatever is going on, and in public, rather than in private. Babies are unclothed, so mothers simply hold their infants in a sitting position to eliminate, and reward them with a hug or some other pleasant activity when they are finished. By 5 months of age, infants are expected to "urinate in position and on command."[32] That Digo children are trained much earlier than American toddlers tells us that control is possible far earlier than our cultural beliefs would predict. But Digo mothers pay a price for this achievement; they must devote themselves to elimination training during their infant's first few months of life.

Infants in most foraging and agrarian societies are not diapered and usually wear no trousers until they have achieved bladder and bowel control. A Rajput mother in India simply holds her infant away from her body when he voids, and he soon understands that his mother does not wish to be soiled by him.[33] Wandering the streets of rural China, one sees countless toddlers riding on their father's shoulders in crotchless trousers. The Gusii of Kenya keep their infants naked until they have mastered bladder and bowel control.[34] There are no diapers to prevent a child from receiving feedback about his behavior, and no buttons or zippers to slow him down.

In the United States, many methods of toilet training have been touted by experts, ranging from rigidly scheduling bowel movements to passively waiting until children show an interest in mastering bladder and bowel control.[35] Some experts emphasized that toilet training should not begin before children were able to control their sphincter muscles, something thought to occur at around 18 months.[36] That toilet training has been a hot topic in the parenting self-help literature for such a long time highlights the challenge it presents to many parents.

Why is toilet training such an ordeal in the United States? Some of our cultural beliefs put obstacles in the path of efficient toilet training. Because we are particular about where we *don't* want our children to void—on the new carpet, in the back yard, or in front of the neighbors—we use diapers, which eliminate most of the unpleasant feedback that motivates children not to soil themselves. Diapered children eliminate wherever they are, without inconveniencing themselves or their parents. Because there is no compelling reason to attend to the signals to void, babies continue doing what they are doing, blissfully unaware of the need to eliminate.

When we begin toilet training, however, all the rules suddenly change. We ask our children to deposit their feces and urine into a toilet, which means that they have to be acutely aware of the need to void (a signal they have previously learned to ignore), *and* they have to stop whatever they are doing. In addition, they are asked to perch on a toilet, which is scary for some children and inconvenient for others. Because we keep our children fully clothed during the training period, the step of removing clothing further increases the time between the urge to void and the opportunity to do so. We have thus added a series of hurdles to bladder and bowel training that youngsters in other societies do not encounter.

An additional obstacle to toilet training that some parents face occurs when they disagree about how toilet training should be handled. My clients Howard and Janet had very different ideas about how their 4-and-a-half-year-old child, Ryan, should be trained. Their pediatrician had determined that there was no physical reason for the delay in bowel control. Howard and Janet said that they had done everything they could think of, but Ryan was determined to deposit feces only in his diaper. When Ryan screamed in protest when asked to give up his diaper, Janet relented so he would not become upset. Janet empathized with Ryan's anger over being frustrated, since she herself had difficulty coping with frustration. Howard's behavior was very different when Ryan screamed: he yelled right back in an attempt to discipline his son. Janet then shouted at Howard to back off. A loud argument between Howard and Janet ensued, with Ryan left to do as he pleased.

Ryan had learned to use temper tantrums to divide his parents and get his way, whether it was about wearing a diaper or acquiring a new toy. When tantrums continue to work, a toddler tyrant is created. The failure to withdraw care produces a child who cannot cope with frustration and the normal demands of life.

FIGHTING back is normal toddler behavior in all primates. When a tenderly cared for child is confronted with the end of indulgence, he initially cannot believe what is happening. The anthropologists William and Corinne Nydegger, who studied the

Tarong people of the Philippines in the 1950s, describe the weaning experience of a 2-and-1-half-year-old Tarong toddler this way: "he who was master of the household is now a beggar at the gates."[37] Who, after being so deeply wounded, would not fight back?

One strategy young primates use to fight back is manipulation. Sluggo, a clever yearling baboon, was no longer permitted to nurse on demand. He discovered that he could nurse without interruption, however, when his mother fell asleep. So Sluggo patiently groomed his mother to sleep and then suckled to his heart's content.[38]

Even when mothers are already firmly rejecting their youngsters, it is possible to trick them into changing their minds. A rhesus monkey toddler observed by Carol Berman on Cayo Santiago Island was consistently rejected as her mother weaned her from the breast.[39] Once when the youngster screamed at a human observer, however, her mother grabbed her protectively and then allowed her to suckle. From that time forward, this resourceful young monkey learned to manipulate her mother by screaming at humans. And it worked like a charm, at least until her mother resumed sexual cycling.

Temper tantrums are the most effective weapons in a toddler's arsenal, especially at the beginning of weaning. Primate toddlers initially whimper or whine when their mothers refuse them, and mothers often relent. But later on, softer cries no longer work and whining escalates into screaming. Jane Goodall described the tantrum scream of a young chimpanzee as a loud, harsh call that sometimes resulted in "glottal cramping."[40] Screaming, throwing themselves on the ground at their mother's feet, flailing their arms, and kicking their feet are some of the ways human and nonhuman primate toddlers seek their mother's attention and pity. Some infants upset themselves so much that they choke, or even vomit.

Using a tantrum as a weapon is a two-edged sword, however, because although persistent, demanding infant monkeys (in some species) are more likely to be granted the nipple, they also are more likely to be punished. Mother macaques often give in to the tantrums of younger offspring (and perhaps as a result, younger infants have more tantrums), but they don't hesitate to punish older infants.[41] Primate young quickly learn which tactics work and when they work. If resistance consistently produces punishment, it will rapidly decline. Similarly, when human parents learn to ignore the tantrums of their 3- and 4-year-olds, tantrums gradually drop out of their child's behavioral repertoire.

When angry tantrums are no longer effective, nonhuman primate toddlers may express their displeasure passively. In species in which weaning is harsh, such as many macaques, some weanlings may sit quietly, alone and inactive. They don't appear to be as interested in eating as they were previously and seem oblivious to the raucous play of peers. In a huddling posture, these youngsters appear despondent to human observers. They don't like what is going on and there is nothing they can do about it: the formula for depression.

Primate toddlers may also regress, displaying behaviors they had long since given up. Regression occurs at the point when the change in the older offspring's status has become abundantly clear—after the birth of a new sibling. Nonhuman primate toddlers may once again attempt to ride, suckle, or share their mother's nest or bed as Flint, the chimpanzee, did after the birth of his baby sister. Human toddlers may regress to more infant-like behavior as well, such as soiling their underwear or staying closer to their mothers, resulting in less play or exploration. Watching their mother (and other family members and friends) shower attention on the new sibling is difficult for all primate youngsters. Reverting to immature behavior to win back their mother's attention is a toddler strategy that is often effective.

Toward the end of weaning, primate toddlers begin to adapt to the huge changes that have been thrust upon them and eventually turn to different sources of comfort and attachment—their peers or other members of their social group. Both males and females trade "mother time" for play time with peers. Later, they choose companions appropriate for the gender-specific behaviors they adopt as they mature. As youngsters accept the new status quo, their focus turns from their mother to their social milieu.

THE timing of weaning, intimately associated with a species' average interbirth interval, is affected by a variety of factors, including characteristics of the species, the physical and social environment, the composition of the family, and even individual differences among mothers and infants.

The biological characteristics of each primate species affect the timing of weaning and the spacing of offspring. Smaller species, such as marmosets and tamarins, have shorter life spans and correspondingly shorter periods of gestation and infant dependence than larger monkeys and apes. A species's characteristic social organization also influences parental behavior and the withdrawal of parental care. For example, in harem societies such as that of Hanuman langurs, unweaned infants are at the greatest risk for infanticide when a new male routs the current landlord and takes possession of his harem of females and young. Tenure for langur males is only a few years, so the earlier infants can be safely weaned, the less likely they will be vulnerable in the event of a sudden takeover.

There also are species differences in temperament that affect how mothers wean their young. For example, vervets and rhesus macaques are both Old World monkeys that live in large, matrilineal societies in which dominance hierarchies determine a female's position in her group. But vervets are much calmer than rhesus monkeys, and this difference in temperament affects all aspects of parenting behavior, including weaning. Weaning is relatively simple and trouble free among vervets, but macaque infants appear more distressed and throw more temper tantrums in response to the relatively harsh, impatient weaning strategies employed by their mothers.

Danger in the environment also is a major factor in the timing of weaning in both human and nonhuman primates; the more perilous the environment, the older an infant is when it is weaned. Sometimes the danger stems from insufficient food or water; when resources are plentiful, weaning occurs earlier than when they are scarce. The presence of soft foods that are easily consumed by youngsters beginning to sample solid foods also influences the timing of weaning.

When the primary danger is predation, mothers may wean their infants from the breast before they wean them from riding. And many primate parents continue to help their young avoid predators long after they no longer regularly carry them. Human parents also stay closer to their children and transport them longer in unsafe environments. In rural America children roam unsupervised at an earlier age than city kids, who live in an environment teeming with obvious and concealed dangers, such as automobiles and human predators.

Among tree-living nonhuman primates, the risk of falling may motivate mothers to wean their infants from the back later, when they are stronger and more mature. Karen Strier observed a 2-year-old muriqui and her pregnant mother as they approached a gap in the canopy, high above the forest floor.[42] The mother easily leapt across, then turned to wait. The youngster looked at the gap and then at her mother, and began to scream. She carried on this way for several minutes, screaming and running back and forth, making it perfectly clear that she was afraid to jump. Finally, her mother reached across the gap and by grasping branches with her hands and feet, made a bridge for her offspring to scamper across. After the birth of her new baby, however, this muriqui mother will no longer come back for her older youngster, who will have no choice but to overcome her fear. Strier believes that the 3-year spacing between muriqui young reduces the risk of infant mortality.

A striking demonstration of the effects of environmental danger on weaning age comes from Robert Sussman's comparison of two physically similar species of lemurs native to Madagascar.[43] The brown lemur lives in trees while the ringtailed lemur is primarily a ground dweller. Ringtailed lemurs are physically more precocious than brown lemurs and their young become independent significantly sooner. Sussman believes that the danger of falling from trees explains why brown lemurs are in less of a hurry to grow up. Falls also account for a high proportion of human childhood injuries, especially in children under 5.[44]

Nomadic !Kung San mothers wean their children from the breast and back considerably later than other foraging peoples, such as the Hadza, who live in northern Tanzania. !Kung mothers carry their children on their arduous gathering journeys up to (and sometimes, even later than) the age of 4. Hadza mothers, in contrast, wean their children from the breast and back by the age of 2 and a half. Older infants are left in camp, unsupervised by adults, in the company of other young children.

The anthropologist Nicholas Blurton-Jones explains these differences in parenting practices by examining the environments in which the !Kung and Hadza live.[45] The !Kung inhabit a more dangerous environment; the landscape is extremely monotonous (and thus it is very easy for an unsupervised child to become irretrievably lost), and the climate is more extreme. Hadza children, by contrast, live in a safer environment. Camp is located in hilly areas with good vistas, and wandering children are less likely to get lost. Food can be gathered near camp, so children are rewarded for short food-gathering forays away from home. Needing less supervision from parents, Hadza children simply are "cheaper" to raise. The Hadza childrearing strategy allows for the production of more children, a shorter inter-birth interval, and an abbreviated period of dependence, without an increase in mortality.

Danger to young nonhuman primates also lurks in their social environment. The highest risk is among those species in which adult males kill suckling infants in order to mate with their mothers, who afterword become sexually receptive. Another risk factor is group size; in aggressive macaque species, the likelihood that a young monkey will be harassed by other group members increases with group size. When the size of their group increases, rhesus infants stay closer to their mothers and other relatives (presumably because closely related individuals are less likely to harm them).[46]

A mother's social rank also affects the risk that her offspring will be harassed by other group members, which in turn influences the age when offspring are weaned. A vervet mother's high rank not only affords her youngster protection from harassment but attracts countless would-be babysitters looking for an opportunity to associate with a powerful family. Offspring of high-status vervet mothers are doted on by other members of the group and receive excellent care from them, an arrangement that gives high-ranking mothers more time to feed and maintain their own physical condition.[47] It is a different story for the offspring of low-ranking mothers, especially among macaques and baboons. High-ranking females and their families regularly pick on lower-ranking ones. Low-ranking mothers compensate by restricting their youngsters more and weaning them later. The cost of keeping their infants safe is that the offspring's opportunities for social experience are reduced and their independence is delayed.

Social rank issues are also present in human societies. Offspring of

high-status human parents are more likely to be courted than harassed by others in the social group. They also are more likely to live
in safe neighborhoods, which further protects them from harassment. Parents who live in unsafe neighborhoods tend to be more restrictive and controlling with children than parents living in safer areas.[48] In both human and nonhuman primates, encouraging early
autonomy and independence is a good strategy when environments
are relatively safe.

Family composition is another factor in the timing of weaning.
The arrival of a new baby changes the life of its older siblings, and in
turn older siblings affect how the newest member of the family is
treated. For example, rhesus monkey mothers with older daughters
spend less time with their babies than mothers who have sons or no
other offspring.[49] This is especially marked in very dominant mothers, whose almost equally dominant daughters are actively involved
in the care of their younger siblings. Older vervet siblings also interact frequently with their new baby brother or sister, which results in
less contact time between infants and their mothers.[50] Older daughters influence the weaning process in both species; infants with older
sisters are weaned at an earlier age than those without. When there
are no older siblings, a mother may indulge her infant longer and
wean it later.

The death of an infant also can affect the path to independence of
its older sibling. As in the case of Flint, the chimpanzee, the death of
an infant can be associated with behavioral regression in its older
sibling. Dian Fossey described a similar incident among mountain
gorillas when the female named Old Goat lost her baby.[51] Old Goat
allowed her youngest offspring, a 4-year-old male, to resume suckling and riding on her back.

Are siblings rivals or helpers in nonhuman primates? The answer
depends a lot on the interbirth interval between siblings. When an

infant arrives on the early end of the average birth interval of the species, it is more difficult for older offspring to adjust. Jealous older siblings have been observed in nonhuman primates: an older offspring may threaten or nip at the baby, grab her mother's hand away from grooming the baby (and pull it to her own back), or even pull the baby off the mother's nipple.[52] The effects are typically mild, perhaps because mothers are always present.

In most cases, older primate offspring direct their anger or frustration at their mother, rather than their new sibling. As older offspring, particularly daughters, grow up, they typically enhance the lives of their younger siblings. They often are their younger sibling's first playmates and eager babysitters. Infant rhesus monkeys with older siblings are physically more advanced and precocious than those without them, and gain independence more quickly. Infant cotton-top tamarins with a twin or an older sibling are capable of independently scampering about sooner than those without siblings. When younger siblings are weaned, an affectionate relationship with an older sibling may ease the frustrating transition to independence.

In traditional human societies, in which birth spacing still is largely determined by the frequency of nursing, similar patterns of sibling influence are seen. Although older youngsters being weaned are angry and frustrated, these feelings are almost always expressed to mothers rather than acted out with baby siblings. Older siblings in these societies often mature into helpful, affectionate play companions or babysitters for their younger brothers and sisters.

The outcome of sibling relationships in the United States today is more variable. When children are spaced less than 2 years apart, the older sibling, still a baby himself, may not be mature enough to cope with a suddenly smaller share of his mother's attention. His devoted companion has suddenly changed: she offers less positive attention, is less playful, and isn't as interested in organizing fun activities.[53]

Not only that, his conversation with his mother is perceived as more negative, with the mother making demands that he do this or stop doing that. These changes are associated with a decrease in warm feelings between mothers and their toddlers.[54] Lacking the verbal skills of a 4- or 5-year-old, a 1-year-old expresses his frustration, jealousy, and rage the only way he can—physically. He hits his baby sister, pushes her down, and asserts his power by taking things away from her. Rivalries that begin when children are babies sometimes continue, unabated, throughout life.

Individual differences in the temperament and maternal style of human and nonhuman primate mothers affect both how they care for their babies and how they withdraw care from their toddlers. Timid or anxious mothers (who tend to have a low dominance ranking or social status) are more protective and indulgent, and withdraw care later than more relaxed mothers, who usually occupy a higher rung on the social ladder. Flo, a dominant, aggressive, and socially adept chimpanzee mother, began to wean all her offspring, including Flint, on the early end of the weaning timetable. Nope, a timid, socially withdrawn chimpanzee mother also observed by Jane Goodall, weaned both of her offspring at the later end of the weaning spectrum, at about the age of 7.[55]

The timing and style of weaning are also influenced by a mother's age. Older nonhuman primate mothers are less rejecting than younger mothers and suckle their infants longer. !Kung San mothers in their forties, who will not become pregnant again, often wean their last child at the advanced age of 5 or 6. Evolutionary biologists believe that elderly mothers have longer interbirth intervals and suckle longer because it "costs" them little to do so; at the end of their reproductive lives, nursing or indulging their offspring a bit longer won't effect their future reproductive output.[56]

Certain characteristics of infants also affect the process of weaning and its outcome. In all primates that have been studied, mothers are more likely to respond to the protest screams of younger infants. But there is a cost to these mothers who give in to their youngster's demands. In rhesus monkeys, mothers of the youngest infants to be weaned often do not get pregnant when they first return to sexual cycling because their infants are still nursing frequently.[57] Mothers are firmer with older infants, whose increased maturity prepares them better to cope with frustration and to fend for themselves. Older infants quickly adapt to maternal rejection, refocusing their attention on playmates or other members of the group.

Although a baby's gender is not believed to influence the weaning process in nonhuman primates, there is no question that gender may profoundly affect this process in humans.[58] The preference is often based on economics. In societies in which wealth is inherited by sons from their fathers, males are indulged and favored throughout childhood.[59] In those rare societies in which wealth is passed on to daughters rather than sons, however, daughters are the fortunate recipients of preferential parental care.[60]

A fascinating example of how gender favoritism is tied to economics comes from a study of the Mukogodo of Kenya by the anthropologist Lee Cronk.[61] Formerly foragers, the extremely disadvantaged modern-day Mukogodo have closely associated themselves with the more successful Masai pastoralists. Masai families strongly prefer sons, since wealth is passed down through the male lineage in their culture. Although the Mukogodo also pass wealth from fathers to sons and *profess* to prefer sons over daughters, their parental behavior reveals that they favor daughters. Daughters are breastfed longer, taken to medical clinics for ill health more often, and are more likely to survive than sons. Why? It seems that daughters have a much better chance of reproducing than sons, because they can marry up the social ladder and become the primary or secondary wife of a more advantaged Masai. Impoverished Mukogodo sons are much less likely to accumulate enough livestock (required as a bride price) to win a young woman's hand in marriage. Many Mukogodo sons, therefore, grow old without marrying or having children. If the ultimate goal is to maximize lifetime reproductive success, it becomes clear why Mukogodo parents invest more heavily in daughters than in sons.

WHEN the timing is right, youngsters move on to the next phase of development without much difficulty. When mothers withdraw care from their offspring too early, however, feelings of abandonment may preclude readiness for independence.[62] The age of the infant when withdrawal of care begins is a key factor in how well he or she adapts to it.

What does the adult outcome of early rejection and insecure attachment in late infancy look like? My clients Barry and Melissa provide one example of how the childhood experience of premature withdrawal of parental care may affect interpersonal functioning years later.

Barry and Melissa had been happily married for 12 years and had two adored daughters. They came to see me after Barry admitted to Melissa what she had suspected for some time: that he had engaged in a brief affair 9 years before. Melissa was initially extremely angry and hurt. Barry clearly wasn't the man Melissa had thought he was— her island of safety in a turbulent sea. Marital therapy allowed Melissa to vent her feelings of hurt, fear, and anger, and both of them to understand how and why the affair had taken place. Barry and Melissa emphasized that they still loved each other. Their goal was to weather this crisis and emerge with an intact, stronger marriage.

But as the months wore on, Melissa could not heal. Despite regular individual and marital therapy and medication with an antidepressant, Melissa was as angry and frightened as ever. She verbally attacked Barry unpredictably and often, and at those times she was unable to discuss anything rationally or think clearly. She responded instantly to the slightest perceived neglect by Barry with a prolonged verbal attack. When Barry was reduced to tears, Melissa backed down. But this cycle of disappointment, fear, anger, attack, and release repeated itself endlessly. Melissa acted as though she had completely lost her safe base, and was hyper-vigilant for any sign that she would be duped again.

Melissa's early history sheds some light on her bottomless rage at Barry and her fear of trusting him again. Melissa was the second of seven children, all born 1 year apart. Melissa's older brother had attention deficit disorder with hyperactivity and required a lot of his stay-at-home mother's attention and supervision. Then came Melissa, a calm, easy child who "took care of herself." Melissa was followed by two brothers and three sisters.

When Melissa was 2, her family's fourth child was born. Her infant brother died of sudden infant death syndrome at the age of 3 months and Melissa's mother was devastated. Maybe she blamed herself, or perhaps it was simply the loss of her baby that precipitated her depression. As she inwardly withdrew, she still was responsible for the care of three children. Her oldest child needed constant attention, as did her youngest, an infant of 1 year. And soon she was pregnant again, with her fifth child. It is understandable that she had little left to give to Melissa.

A child of 2 does not understand that her mother is depressed. Existing at the center of her own world, she concludes that she is not good enough, or that something she has done has caused this reduction in caring. Melissa couldn't cope with Barry's infidelity because the experience transformed her back into that angry, frightened, 2-year-old whose "perfect" mother had suddenly disappeared.

Withdrawing care too late (or not at all), on the other hand, results in a different set of problems for youngsters. Primate youngsters get the message that they aren't capable of going out on their own. Overindulgent chimpanzee mothers have offspring who are reluctant to leave them and grow up. The son of Nope (a chimpanzee mother mentioned earlier), for example, didn't leave his mother until he was 11, which is quite late for male chimpanzees. And unlike most chimpanzee males, he seemed to have little ambition to become dominant over his peers.

Rhesus monkey youngsters are similarly affected by indulgent and nonrejecting mothers. When Harry Harlow and his colleagues attempted to separate young juvenile rhesus monkeys from their inanimate cloth-covered surrogate "mothers," it was extremely difficult for these youngsters to adjust. Never having experienced rejection or punishment by their terrycloth mothers, the youngsters' attachment to them was extremely persistent.[63] Research on human toddlers and school-age children also suggests that the sons of mothers who overprotect them during their first 3 years of life are excessively passive and dependent.[64]

CHAPTER 6

The Quiet Years

CHARLOTTE was the fourth offspring of a low-ranking mother living in Lynn Fairbanks' colony of captive vervets.[1] Because a daughter inherits a rank one notch below that of her mother, Charlotte had little chance of climbing the vervet social ladder. But Charlotte's mother died when she was 4 months old, and that changed her social destiny. The youngest infant to survive the death of its mother, Charlotte was cared for by her older siblings and was tough and resilient from the start. When Charlotte was 2, she offered her babysitting services to the highest-ranking (alpha) female, who accepted her offer. Charlotte became a favorite of the alpha female, and found that certain privileges accompanied her favored status. For example, Charlotte was not picked on by others of high rank when in the company of the alpha female. When Fairbanks decided to form a new living group, she chose Charlotte, her two older sisters (who, unlike Charlotte, had been reared by their mother), and several other females. Charlotte's older sisters retained their low positions in the new hierarchy, but Charlotte quickly rose to the top rank in the new group. She dominated other females who had formerly outranked her, including the daughter of the alpha female from her previous group. Charlotte's clever strategy of making herself indispensable to a monkey matriarch allowed her to overcome the low rank of her birth.

THE term "juvenile" is applied by primatologists to the stage of early to middle childhood. A juvenile has been weaned, and is therefore (at least, theoretically) capable of surviving its mother's death. Smaller and less experienced than adults, yet too grown up to be cared for by their mothers, juvenile nonhuman primates face a very high risk of mortality.[2]

Why is survival so difficult? Imagine being the size of a 6- to 12-year-old and having to compete with adults for food and safety. Small size, subordinate status, and relative inexperience put juveniles at a disadvantage when competing with adults for food, and increase the likelihood that they will be captured by predators. Juvenile humans also have a high risk of mortality, although less than that of nonhuman primate juveniles.[3] Unique among primates, human parents in most societies provide resources for preadolescent children, who depend on their parents far longer than most juvenile nonhuman primates. What all juvenile primates have in common is that they are neither as cute nor as helpless as they once were, and therefore must learn to make their own way in the world of adults.

Primatologists once believed that juveniles were passive creatures whose behavior was simply a response to the events that impinged upon them. But students of primate behavior now assert that juveniles actively pursue the experiences and relationships that will improve their longevity and their lot in life, much as Charlotte, the vervet, did when she attached herself to the alpha female.[4] The pathway to adulthood is long and perilous for juvenile primates, longer than that of all other mammals of comparable size.[5] How does a juvenile reach adolescence physically intact and ready to move on to adulthood? And how involved are primate parents with their youngsters during this high-risk stage of life?

First and foremost, juveniles must survive. The young primate must improve its ability to feed itself, learn to travel on its own, and become more proficient at detecting and avoiding environmental dangers. Second, juveniles must begin to understand their place in the social group. They adopt the behaviors expected of their age and gender and become skilled at performing them. They form relationships with other individuals that will benefit them throughout life, especially after their mothers withdraw care to rear subsequent offspring. Finally, they climb as high as they can on the social ladder.

And what do the parents of juvenile primates do for their half-grown young? Mostly they stay out of the way, as their youngsters learn from their own experience. But because parents are usually nearby, they may still come to the rescue in an emergency.

By the time they are weaned, young juveniles are already familiar with the type of foods that are good to eat, but still have a lot to learn about how and where to find them. Where is that fruiting fig tree and how do you get there? That nut is delicious, but its shell seems impenetrable. Is that mushroom edible or poisonous? What type of stick is best for termite fishing? Nonhuman primate parents serve as role models rather than teachers. Juveniles become more proficient at feeding themselves by observing their parents, by practicing, and by a process of trial and error.[6]

In most human societies, in contrast, youngsters at this age can still count on a place at the table, with parents supplying most or all of the meal. In preindustrial societies, children are often assigned jobs that help produce the family's food, such as milking or tending the cattle, harvesting food from the garden, cooking, and so on. Hadza parents expect their children to find some of their own food, and youngsters know where tasty roots are buried and how to dig them up. As children consume food that they have helped gather (or prepare), they acquire the necessary skills for the transition to adulthood. In industrial societies, children typically contribute little to food gathering or preparation; instead they focus on acquiring the skills needed to compete for high-status, high-paying jobs when they are grown.

Part of growing up is learning how to safely travel alone. Young primates must learn to swing through the trees without falling or scamper across the savannah without getting lost. Brachiating safely through the trees requires practice, and by the time primate young are juveniles, mothers rarely come to their rescue. Falls are common in species such as gibbons, whose mode of transportation is sailing through the trees. All young primates take a chance that they will be seriously injured as they learn to maneuver through their environment.

Orangutans provide a good example of how the local ecology affects the timing of independent travel by juvenile primates. The long period of dependence of young orangutans, the lengthiest of all of the nonhuman primates, may have a lot to do with the orangutan's picky eating habits.[7] The dilemma orangutans face is how to find enough fruit (their preferred food) to maintain their relatively large size. Fruit is not as plentiful as leaves or as evenly distributed in the forest. Fruit trees are often small and may yield only a few ripe fruits at a time. To find enough fruit, orangutans must master a vast amount of spatial data: they must learn the location *and* fruiting cycle of many different, often rare tree species scattered throughout their large home ranges. So orangutan juveniles travel with their mothers for a very long time, learning the secrets of the forest that will later help them survive on their own.

Young human children learn the route to important local places in their environment: school, their friends' houses, or the local swimming hole. But the safeness of the environment has a lot to do with how much independent exploration parents allow. Juvenile !Kung San, for example, do not participate in gathering food on their own until the age of 15, because of the high risk of becoming lost in the relatively featureless bush environment they inhabit.[8]

Avoiding predators is another task that juveniles face. Since all young primates are vulnerable to predators, youngsters must become aware of the clues that a predator has targeted them: for lunch or other, equally undesirable outcomes. If a juvenile nonhuman primate's primary strategy is to be safe, he stays in the middle of his social group, where he is less likely to encounter predators. But then he risks starvation, because there is also more competition for food in the group's crowded, safer center. If his strategy is to fill his belly, he will spend more time at the group's edge, where there is less competition for food. The latter strategy, however, increases his chances of becoming, rather than eating, lunch. So the dilemma juvenile nonhuman primates face is safety versus starvation.[9]

Most nonhuman primate parents continue to protect juveniles from predators at this stage of development. Nonhuman primate parents know a predator when they see one and quickly respond. They scream a warning, pick up their offspring, and run away. Dangers that human children encounter may not be as obvious to their parents as an eagle swooping toward a juvenile spider monkey in the treetops. Parents in industrial societies such as the United States warn their children to avoid strangers, stay away from drugs, and discriminate "good" from "bad" touch. But human parents are often unaware of the presence of a different kind of "predator" (low self-esteem, suicidal ideation, or easy access to alcohol, drugs, or guns) that threatens their children. Parents cannot protect their children from dangers they do not see.

Because nonhuman primate parents are nearby, they have more opportunity to detect danger than human parents. What nonhuman primate parents see around them gives them the information they need to respond to a predator stalking their youngsters. Human parents in industrial societies, however, are often apart from their children. And children may intentionally conceal information about high-risk activities from parents because they don't recognize that they are in danger. Modern parents must do more than respond to obvious signs of peril: they must take an active approach, which requires investing much of their free time observing and intimately getting to know their children. Parents who are aware that their child has suddenly changed can quickly intervene.

When juveniles have enough to eat, can travel independently, and are more proficient at avoiding predators, they can turn their attention to mastering the social developmental tasks that pave the way to adulthood—acquiring gender roles, forming alliances, and climbing the social ladder.

ADOPTING behaviors expected of their gender is one of the most important developmental tasks of juvenile human and nonhuman primates. Learning how to behave like a competent male or female begins during the juvenile phase of development.

Female juvenile primates are very attracted to other females as companions. Just as elementary-school–aged human females are happiest in the company of their girlfriends and have great disdain for boys, juvenile nonhuman primate females also prefer one another's company for most activities. The behavior and activities of older girls in human societies differ from those characteristic of boys, as they do for nonhuman primates. Cross-cultural anthropological research has confirmed these differences in virtually all human cultures.[10]

Rough-and-tumble play is an interesting exception to the rule of preferring same-sexed companions. The choice of play partners appears to be independent of gender; young females select playmates who are age peers and similar in size, strength, and the motivation to play.[11] But play partners may not be the same individuals chosen as long-term companions, in both human and nonhuman primates.

Practicing mothering is a type of play that appeals more to primate girls than boys. Although young girls happily minister to dolls when no baby is available, both human and nonhuman primate females relish a chance to handle a real baby. Childcare is primarily the domain of primate females, and young females garner most of the babysitting jobs. As juvenile females babysit for infants, they learn to provide care in the company of other females. Staying connected with others of their gender (family or other group members) lays the foundation for forming lifelong friendships or alliances.

Juvenile male primates also pick up on gender-specific behaviors primarily through play. Since young males fare better when they grow up strong, physically capable, and competitive, juvenile males choose play activities that promote physical fitness and fighting skills.[12] Wrestling, chasing, and displays of dominance are favorite activities of all young primate males. Human boys also pursue power, and beg their parents for toy weapons. Even parents who refuse to purchase toy swords and guns are stymied by their sons' determination to transform any neutral object into a weapon. Weapons are symbols of power that allow boys to assume a superior position in dominance contests with playmates, or feel invincible during solo play. Young males also choose play partners on the basis of size, strength, and motivation to play, rather than gender, perhaps because of the benefits of testing one's mettle against equivalent opponents.

Juvenile males also seek out older males as companions during this phase of life. In many species, juvenile males follow adolescent or adult males like eager puppies. They imitate the behavior of their elders, or approach them for comfort or protection. The swagger of a juvenile male chimpanzee is an obvious imitation of the way the adult males behave in grown-up dominance contests. So young males figure out how to be a male by observing, imitating, and interacting with other males. And older males typically are tolerant of the younger males who shadow them. Similarly in most human societies, sons at this developmental stage prefer to spend more time with fathers than mothers, and fathers are more involved with sons than daughters.[13]

How do young males acquire gender-specific behaviors when they have no regular access to fathers or other adult males? Except for a few solitary species, such as orangutans, this is not an issue for non-human primates (although in most species, the identity of "father" is unknown). In all social nonhuman primate societies, there is at least one adult male (and often many males) in the group. When there is only one resident adult male, he is quickly replaced when he dies. It is similar in foraging or agrarian human societies, since widows (or divorcées) quickly remarry or rejoin their own kin (or that of their deceased husband). In countries such as the United States, in contrast, in which remarriage is not a sure thing and extended family members are often widely dispersed, there is no guarantee that children from divorced families will have regular contact with adults of the opposite gender of the custodial parent.

WHEN mothers of older youngsters turn their attention to their new baby, juveniles expand their social networks and create alliances that will benefit them when they are grown. Cooperation with others to achieve goals is one of the hallmarks of human and nonhuman primate behavior. We have already seen that juveniles prefer age peers as play partners. Who else do juveniles turn to when their mothers are unavailable?

Juvenile nonhuman primates set themselves up for the future by building relationships with other individuals on whom they can depend to come to their aid. Juveniles typically look first to their own families, selecting individuals who will either remain in the group with them or accompany them when it is time to emigrate. For most primates this means individuals of the same gender, because in virtually all species the members of one sex stay put, while the members of the other emigrate to other communities. In some species females stay close to home and males disperse; in others males stay home and females emigrate.

Typically, it behooves juvenile nonhuman primates to build relationships or coalitions with individuals of the same gender (except when individuals of both sexes disperse on their own, as in monogamous species). They easily discriminate among the different adults in their living group and seek the company of tolerant adults and adolescents, which usually means family members. But although juvenile female vervets and macaques associate most often with other females in their family, they prefer the company of the most dominant females, related or not, who will tolerate having them around. High-ranking females are desirable companions because of the benefits of friendship with a powerful individual. It is no surprise that it is the females in these species who remain for life in the community in which they were born: why put the effort into building an alliance with another female if she is going to leave with the first attractive male that crosses her path? Young muriqui and chimpanzee males, by contrast, are most attracted to older males as companions. In these species, it is the males who remain in their natal groups.

Within a primate family, who are the most appealing companions for juveniles? In most cases, the answer is siblings, which may come as a surprise to many human parents, who daily encounter fierce rivalry among their children.

There is almost no such thing as serious sibling rivalry among nonhuman primates, or for that matter, among mammals other than humans.[14] Certainly, monkey and ape siblings may vie for their mother's attention, but truly aggressive interactions among siblings are rare. Vervet siblings, for example, fight with one another as frequently as they do with nonkin. But although fighting with unrelated monkeys can escalate to the point of injury, fighting among vervet siblings usually does not.[15]

What type of relationship can a young monkey or ape expect to have with its sibling? First, siblings often are one another's regular grooming partners. Grooming is relaxing, hygienic, and the primate way to solidify relationships. Second, siblings stick up for one another in conflicts with nonkin, and older siblings can be counted on to defend their younger, more vulnerable brothers and sisters.[16] This appears to be true in virtually all social primates.

We have seen that older juveniles will sometimes take care of orphaned younger siblings. But even when an older infant or very young juvenile is not an orphan, it still may greatly benefit from extra attention offered by a sibling. Azalea, a rhesus monkey infant who was born with a chromosomal abnormality similar to Down syndrome, came to depend on the special care offered by her older sister.[17] Although Azalea's mother may have been aware of her disability at some level (since she never rejected her), she showed little interest in her obviously different young daughter. Azalea's older sister, however, continued to tote Azalea around well past the time youngsters are expected to travel on their own.

Juvenile male primates often prefer the company of their older brothers. In species in which males emigrate to other groups, brothers often leave home together as juveniles, adolescents, or young adults.[18] When a resident male is ousted from a langur troop, for example, the conquered male and his sons often depart together. Not only is this an effective strategy for avoiding predators (animals traveling solo are always at the highest risk), but it is a safer way to become integrated into a new community.[19] Brothers attempting to join a new group together will probably encounter less harassment from group members than unrelated individuals.[20] Before they leave home together as adolescents, the time brothers have spent together has strengthened their relationships with one another. Even when males don't emigrate, there are good reasons to solidify the relationships with their brothers. For example, coalitions of related male chimpanzees discourage other males from harassing or challenging them.

What is true of all of these relationships among nonhuman primate siblings is that there is some tangible benefit to be gained when siblings associate with one another. When sibling associations do not produce a win-win outcome, nonhuman primate siblings lose interest in one another. The best example of this is what occurs as siblings of different genders mature. As brothers and sisters grow up, the interactions between them sharply decrease, until they are nonexistent. Because it is inevitable that one sex emigrates and the other remains at home (or that *both* males and females disperse, but not together), there is little payoff for strong, enduring bonds between nonhuman primate brothers and sisters.

How do relationships among human siblings differ from those among nonhuman primates? Not much, at least in most preindustrial human societies. But in industrial societies where siblings are often close in age (a fact that may intensify the rivalry), they don't always benefit from their relationship with one another. Sometimes the success of one sibling occurs at the expense of another (or is perceived to do so). Or a successful sibling may resent the family's expectation that he assist the family ne'er-do-well. The downside of sibling relationships (excessive rivalry or complete estrangement) is confined to our species and, most particularly, to industrialized societies.

Intense sibling rivalry among human juveniles often has something to do with differential parental treatment, real or perceived.[21] The behavioral researcher Brenda Bryant describes two types of sibling rivalry.[22] The first is a direct consequence of parental behavior: the parent clearly prefers one child over another. Sometimes the oldest child is favored; he travels first into uncharted developmental territory, which perhaps makes him more interesting to parents. But more often the favored child is the youngest, who retains the privileges of babyhood far longer than the others. Sometimes the child's gender is the key factor driving parental favoritism.

Even indirect signs of preferred status are hurtful: A child hears her parents discussing the academic achievements of one sibling or the social achievements of another. When baby books come out, the oldest sibling's is virtually complete, while younger siblings may have mostly blank books with a few pictures haphazardly thrown in. Perhaps most hurtful is a parent's comparing a child to his sibling, to motivate him to improve his performance. "Why can't you be like your brother Tom—I never had to remind him to do his homework?" or "Your sister isn't afraid to try out for the cheerleading squad—why can't you be like her?" An underachieving or simply less talented child may encounter such comparisons at school as well. When one child feels "less capable than" another, jealousy and resentment are likely to erupt. And it is less risky to dislike one's sibling than one's parents, the inadvertent instigators of the rivalry.

When a child can't successfully compete for positive attention, she may settle for earning it negatively. Some families narrowly focus on the negative behavior of one child and ignore children functioning at a higher level, as was the case with my 16-year-old patient Brianna. Brianna is the oldest of three children and has heavily used alcohol and drugs since she was 12. Her parents have devoted themselves over the past 4 years to protecting Brianna from herself. They have spent the money earmarked for their children's college education on multiple drug-treatment programs for Brianna. After discharge, Brianna inevitably reconnects with substance-abusing friends and relapses. Brianna's 12-year-old brother, Dale, is a straight-A student. His parents regularly must choose between attending one of Dale's extracurricular activities or tracking down his sister. Brianna's poor choices repeatedly put her at risk, and she is "rewarded" with most of her parents' attention. Dale understands, but resents the devotion of parental time and resources to his sister.

Parental overfocus sometimes occurs when a child is disabled. Mentally retarded, physically disabled, or chronically ill children often require extra attention from their parents and a greater share of the family's resources. Parents raising a special-needs child may find that they scrimp on the time allocated to their other children. Those children may feel guilty about being jealous of a disabled sibling, but guilt does not eliminate their feeling that they are receiving less than their fair share of attention.

When parental preferences are based on gender, the child of the preferred gender walks away with most of the parental goodies. An apparent "mania for sons" in some cultures is manifested by mild to extreme preferences for boys. Selective female infanticide is a lethal outcome of excessive preferences for sons.[23] Such parental gender preferences are not coded in our genes, but arise from economics, specifically how wealth is passed down. Boys are preferred in cultures in which wealth passes from fathers to sons, and girls are preferred when wealth is inherited by daughters.[24]

Do nonhuman primate parents prefer offspring of a particular gender? The relationships between captive vervet mothers and daughters are closer than those between mothers and sons, which raises the question: do vervet mothers prefer daughters to sons? In an experiment to test this hypothesis, Lynn Fairbanks and Michael McGuire learned that how often youngsters approached their mothers was the best predictor of how much time they spent together.[25] Equally tolerant of approaches by both sons and daughters, mothers spent more time with their daughters simply because daughters approached them twice as often as sons.

Another factor Bryant thinks contributes to sibling rivalry is competition for resources among siblings. This again goes back to parental preferences, because of the differences in attention, power, or resources allocated to each sibling. When children are born in rapid succession, for example, older infants may forfeit their parents' individual attention to the new baby long before they are developmentally ready to do so, which builds resentment of their younger sibling. Down the road, children who are born a year or two apart may behave less positively and more aggressively toward one another than more widely spaced children.[26]

Differential power or privileges also contribute to sibling rivalry. For example, an older sibling asked to babysit has the power to control the other children. Or a brother may be freer to do as he pleases than his sister, because their parents believe that boys and girls should have different privileges. I have often heard from young female clients that their brothers are not expected to do housework, while they and their sisters can't go out to play until the bathroom is cleaned, the dishes are washed, and so on. When an older, more powerful sibling is benevolent toward younger siblings, as is common in monkeys and apes, sibling rivalry is less likely to surface. But when older siblings use their power to bully or take advantage of younger ones, conflict escalates and may become intractable.

Rather than experiencing the win-win situation characteristic of sibling relationships among nonhuman primates, human brothers and sisters may find that the good fortune of one translates into misfortune for the other. Parents who don't play favorites are more likely to have children who grow up with affection and tolerance for one another.

ALTHOUGH primate parents offer less care to their juveniles than their infants or toddlers, less is better than nothing. What care (other than protection from predators) do parents still offer? Primate mothers are quick to intervene when juveniles squabble with unrelated opponents, but typically ignore bickering among siblings.[27] Rhesus monkey mothers respond differently to different types of screams uttered by juveniles; when a youngster is fighting with nonkin, its vocalizations are quite different from those uttered when fighting breaks out with a relative.[28] Ape mothers also step in and support their juveniles when they are in conflict with larger, unrelated opponents.[29] Similarly, human mothers are more likely to side with their own children in conflicts with nonkin.

Rank plays a role in a mother's willingness, or perhaps ability, to defend her youngster from other members of the living group. A low-ranking mother baboon, who cannot prevent members of a high-ranking family from harassing her offspring, elects not to intervene in such disputes.[30] But juveniles from high-ranking families can count on many supporters when they clash with members of low-ranking families.

Most of the interactions between juvenile nonhuman primates and their mothers reflect how persistently youngsters pursue their mothers for contact. Young female vervets, macaques, and baboons follow their mothers around, sit next to them, and attempt to groom them, which occasionally results in their mother's returning the favor. Most juvenile apes continue to prefer their mother's company long after they are weaned.[31] Although mothers are no longer offering the parental goodies they once were, they still offer the warmth and security of close proximity. Having permission to be near its mother gives a juvenile the courage to leave her side.

Children of this age in most human societies also have ready access to their parents. But rather than following their parents around, they follow their culture's prescription for appropriate behavior of children of that age: to spend much of their time with the parent (and other adults) of the same sex. From this secure vantage point, girls observe their mothers and their female companions perform tasks expected of women, and boys associating with their fathers learn the tasks their culture assigns to men.

In industrial societies children are not expected to spend as much time with their parents during the day, and at night parents may be unavailable even when they are present. The infrequent one-to-one contact between parents and children in the United States is problematic; what substitutes for the presence of parents is the "kiddie culture of peers and media."[32] Kids can find others who *are* available just by picking up the telephone or turning on the computer. They may talk with a friend or communicate with an anonymous stranger on the Internet. The family therapist Ron Taffel warns that when parents don't have time to know their children intimately, children are at higher risk for emotional problems and self-destructive behavior.[33]

As juveniles mature, the relationship between a primate mother and her young becomes more reciprocal, literally a "you scratch my back, I'll scratch yours" arrangement. Effie, a mountain gorilla observed by Dian Fossey, had been badly bitten by three males from a neighboring family.[34] She suffered deep gashes to her head, back, and shoulders, and Tuck, her 5-year-old daughter, took on the job of nurse. For weeks, Tuck licked, cleaned, and groomed the wounds; 6 weeks later, Effie had completely healed.

Although the support of juveniles by nonhuman primate mothers is often subtle and not necessarily overtly affectionate, extended separations between mother and juvenile may reveal their strong feelings for each other. Carol Berman described an incident that occurred after the yearly removal of excess monkeys from Cayo Santiago Island.[35] To prevent overcrowding on the island, an entire troop of monkeys may be trapped and moved to a different location. One year, a juvenile rhesus monkey was inadvertently separated from her mother when she was trapped with the wrong troop. When the mistake was discovered and the juvenile returned to her mother 6 months later, the keepers witnessed a dramatic reunion. Mother and daughter hugged each other, vocalizing excitedly back and forth. Although we cannot presume to understand the inner experiences of monkeys, there was no doubt that their reunion was, for both, a joyous occasion.

STATUS affects the everyday experience and quality of life of nonhuman primates. If the yin of primate relationships is cooperation and the formation of alliances, then the yang is becoming an effective competitor for status, which ultimately determines one's share of scarce resources. Climbing the social ladder begins as a juvenile, and in primate societies in which mobility up the ladder is possible, it is one of the most important tasks a juvenile faces on the way to adulthood. As a juvenile attempts to acquire rank, the outcome of contests in which she participates depends on who is willing to help her.[36] How do juveniles make their mark in caste societies, where mobility is limited, in societies in which rank is clearly defined, but some mobility is possible, and in fluid societies in which adult rank is a free-for-all, and any outcome is possible? Do parents influence their youngster's position in society?

The societies of Old World monkeys, especially baboons and macaques, are similar to those human societies in which rank at birth, or caste, determines one's experiences and opportunities throughout life. In Old World monkeys the effect of "caste" is stronger for the gender that remains in the home troop (females) than for the one that emigrates (males) into a new community. Mother and daughter baboons or macaques are treated similarly by other group members; if your mother is low- or high-ranking, then so are you. During the time between weaning and adulthood, low-ranking juveniles may be constantly harassed by higher-ranking ones. But how do youngsters actually learn their place in the hierarchy: do they learn by experience (how they are treated), or by observation (how their mother is treated by high- and low-ranking individuals, or how she behaves with individuals of different rank)?

It appears that juvenile female Japanese macaques learn from personal experience (being deferred to, supported, or harassed by others) and by observing the outcome of their mother's interactions with other monkeys.[37] Early on, the timid behavior of a low-status mother communicates to her offspring that there are dangers within the social group and it is best to be cautious. In macaque societies, in which a daughter's rank is linked with her mother's, females improve their lot in life by entering into coalitions with other females in their families. Although this strategy is not as effective in low-ranking families, it is still better than going it alone. And when a female develops a special relationship with an adult male in the group (the more dominant, the better), she and her offspring are further shielded from harassment.

What about males in these species? Although a mother's rank does influence that of her juvenile son, a male's adult rank is determined more by his size, strength, or cleverness than by the identity of his mother.[38] Since males eventually emigrate, they acquire rank in their new living groups by displaying fighting skills that intimidate others and by forming alliances with powerful individuals. Unlike females, the rank they end up with is not directly linked to the circumstances of their birth.

Vervet mothers pass on a specific position in the hierarchy to their daughters, but in their society there is some opportunity to move up for those juveniles who throw their lot in with higher-ranking individuals that are not close kin, as we saw for Charlotte, the juvenile vervet whose story opened this chapter. Juvenile females from different families often cooperate in coalitions against vervets from different living groups, or to keep adult males from their own group in line.[39] If a juvenile female has the courage to approach a female from a high-ranking family, there is some chance that she will be accepted by her as a coalition partner. But though juvenile females have at least the potential to improve their status, the price they pay for associating with powerful females is reduced time with their own families. Rather than being chosen by a powerful female, it is the juvenile who woos desirable social companions by offering to babysit for or groom them. High-ranking adults are more likely to tolerate the attentions of a scrappy juvenile female than to actively seek her out.

If a juvenile's mother is high-ranking, the choice is easy; she will always prefer her mother and her own family. But if her mother is low-ranking, she may choose to associate with a more powerful family. In either case, mothers seem to accept the choices of their youngsters and don't interfere.

In some primate societies, such as those of chimpanzees and bonobos, and in many human cultures, acquisition of rank depends more on size, strength, or cleverness than on the identity of one's parents. A chimpanzee male who ends up at the top of the social ladder may even get there as a result of his wiliness, rather than his brute strength, or the identity of his mother.

Mike was a low-ranking adult chimpanzee observed by Jane Goodall at the Gombe Stream Preserve.[40] At one point Mike was almost bald from losing handfuls of hair to other males during aggressive interactions. Mike deferred to bigger, stronger males, and was the last male in line for the pile of bananas regularly set out by Goodall. Like most chimpanzee males, Mike aspired to the top position, although it seemed to be clearly out of his reach—until one day Mike noticed that banging two large kerosene cans together made an ear-splitting noise. Mike created a dominance charging display in which he came roaring toward the others in his group, bashing the two cans together. The other males were terrified and quickly leapt out of his way. When Mike finished his display, the other males deferred to him and competed for a chance to groom him. Mike climbed to the top of the hierarchy by using his brains rather than his brawn.

Even in a fluid society, a parent's rank can give a child a boost up the social ladder, but this by itself doesn't determine where she will end up. The three adult offspring of the high-ranking female chimpanzee Flo all attained relatively high positions on their respective male and female dominance hierarchies, but maintained their ranks with their own confident, assertive behavior. A human daughter of wealthy parents may begin her climb three quarters of the way up the ladder. But if she does not make some effort on her own behalf (or if she actively sabotages her position), she may find herself back at the bottom.

As we saw for toddlers, providing good care to one's juvenile depends on how well parenting strategies mesh with the demands of the environment. Ape parents are actively involved with their juveniles and remain connected with them for a very long time. Howler and capuchin monkeys, by contrast, parent their young more passively and withdraw care sooner. What determines why the parenting strategies of one species differs from those of another?

Parental investment is high and of long duration in species in which the life span and gestation are long, development is slow, and a female produces only a few offspring over her lifetime. These attributes describe both humans and the great apes. Being unresponsive at any stage of development before independence compromises an ape or human mother's prior heavy investment in her young. It does not benefit a chimpanzee or human mother who has lavished care on her youngster for 4 years to be suddenly unavailable to help him. If her offspring dies, she must start over, with nothing to show for her lengthy investment. Because development is so slow in long-lived species, the parenting behavior of ape mothers is most like that of human mothers: they are the most responsive, persistent, and indulgent of all nonhuman primate parents.

Nicholas Blurton-Jones suggests that successful parenting is exquisitely in tune with the environment.[41] For those species (or populations) in which survival itself is an accomplishment, parents must invest more heavily in their young, particularly during stages of high risk. We have seen that the dangerous environment in which the !Kung San live requires parents to be alert and attentive to their children far longer than other foraging peoples who inhabit less dangerous environments. The responsiveness of !Kung parents and their intensive supervision of youngsters—essentially they "babysit" them until the middle of their teenage years—constitute an unusual strategy, even among humans. Protection and indulgence of offspring, combined with decreased punitiveness or hostility toward them, are components of the active style of parenting that is most successful in dangerous environments.

When survival isn't the key issue, a primate parent's goal (unconscious, of course) shifts to the rapid production of offspring.[42] When gestation is short and maturity is rapid, parenting is more passive and care is withdrawn earlier. Squirrel monkey mothers, for example, are not the most responsive of mothers. Their idea of parenting is transporting their infants on their backs and allowing them to nurse when they are hungry. They don't play with their babies, or even groom them very much. And once youngsters are weaned, they cannot count on their mothers for continued support or care. The squirrel monkey mother's investment of a few months of care is not nearly as significant as the 7 or 8 years that is the standard for orangutan mothers.

Similarly, the relatively safe environment inhabited by Hadza hunter-gatherers allows them to produce many children, rather than devote themselves to the survival of one or two.[43] The more children the merrier for the Hadza, because children require little effort to raise and yet are capable of contributing to the family's prosperity by early childhood. Hadza parents believe that indulgence spoils a child and more frequently punish their children than do !Kung parents, which is consistent with their more lackadaisical approach to childrearing. Hadza children are no worse for wear, however, because all receive similar treatment from their parents.

With neither survival nor production as primary goals, parents may work to enhance the future reproductive success of their offspring.[44] Not characteristic of any nonhuman primates living in their natural environment, this strategy is found primarily in industrialized societies, including the United States. Future economic competition has become key, rather than mere survival or the production of many offspring. The accumulation of and uneven distribution of wealth in industrial societies drives a different kind of parenting behavior than that found in nonhuman primate and human societies in which wealth is not accumulated.

When the accumulation of wealth usurps nature's goal of passing on genes to the next generation, behavior changes to achieve the new goal. As the focus shifts from the survival of offspring to their competitive success as adults, parents have fewer children and invest more heavily in each. Anthropologists use the term "demographic transition" to explain the decline in fertility and associated changes in family composition that typically accompany economic development or industrialization.[45] As the number of children decreases, the amount of resources that can be offered to each child increases. The flow of wealth in human societies in which parents have many children typically is from child to parent: each child makes a valuable contribution to the family's resources or defense. When the direction of flow reverses (wealth now flows from parent to child), it is more difficult for parents to provide adequately as the number of offspring increases. Parents carefully plan their families, choosing to have fewer children.

And what resources flow to these chosen few! Toys, art and science projects, music geared for children, specialized enrichment experiences such as science camps or club sports, and of course, extended and expensive education. Parents worry that someone else's child, with this extra math instruction, or that earlier Suzuki program, will enter adulthood with a better chance of success than their own. Sometimes we sign up our children for so many activities and lessons that they literally have no time to play. Parental care becomes more about transporting children from one activity to another (or working an extra job to pay for enrichment activities) than spending quality time with them. Time is, in fact, a key issue, because in societies in which wealth is abundant, time is often the scarce resource.[46] When enrichment opportunities take priority over parent-child time, a child's experience may be diminished rather than enhanced.

Do we devote such a large proportion of our resources to our children out of the goodness of our hearts? Or do selfish motives explain our determination to boost our children to the top of the heap? Why does it matter so much to us how many hits Johnny gets in his baseball game or what role Jane has in her dance recital? Certainly, we may want to bask in the glory of our child's accomplishments as part of our own quest for status among our peers. But beneath our parental pride may be an unconscious motivation to invest in our children that relates to our own future well-being. In the United States, it won't be long before a life span of 100 years is commonplace. Who will take care of us when we are 90, if not our children? The higher our adult children climb on the ladder of success, the more secure we may be in our old age.

ALTHOUGH passive parenting works well in agrarian societies, in which children are constantly in the vicinity of and under the supervision of parents, in twentieth-century America it is more problematic. When parents are less available, passive parenting can produce a massive hole in our children's safety net. With many unsupervised hours, youngsters are vulnerable to a vast number of influences that may be harmful to them. Whether we choose to be active or passive parents, then, depends both on the level of environmental danger and the extent of parental availability.

Most primate parents initiate far fewer interactions with juveniles than infants, but remain receptive to their juvenile's desire for contact. When we are nearby, our children can come to us when they need us. We can unobtrusively observe them and thus be more aware when problems are developing. We can actively intervene when our alarm antennae are stimulated, and bide our time, allowing our children to come to us, when all that is needed is a cuddle or a chat. Just as Jane Goodall chose to apply the principles of ape mothering when she raised her own child, we can each listen to the monkey mother within, and offer the gifts of time and availability to our children, when they need us.

CHAPTER 7

Emptying the Nest

IN retrospect, my husband's and my first wedding anniversary probably wasn't the best day to change the composition of our cottontops' living groups. But Jessie, a 3-year-old female, had threatened her mother for days and had even attacked her a couple of times. In the wild, tamarins of breeding age leave home to avoid the rivalry that would otherwise develop between parents and offspring of the same gender. In captivity, however, adult offspring can't emigrate without human help. In my experience, once mother and daughter (or father and son) tamarins engage in their first skirmish, fighting escalates quickly. Either parent or offspring must be removed from the family to avoid serious, or even fatal, injury. So I placed Jessie with Ira, a 3-year-old male, whose time also had come to leave his family. To my surprise, a horrendous fight broke out. Jessie fearlessly attacked Ira, who retreated to his outside cage. Jessie and Ira licked their wounds and called mournfully, each answered by its own family. Ira was still outside at dusk. Although our cottontops hadn't previously slept outside, Ira curled into a ball and bedded down for a night under the stars, as did his family, snuggled together outside in the cage next to his. By this time, my husband and I had lost our desire to celebrate. Observing these two obviously frightened tamarins cope with the trauma accompanying their sudden transition to adulthood put a damper on our ardor.

WE all think we know what we mean by the term "adolescence," but the nature and even the existence of this phase of the life cycle has been the subject of lively debate for decades. Most agree that adolescence is ushered in by puberty (associated with the cascade of chemical changes in the bodies of young males and females as they become capable of reproducing). When adolescence ends, however, is debatable.

The length of adolescence among humans is tightly constricted in some cultures and stretched wide in others. A prolonged phase of adolescence reflects a culture's need for an apprenticeship before adulthood, which is driven by the nature of a society's economy. As the United States moves from the industrial to the information age, the time needed to acquire the skills necessary to compete in the adult world is prolonged. With puberty arriving earlier (especially in girls), the stage of adolescence stretches out in both directions; puberty begins as early as age 9 or 10, and adulthood emerges during the mid-to-late twenties.[1] Adolescents in the United States typically live at home, attend school, and interact mostly with peers. Perhaps most important, American adolescents are not autonomous; most still depend on their parents for food, shelter, money, and transportation.

Gender also influences the duration of adolescence. In most pre-industrial cultures, girls are considered to be adolescents for about 2 years after puberty. Adolescence is about twice as long for boys in these cultures, perhaps because it takes longer for a boy to acquire the skills he needs to provide for his family.[2] Boys not only must master hunting, fishing, farming, or herding, but must attain their adult size before they can compete for a wife or defend their resources from others. Girls reach adulthood before boys because they go through puberty earlier and acquire experience with traditionally female tasks at a younger age.

The length of adolescence is influenced less by gender in industrialized cultures. In the United States, for example, expectations for differences in behavior based on gender have decreased and the duration of adolescence for both sexes is similar. Economic success is not as closely tied to physical size or prowess as it is in preindustrial cultures, and girls successfully compete with boys in almost every venue. And although women typically marry at a younger age than men, both sexes are marrying later than ever before.

How does adolescence in nonhuman primates compare to human adolescence? Most primatologists define adolescence as the period between puberty and the onset of reproduction.[3] As in humans, puberty begins later and lasts longer in males than females, for the same reason: it simply takes longer for adolescent males to attain their adult size than females. There is no point in hurrying an adolescent male's entry into adulthood; a male who is not fully grown is no match for adult males high in the dominance hierarchy. Although the risk of mortality is lower in adolescents than in juveniles (because of their larger size and increased experience), there are phases in the lives of adolescent primates that are associated with high mortality.

The transition to adulthood for young primates requires completion of several daunting tasks. In addition to polishing their survival skills, they must forge alliances with others in their group and understand their place in the community. They are confronted with their newly awakened sexuality and its accompanying urges, which can land them in precarious situations. The emerging sexuality of adolescent primates often is their catalyst to leave home, but searching for a new home is perilous, and emigration commonly results in death on the cusp of adulthood.

How do adolescent primates prepare for adulthood? And what role do parents play as their offspring tackle these developmental tasks? The theory of parent-offspring conflict (Chapter 5) holds that parents will continue withdrawing care from adolescent offspring, especially when providing care diminishes the parent's potential reproductive success or livelihood.

NONHUMAN primate adolescents are essentially on their own. They have learned how to survive, and now it is their responsibility to do so. They find their own food and water and do not rely on their mothers to protect them from predators. By adolescence a young primate had better know his way around, because his mother will neither wait for nor go looking for him. As he grows up, an adolescent primate learns from his experiences and his observations of others. Before adolescence ends, he will join a new living group or make his mark within the troop of his birth. The outcome of the journey to adulthood reflects both his ability to fend for himself and his good fortune along the way.

Human adolescents are a far more coddled group; they are both less competent and less autonomous than their nonhuman primate counterparts. In virtually all cultures there is a separate stage of adolescence, the length of which varies considerably among cultures.[4] In industrial societies, the stage of adolescence is prolonged so that teenagers have time to acquire the skills necessary to succeed in life. They must learn to travel independently from their parents, and a 16-year-old behind the wheel of the family car, with the radio blaring and a carload of friends, is undoubtedly more at risk than an adolescent gibbon (with considerable experience and much less to distract him) brachiating through the trees. Human adolescents also must learn to recognize and avoid environmental hazards. Protected by their parents throughout their childhood, teenagers begin to travel, alone or in groups, to places where danger is present but difficult to detect, without the experience that is standard for maturing nonhuman primates. Finally, human adolescents must perform academically or learn a trade, just as young chimpanzees polish their threat display or termite-hunting skills.

THE onset of puberty in humans is signaled by the beginning of breast development in girls and the growth of pubic hair in both sexes. A growth spurt in height and weight usually accompanies puberty and lasts about 2 years. Changes in female hormones usher in menarche (the onset of menstruation) and further changes in body shape, confirming that a girl is becoming a woman. The flood of androgens in boys stimulates growth and maturation of the genitalia, changes in body shape, and the development of secondary sex characteristics such as facial hair and a deeper voice. Adolescents also experience changes in the way they think and feel, and are notorious for their passionate beliefs and fluctuating moods.

The changes accompanying puberty transform children into mysterious, unpredictable creatures. If the 9- or 10-year-old is like the family sedan, the young adolescent becomes like a souped-up jalopy, all shiny paint and jazzy exterior, with an unreliable engine and erratic cruise control. The girl who used to come home from school and compliantly do her homework is now living in the bathroom and agonizing over every perceived imperfection. Getting hair and makeup right are more important than getting to school on time. Adolescent boys obsess as much as girls about hair and couture. And both genders neglect homework in favor of interacting with friends or surfing the Internet. It is easy to sympathize with the parents of an adolescent, who wistfully remember when their child was too old for temper tantrums but too young for tattoos, navel rings, or drugs.

Nonhuman primates also spend a portion of their lives as adolescents, and some even experience an adolescent growth spurt, like humans.[5] Primate females begin reproductive cycling at puberty, and all ape and many monkey females menstruate. Young male primates develop impressive primary and secondary sex characteristics such as large size, vibrantly colored faces or genitalia, and great strength. These changes prepare young primates for their adult roles in life: males, to seek power and dominance (to compete with other males for females, food, or other resources); females, to prepare for motherhood and secure their niche in the female community. Whereas the mantra of adolescent nonhuman primates is "be dominant," for human adolescents it is "be popular," which is a more subtle version of the same thing. Popularity is certainly about dominance, and offers respect, privilege, acceptance, and a safe spot within the group. And dominance over or popularity with one's peers also increases one's attractiveness to the opposite sex. Becoming well connected with others in the group, male or female, is the sina qua non of primate adolescence.

WHEN she was a young juvenile, Fifi, a female chimpanzee, was a disgruntled observer of her mother's sexual encounters.[6] When Fifi's mother, Flo, was in estrus, she was highly sought after by the males in her community. Flo's sexual swelling, a red balloon of swollen skin around her vaginal opening, functioned as a beacon to the boudoir. The arrival of Flo's monthly sexual swelling advertised her receptivity to the sexual attention of males. But while Flo was ready for love, Fifi was clearly distressed by the continuous stream of males taking turns with her mother. Sometimes she covered Flo's sexual swelling with her hand, in a vain attempt to deceive eager males about her mother's sexual readiness. When a male mounted Flo, Fifi vigorously attempted to dislodge him. Although such efforts were usually futile, one was successful: Fifi jumped on Flo's back, faced the male, and pushed him so hard that he lost his grip, and his opportunity.

Fast-forward a few years to Fifi's own approaching puberty. Fifi was now fascinated with the sexuality of adult females. She closely followed estrous females, observing their behavior and all matings that occurred. Sometimes she even jumped on the back of a copulating female, but instead of pushing the male away as she had before, she placed her own bottom as close to the male as possible—a sort of virtual mating. When puberty arrived and Fifi had her own bright pink sexual swelling, she pranced around displaying it as proudly as a well-endowed adolescent girl in a tight shirt. Not waiting for males to make the first move, Fifi eagerly approached them, turned, and presented her swelling—an unambiguous invitation to mate. And it worked.

But alas, all good things must come to an end. After ovulating, Fifi's swelling deflated, the signal to males that there is no longer any "point" to having sex. Fifi herself appeared unaware that anything had changed and continued to pester males for their sexual attention. But the party was over until the arrival of her next swelling.

As absurd as it may sound to human males, sexuality in most nonhuman primates is essentially driven by the sexual receptivity of females.[7] In some species, such as squirrel monkeys, macaques, and chimpanzees, a female is receptive to males only during a short period in her estrous cycle; when she is ready to ovulate, she is interested in sex. In other species, females are (theoretically) receptive most or all the time, whether or not they are ovulating (tamarins, bonobos, and humans). But whether or not sex is limited to a few days in a female's estrous cycle or can occur at any time, both males and females appear to enjoy it. Females send olfactory, behavioral, or visual signals when they are receptive and males are exquisitely responsive, doggedly monitoring females for signs of receptivity. When a male chimpanzee encounters a female who is red-hot, he becomes the last of the red-hot lovers. Obsessed with sex, he abandons his preferred social group of male peers to pursue the female, constantly offering his services. But when her swelling abates, so does his desire (and usually, hers).

Sex is on the mind of all adolescent primates. But for nonhuman primates like Fifi, the fascination with all things sexual begins well before the onset of puberty. Nonhuman primates are uninhibited about sex and copulate comfortably in front of an audience, so youngsters grow up observing sexual behavior. In many monkeys and apes, sex play is common among juveniles and even infants, who are great mimics of adult behavior. There is much touching, sniffing, and exploring of one another's genitalia, and young primates often mount one another, as if practicing for the big event. There is no doubt that human children would engage in similar sex play if it was culturally acceptable.

As human and nonhuman primates go through puberty, they become interested in and capable of having sex. A period of adolescent sterility that lasts for their first few cycles following menarche (or in the case of apes and humans, for a few years after menarche) allows young females to have sex with minimal risk of pregnancy. But being capable of and interested in having sex is no guarantee that it will occur. An adolescent female nonhuman primate, with her low status and small swelling, is not very attractive to the dominant adult male of her dreams. And an eager little adolescent male can't get the time of day from the luscious estrous female with the red balloon on her derrière. Sometimes when an adult female's swelling is small (at the beginning or end of her fertile period) and adult males aren't attracted to her, she will mate with an adolescent male. But adolescents usually have to settle for sex play with one another, or with juveniles.

Human adolescents are as interested in sex as their nonhuman primate cousins. And because ovulation is concealed in our species (women do not have cyclic sexual swellings that turn them on and advertise their fertility), sex is interesting all the time. Like bonobo females, whose large swellings on their buttocks change little with the phases of their menstrual cycle, human females have permanent curves that attract males but tell them nothing about receptivity. Since male primates evolved to respond to the sexual signals (olfactory, visual, and behavioral) of females, adolescent human males are in a conundrum. Human females don't smell different when receptive, and their breasts and bottoms are alluring all the time. Carefully observing a girl's body, although entertaining, tells a boy nothing about her receptivity. Because human females can be receptive at any time, boys must take a more active approach than nonhuman primate males, and quickly learn to offer attention and romance.

Like nonhuman primates, adolescent humans are often thwarted in their attempts to have sex. Human adolescents in many cultures have to contend with parents who want to restrict their sex lives. Human societies vary greatly in their attitude toward adolescent sexuality, from highly permissive to very restrictive. In some Asian and Pacific preindustrial cultures, for example, a special house is designated in which adolescents are expected to have sexual relations with one another, while in some Middle Eastern cultures, a girl who loses her virginity may be punished with death.[8] Though human cultures rarely condone promiscuity, more are permissive than restrictive about adolescent sexuality.

How parents view sexual experimentation by their adolescent children is affected by their cultural beliefs concerning the timing of marriage, the role of marriage in the accumulation of wealth, and the relative value ascribed to each gender.[9] When a culture values girls (because they contribute as much, if not more, to their family than boys, as in hunter-gatherer societies), parents tend to be sexually permissive. A young woman who will provide more than half of the food consumed by her family has more freedom to behave as she wishes. Puberty often occurs late and marriage early, relatively speaking, so that sexual exploration by adolescents during the time of adolescent sterility is often tolerated.

But when marriages are economic transactions and daughters are property to be bartered for a good son-in-law, the rules about adolescent sexuality change. Daughters are betrothed (with a dowry) to a partner not of their own choosing, and virginity is usually mandatory. Because marriage may occur years after the onset of puberty, sexually active adolescents run a higher risk of pregnancy, which is glaring evidence of the loss of virginity. Boys in these cultures also are expected to abstain from sex until marriage. Not only would a premarital pregnancy destroy the deal, but adolescents could become attached to their sexual partners and resist the economically preferable match made by their parents.[10]

In the United States today, puberty arrives earlier and marriage later than ever before. Since marriage is often delayed until the mid to late twenties, the period of adolescent sterility is over well before most young people are ready to tie the knot. But sex remains an irresistible temptation to most adolescents, despite its inconvenience for their parents. Most parents want their adolescent children to avoid early pregnancy and sexually transmitted diseases. But data from the

1997 national longitudinal study of adolescent health, based on interviews with over 12,000 children in grades 7 through 12, revealed that nearly half of teenagers in grades 9 through 12 reported that they were sexually active.[11]

That human adolescents are fascinated with sex is a normal, healthy reflection of their primate heritage. Changes in culture and the environment—the lengthening of the period of preparation for adulthood and the increase in sexually transmitted diseases—compel parents to talk to their teenagers about sex. Studies have shown that talking to adolescents about abstaining from sex is somewhat preventive. Being around after school, when teenagers have the most unsupervised time, is another way for parents to help their adolescents resist doing what comes naturally.

WITH the budding sexuality of adolescent primates comes the risk of incestuous mating. Nonhuman primates generally avoid having sex with closely related family members. Mother-son and brother-sister pairings rarely occur in nonhuman primates. Father-daughter incest is difficult to study, since paternity is unknown in most species. But among those species in which paternity is fairly certain (as in monogamous or harem-dwelling species), matings between father and daughter are rare.

Why do primates (and most other mammals) avoid incest? There is some evidence that breeding between closely related individuals reduces the fitness of their progeny, through inbreeding depression, the reduced viability of inbred offspring: highly inbred young die at higher rates as infants (through miscarriage, stillbirth, and early post-natal death) and every other stage of development. But how does a monkey (or human) "know" not to mate with close kin?

An automatic aversion to sexual intercourse between very familiar individuals predicts the disdain for sexual intimacy with members of one's immediate family.[12] This is true even for unrelated individuals who are reared together. In a fascinating study of human mate choice, researchers found that young Israelis raised on a kibbutz rarely chose members of their nursery peer group as mates.[13] Although age peers reared together were not closely related, their familiarity decreased their attraction to one another, as it typically does among family members raised in the same household. Familiarity may also deter incestuous mating among free-living nonhuman primates. For example, male chimpanzees usually remain in their natal community and are larger and stronger than females. An adult male could easily sexually overpower his mother or sister if he was determined to do so, but this rarely occurs. In those few instances in which chimpanzee sons do attempt to mate with their mothers, mothers scream and appear altogether appalled, which discourages their sons from proceeding further.[14]

Not only are primates averse to mating with close kin, but the desire of females for novel and varied sexual experiences may have evolved to increase the probability that they will select unfamiliar males as sexual partners, which decreases the likelihood of incest.[15] It is not unusual for females to choose to mate with unfamiliar, even low-ranking males, rather than dominant, familiar ones. Female macaques seem to go out of their way to rendevous with unfamiliar males, and sexually receptive adolescent female chimpanzees may roam the countryside to mate with males from other communities.

Sometimes primates avoid incest by emigrating to another community. It is no accident that young nonhuman primates typically choose to emigrate around the time they reach sexual maturity. For example, an adolescent female bonobo's first sexual swelling at around the age of 7 is her signal that it is time to leave home. When integrated into her new community, she becomes interested in mating. The motivation of young male primates to emigrate may be somewhat different from that of females. Even when a male achieves a high rank in his natal community, the females with whom he has grown up may not be willing to mate with him. Primate males sometimes must leave home to find willing sexual partners.[16]

Some strategies that primates use to avoid incest reduce the opportunity for sex between siblings, while others decrease the likelihood of parent-offspring pairings. The weakening of ties between brothers and sisters is one mechanism for preventing incest, and the sexual segregation of brothers and sisters (a universal feature of human societies as well) is another.[17] There is no nonhuman primate species in which siblings of the opposite sex both regularly permanently reside in their natal community.[18] Even before siblings of one gender leave home, the relationship between opposite-sexed siblings has changed; brothers and sisters, who once were each other's playmates, have lost interest in each other by adolescence.

Similar to the declining affiliation between brothers and sisters as they age is the weakening of bonds between parents and young of the opposite sex. This is most obvious between mothers and sons among nonhuman primates, where father-daughter relationships are virtually nonexistent. Many primatologists believe that mother-son bonds weaken as sons approach adolescence to reduce the likelihood of incest. The same pattern is found among the preindustrial societies surveyed in a cross-cultural study of human adolescents.[19] Even before adolescence, girls in virtually all cultures spend far more time with mothers than fathers, and it is the opposite for boys.

Among monogamous primates, such as gibbons and tamarins, the bonds between parents and offspring are severed, rather than merely weakened. Fathers harass their sons until they disperse, and mothers behave similarly with daughters. Because monogamous nonhuman primates defend a territory from which they exclude other adults of the same species, the primary threats to the bonded pair are the sexually maturing members of their own family. When a mother tamarin kicks out her only real rival (her eldest daughter), her pair bond with her mate is secure until the next daughter comes of age.

In contrast to the situation among monogamous nonhuman primates, opportunities to sexually stray abound for human couples in industrial societies such as the United States. Threats to the marital bond are encountered next door, at work, or on the Internet. With mature rivals available to tempt husband or wife, however, adolescent offspring don't pose the same threat to their parents' marital bond as do adolescent gibbons or tamarins.

Nearly all human societies ever studied have an incest taboo, and incest avoidance appears to be a cultural universal.[20] Rather than kicking sexually mature children out of the nest, humans rely on sexual segregation, an incest taboo, and a cultural policy of incest avoidance to discourage close relatives from engaging in sexual activity. But despite all efforts to prevent it, incest occasionally occurs in all primates, including humans.

CAROL BERMAN chuckled as she watched a rhesus monkey mother named Gertrude reluctantly assume center stage in the midst of her five adult daughters.[21] It was time to rest, and Gertrude's daughters congregated around her, as usual. But Gertrude's daughters were a quarrelsome lot, bickering constantly among themselves. After yet another bout of sisterly squabbling, Gertrude roused herself and trudged off alone, settling down again at some distance from her daughters. One by one, Gertrude's daughters left the family circle and wandered back to Gertrude. In no time, Gertrude was right back in the middle of the fray.

What kind of relationships do adolescent primates have with their parents when they remain in their natal community for life? As we saw earlier, the strongest bonds among primates are typically those between same-sex kin, while bonds between opposite-sex kin usually deteriorate by adolescence. How do bonds between mothers and daughters compare with those between fathers and sons?

In many, but certainly not all, primate species, young females remain in their natal community. Female baboons, macaques, and vervets, for example, reside in the same living group as their mother for life. What care do mothers in these species provide as daughters approach adulthood and begin to reproduce?

Many nonhuman primate mothers are a source of comfort to their daughters long after they are grown. Carol Berman observed a poignant incident in which a rhesus monkey grandmother, Anna, watched as her young adult daughter, Reema, gave birth.[22] Labor was prolonged and Reema was in obvious distress. Anna returned periodically throughout the day, accompanied by Reema's yearling and several other group members, apparently to check on Reema. Anna would approach Reema, briefly groom her, and then depart. Monkeys from other groups also came to investigate, a few of which actually attacked the struggling female, who screamed. Anna (and others in her group) returned at these times and chased away the intruders. Anna also threatened Berman whenever she approached to assess the situation—that was all she could do.

When hurt or frightened, an adolescent nonhuman primate may approach her mother for reassurance, just as teenage daughters do in similar circumstances. Most of a young female primate's needs for affiliation are met by her mother and other maternal relatives, such as sisters, aunts, and grandmothers.

There is no evidence that strong mother-daughter bonds hamper the healthy development of a daughter's identity. In fact, close, positive relationships between mothers and daughters enhance the self-esteem and self-confidence of daughters. Anthropologists who have studied the Hopi Indians, a society in which females remain in close proximity to maternal kin throughout their lives, report that the extreme closeness between Hopi mothers and daughters has not produced dependent, clingy adult children; rather, adult Hopi daughters are described as strong-minded and assertive.[23] Students of modern American culture have found the same thing: independent young women who know their own minds and have set solid goals for their future are often those who feel connected and close to their parents.[24]

The bonds between mothers and daughters last a lifetime in many primate species. When daughters temporarily, or even permanently, leave home, there still may be opportunities for visits. Jane Goodall observed many felicitous reunions between chimpanzee mothers and daughters who had been apart for a week or less.[25] They rapidly approached one another, grunted with delight, flung their arms around one another, and settled into a bout of social grooming, the chimpanzee way of saying "Welcome home." Birute Galdikas described a remarkable reunion between an orangutan mother and daughter, whom she believed had not seen each other since the daughter's emigration 10 years before. Even in this solitary species, in which affectionate contact among adults is rarely observed, mother and daughter came together in the treetops and tenderly embraced.[26]

Bonds between nonhuman primate mothers and their adolescent and adult daughters thus may remain strong in species in which females remain in or visit their natal communities, and the same is true in human societies in which daughters stay close to home. In contrast, an adolescent daughter in the United States today can count on less of her mother's time than ever before. She may be in line behind her younger siblings for her mother's attention, as well as her mother's job, husband (or new boyfriend), or aging grandparents.

That daughters continue to need their mother's time and support throughout their adolescence was illuminated for me by the case of Nancy, a divorced custodial mother of four, and her 17-year-old daughter, Kayla. Nancy reported that Kayla was overly concerned with grades (to ensure her admission to the selective colleges in which she was interested) and asked that I help Kayla learn to "lighten up." But when I interviewed Kayla, I heard a different story. Yes, she was stressed and worried, but what troubled her most was the loss of her closest girlfriends, on whom she relied for support. Her friends' interests no longer matched hers, and she saw them less frequently. Kayla felt lost and alone. She said that since her parents divorced many years before, her mother had juggled the roles of primary breadwinner and caregiver. Kayla had been drafted willingly into the role of her mother's helpmate and confidante. She had been reluctant to confide her own problems to her already overburdened mother and had relied on her girlfriends for support. When her girlfriends became unavailable, Kayla suddenly had nowhere to turn.

Adolescent girls today need their mothers as much as they ever have. Modern girls have the world at their feet, but the seemingly limitless choices they face can be overwhelming as well as thrilling. Mother-daughter connectedness is the primate way, and human mothers can offer the gifts of guidance, mentoring, and support.

The bonds between fathers and sons either don't exist or are weaker than those between mothers and daughters in most species of nonhuman primates. But in those few species in which paternity is fairly certain and the tenure of fathers in families is long, fathers play an important role in their sons' lives. Father tamarins, for example, are very involved with offspring of both genders, and adult tamarin sons are welcome to remain with the family until they are ready to breed. It is similar for mountain gorillas; occasionally a son (or brother) of the silverback permanently remains in the group if there is at least one female with whom the silverback will not mate (a daughter, for example), and helps the silverback protect the family from intrusions by other males.[27]

Once nonhuman primate males reach adolescence in multimale multifemale societies, most prefer the company of adult males. Not knowing their father's identity, adolescents accommodate to the absence of one special role model by attaching to some or all of the adult males in their group. An adolescent male chimpanzee, for example, would rather pass the time with the adult males than with his mother and younger siblings. Adult males in these species tolerate the presence of adolescent males, though they rarely initiate interactions with them or pay them much attention.

Like nonhuman primates, human adolescent males associate more often with other males than females. Boys in many societies cluster together on the edge of a group of adult males, where they can easily observe the behavior of their fathers without necessarily being well integrated into the adult group. Human fathers generally are more involved with adolescent sons than daughters (although not as involved with adolescent children as mothers).[28] In a survey of 186 preindustrial societies, anthropologists found that boys spend about 66 percent of their time near their fathers.[29]

How do adolescent boys who grow up without fathers in their lives develop their ideas about manhood? The high rate of divorce in the United States, plus the fact that most children of divorce still are raised primarily by their mothers, leaves many boys without a male role model at home. And in American society, unlike nonhuman primate and preindustrial human societies, there is not necessarily a group of adult males nearby whom teenage boys can observe and imitate.

PARENTS of adolescents who prefer the company of their friends to that of their families may be surprised to learn that adolescent peer groups are found among many nonhuman primate species as well. But adolescent or young adult peer groups are typically a male phenomenon among nonhuman primates; adolescent females associate primarily with female kin of all ages, or go it alone.

Peer groups of young males in nonhuman primate societies, called bachelor groups, serve a variety of functions. In squirrel monkeys males approaching breeding age become social outcasts; their mothers and sisters want nothing to do with them. Young males may travel together separately from or on the periphery of a large troop of monkeys—either of which affords them more protection than traveling alone. In species such as langurs and rhesus monkeys, groups of young males commonly depart together in search of a new living community. Peer groups function differently for male chimpanzees, who don't emigrate. They may patrol their home range together to deter males from other groups from infiltrating their community. They also hunt cooperatively and share the spoils, and groom one another in deference to rank or coalition partnership.

In most human cultures, adolescent peer groups also are more likely to contain boys than girls. In industrial societies, however, girls are just as likely to seek the company of peers as boys. In the United States, adolescents segregate by age rather than gender, spend most of their waking hours with their peers, and are less well integrated into the larger community.

Peer groups of human adolescents form for a variety of reasons. Sometimes they are working groups, such as the adolescent male members of the Masai culture, who cooperate in herding livestock. Some adolescent peer groups in the United States, such as scouts, clubs, or sports teams, may be similarly goal oriented. Other groups, such as cliques of friends or gangs, are far less structured and give teens a place to go where they feel accepted. A key feature that differentiates adolescent human peer groups from one another is whether or not the group's activities are supervised by adults. Adolescent peer groups without adult supervision most resemble the bachelor groups of nonhuman primates.

Consistent with the findings for nonhuman primates, groups of unsupervised human teenagers also have more opportunity to misbehave and may impulsively resort to antisocial behavior to get what they want.[30] For example, stealing is commonplace among groups of adolescent Masai boys assigned the responsibility of herding livestock. Whether we are talking about male peer groups in preindustrial cultures, or male, female, or mixed groups of human teenagers roaming shopping malls in the United States, unsupervised kids are more likely to commit antisocial acts (such as stealing or engaging in violent behavior) than teenagers who spend more time in the company of adults.

Do peer groups appeal more to adolescents whose parents are less available or less willing to supervise them than other parents? The study of human preindustrial cultures lends some support to this idea. To quote the anthropologists Alice Schlegel and Herbert Barry, "the peer group is more prominent in the lives of its participants if young people are less involved in family life." The developmental psychologist Urie Bronfenbrenner concurred when he wrote the following about American children in the 1970s: "It would seem that the peer-oriented child is more a product of parental disregard than of the attractiveness of the peer group—that he turns to his age mates less by choice than by default. The void left by the withdrawal of parents and adults from their children's lives is quickly filled with the less desirable substitute of an age-segregated peer group."[31] But perhaps rather than the culprit being parental disregard, parents in dual-income families simply have little free time to spend with their teenagers, who have become accustomed to hanging out with their peers.

Interactions with peer groups are not always, or even usually, negative. With parental supervision and a strong parent-child bond, peer groups can offer positive, additional social experiences, rather than act as substitute families.

I TURN now to leaving home, a venture faced by most adolescent primates. Adolescent mammals have three primary incentives to leave home: to avoid incest, to find receptive sexual partners, and to improve access to resources, such as food or territory.[32] Among nonhuman primates, leaving home (called dispersal) is highly sex biased: in multimale multifemale species, all youngsters of one sex or the other, but not both, disperse at around the time of adolescence (or sometimes even before). Whether it is males or females who leave is determined by a complex suite of factors that isn't entirely understood. But regardless of which gender disperses, leaving home is dangerous.

What makes the journey to a new home so perilous? Dispersing adolescents leave familiar surroundings, either by themselves or with a few companions, for an unknown, unfamiliar destination. When traveling alone, they are vulnerable to predation. Wandering through foreign territory, they attempt to force or wheedle their way into another living group. Sometimes, if they are persistent and willing to stay on the periphery of the group for a while, they are eventually accepted. But sometimes the only way in is to fight, and the outcome can be rejection, injury, or even death.

How do nonhuman primate adolescents know when the time is right to emigrate? And do parents passively wait until their offspring are ready to depart, or do they boot them out the door? The answer is mixed; in some species, the timing of dispersal, or even the decision to disperse, is up to the youngster, while in others, parents unceremoniously evict their young.

Young primates who leave home voluntarily appear to be attracted to other groups. In these species, the emotional ties between mothers and offspring of the gender that disperses gradually cool. Juvenile and adolescent bonobo daughters, for example, lose interest in spending time with their mothers, and mother-daughter bonds are essentially severed by the time that daughters emigrate. In other group-living species, however, such as the Old World monkeys of Africa and Asia, it is sons who leave home.

In contrast to primate species in which offspring voluntarily leave home are species in which young are evicted as they reach sexual maturity or readiness to breed. Eviction of young is most common in monogamous species. In tamarins, older offspring are permitted to delay their departure past adolescence to help raise their youngest siblings. But captive studies of tamarins indicate that, at some point, older offspring are no longer welcome.[33]

Monogamous gibbons also evict sexually mature young. Gibbon parents begin the separation process with increased antagonism toward same-sex young. Adolescents respond by traveling on the periphery of the family's territory, out of harm's way, until they have an opportunity to emigrate. But gibbon parents may be a little more helpful than tamarin parents in easing their offspring's way out the door—sometimes fathers help their sons compete with neighboring males to establish a territory, if there is a vacancy nearby.[34] Among the solitary orangutans, sons are harshly evicted, perhaps to reduce the likelihood of mother-son incest. Daughter orangutans disperse as well, but are not rejected as strongly by their mothers. They stay closer to home and seem to remain on good terms with their mothers when they cross paths.

Nonhuman primate young also may be driven out of their living group by adults other than their parents. When a new adult male takes over a langur troop, for example, all adolescent males in the troop depart. But sometimes an adolescent (or even younger) female is kicked out by other members of the living group, and there is nothing her mother can do.

Carolyn Crockett described one such incident in a wild group of red howler monkeys.[35] Crockett was watching her howlers bed down for the night on a sultry evening in the Venezuelan wildlife preserve Hato Masaguaral, and noticed something odd. One troop of red howlers she had been observing had split into two, and the two groups were sleeping apart. A closer look revealed deep gashes on the face of an adult female (Marbelis) in one group, and similar facial injuries on an adult female (Ana) in the other. Ana's 20-month-old juvenile daughter, Alia, was missing. Crockett guessed that Marbelis and Ana had fought, and Alia had been evicted from the troop. The next day, a single group reformed and everyone settled down. Crockett eventually located Alia and continued to track her movements. Alia had joined a newly formed troop, but left it after about a year to wander alone. Then Marbelis died. Within 2 months, Alia rejoined her mother's troop, supporting Crockett's hypothesis that Marbelis had evicted Alia from the troop.

Crockett believes that red howler monkeys must be able to count.[36] The monkeys she studied live in small harem societies; in 10 years of observation, Crockett never saw a group with more than four breeding females. When there are only two or three adult females in a group and one of their daughters comes of age, she is most likely to fill the vacancy. Females who breed in their family group have significant advantages over those forced to emigrate; they are more likely to breed earlier and bear more young over their lifetime. They also are more likely to survive. Only about a quarter of female red howlers reach adulthood, compared to nearly 60 percent of males (males emigrate voluntarily, often with companions, and at a later age than females). Emigrating females depart alone as juveniles and

Red howler monkeys *(Alouatta seniculus)*; photo by Carolyn M. Crockett

wander until they encounter "floater" males willing to associate with them. In the meantime, they are at high risk of predation. Most emigrating females die (or disappear), whereas most females known to survive to adulthood secure a permanent spot in their family group.[37]

What makes four the magic number—virtually life or death for a female red howler? Crockett believes that groups with more than four females are more attractive to roaming males looking for a group to take over. Since takeovers are associated with a high risk of infanticide (see Chapter 8), it is not in the best interest of any female to permit extra females to remain in the group.

In the majority of human societies, offspring of one gender also are more likely than the other to leave their natal community.[38] In patrilocal societies, such as the Gusii of Africa, daughters go to other communities and sons remain on the family homestead. In matrilocal societies, such as the Hopi Indians, daughters stay close to home. The transition to adulthood in most preindustrial societies is signaled by marriage, at which time offspring leave their parents' home.[39] There also are human societies in which young are forced to leave at or even before puberty. Early, involuntary leave-taking is often tied to economics, following an arranged marriage that benefits the families of both youngsters.

In the United States, offspring are expected to leave home by late adolescence or young adulthood, but the timing varies with the goals of individual young adults and their parents, and is no longer tied to marriage. Americans define "adulthood" differently than do many preindustrial cultures, emphasizing the ability to take financial responsibility for oneself and make independent decisions, rather than simply the attainment of marriageable age.[40] Adulthood in our culture therefore arrives later and is fairly ambiguous, so it is less clear to parents and young adult children when it is time to depart. When adult children stay too long, conflict is more likely to erupt between parents and children. Human parents sometimes must push their offspring out the door in order to adequately care for younger offspring and themselves, not unlike monogamous nonhuman primates.

We speak of "launching" our youngsters into the world of adults. Webster's definition of launch is "to catapult, propel, push, or thrust," which suggests a certain inertia on the part of grown children to leap into adulthood. It can be very comfortable for young adult children to do as they please while their parents continue to care for them. But sometimes the problem with leaving has more to do with parents than children, when it is to a parent's advantage for an adult child to stay. A poorly functioning or ill parent may desire that an adult child assume the role of caretaker. Or if the parents' marriage is discordant, an adult child can act as a buffer between them. Parent-offspring conflict is lower in such cases, because the benefit to a parent of an adult child's remaining at home is high, relative to the cost.

As we saw for other developmental transitions, such as weaning, co-sleeping, and toilet training, forgoing dependence on one's parents when the time is right is a necessary step toward a healthy adulthood. Leaving home too early and leaving too late are both problematic for offspring.

NONHUMAN primates use the energy, power, and fearlessness mobilized during the adolescent growth period to tackle the challenging tasks of adolescence. The hormonal cocktail of puberty imbues adolescent nonhuman primates with the confidence they need to cope with the danger they now face on their own. Teenagers in preindustrial human societies (especially boys) face similar dangers as they approach the end of adolescence. They are expected to join in the hunt, engage in combat to protect their family's resources, or leave home.

Most teenagers in industrial societies have no similar challenge facing them. They are all revved up with nowhere to go. Their bodies are primed for pushing themselves and taking risks, but their lives continue on, mundane as ever. Getting up, going to school, doing their homework, conversing with friends, and going to bed, is *not* what their bodies are prepared for. Perhaps this sheds some light on the risk-taking that is so prevalent among American teenagers and, to a lesser extent, among adolescents in all human societies. If the body is prepared for challenges that never materialize, an adolescent may utilize his readiness for battle in risks of his own choosing.

Reckless behavior, defined as behavior with a high potential for negative consequences, is a trademark of human adolescence. The development expert Jeffrey Arnett says that adolescence is a time of heightened recklessness in every human culture, past or present.[41] Adolescents are overrepresented in every type of risky behavior examined by Arnett, including drinking and driving, engaging in sex without contraception, using illegal drugs, and participating in minor criminal activities. Boys are more likely to be risk-takers than girls. Boys take more risks than girls for two reasons. First, higher levels of the male sex hormone, testosterone, are associated with reckless behavior. As testosterone levels decrease with age (from the twenties on), males engage in fewer high-risk behaviors. Second, lower levels of monoamine oxidase (MAO) are associated with increased risk-taking, and males have lower levels of platelet MAO than females.[42]

A dramatic rise in the frequency of reckless behavior among adolescents in the United States has occurred over the past 30 years, and the number of dangerous choices available to today's adolescents increases the likelihood that an impulsive decision will have a fatal consequence. Although young people between the ages of 16 and 24 constituted only about 19 percent of licensed drivers at the time of Arnett's study, they accounted for almost 40 percent of drunk drivers involved in fatal accidents.[43] When Arnett analyzed pregnancy-prevention techniques among sexually active 15- to 19-year-old girls, he found that only a third consistently used contraception (but this percentage has substantially increased since 2002).[44] Arnett's findings for illegal drug use were similar; adolescents had the highest rates of illegal drug use, for virtually every kind of substance. And the prevalence of delinquency and minor criminal activity was higher during early adolescence than other developmental periods, regardless of education or occupation of parents, family size, or quality of home life.[45]

Arnett says three factors contribute to risk-taking in American adolescents. First, adolescents are "sensation seekers" who thrive on novel, varied experiences. Sensation seekers feel excited by risk (rather than anxious, like their middle-aged parents) and underestimate the risk associated with desirable experiences. Underestimation of risk is linked to the second factor Arnett cites, which he calls the "personal fable" of adolescence; adolescents are convinced that, somehow, they are magically exempt from danger.[46] Viewing oneself as the center of the universe and virtually invincible leads to errors in judgment that result in poor choices. This explains why a teenage boy believes that *he* can safely drive while intoxicated, or why an intelligent girl who knows how to prevent conception and avoid sexually transmitted diseases chooses to have unprotected sex.

The third factor that fuels adolescent high-risk behavior is the influence of peers. During the past 30 years—the same time in which the reckless behavior of American adolescents has sharply increased—there has been a mass exodus of mothers out of the home and into the work force. Not well integrated into the larger community, adolescents are often unsupervised after school, and peer groups have moved in to fill the void. The drive of adolescents for novel experiences and their less than reliable judgment, plus virtually unlimited opportunities for impulsive behavior and the lack of adult involvement or supervision, are a dangerous combination. Risk is compounded for the highest sensation seekers, who are attracted to one another as companions.

How can parents protect their adolescents during these "normal" but tumultuous times? The best protection appears to be family connectedness and closeness. A study of more than 12,000 adolescents revealed that what protected against almost every risk factor studied was parent-family connectedness, with perceived school connectedness coming in second.[47] Teenagers who felt close to their parents and a part of their school community were least likely to engage in high-risk behaviors. Teenagers need to feel loved and valued by their families, *and* that they fit within their peer group.

Some parental behaviors may actually increase their children's level of risk.[48] Parents who engage in high-risk behaviors or keep dangerous items at home place their children at risk in their own homes. For example, over 25 percent of American teenagers regularly smoke cigarettes; when parents smoke at home, their children are more likely to do so. Similarly, when alcohol or drugs are available at home, a child is more likely to sample them. Alcohol intoxication, in combination with depressed mood, greatly heightens the risk of suicide. In a study of 16,000 high-school students aged 15 to 18, 20 percent reported that they had seriously considered suicide during the past year. When both alcohol and firearms are kept at home, the risk of adolescent suicide greatly increases.

Adolescents who feel they are invincible or that what they are experiencing is catastrophic are every bit as much in need of the time and attention of loving, attentive parents as younger children. Adolescents look grown up, but in reality they still have a long road to adulthood, especially in our culture. Listening to and spending time with teenagers is the best way for parents to keep them safe.

WHEN offspring are physically and emotionally grown and ready to fly the coop, parents experience a mixture of relief and sadness. Yes, it is great to have one's life back and to do as one pleases, but there also are feelings of loss as parents struggle to refocus on themselves and their spouses. Nonhuman primates do not experience the empty-nest syndrome because their nests are never empty; nonhuman primate females do not go through menopause and continue to reproduce until they die. Perhaps having one offspring after another helps monkey and ape mothers separate from their grown young, since the demands of infant care ensure that parents disengage from older offspring. For nonhuman primates, active motherhood never ends.

In preindustrial societies, in which offspring of at least one gender stay close to home and strong connections endure between members of extended families, the transition to the empty nest also may be less difficult. Children grow up and are replaced with grandchildren to nurture and enjoy. In industrial societies, however, grown children may disperse across town or around the world. Once children leave home, parents are no longer assured of regular contact with them.

IMAGINE a glorious day at the beach, with streaming sun and pounding surf. When you take your baby to the beach, you slather her with sun-screen, keep her under an umbrella, and hold her snuggled against you while you dangle her toes in the surf, amid screams of delight. When you visit the beach with your 3-year-old, you have to keep an eye on him every second because he can't wait to experience all the beach has to offer. He wriggles as you apply sun-screen and charges ahead of you into the water. You hold his hand in the shallow surf, for what seems like an eternity, as he joyously leaps over every tiny wave. You accompany your 10-year-old to the beach, but hand her the sun-screen to apply herself. You admonish her to be careful and then contentedly watch from the shore, secure in her knowledge of the sea and her ability to swim. When your 16-year-old asks permission to go to the beach with his friends, he pointedly does not invite you to come along. You hand him the sun-screen, knowing that he may forget to use it, and tell him when to be home. You are at home, reading a book, when your 22-year-old goes to the beach, unaware that she has gone.

We have seen that primate parenting across the life span is about the gradual withdrawal of care in tune with the growing capabilities of young. Withdrawing care, however, is not synonymous with disconnecting from offspring. Human and nonhuman primates often maintain long-term relationships with parents or other family members for life. Even when parents are no longer providing care, they may still be a source of comfort or support to their adolescent or young adult offspring. This is not to say that maintaining connections with maturing young is easy, because as adolescents and young adults try their wings, they may distance themselves from their parents. The difficulty parents experience in navigating the choppy waters of adolescence with their teenaged children is reflected in a tongue-in-cheek notation made by psychiatrists in the charts of troubled families: "Two teenaged children. No other abnormalities."

The goal of successful parenting is to withdraw care neither too early nor too late. Discerning the optimal timing, however, is not as clear as it used to be. As we adapt to the demands of an increasingly complex society, the signs that it is time to make the transition from one phase of development to the next may be obscured.

Parenting with Partners

AT the first whimper of her 2-month-old son, 26-year-old Jamala quickly offers him her breast. She cradles him protectively, anxiously examining him for signs of discontent, but there is no cause for concern. He nurses vigorously, then drifts back to sleep. Jamala's worries dissipate. After all, a Gusii mother's mantra is that a quiet baby is a healthy one. Jamala's first child died when he was 4 months old, and her second succumbed at 7 months. As her husband's third wife, Jamala is disconcerted that she has not yet borne a child who survived—Gusii wives are expected to produce many healthy children who will some day contribute to their family's prosperity. Jamala is determined that, this time, she will succeed.

I often chuckled as I watched my three cottontop tamarin families bed down for the night. There was a flurry of activity within the small wooden nest boxes in which the tamarins slept, with one furry body scrambling over the next. But the final positions were always the same—fathers settled down directly in front of the entrance, and mothers and young cuddled up behind (or on top of) them. Fathers vigilantly monitored any activity near their cage and jumped out of the nest box, with an impressive frown and topknot erected in a warning display, whenever they perceived the presence of a threat to their family.

THE type of pair bond typical of a species (or population) of primates tells us something about the type of parental care that will be offered by mothers and fathers. Among nonhuman primates, exclusive pair bonds are the exception rather than the rule, and mothers in many primate species raise their young with virtually no help from others. In contrast, some form of pair bond, either permanent or serial, is a cultural universal among humans.[1] Primates may bond with multiple mates at the same time (polygyny or polyandry), or with one mate at a time (monogamy). Polygyny and monogamy are far more common than polyandry among primates, and thus are the focus of this chapter.

Although the type of pair bond influences parenting behavior, the help mothers receive with childrearing doesn't always come from their mates. Who is responsible for parenting and childcare in polygynous societies?

POLYGYNY is common in human and nonhuman primates. Polygynous nonhuman primates live in family groups consisting of a patriarch, his mates, and young, and are not members of a larger community. The practice of polygyny by nonhuman primates usually has more to do with the tendency (or willingness) of females to live in groups than it does with a male's inclination to round up and guard a group of unwilling females. When enough food is available for females to reside in groups (patches of food are large enough to support more than one female), polygynous males simply capitalize on the opportunity to mate with several females.

The australopithecines, pre-hominids who roamed the African plains 4 million years ago, probably were polygynous.[2] And throughout recorded history, human males have eagerly taken more than one spouse. Today, polygyny is most often found in preindustrial societies. In rural, agricultural societies, for example, a man with many wives and children can cultivate more land, and thus accumulate more wealth.[3]

Much of the world's population today lives in societies in which polygyny is legal, or at least permitted. But only 10 to 25 percent of men in polygynous cultures actually have more than one wife, and most of these have only two.[4] Polygyny is practiced by societies as diverse as the Bedouins of the Middle East, the Yanomamos of Brazil and Venezuela, and the fundamentalist Mormons living in Arizona and Utah, to name a few. Unlike polygynous nonhuman primates, human polygynous families are usually integrated into a larger community.

Do mothers who share a mate cooperate in the care of all offspring, or do they compete for a larger share of the resources for themselves and their own young? And what role do fathers play in parenting their numerous offspring—are they "Cads" or "Dads"?

Sarah Blaffer Hrdy studied polygynous Hanuman langurs in northern India, on the forested hills of Mount Abu and near villages, for about 9 years.[5] The langurs from this region are scavengers and are regularly fed by villagers, tourists, and religious pilgrims. These lean, long-limbed primates, the sacred monkeys of India, are named after the Hindu monkey-god, Hanuman.

Food competition is minimal among these leaf-eating langurs, and females and their young peacefully coexist. Females are permanent family members, but the current male resident has a limited tenure as family patriarch—at Abu, it averages less than 3 years.[6]

Care of langur young is strictly the domain of females. Female langurs are smitten with babies, and newborn langurs are an instant magnet for females of all ages. We have seen that langurs make good use of babysitters (Chapter 4), and that mothers' helpers are other females (who are closely related, and thus benefit, genetically speaking, from the survival of all young in the family), rather than the family patriarch. Both fertility and infant mortality are relatively high among langurs, and infants who survive grow up quickly. Langur mothers are far from indulgent with their infants. Hrdy described her dismay at having to watch langur mothers ignore "the most desperate cries" from their infants, while continuing to feed.[7] When an infant is endangered, however, its mother quickly retrieves it.

The primary role of Hanuman langur fathers in polygynous populations is that of protector of infants, although the protection is indirect. When the patriarch defends his family against incursions by rival males, his progeny gain a reprieve from infanticide. Beyond an occasional heroic rescue of an infant, however, male langurs are detached fathers who provide virtually no parental care. Conceiving young and retaining ownership of a harem for as long as possible, which benefits both the patriarch and his offspring, are the essential components of fatherhood in polygynous langurs. Like most polygynous fathers with many mates and offspring, langur patriarchs are better described as Cads than Dads.

Although langur fathers do not provide care for dependent young, they may remain part of their son's lives later on, when a new male langur assumes possession of the harem. At that point, a father and his juvenile or adolescent sons are summarily evicted from the group. They often stay together, as members of a bachelor group, for some period of time. On rare occasions, fathers may even come to the defense of older sons when threatened by bands of rival males.

Human mothers in some polygynous societies also cooperate in the care of young. The Cagayan Agta, mobile hunter-gatherers of the Philippines, practice both monogamy and polygyny, but a husband typically takes a second wife only if the first is infertile. About 20 percent of men have two wives, and the rest have one (or none).

We have seen that passing a newborn from one individual to the next is standard behavior for langurs, although generally uncommon among most other primates. The Agta care for their children in ways that are somewhat reminiscent of Hanuman langur methods. To quote the anthropologist Jean Peterson: "The infant is eagerly passed from person to person until all in attendance have had an opportunity to snuggle, nuzzle, sniff, and admire the newborn . . . A child's first experience, then, involves a community of relatives and friends."[8]

Members of Agta foraging communities are closely related through blood (like langurs) or marriage. Typical groups contain, on average, 15 to 35 people, and are comprised of a few nuclear families. Entrance to the group is dependent upon the presence of a "kinsperson to bond to," typically a sister or brother.[9] But in this society, unlike the langurs', either fathers or mothers can be closely related to the others in the community. Grandparents are a part of these communities, although they rarely survive to advanced age.

As with langurs, both high fertility and relatively high infant mortality are characteristic of Agta groups. The interbirth interval is short, but 49 percent of children do not survive to puberty.[10] When only children who survive to the birth of their next sibling are counted, the average interbirth interval is about 3 years.[11] Agta families are often caring for a toddler and a newborn at the same time.

Agta women hunt and fish like the men, unlike women in many

foraging societies. In fact, women are responsible for bringing in a third of the wild pigs and a fifth of the wild deer consumed by the community.[12] Among the Aka pygmies, we saw that mothers were equal participants in the net hunt and fathers were very involved with children. But childcare is handled differently among the Agta.

Agta mothers, like mother langurs, are primarily responsible for childcare. They carry their infants in a sling during their first 12 months, and then transport and care for young children in camp, until the age of 2 o 3, when youngsters become more independent. Mothers breastfeed on demand, and the entire family sleeps together at night. Hunting and dispatching prey with infants on their backs is standard behavior for Agta mothers. Mothers with two or three small children often hunt together and assist one another with the children, although they typically don't hunt and fish as much as mothers with independent young.[13]

Like young langurs, Agta youngsters grow up quickly; unsupervised, they are allowed to handle knives and play in rivers and near open fires as small children. As they get older, they often spend the night with friends (usually cousins and their parents), and sometimes take over a vacant dwelling, where they sleep with peers under the watchful eye of an adolescent sibling.[14] As in other polygynous societies, which characteristically are very fertile, parenting among the Agta is not indulgent, and children rapidly become independent.[15]

Polygynous Agta fathers contribute more to childcare than langur fathers, but they also have only two mates and about the same number of children as monogamous fathers. Agta fathers are active in childcare most often, however, when there is no other alternative, despite the fact that food contribution by mothers is significant. The level of involvement of Agta fathers with children depends on three factors: whether they have one wife or two, how old they are, and the interbirth interval of their children.[16] Agta men say that they take a second wife only if their first is infertile; when only one wife bears children, childcare is easily be handled by the two co-wives, who willingly help each other and do not have to compete for resources. Older fathers are much less involved with children than younger fathers, offering little more than a quick cuddle or kiss, and leaving the childcare to their wife (or wives) or older offspring. A young, monogamous father with several children close in age, in contrast, is more involved with the care of his children, although his contribution does not rival that of his spouse. He has no second wife to help, and if he has no daughter old enough to babysit, there is no one else to take up the slack.

Besides fathers and mothers, other siblings (particularly daughters) and grandparents are trusted to babysit. Over their first year of life, babies are increasingly handed to other caretakers. Babysitters tend infants for 1 or 2 hours, but distressed infants are promptly handed back to their mothers. Grandmothers and grandfathers are willing helpers when they are no longer able to hunt and fish, but fairly young grandmothers would rather be out hunting in the forest than caring for grandchildren. Most grandparents die, however, before they can no longer contribute food to the community.

Grandparents and older sisters together provide about 19 percent of childcare (compared to over 50 percent by mothers), while the contribution of fathers is less than 5 percent.[17] Aunts and other community members also help out, and if an infant is orphaned, close kin take over its care. In closely related Agta communities, virtually everyone is involved in raising the children.

Some mothers in polygynous societies, like that of mountain gorillas, compete rather than cooperate with each other in childrearing. Dian Fossey at first studied, and then actively worked to protect, the mountain gorillas that inhabit the Virunga Volcanoes in Rwanda,

Gorillas *(Gorilla gorilla;* photo by Noel Rowe

until her murder by poachers in 1985. Fossey's work lives on, how-ever, and her book, *Gorillas in the Mist,* provides a fascinating look at parenting in a polygynous ape society.

Like Hanuman langurs, mountain gorillas are primarily vegetari-ans. Almost 90 percent of their diet consists of leaves, shoots, and stems, which are plentiful. Gorilla females are amenable to group living, like female langurs, because plentiful food reduces the need for females to compete with one another. And mountain gorillas, like langurs, live in family groups that are not integrated into a larger community.

But here is where the similarities between langur and gorilla families end. Unlike female langurs, who remain in their natal troop for life, gorilla females leave their families when they are mature and ready to breed. Unrelated females join a silverback's family, one at a time, and compete with one another for his attention. The silverback male is the most permanent member of a mountain gorilla family and is extremely attractive to all of its members. Adult females groom and mate with him, and youngsters of all ages like to cuddle, play with, or simply be close to him.

In contrast to the relaxed dominance hierarchy among langur females, the hierarchy among female mountain gorillas is more rigid and based on the order in which females originally joined the silverback patriarch; the first female has the highest rank, followed by the second, then the third, and so on. Although mountain gorillas generally don't compete for food, the dominance hierarchy predicts the order in which individual group members have access to the few highly preferred foods that are in short supply.

Mountain gorilla females sharing a silverback are rivals rather than comrades. They typically aren't fond of one another (or of one another's offspring), and high-ranking females often behave aggressively toward low-ranking ones. Fossey believed (but was unable to document) that infants of low-ranking females were even at risk for fatal abuse at the hands of other females.

The differences in the nature of female relationships in langur and gorilla families (langur females are closely related, and female gorillas are not) might lead us to predict that the behavior of mothers might also differ in these two polygynous societies. And, indeed, female gorillas do parent differently than female langurs. First, gorilla mothers do not share their infants (who mature far more slowly than langur infants) with other females. Once a baby is born, it is carried only by its mother for a very long time.

Second, gorilla females are reluctant to allow any other individuals, even their own daughters, to handle newborns. After infants have matured beyond the most vulnerable stage, however, mothers may allow their older daughters (who are their only close female kin in the family group) to participate. But inexperienced daughters lack good babysitting skills, and mothers are quick to retrieve distressed infants being carried upside-down or riding backward on the backs of their older sisters.

The indulgence of infants by mountain gorilla mothers, unusual in polygynous groups, might be predicted by this species's low fertility (the average interbirth interval between surviving young is about 4 years) and slow maturation of young. When few offspring can be produced, it makes more sense to invest heavily in each one.

As we saw for langurs, the presence of a strong silverback protects his offspring from infanticide by rival males. Gorilla fathers, however, are far more involved with young than langur fathers, and are more accurately viewed as pinch-hitting Dads than Cads. For example, gorilla fathers more actively protect their kids than langur fathers. A distressed youngster provokes an intimidating charge by the silverback toward the perceived threat. Fossey described one such incident in which a silverback led a screaming charge directly at her. A young juvenile gorilla named Icarus had been climbing a tree when he suddenly fell, crying out in distress. The silverback male, Beethoven, and his blackback cohort, Bartok, charged Fossey, roaring and screaming, as if Fossey were to blame for Icarus's predicament. When Icarus clambered back up the tree, obviously unhurt, the gorillas halted their charge—just 10 feet in front of Fossey.

Unlike a male langur, whose tenure with his family is short, a silverback patriarch typically remains with his family until he dies, after as long as 20 or 30 years. And in contrast to langur fathers, mountain gorilla fathers are openly affectionate and indulgent with their youngsters, although they perform little routine care. But when a young gorilla is orphaned (after it is weaned, but while it is still dependent on its mother's care), it is the silverback, rather than his mates, who typically assumes the role of caregiver.

Fossey related the story of a 37-month-old juvenile female named Simba, whose mother suddenly left the family to join another silverback. After her mother left, Simba changed from happy and outgoing to withdrawn and forlorn almost overnight. Simba's father, a silverback named Uncle Bert, took over her care. Simba initially refused to play with other youngsters and preferred to spend her days and nights in close contact with her father. Uncle Bert tenderly cared for Simba, and within 2 months she was once again her playful self. For over a year, Uncle Bert shared his night nest with Simba and intervened on her behalf whenever she squabbled with other playmates, "spoiling" her completely, from Fossey's perspective. Fossey saw this pattern repeated many times; weaned mountain gorilla orphans depended on their fathers for comfort and care.

As good-natured and indulgent as silverbacks are with their own offspring, like langur males, silverbacks do not tolerate the presence of unrelated dependent youngsters. Fossey documented nine cases of observed infanticide and suspected many more. Infanticidal silverback mountain gorillas, like langurs, never abuse or kill their *own* young. Sometimes infants are killed when one silverback challenges another for possession of an adult female, but the perpetrator is always the unrelated male. Infanticide often occurs shortly after a resident silverback dies, when his females and their dependent young transfer into a new group. For example, 27 days after a silverback named Rafiki died, Uncle Bert, the leader of the family that one of Rafiki's females had joined and the father who had painstakingly cared for his orphan daughter, killed the female's 11-month-old infant. Fossey remarked "it seems likely that all sexually mature males at some time in their lives carry out infanticide, and most females have at least one infant that falls victim to attack by a silverback."[18]

Infanticide committed by unrelated silverback gorillas or male langurs is explained by most primatologists in the same way: as an effective reproductive strategy for males who don't "know" how long they will possess their harem. Females whose infants die become sexually receptive shortly thereafter. With an interbirth interval of about 4 years in mountain gorillas (when the young survive), silverbacks presumably can't afford to wait until unrelated youngsters are weaned and their mothers become receptive again. In polygynous nonhuman primates in which a patriarch's tenure is unpredictable, it is the male's biological clock that is ticking.

One version of polygynous parenting in humans is found in agrarian societies in which many wives and children are needed to work the fields. These are mostly highly fertile, patriarchal societies in which men completely control family finances and make all important family decisions. With more wives sharing a husband, there is less of him to go around and more competition for his attention (and a share of the resources he controls).

We have seen that human mothers need help rearing young. Who helps mothers in large polygynous families in which mothers typically are not closely related? The Gusii of precolonial Kenya and polygynous fundamentalist Mormons living in isolated communities in the United States present an interesting contrast of how polygynous families with competing mothers function when they are in synch with the environment, and when they are not.

Until about 1930, the Gusii were mobile agriculturalists; as they moved, they acquired more land to satisfy their desire for more fields to plant and more pastures for livestock. They lived on homesteads that included a patriarch, his wives, dependent children, and grown sons (and eventually their wives and children). Almost half of the men had more than one wife (a high proportion compared to that in most polygynous societies), probably because of the abundance of land that could support large, rapidly growing families.[19] In fact, multiple wives and high fertility were the most direct route to status and wealth; the larger the family, the more land that could be tilled, animals tended, and resources protected. The fertility of the Gusii was higher than that of nearly all other human populations at that time.[20]

Everyone in a Gusii family had an essential role to play in support of the homestead and a clear position in the family hierarchy. The patriarch was the undisputed king of the castle; he protected and managed the homestead, made decisions and enforced rules, refereed conflicts among his wives, and regularly impregnated them. One rung down in the hierarchy were his wives, who ruled the roost (except when their husband was home). A good wife bore many children, carefully tended her infants, managed her home, cooked meals, and worked in the fields. Children were at the bottom of the hierarchy and learned early to obey their elders.

Gusii parenting beliefs and behavior were in tune with the demands of the environment in which they lived. Infant mortality was high, so infant survival was a Gusii mother's top priority. Mothers indulged their infants, instantly responding to any sign of distress. Crying babies, for example, were promptly held and comforted. Infants were in almost continual contact with their mothers during their first year of life. Mothers nursed their babies on demand (every few minutes throughout the day or night), and slept with them at night. A mother's job was to soothe, nurture, and protect her baby, not to teach, play with, or stimulate it. With high infant mortality and the desire for many children (sons to eventually work the fields and daughters to earn bridewealth for their families when they married), Gusii mothers focused more on signs of infirmity, weakness, or developmental delay than they did on precocity, so sickly babies got more attention than healthy ones.

After she weaned her infant (and the threat of mortality had decreased), a Gusii mother's indulgent ways disappeared as she refocused on molding her child into a compliant worker. She held her youngster considerably less, was less attentive to him, and trained him to be obedient. Mothers reacted swiftly to disobedient children and used threats to keep them in line, such as "I'll beat you" or "I'll throw you out in the darkness and you'll be eaten by hyenas."[21] Children soon learned to avoid their mothers' unpleasant words with rapid compliance. Their job was to become independent relatively quickly and begin to contribute to their families.

Like gorilla mothers, Gusii mothers did not cooperatively care for one another's children. Wives lived with their own offspring in separate dwellings, where they were visited by their husband. Mothers were very involved with infants, but after a child was weaned (at around 17 months), mothers expected their older children to handle much of its care. Older children were a mother's most valued helpers. If daughters were available, they were assigned primary responsibility for childcare, but when there were no elder daughters, sons were called into service. When no older children were available, younger sisters, other children in the homestead, or an infirm elder might pitch in. The assistance of older siblings with younger ones allowed mothers to produce many children *and* work in the fields.

Like the silverback gorilla, the Gusii patriarch was a permanent family member, the most powerful individual in the family, and dominant over all others. His duties were to lead and provide for his family, defend the homestead, conceive children, and administer discipline, rather than provide childcare. Fathers became a bit more involved in the lives of older children; they arranged marriages for their daughters and directed their sons in their duties, on and off the homestead. But unlike the silverbacks, Gusii fathers did not become substitute mothers for orphaned youngsters.

In fact, no one was eager to take on the care of orphans. Adoption was undertaken reluctantly and haphazardly, if at all. Gusii women do not nurse infants other than their own, so unweaned infants usually died. The Gusii saying "Another woman's child is like cold mucous" says it all: women were unwilling to help raise one another's children.[22] Orphans were at exceptionally high risk of disease, malnourishment, and neglect.

Gusii parenting resembles that of gorillas in some ways and that of langurs in others. Like gorillas, Gusii mothers are especially protective of their babies during infancy, and prefer to allow older siblings, rather than the patriarch's other mates, to interact with older infants. But more like langurs, Gusii mothers have lots of help with childcare.

Today, monogamous Gusii households outnumber polygynous ones, perhaps because the ecological conditions that were associated with polygyny in precolonial Gusiiland have changed drastically. Land is no longer abundant, so homesteads are smaller and cannot support as many wives and children. Some family members eventually leave home to work in cities. Because family members today cannot entirely depend on the patriarch, he no longer rules the family with an iron fist. The family hierarchy, based on obedience and conformity, has broken down.

Although polygyny is less commonly found in industrial societies, about 50,000 members of the Fundamentalist Church of Jesus
Christ of Latter-Day Saints (FLDS) practice polygyny in small, isolated communities in the United States, Canada, and Mexico. Despite
the fact that marriage to multiple partners (polygamy) violates federal law and the Arizona constitution, was outlawed in Utah in 1896,
and prohibited in 1890 by the Church of Jesus Christ of Latter-Day
Saints, fundamentalist Mormons continue to practice it today because they believe that God has commanded them to do so. FLDS
Mormons believe that a righteous husband and his wives will live together as a god and goddesses in the Celestial Kingdom, surrounded
by their progeny, and rule over the planets for eternity.

After polygamy was outlawed, polygynists moved to small, geo-
graphically isolated communities in an attempt to continue their lifestyle unmolested. Many settled in the neighboring towns of Hilldale,
Utah, and Colorado City, Arizona, close to the Utah-Arizona border.
Patriarchs circumvented the law against polygamy by legally marrying only their first wives, and entering into a "spiritual union" with
the others.

The isolation of these two communities has allowed them to persist, without significant change, for over 100 years. Access to the outside world is severely restricted; no public transportation serves these
communities, and since all vehicles are owned by the church it is difficult to leave without permission.[23] Education ceases after the eighth
grade for both boys and girls, and book censorship and limited access to television keeps residents uninformed about the rest of the
world.

As among gorillas and the Gusii, there is a strict dominance hierarchy in this highly patriarchal society, with husbands at the top,
wives in the middle, and children at the bottom. There may or may
not be status differences among the wives—much depends upon

how the patriarch manages his family. The first wife has a huge advantage over (and often more power than) the others, however, in that only her marriage is legal.

Like Gusii, gorilla, and langur mothers, FLDS mothers are in charge of home and hearth. Some co-wives live in separate dwellings with their children, but others live communally with their husband, and some co-wives are related, but most are not. Mothers are their children's caregivers, teachers, and role models. They nurture them, teach them life skills, discipline them, and protect them. Mothers are responsible for managing their own homes and children when co-wives live separately, but share in home and childcare tasks when living communally. Mothers are most closely bonded to their own children, however, and may resent co-wives who discipline their children. Helping with food preparation, clean-up, and other household tasks is smoothly accomplished by most communally living co-wives, but they are less satisfied about sharing childcare.[24] Because many co-wives today must work outside the home, there is greater need for communal childcare and more resentment about how it is done.

Like Gusii children, FLDS children are expected to do as they are told. Parents reward obedience and cooperation, rather than individuality and assertiveness. Older children of both sexes are often responsible for babysitting younger siblings, and children of different co-wives are expected to behave like full siblings and care unconditionally for one another. Younger children soon learn to comply with the one directly above them in the chain of command.

The goal of polygynous FLDS families is to produce many children. We have repeatedly seen the link between high fertility and less indulgent maternal behavior—a strategy of quantity versus quality.[25] Like offspring of langurs, the Agta, and the Gusii, FLDS children become independent at a relatively early age. Their schooling is limited and completed early, and girls often marry and begin to reproduce during their mid to late teens.[26]

Like gorilla silverbacks and Gusii husbands, Mormon patriarchs are dominant over other family members and the center of the family's attention. Their needs are met promptly, and they are revered and obeyed by other family members. They are expected to provide for their families, control family resources, make family decisions, and defer only to the current Prophet (who is considered to be the most powerful man on earth). They are also expected to be active in the church and act as a source of religious wisdom and righteousness.

FLDS fathers can be Cads, Dads, or anything in between. Fathers are admired, respected, or sometimes feared, but essentially uninvolved in the care of small children. Some fathers are spiritual leaders, affectionate with their children, and fair with their wives. These fathers are like silverback gorillas in that they are sources of safety and emotional support for their youngsters. But other fathers have formal or aloof relationships with their children. Men with many wives and children may not know exactly how many children they have, much less be able to accurately match names with faces. In these families, the father may behave more like langur males than silverback gorillas.

Polygyny is not a good fit with the characteristics of a modern industrial society, so fundamentalist Mormons pay a high price for their lifestyle: they forfeit economic prosperity. Living in an economically deprived, barren, desert environment, they have few opportunities for career advancement or the accumulation of wealth. Because large families eat up rather than add to a family's resources in industrial societies, Mormon polygynists typically aren't wealthy, and many families live in poverty. More than one third of the polygynous Hilldale–Colorado City families depend on food stamps, compared to less than 5 percent of other Utah families.[27] Although there are a few very wealthy men (with many wives) in these communities, it is not unusual for poor husbands also to have more than one wife (which does *not* occur when polygyny is an adaption to the environment).

Polygyny among fundamentalist Mormons is crumbling under the strain of pressures from every side. Polygyny is illegal in the United States *and* banned by the mainstream Mormon church. The economy that supports plural families is poor, so tax dollars from the people of Arizona and Utah are necessary to subsidize the community. Fathers cannot provide for their families, mothers compete with co-wives for scarce resources for their children, and children have fewer years of schooling than other kids in the United States, which decreases their potential to succeed (should they leave the confines of their community). In addition, the cultural beliefs that support polygyny clash with the mores of Western culture, which champion the rights of freedom of speech and individual liberties.

The cost of practicing polygyny—acceptance of rigid gender roles, absolute compliance with male prerogatives, isolation from the outside world, and a life of poverty—is too high for most modern women. In fact, many FLDS co-wives attempt to flee their plural marriages, and adolescent girls are starting to fight back against those who would coerce them into early, plural unions. A support network, called the Tapestry of Polygamy, assists women who wish to leave this lifestyle behind.[28]

Most inhabitants of industrial societies (in which infant mortality is low) have exchanged high fertility for a greater investment in fewer children. Although polygyny may be common among our primate ancestors, the primary functions of the polygynous patriarch—to protect his offspring from infanticide by rival males in nonhuman primates (an offer his mates cannot refuse), or to oversee a large family of workers in human agrarian societies—are not essential components of fatherhood in industrial societies today. Polygyny is part of our past, but is unlikely to be part of our future.

MONOGAMY is about five times more common in nonhuman primates than in other mammals, although still less common than polygyny. In hunter-gatherer societies like the Aka pygmies and the nomadic !Kung San, and in modern Western industrialized societies, most husbands have only one wife. Monogamy is the only system of marriage most Westerners have ever known, and it is the most common human mating system today in terms of the actual number of people who practice it.[29]

Families of monogamous nonhuman primates typically isolate themselves from one another, protecting the reproductive pair bond by excluding all potential sexual rivals. In contrast, humans attempt to maintain their monogamous pairings in a sea of potential sexual rivals. Although monogamous pair bonds in nonhuman primates are fairly permanent, human pair bonds are often temporary, and divorce and remarriage are facts of life in nearly all human societies. Since the legalization of divorce in Chile in 2004, there are only two countries—Malta and the Philippines—in which divorce is illegal.[30] The term "serial monogamy," or having one spouse *at a time*, more accurately describes the human version of monogamy.

We have seen that ecological factors, such as the availability and distribution of food, influence mating systems. In contrast to polygynous primates, who typically consume abundant, fairly evenly distributed foods, monogamous primates prefer foods, such as fruit, that are found in small, scattered patches.[31] When desirable foods are clumped in patches too small to sustain a group of females, the species that eat them are more likely to be monogamous (or solitary, like orangutans). To capitalize on small food patches as they become available, most monogamous primates defend a territory against other families. The family's territory contains enough resources to meet the needs of the nuclear family, but not enough to support unrelated individuals.

Mating systems also are influenced by biological factors, such as how many adults are needed to raise young successfully, and how long it takes for offspring to become independent. We have seen that many nonhuman primate mothers are capable of rearing offspring without help from a mate. Do primate mothers with monogamous pair bonds *still* have the primary responsibility for childcare? How do mothers balance taking care of themselves and rearing young? And if monogamous mothers are still responsible for childcare, what is the role of "Father" in bringing up baby?

Female primates have always been dual career mothers.[32] All nonhuman primate females and most human mothers manage to raise their offspring while continuing to maintain their physical condition, avoid predators, forage for food, and otherwise contribute to their own (or their family's) subsistence. It may be a bit easier for nonhuman primates than their human counterparts to work and raise kids simultaneously because their young are always along for the ride until they become independent.

Mothers in hunter-gatherer societies gather plants, fish, hunt, collect firewood, cook, and manage the family dwelling with their babies riding in a sling attached to their bodies. In the United States, infant care became incompatible with work only after the industrial revolution, when salaried work usually could not be done at home; fathers became specialists in provision, and motherhood was suddenly defined as "a full-time job."[33] As more women took jobs outside the home during the twentieth century, however, they once again faced the challenge of caring for their children while contributing to family income, which required a reevaluation of the traditional division of labor.

Chinese white-cheeked gibbons *(Hylobates leucogenys)*; photo by Noel Rowe

In some primate societies, monogamous fathers and mothers make different, but crucial contributions to family functioning. Mothers are the primary caretakers of young in these societies, while fathers specialize in protection and/or the provision of food or other resources.

The behavior of fathers in the large, monogamous primate species of southeast Asia, the gibbons and siamangs, differs greatly from that of mothers. Gibbon fathers are essentially uninvolved in childcare, and siamang fathers offer no care during their infant's first year of life. The contribution of a gibbon father to his young is indirect; by fiercely defending his family's territory against intruders, some primatologists believe that he ensures that there will be sufficient food to feed his family.[34] Others, however, theorize that the gibbon father's continual presence keeps his youngsters safe from roving bachelor males, who could be a threat to their lives.[35]

Gibbons inhabit rainforests and search for small patches of food (fruit is preferred) in an arboreal environment. A monogamous mating system, organized around territorial defense, is well adapted to these conditions. Patrolling a familiar area allows gibbons to better exploit food sources as they become available and simultaneously exclude other adults (who might compete with them for food or mates) from the vicinity.

Despite being monogamous, gibbon fathers offer virtually no parental care, perhaps because gibbon mothers can manage perfectly well without help. Gibbon mothers carry their young throughout their babyhood, with apparently no ill effect, because gibbons give birth to only one infant at a time, and the weight of a gibbon infant is low relative to that of its mother.

The question, then, is why does a female gibbon accept a permanent partner, rather than lead a solitary life, like female orangutans? What do males contribute that makes them desirable, or even, indispensable members of gibbon families? Carel van Schaik and Robin Dunbar pondered this question and devised some clever experiments to answer it. They analyzed movement patterns of adults, instances of predation, physical proximity of mated pairs, and the haunting vocal duets sung by mated pairs at the boundaries of their territory.[36]

Van Schaik and Dunbar found that their data did not support the most prominent hypotheses about monogamy in large primates.

One hypothesis asserts that males are monogamous because they are unable to defend a territory large enough to support more than one female and her young. Instead, their data suggested that a male gibbon *could* conceivably defend an area large enough for as many as seven females and their young. Another hypothesis suggests that the presence of an adult male substantially reduces the risk of predation. But the agility, speed, and large size of gibbons, plus their preference for traveling in the treetops, make them virtually immune to running predators such as large cats or avian predators such as eagles. Thus the safety-in-numbers hypothesis seems an unlikely explanation for monogamy. A third hypothesis is that territorial defense by males gives females more time to feed and perhaps allows for a larger territory to exploit. But there is considerable overlap (up to 25 percent) of gibbon feeding territories, and the most efficient territorial protection would occur if males and females were apart, simultaneously defending different parts of their territory. Instead, mated pairs invariably travel together.

Van Schaik and Dunbar proposed a fourth hypothesis: that the presence of gibbon fathers might protect their infants from infanticide. But why even suspect that infanticide might occur in gibbons? No instances of infanticide have been observed, and this phenomenon has most often been documented in polygynous species.[37]

The evidence for monogamy as a defense against infanticide in gibbons is threefold. First, although female gibbons are the same size and strength as males and vigorously defend their territories against other females, they are generally wary of male intruders and are reluctant to engage in territorial defense against them.[38] Second, females carrying dependent infants are even less willing to engage in territorial disputes with unfamiliar males. Finally, widowed females do not sing when carrying dependent infants, but continue to defend their territories against intruders. If a gibbon widow wanted to attract a new mate, one would predict that she would sing to advertise her location and widowed status. Her song would be a solo rather than a duet, alerting neighboring males that the resident male was absent. Van Schaik and Dunbar argue that gibbon widows do not sing when they have dependent infants because attracting unfamiliar males might increase the risk of infanticide.

The primary contribution of gibbon fathers, therefore, may be the (indirect) protection of their genetic young from rival males. The presence of human fathers, regardless of their fathering skills or ability to provision their young, similarly may indirectly protect their offspring from the murderous behavior of unrelated men, who might otherwise become involved with their children's mother.

An extensive review of human infanticide revealed that of 60 cultures surveyed from the Standard Cross-Cultural Sample (a sample of 186 preindustrial societies compiled by George Murdock and Douglas White in 1969), infanticide occurred in 39.[39] It is not uncommon for mothers to abandon or even kill newborns when they believe that they are unable to care for them, or that their babies are somehow defective (see Chapter 10). The remainder of infanticides typically are committed by men who are not genetically related to the infant, in one of two circumstances. When a husband suspects that he has been cuckolded, or he *knows* that he is not the father of a newborn (for example, his wife was pregnant when they married), he may feel that infanticide (or child homicide, in the case of older children) is justified.[40]

Infanticide on the basis of paternity (or the lack thereof) is not restricted to preindustrial societies and nonhuman primates. A chilling tale of increased childhood mortality associated with the presence of a step-parent in the home has been documented in industrial societies as well, by the evolutionary psychologists Martin Daly and Margo Wilson. Analyzing statistics of child mortality in Canada from

1974 to 1983, they found that in the first 2 years of life, stepchildren were 70 times more likely to be victims of fatal child abuse than children living with two biological parents, although the overall incidence of fatalities was relatively low.[41] Rival males who harm unrelated children are not always married to the mother; newspaper headlines reporting the fatal abuse of babies or small children by the mother's new boyfriend are a daily occurrence in the United States. The presence of monogamous primate fathers thus protects their genetic offspring from unrelated adult males who might otherwise harm them.

Another way that human couples divide duties is for fathers to specialize in the provision of resources and mothers to assume primary responsibility for childrearing. In all human societies a key contribution of fathers to the family is the provision of (tangible) resources, a form of care that is not offered by nonhuman primate fathers.[42] The commitment of fathers to work for resources reflects a different, but essential form of caregiving that is crucial to the survival of children. Fathers spend time away from home in order to provide necessary resources for their wives and children—meat in many hunter-gatherer societies and money for food, shelter, and the like in industrial societies.

After the industrial revolution began in the United States, fathers had to leave home to earn an income to support their families. Both fathers and mothers became specialists in a gender-based division of labor—fathers as wage earners and providers of resources and mothers as homemakers. Father returned at the end of his work day to a clean house, hot meal, well-cared-for children, and an attentive mate. He decided how the money was spent and often was called upon to discipline the children. The division of labor by gender worked well, as long as only one spouse assumed the role of provider.

By the close of the twentieth century, however, the sexual division of labor had begun to disintegrate. Changes ushered in by the industrial revolution had radically altered how we earn a living and how we parent our children, and lengthened the period of childhood dependence, owing to the extra time needed to prepare for adulthood. Two tired parents now return home from a full day's work to face an evening of home and childcare duties. Children reside at home longer, contribute little or nothing to their own upkeep, and need more supervision than when they toiled alongside their parents on the family farm. Rather than encouraging early independence, we may support our children while they earn advanced educational degrees to enhance their future earning power. Parents invest more time, effort, and resources to raise children today than ever before.

Americans (and parents in other Western industrial societies) are having fewer children today than at any other time in history.[43] As in other societies where fertility is low, parents are indulgent with their children.[44] The anthropologist Monique Borgerhoff Mulder argues that lower fertility rates, first seen in the nineteenth century (before contraceptives were available and well before the conservation movement began to preach human population control), may be associated with our drive as a species, rooted in our ancient past, to maximize wealth.[45] No longer valuable helpers to their parents, young children today are voracious consumers of resources. Adult humans may decide that they prefer the trappings of wealth, such as expensive homes, automobiles, and vacations, to the patter of (multiple) little feet. So parents have fewer children, but invest more in each child.

When women began to contribute equivalently to family income, the divide-and-conquer strategy was less successful, even with smaller families, and women who tried to do it all became overloaded and overwhelmed. The majority of mothers in the United States today with children under the age of 18 are employed outside the home, and most mothers still take primary responsibility for "the second shift" at home.[46] Domestic duties add approximately an extra month per year to the work mothers actually get paid for. But, as mothers have become more committed to their paid employment and their contribution to family income has become more substantial, they have increasingly demanded that their spouses share the work of raising a family and managing a household. A new kind of marriage is emerging (although still uncommon), in which both spouses equally share the responsibility for provision and childcare.

In a massive study of the relationships between American couples initiated in 1983 and followed up over the next 10 years, the sociologist Pepper Schwartz found a mere 56 couples who fit into a category she described as "peer" marriage.[47] Men performed 40 percent and women 60 percent of domestic duties, but both sexes had an equal voice in decision making, and an equal say about how money was spent. The father's income typically was insufficient to support the family, and both spouses sacrificed career goals in exchange for the flexibility required to share domestic duties. There were few "power couples" in this sample; the decision to cooperatively care for their families often put both spouses on the slow track of career advancement. Although spouses who shared home and childcare described themselves as best friends and said that their partner was irreplaceable, they also revealed that they felt more like friends than lovers.

Egalitarian marriage is also found in some nomadic hunter-gatherer societies, such as the Batek of the Philippines, studied in the mid-1970s by the anthropologist Karen Endicott.[48] Most Batek marriages are monogamous, but divorce and remarriage are common. Men and women contribute equivalently to subsistence; although men do more of the blowpipe hunting and women more often dig for wild yams, both sexes engage in both activities. Although nuclear families sleep, cook, relax, and do much of their work together, the inclination of all members of the community to share food facilitates childcare for individual caregivers, allowing both parents the flexibility to attend to their children, instead of their bellies, when extra care is needed.

Batek husbands and wives are free to make their own decisions and engage in activities as they wish. Neither gender has power or social advantage over the other, and the egalitarian relationship between husbands and wives is reflected in their parenting behavior. Although mothers are the primary transporters of infants, fathers also are very involved with babies, and "hold, cuddle, and chatter to their sons and daughters" with obvious enjoyment.[49] They cook for older children, bathe them, supervise them, and retrieve them, just as mothers do. And when a new baby is born, Batek fathers are reliable sources of comfort and attention for older offspring, while mothers tend to newborns. Batek children appear to be equally attached to both parents.

Like Batek parents, some nonhuman primates who live in monogamous (or sometimes, polyandrous) families also are experts in the communal care of young. One group of nonhuman primates who cooperatively care for young are the Callitrichidae, a family of about 30 species of marmosets and tamarins who inhabit the steamy rainforests of Central and South America.

Marmoset and tamarin males are full parenting partners with their mates, and the intensive caretaking characteristic of marmoset and tamarin fathers is crucial to the survival of their young. The contribution of callitrichid fathers is equal to, or perhaps, even greater than that of mothers, whether or not the criterion is intensity, duration, or the number of caretaking behaviors performed by parents.[50] Fathers may even assist in the birth process; they have been observed to help pull infants from the birth canal, clean membranes and blood from newborns, and consume the placenta with the mother.

Female marmosets and tamarins may carry newborns extensively during the first week of life, but from then on (and in some species, from birth) fathers carry infants more often, and until a more advanced age than mothers. Fathers generally are more tolerant of and involved with infants than mothers; they reject infants less and at an older age, share food with and play with them, groom them, and protect them, while a mother's primary job is to nurse them.

Callitrichid fathers are definitely Dads. They are among the most devoted of all mammal fathers and are far more involved with their offspring's care than most human fathers. Although the distribution of preferred foods in small patches in typical callitrichid habitat would predict monogamy, it would not necessarily predict superdads.

What then does account for callitrichids' egalitarian, cooperative sharing of childrearing? Callitrichids are unique among primates in that they regularly give birth to twins. A pygmy marmoset mother, who weighs 130 grams (less than a third of a pound), gives birth to twins whose combined body weight of 30 grams amounts to almost a quarter of her body weight. Charles Snowdon, a primatologist who studies callitrichids, likens this to a 120-pound human female giving birth to a set of 15-pound twins.[51] How could a beleaguered callitrichid mother produce enough milk for two enormous babies, transport them through the trees, find enough food for three, and evade predators? No wonder superdads evolved in callitrichids.

In fact, having a superdad isn't always enough to ensure the survival of young. Anne Wilson Goldizen and John Terborgh studied saddleback tamarins in the Manu Biosphere Reserve in Peru for several years. Goldizen observed the formation of several new families and reported that she never saw a new pair successfully rear their first set of twins by themselves. Indeed, Goldizen believes that a male and female are unable to do it alone. She suggests that for saddleback tamarins to raise their first set of twins, there must be at least three adults in the family—two males and one female. She calls this mating system cooperative polyandry, and has observed that both males mate with the female.[52] Since either male could be the father, both are willing to care for infants. The assistance of the extra male appears to be the key factor in the survival of young.

Saddleback tamarin family dynamics, however, change as the family matures. Once youngsters are about a year old, their parents breed again. When the second set of twins arrives, their older siblings help to care for them. We saw in Chapter 4 that tamarin young remain with their families for a year or two after they become sexually mature and are heavily involved in the care of younger siblings. Once a family has three sets of young, the father's share of childcare duties declines as the contribution of older offspring increases. Indeed, the term superdad no longer applies, since the efforts of fathers no longer exceed those of other family members. Studies of captive cottontop tamarins produce similar results: as family size increases, the contribution of fathers decreases.[53] And the number of offspring that survive (in the wild or in captivity) increases with the number of available helpers.[54]

Callitrichid biology provides an intriguing example of how mating systems can vary with the ecological constraints of habitat, the biological parameters of each species, and the differing needs of the family in different stages of the life cycle. In captivity, monogamy is a better fit with the characteristics of the environment than polyandry. With no predators, high-quality food consistently available, and restricted living space, there appears to be little need for an extra male, and indeed aggressive behavior commonly occurs when two adults of the same gender are housed together. When an extra individual is not needed to ensure the survival of young, jealous behavior replaces cooperative parenting. And jealous, aggressive behavior keeps potential sexual partners away from one's mate in nonhuman primates, just as it does in humans.

Aᴌᴛʜᴏᴜɢʜ monogamy works when neither parent is unfaithful and both perform their expected roles, the high rate of divorce in first and second marriages in the United States—50 and 60 percent respectively—leaves many parents without a partner.[55] Most single parents in industrial societies wish to remarry; unlike many hunter-gatherers, they don't live with extended family, and it is difficult to raise children alone and on only one income. Remarriage is a direct pathway out of poverty, especially for single mothers, in industrial societies such as the United States.[56] A single mother has a lot to gain by remarriage (increased income and help with childcare), but like the widowed gibbon mother, she may also have a lot to lose.

Remarriage often produces a negative outcome for children, beyond the higher risk of fatal abuse mentioned earlier. Studies of preindustrial societies reveal that children commonly grow up with a step-parent, owing to the high rates of adult mortality and divorce in these societies.[57] The experience of stepchildren in some preindustrial societies is similar to that of their counterparts in modern industrial societies: the care they receive is somehow less than that offered to biological children.[58] In the Grande Anse of Trinidad, for example, fathers interact more with genetic than stepchildren, but have more agonistic encounters with stepchildren than biological children.[59] Grande Anse fathers report that it is "natural" to care more for biological offspring than stepchildren.

In the United States, outcomes for children in blended families are often negative. Children in remarried families permanently leave home at an early age, perhaps because of the high levels of tension that are a fact of life for many, if not most, remarried families. Children in remarried families have more emotional and behavioral problems throughout their childhood, higher school-dropout rates, and higher rates of school suspension or expulsion.[60] The stresses generated by remarriage may cancel out the benefits of an additional income.

The union between remarried spouses in the United States is less likely to endure when children from previous marriages are present. Not only are remarriages shorter when stepchildren are present, but as the number of stepchildren increases, the average duration of the remarriage decreases.[61] And when the remarriage ends, so typically does the investment in stepchildren.[62] These findings are not surprising given the predictions of evolutionary biology: a step-parent is not expected to invest eagerly in children that do not carry his or her genes.[63]

The rivalries between a new spouse and stepchildren, and between the two sets of children who are expected to accept one another as family, are the primary sources of conflict between remarried spouses. Parents are evolutionarily programmed to prefer their biological children. In a 1975 study of parenting in blended families, almost 50 percent of stepfathers and 75 percent of stepmothers admitted that they did not have parental feelings for their stepchildren.[64] Even in blended families that have been together for a long time, favoritism of biological offspring regularly occurs.[65]

The behavior of stepchildren is also responsible for some of the animosity with step-parents; for example, stepchildren are both less warm and more negative with stepfathers than biological fathers.[66] Adolescents, in particular, have a difficult time accepting a parent's remarriage and may make life miserable for a step-parent.[67]

The remarried couple, in an attempt to strengthen and stabilize the new family, may decide to have a child or two together. Sometimes this works, but often it doesn't. Rather than lessening conflict, the new child may intensify the resentment of children from previous marriages, who may view the newest family member as the recipient of extra love and resources. My patients Cindy and Ned had a child of their own when Cindy's two children from her first marriage were still in elementary school. Ned was so infatuated with his biological son that he focused most of his attention on him, essentially ignoring the older children. Cindy's children became jealous and resentful, which caused discord between Ned and Cindy and drove them into marital counseling. Adding more children requires more sharing, and when sharing isn't even, everyone notices. The second divorce occurs when these issues cannot be resolved.

If there are drawbacks to remarrying after the death or departure of the first spouse, wouldn't it be advantageous for human mothers to remain unpaired, like gibbon widows, until their children are no longer vulnerable? The answer may be yes, *if* a mother is able to obtain help with childcare and generate enough income to support her dependent children. Some women with high-paying jobs can do this, and a rare few are choosing to start their family without a partner, through adoption or the use of a sperm donor. But most single mothers don't have these resources, so they take a chance on remarriage. They tolerate the increased risk that their new partner (or another member of their blended family) will physically or emotionally harm their children, in the hope that the new pair bond will offer a higher standard of living and a brighter future.

MONOGAMY is well adapted to some environments, and polygyny to others. What is crucial for the rearing of human children is that mothers have reliable help raising their children. That help typically comes from fathers, older offspring, co-wives, grandparents, or others in the community. Among the Mosuo people of southwestern China, however, mothers turn to their brothers for help.

Perhaps unique among humans, the Mosuo do not formalize their marriages.[68] Marriage is between friends and lasts only as long as a woman opens her door at night for her mate. Husbands are strictly overnight visitors and assume no responsibility, fiscal or otherwise, for raising their children; in the morning, they return to their natal family. Some fathers and their children, however, enjoy close relationships and are fond of one another.

In a culture in which "walking" marriages last only as long as the feelings of love, and fathers are visitors rather than residents, a mother's brothers are the men in her life committed to help her. The philosophy of the Mosuo is that a mother's children remain closely linked throughout life; adult sons make money for their mother and assist sisters and their children. An uncle's care of his nieces and nephews is reciprocated later in life, when it is their obligation to care for him.

We have seen many examples of primate societies in which other community members lend parents a hand with childcare. In many human preindustrial societies, parents receive even more help when they have too many children to raise. Foster care of young, or temporary adoption, is a common solution for families in preindustrial societies who have too many (or too few) children.[69] Fostering differs from adoption in that the bond between biological parents and children is not severed. The child goes to its foster parents (who seek the opportunity to raise it) after weaning, but can return to its biological parents at any time if the arrangement doesn't work out. Biological parents continue to interact with children they have fostered out and remain concerned about and interested in them, but allow another family to raise them. In this way, children do not lose their biological parents *and* are raised by individuals who are better able to care for them. Permanent adoption, with a complete severance of the parent-child bond, is rare in these societies.[70]

Cooperative care of young is found in all human societies and may have been present among the earliest hominids.[71] Males and females in many nonhuman primate and in virtually all human societies rely on some sort of pair bond to raise young. In polygynous primate families, help with dependent offspring typically comes from older siblings (or sometimes from co-wives), rather than from fathers. Monogamous primate fathers help their mates with childcare more often than polygynous fathers. How much primate fathers help, however, is closely linked to their mate's need for assistance, the unavailability of other helpers, and sometimes to their mate's contribution to subsistence.

CHAPTER 9

Parenting Solo

O N a steamy December day in 1983, Karen Strier was tired and sweaty after following a troop of 23 muriquis up and down steep slopes all morning.[1] She was ready for a break when the monkeys settled down for a midday snooze. Suddenly, an adult male from a different troop approached and threatened her. Barking loudly, swinging through the trees, and breaking and dropping branches all around her, he alerted the other monkeys to the stranger in their midst. Four of the females from the troop Strier had been observing, who over the past 6 months had become habituated to her constant presence beneath them, rushed over to the male and threatened him. He fled the scene, with the four females in hot pursuit. Moments later the females returned. Hanging by their thick charcoal tails, they chuckled softly as they embraced one another and held hands. When they extended their arms toward her, a muriqui gesture of reassurance, Strier knew that she had been truly accepted.

NOWHERE to be found among the preferred mating systems in human cultures is the most common mating system of nonhuman primates: the multimale multifemale society, in which adult males and females live together, without permanent pair bonds, in one cohesive community.[2] Although humans prefer some type of pair bond, the high divorce rates in many industrialized societies plus the increasing number of adults who never marry are creating a way of life somewhat like that found in multimale multifemale societies of nonhuman primates: solo parents rearing offspring on their own (with no mate at the ready to protect, provide care for, or provision offspring), while living in a larger community of other adults and children.

Of the nonhuman primate parents who are permanently single, 100 percent are mothers. Single parenthood is the status quo for these species, and for millions of years, mothers have had full responsibility for raising their young. Although males in these species don't help with the routine care of youngsters, their presence does ensure that young have role models of both sexes, as well as front-row seats to the behavioral interplay between the sexes.

We have seen that parents frequently lose their partners to death or divorce in preindustrial societies, but that parents without partners quickly remarry, return to their family of origin, or rely on extended family members for help with childrearing. Single parenthood in industrial societies today, however, isn't always temporary. Before industrialization, it was virtually impossible for a human mother to raise her children without a mate (plus a stable of extra wives, older offspring, or extended family) to help out. But today, single parenthood is gaining ground on two-parent partnerships and soon may overtake traditional marriage as the status quo for childrearing in the United States, by default if not by choice.[3] Since the early 1970s, the proportion of families with children headed by single parents has doubled in the United States, Great Britain, Japan, and Australia.[4] About a third of American children will experience at least one divorce as they grow up, and 10 percent of children will experience at least two divorces of their residential parent before they are 16.[5]

Worldwide, most human single parents who have the primary responsibility for childrearing are mothers.[6] Seventy-five percent of single parents in Japan, 81 percent in the United States, 86 percent in France, 88 percent in Australia, and 95 percent in Great Britain are mothers.[7] Single mothers have to contend with financial stress, the stigma of unmarried motherhood or divorce, and societal views that they are somehow either deficient or overwhelmed with problems.[8] Working single mothers are criticized for not being home with their children, and stay-at-home single mothers on public assistance are reproached for not setting an example of personal responsibility for their children.[9] In the arena of public opinion, single mothers simply can't win.

How do nonhuman primate single mothers, "experts" in single parenting, raise their young? As we have seen, mothers in some species rely on helpers (like their counterparts in preindustrial societies, whose mates have died or left them). But how do mothers who typically do *not* use helpers manage solo parenting? Three species without helpers present an interesting contrast: the orangutan mother, whose social world consists primarily of herself and her dependent young; the muriqui mother, who lives in a community of males and females high in the rainforest canopy; and the bonobo mother, who lives in a large, complex, and highly interactive mix of males, females, and young.

O F late it had been difficult for the mother orangutan Bella and her two offspring to find enough food. It was an especially dry year in the Bornean rainforest, and there was little fruit available on Bella's home range. It would take another long day of travel through the forest to find enough food to fill three bellies. Soon it would be time for Bella to "encourage" her 8-year-old son to leave the family—Bella's home range could no longer provide enough food for three.

Students of orangutan behavior often comment on the harshness of life in the forest for these bright orange, highly intelligent apes, the largest of all tree-dwelling primates. Orangutans prefer to eat fruit, and since fruiting trees produce fruit seasonally and are widely distributed throughout the forest, foraging is an arduous and often unrewarding endeavor. For these large apes to specialize on fruit, they may have had to forgo the social communities in which most monkeys and apes live in favor of a more solitary lifestyle, focused on traveling from one fruiting tree to the next.[10]

How do solitary orangutan mothers care for their young alone in the forest? The answer is, one at a time. We have seen that low fertility is often linked with indulgent parenting, and orangutan mothers are no exception. Females raise an average of only three offspring over their reproductive lifetime and take full responsibility for child-

Borneo orangutans *(Pongo pygmaeus);* photo by Noel Rowe

care, devoting years of their lives to each offspring. Orangutan infants have no rivals for their mother's attention.[11] Mothers do not even allow older offspring to help care for a new sibling; during its first year of life, an infant never leaves its mother's body. Mothers and their dependent young (usually one infant and one, or less commonly, two older youngsters under the age of 9) spend their days traveling and foraging for food, with only each other for company.

Weaning drastically changes the status quo for the young orangutan, particularly if the youngster is male.[12] The mother who lovingly catered to her son as an infant now ignores his efforts to suckle and may roughly reject him if he persists. Temper tantrums not only do not sway his mother, but may result in even harsher treatment. Suddenly, it is clear that it is best for him to keep his distance from his mother. By the time his new sibling is born, he is accustomed to being ignored.

As male orangutans reach adolescence, their relationship with their mother deteriorates even further. Mothers are less tolerant of their sons' presence and may vigorously chase them away. This sounds harsh, but mothers are preparing their sons for a life of solitary wandering through the forest and encouraging them to leave their family of origin before they reach breeding age (perhaps to avoid incest).[13] No longer receiving the care or affection of another living creature, an adult male orangutan must tend solely to his own needs. Twice as large as adult females, he pursues and mates with estrous females (with or without their permission), and otherwise ignores them. It is a simple and self-focused life, devoted to finding enough fruit to survive.

Orangutan mothers are more tolerant of their maturing daughters than their sons. Daughters are not summarily rejected, but they certainly are not a focus of attention and are not sought out by their mothers. An adolescent daughter gradually loses interest in being near her mother and infant sibling, preferring the company of other adolescent males and females. When it is time to select her own home range, however, a daughter often chooses to settle in an area that borders on or even overlaps that of her mother.[14] Although she may see her mother infrequently, she remains on friendly terms with her.

Orangutan mothers thus manage single parenthood by raising one offspring at a time, indulging them essentially as "only children." Adult males come into the picture only when mothers are sexually receptive, so the risk of infanticide is low. Dependent young are the recipients of their mother's devoted care and attention, but adolescents are more or less harshly evicted from family life. Because orangutans prefer food that is scarce, they don't have the luxury of avoiding social isolation (and neither do their dependent offspring, who have no play companions). The extreme social isolation that comes with the territory of orangutan single parenthood is something that human beings, a highly social species, would find difficult to endure.

ALL Karen Strier had to do was follow her nose. She took 20 steps, then stopped and sniffed the thick, humid air of the Atlantic Coastal Forest of eastern Brazil. Smelling cinnamon, Strier knew she was closing in on a troop of muriquis. Muriquis regularly feast on cinnamon leaves, and their bodies and even their feces exude its spicy, sweet scent. When Strier saw her first muriqui in the wild in 1982, almost nothing had been written about them. Strier decided to learn all she could about these appealing pot-bellied monkeys the color of charcoal. Virtually all the information we now have about muriquis comes from the work of Strier, her Brazilian colleagues, and her students, much of it chronicled in her book *Faces in the Forest*.[15]

Muriquis live in mixed groups of males and females, and both

Muriquis *(Brachyteles arachnoides)*; photo by José Caldas

sexes prefer companions of the same gender. Muriquis prefer to eat fruit, which is seasonally available on widely dispersed fruiting trees. When fruit isn't available, muriquis make do with a lower-quality diet of leaves, abundant in the forest. The distinctive pot belly of both males and females makes room for the large intestinal tract needed to absorb the nutrients from leaves.[16]

Muriquis are strikingly different from other primates because they seek peace, not power. Although there is equality between the sexes in a few species of monogamous primates, no other nonhuman primate living in multimale multifemale groups exhibits the muriqui's characteristically peaceful, nonhierarchical way of life. Not only is there virtually no strife between males and females, but also hostile interactions between individuals of the same sex are rare. The unique greeting between muriquis—dangling upside down by their tails as they engage in a full body hug, face to face, with arms and legs entwined—is in stark contrast to the seemingly cool response of one orangutan to another.[17]

Male and female muriquis are similar in size, which is unusual in species that are not monogamous. In fact, the only way a human observer can discriminate males from females is to catch a glimpse of an individual's genitalia: male muriquis have testicles "the size of billiard balls."[18] Rather than compete with other males for mating privileges, a male who is both desirable to and the last to mate with a female will be the winner in the lottery to impregnate her. Perhaps because fighting with other males for the privilege of mating risks a potentially lethal fall from the tall trees muriquis inhabit, males patiently await their turn to mate with estrous females. Females, however, are by no means passive sperm receptacles and prefer some males over others, for reasons not clearly understood. After coitus, the semen coagulates and hardens to form a plug. But the plug is easily removed (by the female or the next male in line), so that females can mate as often as they like. When a male has the good fortune to be the last to mate with a particular female, the plug keeps his semen in place, increasing his likelihood of paternity. In muriquis, the sperm do the competing, rather than individual males.[19]

How does this unusually peaceful coexistence between the sexes influence muriqui parenting? As is the case for other nonhuman primates living in multimale multifemale societies, mothers assume all responsibility for infant care. To quote Strier, "Muriqui mothers don't compromise on their kids."[20] Mothers are very responsive to their infants, feeding them on demand and rescuing them from danger. Mothers are accompanied by older offspring as well, who mostly observe their mother care for the family's newest addition. When a mother needs a break from her infant, she may park it high in a tree, sometimes near other infants whose mothers have done the same thing, while she feeds below. She vocalizes often, perhaps to reassure her infant that she is still there, and her infant makes the most of its opportunity to play with others while she is gone. As her youngster matures, its play companions are most likely to be the offspring of her female companions.

Weaning comes as a shock to the older muriqui infant, who resists loss of the breast as vociferously as any other infant primate. Whining and petulant screaming fills the air, and other muriqui females may "neigh when a juvenile has been whining too long, as if to reprimand the mother for not being more attentive."[21] Weaning is a gradual process, with mothers often giving in to the demands of their offspring (perhaps in response to the disapproval of their peers). After weaning is completed, a young juvenile still travels with and sleeps beside his mother, who remains attentive to him.

Between the ages of 2 and a half to 5 years, the preference of young muriquis to be near their mothers begins to wane. Because young females will eventually emigrate, their ties with their families gradually weaken, and daughters begin to distance themselves from their families and other troop members. By adolescence, mother-daughter bonds are completely severed.

Muriqui sons, however, never leave home. Unlike orangutan mothers, whose sons become persona non grata, muriqui mothers do not reject their sons. Juvenile sons, however, turn their attention to the troop's adult males and attempt to follow, play with, or simply be close to them. Although adult males neither engage in raucous play with nor provide care to these active juveniles, they may allow them to swing on their tails and are generally tolerant of their company. As young males build relationships with other males in their troop, they secure their place in muriqui society.

The egalitarian way and peaceful disposition of muriquis reduce the need to protect youngsters from aggression. Food is abundant, so competition isn't much of an issue for muriquis. Rather than potential infant killers, males are benign members of the community who serve as role models for younger males. Muriqui mothers (and all other nonhuman primate mothers who live in groups) parent in front of an audience, and other group members may vocalize in dismay in response to a mother's parenting behavior. Finally, muriqui mothers raise their youngsters in the midst of a sociable, friendly group of females and young. With so few stressors, solo parenting among muriquis is a breeze.

BONOBOS, formerly called pygmy chimpanzees, truly deserve the label "uncommon chimpanzees" for the remarkable way in which they resolve conflict and for the power wielded by adult females over males—unique among the great apes.[22]

In 1973 when Takayoshi Kano began his study of bonobos in the tropical lowland forest of the Republic of the Congo (formerly Zaire), almost nothing was known about them. Jane Goodall's work

Bonobos *(Pan paniscus)*; photo by Noel Rowe

on the chimpanzees of Gombe had produced a wealth of information about the common chimpanzee, *Pan troglodytes,* and Kano wondered if the behavior of bonobos, *Pan paniscus,* was similar. Goodall had written about same-sex linear dominance hierarchies, aggressive behavior by males who frighten their subordinates (including all females and young) into submission, and coalitions of adult males who hunt down and murder individuals from other communities. Like bonobos, common chimpanzees live in large "fission-fusion" societies, but daily break up into smaller groups, called parties, to travel and forage for food.

It didn't take Kano long to find huge behavioral differences between the two superficially similar chimpanzee species. Unlike the larger, more heavy-set common chimpanzees, who spend most of their time on the ground, bonobos are equally at home in trees and on the forest floor. Bonobos prefer to spend their days in relatively large (rarely less than 20 individuals), mixed parties of males, females, and young, while adult male and female chimpanzees prefer smaller parties, and most often seek one another's company when females are sexually receptive.[23]

How conflict is resolved is the most striking difference Kano observed between bonobos and chimpanzees, evident from the first time he watched a group of bonobos feed together on some sugarcane he had given them. Common chimpanzees would react to a sudden bounty with competition; dominant males would aggressively threaten the others and hoard food, and females and young would beg the dominant males for whatever crumbs they were willing to share. When the bonobos discovered the sugarcane banquet, however, they screamed with excitement and plunged into a sexual orgy. Males rubbed rumps with each other, females lay on their backs and rubbed genitals with one another, and males and females had sex.[24] The bonobos used sex to reduce tension and conflict, and then shared the treat without squabbling.[25]

Bonobos are unique among the apes (and perhaps, among all primates) in their ability to resolve conflict without violence. Compared to the societies of other apes, theirs is a relatively egalitarian society in which the slightly larger and stronger males have no advantage over the females. Although contrary to the case of muriquis there *are* status differences among both male and female bonobos, dominance is expressed more subtly, and less dominant animals are able to ingratiate themselves with higher-ranking individuals in order to claim a share of the resources. It isn't true that aggression never occurs among bonobos, but when it does, it is typically short-lived.[26] Male bonobos are more aggressive than females; shrill screaming and violent movements accompany squabbles between males, but a little rump-to-rump contact or mounting soon ends the skirmish, appeasing both participants. The tension-relieving behaviors of male bonobos not only quash conflict but help prevent its recurrence.

Another way in which bonobos differ from the other great apes is that unrelated adult females become one another's allies and companions. When an adolescent female bonobo attempts to permanently join a new troop, her first order of business is to develop a close friendship with an old adult female.[27] Elderly females typically are the highest-ranking members of bonobo societies, so having an old female as a friend (or perhaps as a partial substitute for her mother) eases an immigrant's entry into the group and improves her access to good feeding sites.[28] So adolescents shadow these senior females, gazing at, grooming, and offering to rub genitals with them.[29] Allowing young females to associate with them thus has its rewards for old females as well. These friendships continue, fueled by the ardor of the adolescents, until young females first give birth. At that time, young mothers devote themselves to their infants and spend less time with other females.

Why do female bonobos develop alliances with unrelated females when no other apes do so? The alliances that develop among females apparently prevent individual males from bullying them.[30] Cohorts of bonobo females can dominate males (who don't form alliances) and thus control access to food, which is the pathway to power. But why don't male bonobos join forces, like male common chimpanzees, and gang up on the females? Primatologists believe that male primates form alliances to ensure access to food and to sexually receptive females.[31] But food is abundant in typical bonobo habitats, so there is no need to hoard it. And like women, bonobo females are sexually receptive much of the time, regardless of when they are ovulating. The sexual swellings of bonobo females reappear 1 year after they give birth, although ovulation does not resume for 4 years after parturition, so females obviously are available for sex again long before they are capable of becoming pregnant.[32] With so many females interested in and available for sex, males do not have to compete for mating opportunities. Like muriqui males, male bonobos are not pushy about food or sex and seem to get enough of both to keep them satisfied.

In this unusual primate society, how do mothers rear their young? Like muriquis and orangutans, bonobo mothers are responsible for essentially all childcare. They are also very indulgent, because fertility is low and each offspring requires a major investment of time and effort to raise. Life in bonobo groups is centered on its youngest members, and while mothers don't rely on the assistance of others, everyone in the troop watches out for youngsters. Kano described one incident in which gunfire was heard in the forest.[33] A frightened older infant that was off of its mother's back jumped onto the closest available body—that of an adult male. The male firmly held the baby to his chest, scanned the forest, and carried the infant until its mother retrieved it. Adult males are tolerant of infants and juveniles, often invite them to play, and groom the youngsters of females who are grooming them.[34] Since any male could be the father of any infant (except for his own siblings, since he does not mate with his mother), it behooves each male to protect youngsters.

The indulgence of bonobo mothers continues during the weaning process and throughout later stages of development. Kano has never observed a mother bonobo behave aggressively toward her infant.[35] At around the age of 4, when bonobos are weaned, mothers gently refuse to nurse or carry them. A year later, mothers more strongly reject especially persistent youngsters. But when a juvenile bonobo throws a temper tantrum, its mother either hugs it firmly to her chest or presents her derrière for mounting, offering sexual stimulation for comfort.[36] Mother bonobos continue to protect offspring as juveniles and share food with them. Although they don't offer much assistance to their mothers, older juvenile and young adolescent bonobos have the opportunity to observe their mothers care for younger siblings.

As among muriquis, the most enduring bonds among bonobos are between mothers and sons.[37] Adult sons stay in their natal group for life, and their relationships with their mothers remain strong throughout their lives. As long as their mothers are alive, sons have access to the central core of the group, which is the best place to be as far as food and safety are concerned. In addition, sons are treated well and often are chosen as sexual partners by their mother's female companions, who also inhabit the group's central core.[38] Since a mother's dominance rank influences that of her son, adult sons improve their lot in life by associating with their elderly, powerful mothers for as long as they can, rather than allying with other males. The status of a male actually plummets upon the death of his mother.

It is a different story for adolescent females, who emigrate between the age of 7 and 9. No outright aggression has been observed between mothers and daughters; rather, daughters gradually appear to become aloof, isolate themselves from their natal troop, and finally set off on their own to find a new home, much like adolescent female muriquis.

The bonobo mother's secrets for successful single parenting are that she doesn't need a male partner to protect her young from infanticide and that she has a great female support system, all the food (and sex) she desires, help from males when she needs it, and widely spaced young, which allows her to invest in only one dependent youngster at a time. There are plenty of adult males to act as role models for sons, and to allow offspring of both sexes to observe how males and females relate. It has often been said that bonobos live by the adage "Make love, not war," which appears to facilitate the job of single parenting in this species.

A SURVEY of the anthropological record reveals no human culture in which single parenting without helpers is the norm. Although we can't be certain about our primal past, the fact that modern-day relics of ancient human societies, the hunter-gatherers, all partake in some form of marriage leads us to reject the possibility that ancestral hunter-gatherers might have lived in multimale multifemale societies like those of bonobos or muriquis. Relatively permanent single parenthood has only recently become an option for humans.

We have seen that the initial helplessness and especially long dependence of human infants requires help with parenting, and that husbands have traditionally been available as protectors, providers, and part-time (or, rarely, almost full-time) parenting partners. The contribution of human fathers (and additional helpers) to childcare has been sufficient to produce a successful outcome, maintaining the human strategy of relying on some form of pair bond.

Nonhuman primates living in multimale multifemale societies have been designed by evolution for single parenthood, and single parents in preindustrial societies either quickly remarry or receive help from extended family. In the United States, however, single parents stumble through the minefield of single parenthood without a map. The pathways to human single parenthood vary, and some are easier to manage than others. In addition to divorce and unplanned pregnancy, single-parent families are created by the death of a parent or by an active choice—a woman (or, rarely, a man) decides that the time is ripe to have a child, despite the absence of a partner.

How do parents in industrial societies cope with the demands of relatively permanent single parenthood? We will see that many of the protective factors on which nonhuman primate single mothers rely—being able to provide sufficient food and resources for themselves and their offspring, avoiding social isolation, living in a mixed community of males and females so that young are exposed to individuals of both genders, and relying on other females for support and companionship—are missing among their human counterparts in Western industrial societies.

Although certainly not a byproduct of millions of years of evolutionary history, single parenthood by choice is most similar to single parenthood without helpers among nonhuman primates, in that a spouse was *never* part of the parenting plan. This route to single parenthood is most often traveled by older, well-educated, financially well-off unmarried women, who involve a man only for his donation of sperm.

In her book *Single Parenting by Choice*, Naomi Miller reviews the research on single mothers who deliberately embark on parenting without a partner, and includes interviews with several such mothers. By and large, these are women nearing the end of their reproductive years—the Murphy Browns of the 1990s. Many have been married before. Most grew up in stable, intact families, although many describe their parents' marriages as unhappy. They report that their romantic relationships with men were generally unrewarding, and often comment that they would rather be alone than trapped in a relationship similar to that of their parents. It isn't that these women would rather not have a partner; instead, the time has arrived for motherhood and there is no acceptable partner available. What these mothers have in common is a strong desire to be a mother and an enormous commitment to parenting.

Because these mothers have chosen to single-parent (rather than being thrust into single parenthood by an unplanned pregnancy, divorce, or widowhood), their attitude is positive, energetic, and hopeful. Like bonobo and muriqui mothers, they become pregnant knowing that they will raise their children on their own, so they face none of the losses and avoid most of the negative feelings that accompany the other routes to human single parenting. Because there is no resident father, there are no conflicts about parenting decisions, household duties, or family finances. Like nonhuman primates, these human mothers can raise their children without the help (financial or otherwise) of a husband. They typically can afford good-quality childcare, which allows them to put in a full day's work knowing that their children are well cared for. Human single mothers by choice, like bonobo and muriqui mothers, typically have a strong network of friends on whom they can rely for support, assistance, or companionship. In fact, the only thing that may be missing in these families—the only thing different from single-parent group-living nonhuman primate families—is a group of friendly adult males on hand to act as role models for sons, show youngsters how men and women interact, and lend a hand in an emergency.

Single mothers by choice suffer fewer disadvantages than other types of human single parents, but their lives are by no means free of stress. Many of these mothers express sadness about not having a partner with whom to share the joys of childrearing—one who was intensely interested in the child's first step, funny expressions, or endearing ways. The downside of having no one to argue with about childrearing is that there also is no one to consult when problems arise. From conception on, these mothers have all the responsibility for raising their children, which can be lonely and exhausting. And when their children get older, they may barrage their mothers with questions about the identity of their father and why he isn't around. Even though a father was never part of the plan, children may nonetheless feel disappointed or even rejected because he is absent.[39]

Although single mothers by choice bear the greatest resemblance to group-living nonhuman primate single mothers (in that they are committed to single parenthood, have more resources and fewer stresses than other types of single mothers, and often have a network of good friends to support them), it is still difficult for them to cover all the bases. In a culture in which families live in closed dwellings (rather than in an open, interactive community of men and women like many hunter-gatherers), there is no guarantee that children of single mothers will be sufficiently exposed to men (and to relationships between the sexes) to guide them in their own adult relationships later on. Single mothers by choice have a decent shot at a successful outcome, but still may come up a little short.

COMPARISONS between nonhuman primates who are *always* single parents with humans in industrial societies who are thrust into single parenthood by misfortune may make little sense. Unlike nonhuman primate single mothers, who typically have only one dependent youngster to raise at a time, suddenly single human parents in industrial societies may have several dependent young to care for (and no extended family nearby to help out). A parent's workload increases with multiple dependent children, which decreases the likelihood that he or she will have the luxury of providing indulgent care.[40]

One strategy for human single parents by misfortune might be, whenever possible, to adopt the tried-and-true coping mechanisms of nonhuman primate single mothers living in multimale multi-female societies: become self-sufficient, take advantage of the safety and sociality that come with being part of a larger community of men and women, avoid social isolation, have no further young until the youngest is fairly self-sufficient, and devote oneself to the provision of resources and parenting.

Widows and widowers have a better prognosis for successful single parenting in some primates than others. The death of a nonhuman primate mother is an automatic death sentence for her unweaned offspring, but in most species, the death of a father has little impact on the survival of his young. Among callitrichids, however, we have seen that it takes both parents (plus other helpers) to successfully rear young.

Among humans, parenting partnerships and the availability of extended family make for smooth childrearing among hunter-gatherers such as the nomadic !Kung San, especially when a parent dies. Because !Kung spouses typically live with either the wife's or husband's family rather than as a nuclear family, the availability of kin to help lessens the impact of the death of a spouse on childrearing.[41] Among the Gusii, in contrast, the absence of either parent places a child at high risk. Gusii children without fathers often are ostracized by the community and not well cared for by their mothers. When Gusii mothers die (or desert their families), unweaned infants usually die too, and older children receive minimal care from other family members. The outcome is even more dire for Aché widows. Since the contribution of fathers is crucial for childrearing in this culture and unrelated fathers are unwilling to invest in the progeny of other men, a mother may commit infanticide if her spouse dies before or shortly after a child's birth, or the community may take care of the problem of father absence by burying the infant alive with its father.[42]

In a modern industrial country such as the United States, the death of a parent typically is not a disaster, and families cope with parental death without the shame that often accompanies divorce or unmarried motherhood.[43] Because a history of high conflict (which typically precedes divorce) is not a given in families which have been disrupted by death, relationships with a deceased spouse's extended family are rarely jeopardized, and surviving spouses and children can usually rely on the continued affection and assistance of family members on both sides.[44]

The literature on the pathway to single parenthood via widowhood in the United States is fairly sparse, perhaps because there are far more never-married or divorced single parents than there are widows or widowers. There is some evidence, however, that the outcome for children whose parent has died is not much different from that of children who grow up in intact, two-parent families.[45] But when children do experience significant problems in adjustment, that typically has more to do with impaired parenting *after* the loss, rather than the loss itself.[46] Girls seem to be more adversely affected by the death of a parent than boys (especially if the mother dies), and are at higher risk than boys of becoming seriously depressed as adults.[47] Other reasons the risk for girls is higher may be that they are more often expected to help out at home, feel more burdened by the living parent's need for social support, or simply need more nurturing. Community programs focused on teaching widowed parents more effective parenting skills could enhance the adjustment of their children.[48]

If the surviving parent can, with a little help from family and friends, go on with his or her life and provide adequate, supportive parenting, the prognosis is good. The loss of a beloved spouse, through no fault of one's own, may be easier to recover from than the shame associated with being abandoned by a spouse or the guilt stemming from the decision to break up one's family. Parents who recover from the loss of a spouse function better and do a better job of raising their children.

Unmarried motherhood resulting from an unplanned pregnancy is not a preferred pathway to parenting in most cultures. Unmarried girls or women who become pregnant must cope with the financial and physical burdens of raising children solo *and* face the stigma attached to unmarried motherhood. They may be shamed, punished, or even killed in some cultures for having premarital sex, and on top of that, an unmarried mother may feel abandoned by a man she believed truly cared for her. Family and friends are rarely happy for these mothers, and there may be no celebration of the pregnancy or birth. The message they usually receive is that they have done something wrong, and the child is a daily reminder of the choices they made and the opportunities they will miss.

In the United States, unplanned pregnancy as a cause of single parenthood is common among very young (often adolescent) mothers who grow up in poverty. Though the overall rate of teenage pregnancy is lower now than in the 1960s or 1970s, today's teenaged mothers are less likely to be married; 79 percent of mothers between the ages of 15 and 19 in the United States today were unmarried in the year 2000, compared to 15 percent of teenaged mothers in previous decades.[49] This figure is even more striking when compared to the proportion of unmarried mothers in other age categories. For example, 23 percent of mothers aged 25 to 29, and 14 percent of mothers aged 30 to 34 are unmarried.[50] Statistics also show that young, unmarried mothers are likely to have more children out of wedlock, during their twenties.[51] A high percentage of very young mothers live below the poverty line, and most receive little or no financial or emotional support from the baby's father.[52]

We have seen that adolescent nonhuman primate females rarely become pregnant, and when they do, are less able to provide adequate care to their offspring than fully grown females. How do very young, human single mothers cope with motherhood? First of all, the birth of their babies may disrupt their education—adolescent mothers have only a 50-50 chance of graduating from high school (although many of these girls drop out of school *before* they become pregnant), which reduces their chance of earning a comfortable income.[53]

Young, unmarried women who are on their own to take care of their children often must take low-paying jobs with inflexible hours. They are less likely to be able to afford quality childcare, and may feel that they have no choice but to leave their children with babysitters who don't charge—their current boyfriends. We have seen that men are far more likely to abuse (sometimes fatally) children sired by other men than their own biological offspring (Chapter 8).

In addition to the stigma of single parenthood and a multitude of stressors, adolescent mothers simultaneously face the developmental leap from childhood to adulthood. At the time they should be focusing on their own identities and becoming independent from their parents, they are responsible for meeting the needs of another, helpless human being. But like every other teenager, adolescent mothers are often preoccupied with themselves. They may find it difficult to empathize with the needs of their babies and often put their own desires ahead of their infants' needs.[54] Perhaps because of their lack of knowledge about child development, their expectations about their baby's behavior may be unrealistic, and they perceive their babies as difficult.[55] Very young mothers frequently are relatively punitive with their youngsters, and often see their role as a disciplinarian rather than a nurturer.

Children raised by single teenage mothers (or even single first-time mothers in their early twenties) have poorer developmental outcomes than children of older or married mothers. For example, preschoolers of very young, unmarried mothers have more behavior problems, are more aggressive, and have poorer impulse control. During adolescence, these children are more likely to engage in delinquent behavior, be incarcerated (boys), and be sexually active (girls).[56] These effects are even stronger for later-born than first-born children of single teenage mothers, so over time these mothers apparently perform worse, rather than better.[57]

The outcome for children of young, unmarried women living in poverty, however, is not a foregone conclusion. In a study of almost 300 families on public assistance, headed by adolescent single mothers with preschool-age children, developmental psychologists discovered several factors that mitigated against the severely depressed outcomes typical of children growing up in these families.[58] Two factors that predict how well children do in school were measured. The first factor, school readiness, is a measure of a child's cognitive development, and the second, behavior problems, reflects a child's social development. Several characteristics of children, communities, and parenting practices were found to reduce the detrimental effects on children of growing up in poor families headed by young single mothers.

Some of the protective factors reside in the personality of the child; sociable, friendly children without attention problems do better in school than those who do not easily interact with others or are easily distracted. It is helpful when fathers or extended family members offer financial and emotional support. A close relative or friend or a reliable after-school program may relieve the single mother's heavy burden of round-the-clock childcare responsibility, and provide an additional positive environment for her children.

Certain parenting practices in these high-risk families also predict more positive outcomes; for example, parenting that is warm and positive, rather than harsh and punitive, is a robust predictor of better adjustment. But being warm and positive isn't easy under the constant stress faced by many of these young single mothers.[59]

Divorce, a fact of life in virtually all human societies, is a route to single parenthood untraveled by nonhuman primates. Part of the problem of divorce for children is the difficulty of blending remarried families, as we saw in Chapter 8. But divorce, by itself, is linked with many risk factors for children.

Divorce, like parental death, is less problematic in some cultures than others. For example, among the gentle, egalitarian Batek people of Malaysia, divorce is common and simply "enlarges the social world" of children.[60] Batek children of divorced parents remain closely connected to both parents. The Batek community's way of sharing food and resources provides an additional safety net for children. Older children decide for themselves with whom they will live; they can alternate between parents, live with older siblings, or even reside with a step-parent no longer married to the biological parent. At the other extreme, we have seen that in some cultures, such as the Aché of Paraguay, father absence through death, divorce, or abandonment is often a prescription for infanticide and higher mortality rates for children (up to the age of 5). Despite the huge cost of divorce for children, the average Aché woman remarries more than 12 times.[61]

The effect of divorce on children in industrial societies is variable, depending on the presence of a host of risk factors. My client Corinna endured the bitter divorce of her parents when she was 16, and her experience illuminates the disadvantages of divorce for kids. Corinna remembered well the acrimonious fighting between her parents, both before and after the divorce. After the divorce, Corinna's mother was alternately angry with her ex-husband for leaving, and sad that he was gone. Corinna soon filled the position of mother's helper and confidante; she rushed home from school to supervise two younger siblings and listened to her mother's nightly diatribe about her father. Corinna married Joe when she was 19, primarily to escape from home. But after 5 years of marriage and two children, her husband had a serious drinking problem. There often were ugly arguments in front of the children, and Joe had even shoved Corinna a few times. "I want to leave Joe," said Corinna. But remembering her own past, she added, "If I leave him, will it hurt the kids?"

The families of 1 million children in the United States divorce every year, and it is projected that over half of the children born in the 1990s will spend part of their childhood in single-parent families.[62] Like unmarried mothers, divorced single parents have more losses to deal with than widowed parents. They either left or were left by their spouses, and often feel ashamed, guilty, sad, or regretful. They may be estranged from the family of the ex-spouse, which results in further emotional losses for their children. Most experience a significant drop in income and leisure time. And divorced parents often have angry or sad children to care for, who need more attention than contented children.

The first two or three years following divorce are difficult for most families, but the majority eventually restabilize and function fairly well.[63] Although children from divorced or remarried (step-) families have a twofold higher risk for problems in adjustment than children from intact families, about 75 to 80 percent of children from divorced and step-families have no significant adjustment problems. The vast majority of them grow into healthy, competent adults who function normally. Just as growing up in an intact home doesn't guarantee a successful outcome for children, growing up with divorce or parent remarriage does not guarantee an unsuccessful one.[64]

"Should I stay for the sake of the children?" is a question commonly asked of therapists treating families considering divorce. The answer emerging from years of careful research on over 1,000 families is, "It depends."[65] Sometimes it is best for a parent to sacrifice his or her own happiness and remain in an unhappy marriage until the children are grown; in other cases, however, divorce is the best option for the entire family.[66] On what basis can this decision be made?

The consequence for a particular child is influenced by a host of risk factors associated with divorce. First, the income of custodial mothers declines by one quarter to one half, compared to a 10 percent decline, on average, for custodial fathers.[67] In 1995, the median income for two-parent (biological or remarried) families with dependent children was almost three times that of single-parent families headed by mothers.[68] Less money may mean that the custodial parent has to move. Moving often isolates single parents from friends and family at the time they most need to be connected to others. Relocating is difficult for children as well. They must simultaneously adjust to the divorce, a new home, and a new school. Perhaps most important, moving far away can greatly reduce or even completely eliminate interaction with the nonresident parent, which may have long-term consequences such as reduced financial or emotional support.[69] And friends are across town instead of next door.

Children with multiple stressors whose parents are frazzled and distraught may fall in with a deviant peer group in search of a surrogate family that has time for them, which adds additional problems to the mix. These changes in a child's living environment and peer group often are linked with earlier sexual activity, adolescent pregnancy, poor academic achievement, substance abuse, or other destructive behaviors.[70]

If the conflict between parents does not abate after the divorce, the risk to their children's psychological adjustment remains significant.[71] When youngsters are caught in the middle between warring parents (whether or not they are married or divorced), the potential damage to their psychological well-being is enormous. When conflict will remain high, even after divorce, children actually do best when their parents stay together—the conflict is no less harmful, but other risk factors are avoided such as economic decline and the presence of only one parent.[72] When a divorce does reduce conflict between parents enough so they can amicably co-parent, the outcome for children improves after divorce.[73] But since chronic high conflict precedes only a minority of divorces, divorce may help fewer children than it hurts.[74] Without a crystal ball to show us exactly how we will function in the aftermath of divorce, it is difficult to know which option to choose.

When parents are both willing and able to minimize the conflict to which their children are exposed and stay together for the sake of the family, children clearly benefit. But when parents who rarely expose their children to conflict do decide to divorce, it can be very confusing for their children, who feel surprised and puzzled by the seemingly inexplicable behavior of their parents. When marital conflict is not observed by children, even when marriages are unhappy, divorce produces a poorer outcome for children.[75]

Finally, the individual characteristics of children and parents influence the impact of divorce on children. Children with difficult temperaments who have trouble coping with change have a much harder time adjusting to divorce than children with easy, calm temperaments.[76] Intelligent, socially mature children adjust better to divorce, perhaps because it is easier for them to make positive connections with other children or supportive adults. A parent's response to stress also affects how children adjust to divorce. Parents who are depressed or anxious, easily angered, or abuse alcohol are more likely to cope poorly with divorce. And as parental functioning declines, so does the adjustment of children.[77]

The most significant determinant of how children psychologically adjust to divorce is the quality of parenting they receive afterward.[78]

Parenting is the filter through which the residue of risk flows. When parents can minimize the conflict to which their children are exposed, monitor their activities, warmly respond to them, and resist the temptation to lean on them excessively for help or emotional support, children have a good chance of emerging from divorce relatively unscathed.[79] But precisely because it is so difficult to parent effectively when one is under unrelenting stress, children whose parents divorce or remarry have a higher risk of poor adjustment. Parenting programs for divorced parents can improve the parenting skills of the resident parent, which decreases the risk to the children's long-term adjustment. One such program in Arizona teaches anger-management techniques to reduce conflict between ex-spouses, as well as listening skills and discipline strategies to improve the relationships between divorced parents and their children.[80]

ALTHOUGH most single parents today still are mothers, the number of single fathers is growing. In 1970, there were just under 400,000 households in the United States headed by single fathers, but by 2000, the number had quadrupled.[81] About 19 percent of all single-parent families in the United States are currently headed by fathers.[82] Among nonhuman primates, we have seen some examples of co-primary caregiving, but many more of fathers (or adult males) as occasional helpers or tolerant bystanders. There is no precedent for permanent single fatherhood among nonhuman primates.

Custodial fathers in the United States, as a group, are generally considerate, competent caregivers.[83] While custodial mothers run the gamut from immature, inexperienced adolescents to competent, financially comfortable single mothers by choice, custodial fathers are more uniformly capable: they rarely are adolescents, are usually employed and earn a higher income than single mothers, generally have had considerable experience with childcare before obtaining custody, and have actively sought custody of their children. Unlike absentee fathers or fathers who disengage after divorce, custodial fathers have been heavily involved in childrearing from day 1. But because custody is still more routinely awarded to mothers, fathers pursuing full custody face an uphill battle and usually must prove that they are better equipped to care for children than mothers.

My client Sam had been a very involved father before his wife, Robyn, left him and their 5-year-old son, David. Robyn became pregnant shortly after she and Sam started dating. Considerably younger than Sam, Robyn had never shown much interest in parenting, but Sam took fatherhood seriously. In fact, one reason Sam had decided to marry Robyn when David was a year old was to legally ensure that he would always remain an integral part of his son's life.

During the first year after Robyn left, she regularly canceled plans to see David at the last minute and spent little time with him. Sam was astounded when Robyn suddenly announced that she was filing for divorce and asking for full custody. She was unemployed and apparently coveted the financial aid, tax relief, and child-support payments she would receive as her son's custodial parent. Although Sam had always been David's primary caretaker, he worried that the court might award custody to Robyn, out of a bias in favor of mothers as primary caretakers.

Are mothers really best suited to raise children? It may be surprising for some to learn that the outcome for children raised by custodial fathers is better, on average, than that for children raised by mothers. Fathers experience less childrearing stress and have better relationships with their children, and children have fewer behavior problems when they live with their fathers than with their mothers.[84] What could explain the fact that fathers, who are regarded by many as less prepared for parenting than mothers, do as well as or better at single parenting than mothers?

First, both parents are more likely to be involved with the children in father-headed families, which reduces the losses the children have to bear. Nonresident mothers are far more likely to stay connected to their children and remain significant figures in their lives than nonresident fathers.[85] Nonresident mothers also are generally more effective parents and more available to their children than nonresident fathers.

Second, single fathers and mothers have similar parenting styles. Left alone to manage the house and children (when income and resources are equivalent), single fathers and mothers tackle their responsibilities similarly.[86] Like the rhesus monkey fathers forced into fatherhood in Chapter 3, human fathers who take on the task of raising their children are fully capable of doing so.

Third, the income of custodial fathers declines far less than that of custodial mothers. The percentage of single fathers who live below the poverty line is less than half that of single mothers, and the median income for single-father families is about one and a half times greater than that of single-mother families.[87] Economic decline is linked to many other risk factors to adjustment and greatly increases parental distress, which disrupts parenting. When the income and resources of fathers and mothers are equivalent, fathers lose much of their parenting advantage.[88]

Finally, like widowed single parents, custodial single fathers elicit compassion and support from others and are publicly admired for embracing the challenge of single parenting. In fact, custodial fathers are often accorded hero status because of their (unexpected) willingness to raise their children. But because many consider them to be inherently less competent than mothers, single fathers also benefit from the help that friends or kin regularly offer them.[89] Single mothers, by contrast, usually cannot count on the same level of support and compassion from others.

Despite the fact that custodial fathers have fewer risk factors than mothers, single parenthood isn't easy for them, especially during the first 2 years after the divorce. In contrast to mothers, who initially tackle single parenthood by trying to overcontrol their children's behavior, fathers initially restrict their children's activities too little and assign them too much responsibility for household tasks.[90] Both mothers and fathers eventually move closer to the middle, providing a good balance of control and opportunity for independence. It seems to be easier for fathers to manage the household than mothers, but harder to communicate effectively and monitor their childrens' activities.[91] And fathers have an especially difficult time raising daughters.[92] They feel less confident about parenting daughters and often lean on them too strongly as confidantes or for help with housework.

When risk factors are similar for custodial mothers and fathers, children may do better when raised by the parent of the same sex.[93] Daughters raised by competent mothers and sons by capable fathers each have a high-functioning adult of the same gender as a role model. But because custodial mothers are usually at an economic disadvantage, the advantages of growing up with a parent of the same sex may be offset by the risk factors caused by by reduced income.

We have seen that it is not unusual for nonhuman primate males in several species to adopt and raise weaned orphaned infants. Similarly, human fathers without partners are capable of adequately caring for their children. And because nonresident mothers typically remain a part of their children's lives and custodial fathers often reap the benefits of support by other women, the children of single fathers have a good chance of regularly interacting with adults of both sexes.

ONE parent is sufficient to raise young in those nonhuman primate species in which single parenthood has evolved. But in species in which a relatively permanent pair bond between the sexes has evolved, whether we are talking about tamarins, gorillas, or human beings, parents are not as prepared to cope with the challenges of single parenthood. If a father tamarin dies shortly after the birth of his first set of twins, it is unlikely that the infants will survive. And the death of a silverback gorilla spurs his mates to quickly join the family of a new patriarch (even if it means the death of their un-weaned infants), rather than try to carry on alone.

Since single custodial parents usually are mothers, the crucial question becomes, "How does growing up without a father affect children?" In preindustrial societies in which childcare is offered by individuals other than the child's biological parents (the Efé, the Agta, and the Mosuo, among others), the absence of a biological father minimally affects his children. Other men in the community are regularly in view, interact with children, act as role models, and occasionally lend a hand, so that the presence of a father is less crucial. In an industrial society with closed dwellings and isolated families, however, youngsters may not have similar access to men.

In the United States, the effects of the father's absence are completely intertwined with the risks associated with economic decline.[94] For example, absent (or disengaged) noncustodial fathers may pay little or no child support.[95] Absentee fathers are less likely to contribute to college expenses and this may be a key factor in the lower educational attainment (and subsequent poorer earning ability) of their children.[96] Even when fathers stay in the picture, available resources for their children are reduced when they remarry.

If two (or more) parents are better than one, will any capable couple (or threesome or foursome) do? Can a mother and grandmother, a gay couple, a group of male or female friends, or a mixed group of unpaired men and women with children provide a healthy environment for childrearing, or is it vital for children to grow up with a mother and a father? Some researchers believe that children do best when raised by parents of both genders, each of whom makes a unique contribution to a child's experience of growing up.[97] Others believe that gender is not the crucial issue; what counts is that children are cared for by responsible, loving adults on whom they can rely.[98] A family with more than one capable adult sharing the responsibility for children, regardless of gender, has a better chance for a positive outcome.

SUCCESSFUL human parents without partners have, for the most part, adopted the principles that underlie single parenting among nonhuman primates; they are self-reliant, avoid isolation, ally with others, obtain companionship and help from others (kin or nonkin, males or females) with childcare, make sure that their offspring are exposed to adults of both sexes, and devote most of their energy to the care of their children and themselves. Parenting without a male partner can succeed only when a woman does not need help from a mate to share childcare duties, provide offspring with resources, or protect them from the sometimes malevolent intentions of unrelated males.

Humans have neither the essential equipment nor the thousands of years of practice, evolutionarily speaking, on which nonhuman primates rely to bring off single parenting without a hitch. Our babies can't cling to us unsupported while we go about our daily work, or take the initiative to suckle when they are hungry. We don't raise our children one at a time, like orangutans, and the time it takes our children to reach adulthood is extraordinarily long. And few of us live in open communities of family or friends, like bonobos.

Like tamarins, humans have evolved as cooperative breeders who depend on the help of multiple caregivers to rear young. Successful single parenting in humans, therefore, must be a group project. The multimale multifemale structure of nonhuman primate societies is one strategy for solo parenting we might consider.

CHAPTER 10

The Dark Side of Parenting

$\mathbb{B}$ASSA, a captive rhesus macaque living in a large social group, was contentedly sitting with her infant, who was beginning to show an interest in exploring the environment beyond its mother's lap. When her baby ventured a few steps away from her, Bassa retrieved it. But her infant was persistent, and tried again and again to leave her. Bassa pursued her infant, roughly dragged it back and sat on it, appearing to be oblivious to its cries.

THE famous first line of Tolstoy's novel *Anna Karenina* says it well: "All happy families are alike, but an unhappy family is unhappy after its own fashion." The same notion can be applied to parental care. Adequate parental care is similar among human and nonhuman primates and very basic: provide a youngster with warmth, food, shelter, and comfort, rapidly respond to his distress, and protect him from harm, and it is likely that he will mature into a healthy, competent adult. Inadequate care, however, is more idiosyncratic. Of all primates, humans have the dubious distinction of possessing the most varied behavioral repertoire for maltreating their own offspring, and the human parent's capacity for neglect and abuse surpasses any maltreatment nonhuman primate parents are known to inflict on their young.[1]

We will see that there are multiple paths to parental maltreatment, and that no single risk factor invariably produces this outcome. Early childhood experiences, temperament, the presence or absence of social supports, acute or chronic stress, and cultural practices all combine to produce parents that may fall anywhere along the continuum of parenting, from superior to abysmal.

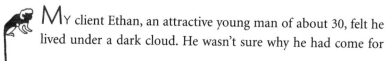 MY client Ethan, an attractive young man of about 30, felt he lived under a dark cloud. He wasn't sure why he had come for

therapy, but he knew that he was unhappy in just about every area of his life. He boss intimidated him, and he worried incessantly about what his coworkers thought of him. He couldn't find any leisure activities that interested him. He had few friends, and no one he felt close to. His relationships with women were infrequent, short-lived, and invariably disappointing. Although he longed for a committed relationship with a woman, he had never gotten to first base. Everything and everybody seemed to let him down.

Ethan is the oldest of five brothers. His father, mentally ill and low functioning, contributed little to the care of the children, who were raised primarily by their alcoholic mother. Ethan vividly remembered a time when his mother took him and his brothers to an adult party. The brothers fell asleep on a pile of jackets while their mother partied with her friends. In the morning when Ethan and his brothers awoke, their mother was gone. Ethan collected his brothers and managed to lead them home. He learned early that he couldn't count on anyone else to watch out for him, and that people he loved regularly let him down. By the time Ethan was an adult, it was impossible for him to trust anyone else enough to take a chance on becoming involved in an intimate relationship.

Of the 903,000 children who were victims of maltreatment in the United States in 2001, up to 63 percent were physically neglected, 19 percent were physically abused, 10 percent were sexually abused, and 8 percent were emotionally abused. Children under the age of 3 accounted for 28 percent of the incidents of maltreatment.[2] Eighty-four percent of these children were maltreated by their parents.

Neglect is a sin of omission; neglected children are ignored, as if they are of utterly no value, rather than beaten. They are easily distinguished from children who are adequately cared for in that they have poor hygiene, are often dirty, unkempt, thin, or ill. They roam their neighborhoods unsupervised, and when they engage in dangerous behavior, no one is around to notice or care. Their parents rarely interact with them, and their speech and gross motor skills are often delayed.

Parents who neglect their children are essentially indifferent to their welfare.[3] They typically lack knowledge about child development, aren't interested in acquiring good parenting skills, and have little inclination to look at, talk to, or touch their children. They ignore their crying infants and may believe that responding to a child will spoil him. When neglect is severe, as in the failure-to-thrive syndrome, parents are detached and literally oblivious to the needs of their babies. These infants are left on their backs in their cribs for so long that their heads become flattened, and they are so malnourished that they may suffer brain damage and permanently stunted growth.[4] Many who study child maltreatment believe that the experience of neglect is even more harmful than that of abuse.[5]

The second way parents maltreat their young is by physically harming them. I focus on physical, rather than sexual or emotional, abuse because there is enough information on physical abuse perpetrated by both human and (captive) nonhuman primates to permit a comparison between them.

The signs of abuse may not be as easy to recognize as those of neglect. To understand abuse, first we must be able to recognize what it is, and what it is not. For example, we often read of mothers who abandon their newborns in dumpsters or kill them immediately after birth. But rather than abuse, the abdication of parenting is best viewed as one of many ways (putting a child up for adoption is another) a mother "copes" with her lack of readiness to parent (or in some cases, her perception that her child is defective). Both abandonment of young and infanticide usually occur within hours of an infant's birth and are committed before any attachment between parent and child has developed. The feelings that accompany infanticide or abandonment are sadness, resignation, or even indifference, rather than anger, the emotion that more typically accompanies abuse. These acts thus function as a method of birth control that occurs after the birth of the infant, rather than before.

Abandonment and infanticide are both commonly practiced in human societies in which prenatal methods of birth control (contraception and abortion) are not readily available. Both abandonment of unwanted children (on the street or in foundling homes) and infanticide were facts of life in Europe before the twentieth century.[6] In many preindustrial societies today, if food or social support is scarce, a father has died or abandoned his family, a newborn is a twin, in poor health, appears deformed, or is too close in age to the next oldest offspring (so that the mother's investment in the newborn might compromise the health of its older sibling), infanticide may be the outcome.[7]

When a !Kung San mother goes into the bush alone to deliver her baby, she has a decision to make. If she became pregnant before her older child was ready to be weaned, she may dispose of her newborn in the bush and return to camp alone, because she cannot simultaneously care for two suckling children.[8] Infanticide is infrequent among the !Kung, and it is committed only out of perceived necessity. Whether we are talking about the rise in female infanticide in twentieth-century China after the institution of the one-child-per-family policy or abandonment of infants by young single mothers in the United States, we are referring to a decision to refuse to parent, rather than to physical abuse.[9]

If abandonment and infanticide are not examples of abuse, then what is? Non-Western peoples might believe that for a mother not to sleep with her infant is abusive.[10] Members of Western industrial societies might view as abusive the ritualized, socially sanctioned practice of circumcision without analgesia for young boys (commonly practiced in Central Asia) or the intentional scarring of the faces of youngsters by some East African traditional peoples (as part of their society's initiation rites). Many societies subject children to physical pain to teach them to be strong and to control their impulses. The Machiguenga of southeastern Peru, for example, ritually bathe children in scalding water (without injury or damage to the child), to prepare them to endure the pain they will later encounter in life.[11]

The anthropologist Jill Korbin, who has studied child abuse cross culturally, suggests that behaviors of which a culture approves, performed by most or all of the individuals in the society, should not be labeled abusive.[12] Rather, idiosyncratic and physically harmful behaviors that are *not* culturally sanctioned (and are performed when a parent is extremely angry, to vent unpleasant feelings) better meet the criteria for abuse.

The hallmark of physical abuse, the battered-child syndrome, is not condoned by any culture and includes a variety of injuries inflicted by parents. A baby suffers spontaneous subdural hematoma when she is shaken like a rag doll to make her stop crying. Abusive parents fracture skulls, break bones, punch and kick abdomens (causing ruptures of liver, spleen, or intestine), burn skin with cigarettes or scald it with boiling water, beat and whip buttocks and legs, bite limbs, slap faces, and pull hair. Maltreatment of human children varies from mild to severe and is sometimes fatal (although homicide is not usually the abusive parent's conscious intention). Cases of moderate to severe child abuse involve injuries that typically require medical treatment and may result in permanent damage.

After the battered-child syndrome was described by the American physician C. Henry Kempe in the *Journal of the American Medical Association* in 1962, the issue of child abuse became a legitimate topic of discussion among professionals working with children: physicians, nurses, teachers, social workers, counselors, and psychologists.[13] Kempe's article stimulated a vast body of research in the United States dedicated to describing, analyzing, treating, and preventing child abuse. As a result of the efforts of Kempe and many others, the battering of children in the United States today no longer masquerades as "corporal punishment," and is now viewed as an aberrant behavior.

Corporal punishment is defined as "the use of physical force with the intention of causing a child to experience pain but not injury for the purposes of correction or control of the child's behavior."[14] Ninety-four percent of American parents use corporal punishment (mostly in the form of spanking) by the time their children are 4 years old.[15] But in Austria, Croatia, Cypress, Denmark, Finland, Germany, Israel, Latvia, Norway, and Sweden, corporal punishment has been banned by the government.[16] Does corporal punishment "work"—stop the undesirable behavior now *and* prevent its recurrence—or is it merely a way for parents to let off steam that can escalate into abuse?

In a meta-analysis of 88 studies, the psychologist Elizabeth Gershoff found that corporal punishment produced only one desirable behavior: immediate compliance. But physical punishment did not produce long-term compliance; children who were spanked were less likely than those not spanked to embrace the idea that their behavior was inappropriate, to feel guilty about it, or to attempt to make reparations for what they had done. So the primary goal of discipline— permanent behavior change—is not achieved through the use of corporal punishment.

Rather than being an effective method of discipline, corporal punishment is linked with ten highly undesirable consequences, including increased risk of physical abuse; increased aggressive, delinquent, and antisocial behavior as a child; increased aggressive and antisocial behavior as an adult; poorer mental health as a child and as an adult;

and decreased quality of parent-child relationships, among others. The most significant negative consequence is the strong link between corporal punishment and physical abuse: when parents are very angry, it is easy for physical punishment to escalate into abuse. Gershoff concluded that "corporal punishment and physical abuse are two points along a continuum, such that if corporal punishment is administered too severely or too frequently, it crosses the line into physical abuse."[17] Indeed, abusive parents frequently mention that an abusive incident began with an attempt to use corporal punishment to discipline their children.[18]

Why doesn't corporal punishment work? Because children will do whatever is necessary to escape or avoid pain, spanking does produce immediate compliance. But the anger and resentment triggered by the pain of physical punishment makes a child less open to learning from his parents, and in fact, may make him resistant to and aggressive toward them. The strategy that emerges is not to perform the behavior in question when parents are around, and to defy them when they are absent. Rather than internalizing moral norms and social rules, a child learns only to avoid punishment.

Abuse traumatizes children and has long-term consequences for the rest of their lives. My client Gabriella illustrates how the damage inflicted on children by abuse accompanies them into adulthood. A raven-haired, green-eyed, and strikingly beautiful 27-year-old, Gabriella confided to me that she has never had a decent relationship with a man. Many men pursue her, but when dating becomes exclusive, her boyfriend invariably "turns mean" and physically harms her. All of Gabriella's boyfriends have seriously abused alcohol, and she commits herself to each relationship knowing that her boyfriend's modus operandi is to become intoxicated, and then violent. Each time, however, she imagines that her love will transform her boyfriend into the man she has been searching for all her life. This hope compels her to stay in a relationship even after it becomes abusive. Gabriella has been hospitalized several times after serious beatings.

I asked Gabriella if she knew why she clings to men who hurt her. She shared with me her memory of Christmas Eve when she was 4 years old. Her father was a mean drunk, and Gabriella and her siblings had learned to make themselves scarce whenever he staggered inside. But this was Christmas Eve. Her father came home drunk, but smiling. He told the children that Santa Claus had come and that presents awaited them upstairs. The children raced upstairs, their mother close behind them. Gabriella's father locked the door behind the children before their mother could enter. He then beat the children, without explanation, for 2 hours, while their mother helplessly pleaded for him to stop. Gabriella recognized that as an adult she still associated love with violence. Her attraction to violent men, as well as her childlike fantasy of rehabilitating them, stemmed from her need to redo her past. But unlike the fairy tales she loved as a child, her love stories always had unhappy endings.

Maltreatment of children increases their risk of domestic violence later on. So twice as many men and women maltreated as children (compared to children who were not maltreated) are later involved in violent intimate relationships.[19] Maltreated children, who are characteristically aggressive and unempathic, are more likely to be arrested as juveniles and as adults, and are arrested for violent crimes more often than individuals who were not maltreated.[20] They perform more poorly in school, show lower levels of achievement, and suffer more from mental problems (such as post-traumatic stress disorder) than others without this background.[21]

Maltreatment as a child may even affect adult longevity. As adults, people who have been maltreated when they were young have a higher risk of serious health problems such as alcoholism, drug abuse, depression, suicide, severe obesity, and certain chronic diseases, than other adults.[22] Some of the health problems that develop relate to the "coping" skills used by maltreated youths, such as smoking or alcohol consumption. For example, abused and neglected children are more likely to begin to smoke by the age of 14 than youngsters who are not mistreated, because they feel that nicotine helps them regulate their often volatile emotions.[23] Years later, illnesses such as emphysema, cardiovascular disease, and lung cancer are the repercussions from the use of dangerous substances for short-term coping.

NOWHERE in the literature on wild primates living in undisturbed populations is there anything remotely resembling the abuse and neglect of young that we read about so often in our newspapers or hear about in our consultation rooms.[24] The field primatologists whom I interviewed, who collectively have observed hundreds of nonhuman primates for thousands of hours over many years in the wild, could not come up with a single example of parental behavior that fits the definition of abuse.

Alas, however, we have learned two ways to produce monkey and ape mothers in the laboratory who are capable of abuse or neglect: raise them in social isolation, away from their own kind, or place them in a living situation so different from that in which their species evolved that they are unprepared to meet the demands of motherhood.

In the late 1950s and early 1960s, Harry Harlow and his students at the University of Wisconsin initiated an ambitious research program to understand the effects of early social deprivation on the adult social and parental behavior of rhesus macaques. Newborn infant rhesus monkeys were separated from their mothers at 3 days of age and raised for 6 months under three conditions. Two groups were raised in total social isolation with either an inanimate surrogate "mother" made of wire or one covered with soft terry cloth to cling to. In the third condition, infants had the opportunity to grow up with other live, warm, interactive rhesus monkeys—peers, rather than their mothers.

As adults, the first two groups differed from normal monkeys in every conceivable way. Their social behavior was bizarre, their sexual behavior was abnormal, and they were clearly overstimulated when placed with other monkeys. But the most profound effects of being raised in social isolation were revealed when females first gave birth. Over 75 percent of these "motherless" mothers were indifferent to or brutally abusive to their infants.[25]

What does the term "abusive" mean among rhesus monkey mothers? Abusive mothers violently rejected their babies, stepped on or jumped on them, bit them, mutilated them, and sometimes immediately killed them. Interestingly enough, monkey mothers who committed infanticide were behaviorally quite different from those who merely abused their infants. Infanticidal mothers ended their infant's lives with a seeming lack of hostility, as if they were not aware "where the placenta ended and the infant began."[26] They chewed through the umbilical cord, as a normal monkey mother would, but then continued to chew through the baby as well. These murderous mothers (like the infanticidal human mothers mentioned earlier) were completely indifferent to their newborns and behaved as though they did not recognize their babies as living beings.

Females who had been removed from their mothers at birth and raised with peers later parented far better than the social isolates. Seventy-five percent of them adequately cared for their babies (they fed them, carried them, and neither neglected nor abused them seriously enough to require intervention by laboratory staff), compared to less than 25 percent of the isolate-reared mothers.[27] Although more skilled than isolate-reared mothers, peer-reared mothers still did not approach the 95 percent rate of adequate care set by wild-caught rhesus monkey mothers living in captivity.[28]

Harlow's research showed the enormous effect of early social experience (or the lack thereof) on parental care by rhesus monkey mothers. Almost as important as "mother love" was experience with other monkeys during development: parenting by peer-reared monkey mothers was nearly as competent as that of mother-reared mothers.

The psychologists Steve Suomi and Chris Ripp, who summarized the findings of two decades of work on motherless monkey mothers, concluded that "there is more to macaque mothering than instinct."[29] But are the effects of early social experience immutable? To find out if parenting improved with experience, motherless monkey mothers were observed with successive infants. Neglectful mothers, who essentially abandoned their first offspring, greatly improved with subsequent infants, provided that they had been exposed to their firstborn for at least 2 days. This minimal exposure, even if mothers essentially ignored their infants, was sufficient to produce adequate mothering the second time around. Abusive mothers, however, showed little (if any) improvement over time.[30] Mothers who immediately killed their babies (or whose infants were instantly rescued by laboratory staff) also did not improve, perhaps because they did not have the requisite 2 days of experience with infants that was linked with improvement by neglectful mothers.

What are the long-term effects on rhesus monkeys of being neglected or abused? Behavioral differences between normally reared and maltreated offspring are seen at all stages of development.[31] Abused or neglected infants are clingy, reluctant to leave their mother's side, and cry more than mother-raised infants. They are less playful and begin to play at a later age than mother-reared babies. By their second year of life, they are hyper-responsive to change and highly emotional. As adolescents, they are very aggressive with unfamiliar peers.[32] Extremely wary, they appear to be insecure and frightened, perhaps because they were on their own, unprotected, at far too early an age.

Growing up without a mother (or other live members of one's species) thus produces long-term behavioral and emotional deficits in captive female rhesus monkeys that negatively impact their parenting behavior as adults. Is the parenting behavior of wild adult macaques who were orphaned at an early age similarly affected?

When Mariko Hiraiwa was collecting data on maternal care in a troop of wild Japanese macaques, she noted the usual findings; first-time mothers were awkward or even inept with their babies, compared with older, more experienced mothers.[33] But some of the first-time mothers were unusually neglectful. They didn't regularly support their babies with their hands during the first days of life, left them behind (sometimes over considerable distances) while they searched for food, and did not restrict them as much as other first-time mothers. These behaviors inadvertently increased the risk that their infants would be kidnapped by other troop members, taken by predators, hurt by environmental hazards, or simply lost.

Neglectful mothers also were more aggressive with their babies than other first-time mothers. One mother yanked her baby off her breast by its hair, and others did not allow their infants to nurse as frequently or for as long as they wished. Neglectful mothers roughly pushed their infants off them or bit them. Almost one half of the infants of these neglectful first-time mothers died during their first year of life, in contrast to infants of merely awkward and inept mothers, all of whom survived.

What could explain the neglectful, aggressive, and sometimes bizarre maternal behavior offered by this group of monkey mothers? Perhaps it had something to do with the fact that *all* the mothers in this group had lost their own mothers when they were between 1 and 5 years of age. In the years before Hiraiwa's study, many of the mothers of these now inadequate new mothers had been captured by humans (before their daughters were mature). In a few cases, the mothers of the neglectful mothers disappeared (and presumably died) before their daughters were grown. Although the daughters were old enough to survive without milk, they might not have been prepared for the complete disappearance of their mothers from their lives. Since female macaques enjoy a close relationship with their mothers even after they are grown, and coalitions of related females form the core of macaque society, the absence of a mother would place her daughter at a serious disadvantage.

Despite growing up in their natal troop (in the company of adults and peers), and having opportunities to babysit and to observe other mothers care for their young, these Japanese macaque mothers who had lost their own mothers at an early age neglected their first babies. But they improved with experience. They neglected their second or third infant less than they did their first (although they continued to behave more aggressively with their babies than other mothers), but later-born infants were no more likely to die during their first year than those of other experienced mothers.

Hiraiwa concluded that being the recipient of adequate maternal care determines whether or not an infant Japanese macaque survives its first year, and that a mother macaque's ability to care for her first infant is seriously impaired when her own mother died or disappeared before she was grown. What was missing in the development of these neglectful mothers? Did they suffer from the absence of a safe, secure, harbor that later hampered their ability to care for their own young, or were they inadequate because they could not intimately observe their own mother care for a newborn? This "natural" experiment cannot explain why these mothers failed; rather, we learn only that wild monkey mothers are capable of severe neglect when the conditions under which adequate motherhood evolved are disrupted.

Maltreating monkey mothers thus can be created in the laboratory or in the wild when they don't have the developmental experiences necessary for adequate parenting. Are abusive or neglectful human parents "created" the same way?

Neglectful human parents often have a history of severe emotional deprivation during their own childhoods.[34] The consequences of being neglected by one's parents are vast. When neglected children grow up, they are generally unhappy, needy, lonely, and dependent.[35] Many are chronically depressed and are focused more on their own pain than on their children's needs. They have low self-esteem and a deep sense of worthlessness or ineptitude. Because their experience was that they had no impact on their environment, they learned to give up when they couldn't manage, rather than to ask others for help. The demands of parenthood may feel so overwhelming that they simply withdraw. Because they did not feel valued by their own parents, they often are ill equipped to meet the demands of parenthood.

Similarly, parents who physically abuse their children often were neglected or abused by their own parents.[36] Imagine the following scenario. As a child, the abusive parent feels unloved by her own parents. She believes that her parents are neither interested in nor concerned about her. Because her parents maltreat her, she never develops the sense that she can expect to be treated well and not intentionally harmed by others.

As she grows up, her transition from one developmental stage to the next is difficult. Without basic trust, it isn't easy to separate from her parents, a task that begins as a toddler. Like abused nonhuman primates, she is clingy, reluctant to leave her parents and hesitant to explore her world.

In her adolescent years, her inability to trust makes her suspect the motives of others. She anticipates and fears criticism and is reluctant to ask for help. She avoids authority figures (in anticipation of being criticized by them), and may isolate herself to avoid hurt or disappointment. When she becomes involved in a relationship, her fear of harm or abandonment and her lack of independence make her cling, even to an abusive partner. Because she has learned to associate love with violence, violent relationships are eerily familiar to her, and she is drawn to them like a moth to a flame.

Her early history of abuse or neglect is linked to her poor self-esteem. She suffers from a low-grade chronic depression and typically sees the glass as half empty. Unable to regulate her emotions, she experiences intense, extremely negative emotions. Tolerating frustration is extremely difficult for her, and she often acts impulsively, in a frantic but usually futile attempt to make bad feelings (which are intolerable) go away.[37] Because she has learned to impulsively grab for anything that might make her feel better (even if only in the short term), she begins to abuse alcohol as a teenager.

When she becomes a parent, her frustrated need to be nurtured is placed, inappropriately, on her own child. Rather than offering unconditional love to her child, she reverses the roles and expects to be nurtured by her child.[38] When her child does not meet her unrealistic expectations, she is disappointed. And disappointment, like any other negative emotion, is intolerable. Disappointment and frustration turn into rage when her child fails to obey her or otherwise meet her expectations, and abuse is the unfortunate outcome of her attempt to discipline her child, especially when she is isolated and her stress level is high.[39] Not having experienced unconditional love or empathy from her own parents, she is unable to empathize with her own child's pain and sorrow. Her focus is on herself, rather than on her child.

THE possibility that abuse or neglect might pass from one generation to the next has sparked a lively controversy for many years among those who study these phenomena in humans. Because the issues surrounding child maltreatment are very complex, the primatologist Dario Maestripieri looked at maltreatment of off-spring by captive monkeys and asked the following question: "Is a nonhuman primate mother, who was abused or neglected as a youngster by *her* mother, more likely to maltreat her own young than a mother who was not maltreated?" Maestripieri analyzed abuse and neglect by captive macaque monkeys to see if maltreatment occurred more often in some families than others. The data he reviewed included observations of mildly to moderately abusive parental behavior by mother macaques living in relatively undisturbed conditions in captivity, as well as over 30 years of colony records from the Yerkes Regional Primate Center, near Atlanta, Georgia, where examples of severe infant abuse or neglect by captive macaque mothers were documented.[40]

Maestripieri observed captive monkey mothers and their infants housed in large groups for the infants' first 3 months of life.[41] He defined abuse as dragging, throwing, crushing (pushing an infant to the ground with both hands), and sitting or stepping on an infant. These behaviors did not occur during aggressive interactions between adults or unrelated animals: they occurred only in the context of infant abuse.

Severity of abuse was predicted by how frequently the behavior occurred, rather than by the specific type of abusive behavior.[42] Each incident lasted only a few seconds, but a frequently abused infant was more likely to be seriously injured (or even killed) than one who was infrequently mistreated. Abusive mothers were generally more aggressive than other mothers and reacted quickly and more negatively to stress. For example, abuse sometimes followed the harassment of a mother (or her infant) by another group member. Although abusive mothers and their infants were not targeted for harassment more frequently than other mother-infant pairs, abusive mothers often responded to provocation by maltreating their babies, which suggests that it was difficult for them to regulate their emotions when stressed.[43]

Abuse appeared to be disconnected from the characteristics or behavior of a particular infant: abused youngsters seemed normal and healthy before maltreatment and did nothing to provoke their mothers to harm them. A maltreated (screaming) baby, however, does upset other group members, who often approach and attempt to retrieve the infant. The presence of an audience and rapid intervention by others shortens the period in which a mother can freely abuse her infant.

The characteristics of macaque mothers who abuse their babies are different from those of mothers who neglect their infants. Unlike neglectful mothers, abusive mothers typically are neither young nor inexperienced. And rather than ignoring their babies, abusive mothers appear to overrespond to them; Maestripieri and others have described the behavior of abusive monkey mothers as possessive or controlling.[44] The abusive mother's determination to control her infant's behavior may culminate in abuse, while other aspects of her maternal behavior are satisfactory (such as providing food, warmth, and protection). Unlike normal mothers, abusive mothers aggressively (and more frequently) restrain and reject their infants from a very early age. A mother may become abusive when her infant attempts to leave her, plays with a peer, or fails to respond quickly to her signal to return.[45]

Some researchers who study infant abuse among captive rhesus monkeys suggest that excessive maternal anxiety, rather than hostility, is the primary cause of the abuse of infants.[46] Because most of the abusive behavior directed at infants is not part of the rhesus monkey's normal repertoire of aggressive behavior, and because mothers seem indifferent (rather than hostile) to their infants when abusing them, abuse by captive macaques may be predicted to occur when highly emotional mothers have neglible skills for coping with anxiety, rather than aggression. When researchers treated one of the abusive mothers with a tranquilizer to reduce her anxiety, she behaved more like a normal mother with her infant.

But regardless of whether or not abuse by macaque mothers stems from anxiety or aggression, abuse affects the functioning of their offspring throughout their lives. Their mother's behavior is undoubtedly confusing: one moment she restrains them and holds them close, and the next she harms or aggressively rejects them. Babies who are rejected harshly, unpredictably, or too soon become anxiously attached to their mothers. Anxiously attached youngsters are more clingy as infants and more aggressive as adolescents than individuals with secure attachments. It may well be that the increased aggression shown by these harshly treated youngsters as they mature, along with their poor ability to tolerate stress, sets the stage for permanent hyper-aggressiveness (in both males and females), which perpetuates the cycle of infant abuse.

The concentration of abuse in certain families of macaques studied by Maestripieri lends support to the idea that abuse may be transmitted from one generation to the next. Of the 10 abusive rhesus monkey mothers identified in the observational studies, 5 were mothers and daughters.[47] The records of fatal abuse from the Yerkes Center paralleled those of the observational studies: fatal abuse was more commonly found in some families than others.[48]

The results for neglect in captive macaque mothers differed from those for abuse. Monkey mothers who fatally neglected their babies showed no interest in them whatsoever, rather than attempting to control them. There was never more than one neglectful mother per family, and mothers who neglected their babies were not closely related.[49] Most of the mothers who neglected their babies were first-time parents and rarely were neglectful with subsequent infants. Like the motherless mothers in Harlow's laboratory, neglectful mothers improved with experience while abusive mothers did not. Contrary to the human pattern for child maltreatment, abuse and neglect typically were *not* committed by the same mother, and thus appear to be elicited by different circumstances in captive macaques.[50]

These data make a convincing case for the possibility of intergenerational transmission of physical abuse, but not neglect, in captive macaque monkeys.[51] This suggests not that every monkey mother abused as an infant is destined to abuse her own offspring, but only that mothers who abuse their young are likely to be closely related to other abusive individuals. It isn't clear if abusive behavior is passed on by imitation or learning, or if an aggressive, irritable, temperament (perhaps exacerbated by the experience of abuse) is the key factor. But poorly functioning monkey mothers cope poorly with environmental stress, which may heighten an already elevated state of arousal and precipitate abuse. And because a poorly functioning monkey has a better chance of surviving and reproducing in captivity than in the wild, her aggressive or anxious temperament passes to her offspring, which perpetuates the cycle.

Like the controlling rhesus monkey mothers, abusive human parents also expect their children to instantly comply with their wishes. When their child is "good" (defined as obedient, well-behaved, and loving), all is well. But when their child's behavior does not meet their expectations (which often do not mesh with the child's stage of development), they begin to feel like failures. In their need to feel competent, they ignore their children's feelings (as *their* feelings were ignored as children) and force them to comply with their demands, repeating the experiences of their own childhood. Instead of learning empathy from their parents, adults abused as children have learned that children *must* comply with parental wishes, and thus may repeat the abusive behaviors they experienced at the hands of their own parents.

The brain chemistry of women abused as children is permanently altered as a consequence of maltreatment; women with a childhood history of abuse have greater pituitary-adrenal and autonomic responses to stress than women who do not.[52] Maltreatment as a child thus results in permanent changes in the body's response to stress, such as heightened emotional reactivity, which may increase the risk of mood and anxiety disorders later in life. Since both depression and anxiety reduce an individual's capacity to cope with life (which includes parenting), it is likely that the experience of abuse, and the resulting changes in body chemistry, play a role in the perpetuation of maltreatment in the next generation.

Do all parents with a childhood history of abuse maltreat their own children? Certainly not. But the risk of abuse is clearly elevated among parents who were victimized by their own parents. About a third of these individuals go on to abuse their own children, but more intriguing, two thirds do not.[53] Even with a predilection for abuse, most victims of child abuse do not, as adults, abuse their own children. The presence of certain protective factors, such as having one parent who was loving (and not abusive), having a loving, supportive spouse, and working through the trauma of abuse in psychotherapy may help to break the cycle of child abuse, sparing the next generation.[54]

Negative early childhood experiences thus increase the probability that primates will maltreat their offspring. The addition of chronic stress further increases the potential for parental abuse or neglect.

SUCCESSFULLY breeding gorillas in captivity isn't easy. Of the first 29 live infant gorillas born in zoos, less than half were properly cared for by their mothers.[55] Some of the infants initially accepted were later injured severely, or even killed by their mothers. Wild gorilla mothers are characteristically gentle, patient, doting mothers. What was going on?

Virtually all of the mother gorillas had been captured in the wild during their first 2 years of life. These captures are invariably traumatic, because wild gorillas do not give up their young to human hunters without a fight; trappers usually kill mothers (and other family members) in order to capture youngsters. The reason that the gorilla mothers parented poorly, however, was ambiguous: was early trauma responsible, or was it that they had grown up without appropriate role models to imitate?

Further review of the gorilla breeding data revealed that sometimes an infant had been removed from its mother before her parenting potential had been carefully assessed.[56] But in the remaining cases, there were huge differences between the mothers (all of whom had been captured and permanently separated from their mothers as youngsters) who provided good care and those who did not. Seven of eight adequate mothers were housed with other adult gorillas, while eight of nine abusive or neglectful mothers were housed alone with their infants.

Despite two strikes against them (traumatic early experience and loss of their mother), several wild-born female gorillas did not become unfit mothers; a supportive social environment apparently mitigated the effects of their early losses. Mothers with three strikes against them (traumatic early experience, mother loss, and improper housing), however, performed poorly. Nonhuman primate mothers forced to live in an environment that is socially dissimilar from that in which they evolved (such as an environment where females and young are housed in isolation rather than in a family group) have a higher risk of maltreating their young.

Abusive or neglectful parenting, therefore, is not difficult to elicit from captive nonhuman primate mothers. Any stressor that increases the general level of tension among group members can negatively impact parenting. For example, conflict within a captive group (in which escape or avoidance, of course, is impossible) increases tension among all group members and may trigger abuse. Housing nonhuman primates in isolation, with too many or too few companions, or the "wrong" companions (not those that they would associate with in wild populations), can produce abusive or neglectful parental behavior.[57]

In recent years, captive breeding of nonhuman primates has significantly improved. It is now mandated by law that breeders house captive animals properly, taking into account the characteristics of social groupings typical of each species. In the United States today, virtually all laboratory populations of nonhuman primates are maintained by captive breeding (rather than by wild capture), which has diminished the role of early trauma associated with later maltreatment of infants in these settings.

Like nonhuman primates, human parents under high stress also are at greater risk of maltreating their children. One type of parent who abuses his or her children lives in a chaotic, high-stress environment and has a childhood history of early trauma or loss, two conditions that are often directly related. We have seen that adults maltreated as children function more poorly than their adequately treated peers in many ways, some of which actually may increase the number of stressors they face.[58] Common stressors linked with child maltreatment are poverty, unemployment, abandonment by or death of a spouse, isolation, and the absence of helpers. Poverty is the stressor most predictive of neglect; when resources are meager, there simply may not be enough to go around.[59] Unplanned children and children from large families are at higher risk when resources are limited.[60] And very young, poor single parents (with the risk factors of poverty and lack of social support) are at the highest risk for maltreating their children.[61]

Substance abuse by parents (typically elevated in high-stress environments) is one of the primary stressors implicated in the increase in child maltreatment in the United States. Parents who regularly use drugs or excessively consume alcohol are almost three times more likely to abuse, and over four times more likely to neglect their children as parents who do not depend on these substances to cope with life.[62] In a study of parents addicted to alcohol or opiates, researchers found that all of their children were mildly to moderately neglected, and 41 percent of them were both abused and neglected.[63]

Stress is a precipitating factor for child maltreatment, but most stressed parents do not abuse their children. Similarly, although poverty and lower socioeconomic status place added burdens on parenting, most poor parents do not abuse their children.

ANOTHER type of stress that impacts parenting is precipitated by the need to accommodate to rapid changes in one's living environment. Adjusting to captivity by wild-caught nonhuman primates is an example of this type of acute stressor. Newly captive primates are stressed because the way in which they normally operate is severely curtailed by their loss of freedom. For starters, they have suddenly lost their mothers or other family members, as well as their rank and place in their social group. Their new social companions are unfamiliar (and potentially dangerous), so earning a spot in the new group's hierarchy is a top priority. Perhaps most distressing, captives are suddenly in constant contact with humans (who, from their perspective, are feared predators). Because danger is always present and escape is impossible, wild-caught nonhuman primates initially are extremely wary and fearful, exhibiting emotions that can disrupt parenting. In contrast, infants born in captivity to captive-born mothers are used to the presence of humans and are not as frightened of them. When they grow up, they do not behave as if perpetually on guard and, for the most part, adequately care for their young.

Even primates who are adapted to captivity are at risk for poor parenting when their environment suddenly changes. Managers of captive primate colonies learned the hard way that moving mothers with young infants into newly formed, unstable groups often resulted in an increase in infant mortality—from skull fractures, or injuries to hands, limbs, or trunk.[64] A change in composition temporarily upsets a group's balance, triggering fear, agitation, or hostility.[65] When a mother is frightened or agitated, anticipating harm to herself or her offspring, she is less apt to be calm or patient and more likely to maltreat her young.[66]

Human parenting is likewise impaired when cultural ways are disrupted, and parents lack the community supports on which they have traditionally relied. For a fascinating but tragic example of how parenting deteriorates when support from the community suddenly disappears, consider the Maori, the indigenous people of New Zealand.

The Maori inhabited New Zealand long before European settlers arrived, and their parenting practices evolved in harmony with the environment. As with other native Polynesians, parenting was a community project among the Maori. In the small villages in which they traditionally lived, children called every woman *whaea* (mother), and every man, *matua tane* (father), exemplifying the interest of all community members in the well-being of every child.[67] Fostering was common among the Maori, ensuring that households contained neither too many nor too few children.[68] The Maori also regularly used babysitters; older children were responsible for their younger siblings from a tender age. In the environment in which the Maori lived, these practices were efficient and completely safe.

Maori children were indulged by their parents until the age of 2, when they were first considered to be "trainable." When parents became less responsive to their toddler's demands, children looked elsewhere for comfort. From the age of 2 on, they frequently visited the homes of other villagers, often spending the night. Maori children grew up in an environment that fostered early independence and socialization. They were intimately known and loved by their parents and watched over by other members of their community. Maltreatment of children was virtually nonexistent.

When many Maori migrated to New Zealand cities during the twentieth century, the supportive, low-stress environment of their rural or island villages was exchanged for a high-stress urban environment characterized by poverty. The rate of reported child abuse among Maori living in cities skyrocketed: a report published in 1972 revealed that child abuse was six times as frequent among the Maori (and nine times more frequent among other Pacific Islanders who had recently emmigrated to urban environments) than among families of European ancestry.[69] Although Maori and other Pacific Islanders made up a small fraction of the population in New Zealand at the time of this report, they accounted for almost two thirds of the incidents of child abuse. How did the Maori, in one generation, shift from a culture in which child abuse was negligible to one in which it was a fact of life?

Anthropologists who study the Maori explain it this way: When Maori families moved to the city, community support for parenting disappeared. Suddenly, parents had no backup for childcare, the converse of traditional Maori ways. Early independence for children wasn't safe in urban environments, nor was the reliance on very young children to babysit for even younger siblings—leaving a 5-year-old to care for a crawling infant was now viewed as "neglectful."

Maori families in cities lived among families who had come from

Europe, where parenting practices differed greatly from their own. Parents of European ancestry did not parent collectively and neither understood nor approved of group parenting.[70] Maori mothers mimicked their white neighbors in an attempt to assimilate; they did not ask for help and began to expect more from their infants. Indulgent behavior decreased and parents became more demanding.

Perhaps most important, parenting no longer occurred in front of an audience: maltreatment could now occur behind closed doors. With no one around to observe or intervene, the Maori lost two protective factors—public scrutiny and communal responsibility for children—in one fell swoop. The parenting support on which the Maori had depended for generations had suddenly vanished, with nothing to replace it. Poverty, easy access to alcohol and drugs, and European-style housing (which resulted in the isolation of mothers and young children within their dwellings) perhaps explain how the incidence of abuse and neglect could increase so precipitously in just one generation. "Where is the taro patch to which she (a mother) can retire to share her troubles with other women and do useful work while a solution is being worked out? Where is the lagoon, the beach or the reef where children can have fun, find food, and escape from parental surveillance? Where are the elders who will direct that someone give assistance? Where are the dwellings of kinsfolk to whom a frightened child may run for comfort?"[71]

The Maori were unprepared for the enormous changes in their way of life. Like nonhuman primate mothers who had to suddenly adjust to captivity, Maori parents who were suddenly isolated, without the social supports on which they relied for generations, were at increased risk for maltreating their young. Child maltreatment is thus a predictable outcome when parents must rapidly adapt to massive changes in their environment without adequate resources to cope with the demands of parenting.

We have seen that the Maori rarely maltreated their children before their massive migration to an urban environment. Are children more likely to be abused or neglected in some cultures than others?

ARE victims of battered-child syndrome just as likely to be found in one culture as another? Jill Korbin sought to answer this question by surveying a variety of preindustrial and industrial societies around the globe. She found that examples of brutal abuse can be found in almost every culture, but that it occurs much more often in some cultures than others. Contrary to expectation, parents in "violence prone" cultures, such as the indigenous people of New Guinea, typically are not aggressive, much less abusive, with their children.[72] Similarly among the Gusii, husbands beat their wives, but not their children.[73] And the Yanomamo of South America, who reputedly beat their wives and sometimes kill children from other communities, do not abuse their own children.[74]

How do cultural practices protect children from maltreatment, and conversely, how might they place children in harm's way? Several cultural conventions are quite effective in preventing child maltreatment. As strange as this sounds, one of the "protective" factors against child abuse and neglect in some cultures is the decision to abdicate parenting (by abandonment or infanticide). Infanticide and abandonment essentially "weed out" unwanted children on the day of their birth. For example, children who are abandoned or targeted for infanticide at birth are similar in many ways to those children most at risk for maltreatment in other cultures—children considered to be deformed, defective, or ill, orphans, children of the "wrong" gender, children too close in age to the next oldest offspring, one of a pair of twins, children with absent fathers or of suspect paternity, children of very young mothers who lack sufficient social supports or resources, or children from very large families.[75] Children not abandoned or killed are, by definition, wanted and valued, and are unlikely to be mistreated as they grow up.[76]

A second protective factor (and a more benign form of the refusal to parent) found most often in preindustrial societies is the practice of fostering, described in Chapter 8. When a family can't manage an extra mouth to feed, another family with too few children is more than willing to take responsibility for rearing that child. Because children in preindustrial societies make a significant contribution to their family's economic well-being (either as youngsters or as adults), foster families actually obtain some benefit from rearing nongenetic children. And because fostering is temporary rather than permanent, a placement that isn't working out is easily remedied.

A third protective factor against child abuse characteristic of many cultures is that childrearing is often a community project, rather than a burden born solely by parents. Even in cultures characterized by high fertility, the help of extended family, older children, and other community members decreases pressure on parents. Child abuse is rare in cultures in which mothers are not routinely isolated from other adults. Similar to the rhesus monkey and gorilla mothers described earlier, human mothers whose only companions are their offspring are more likely to maltreat them than mothers living in more natural social groupings. Securely embedded in their communities of close kin or companions, human and nonhuman primate mothers not only enjoy the company and help of other adults, but have the added benefit of a fourth protective factor: exposure to public scrutiny. Other community members are aware when a parent is overwhelmed and are willing to intervene. Primate parents who abuse their youngsters in private do not have to face the stigma of community disapproval.

A culture's expectations for the behavior of children may also protect against child abuse. The indigenous people of New Guinea, for example, believe that children are unable to reason before the age of 6 or 7.[77] Younger children are rarely punished for misdeeds because they are not expected to know better. And culture-wide disapproval of the use of corporal punishment ensures that discipline does not escalate into abuse. The contributions of children to their families in preindustrial cultures additionally protects them from maltreatment by their biological parents, just as it does with foster parents.[78]

Cultures that are tolerant and accepting of the behavior of young children usually expect older children to conform to society's expectations for appropriate behavior, and the methods they use to obtain compliance are quite effective. Expectations for behavior at each stage of life are clear (and developmentally appropriate), as are the consequences for infractions. With culturally sanctioned practices for discipline understood by both parents and children, parents are not as likely to "lose control" and beat their children. Consistency of parental discipline socializes children to understand their culture's prescription for what is acceptable behavior and what is not.

Battered-child syndrome, unfortunately, is more common in the United States than in many other cultures, and there is some evidence that the incidence is rising.[79] If the increase in abuse is simply due to more thorough reporting or to better recognition of abuse, we would expect to see all types of abuse rising at the same rate. But the level of moderate abuse has stabilized, while the incidence of severe abuse quadrupled between the mid-1980s and early 1990s.[80] There are more serious cases of child abuse in the United States today than ever before.

Why are children in the United States today at higher risk for abuse than children in many preindustrial cultures? One reason may be that, as a society, we have adopted none of the three forms of parental abdication regularly practiced in other cultures: infanticide, infant abandonment, and fostering. Although other forms of prenatal birth control (such as contraception or abortion) are available, the young, poor, single parents at most risk for child maltreatment may have the least access to these means of refusing to parent.

Infanticide is illegal (as well as morally repugnant to most individuals in American society), and until recently there was no socially acceptable way in the United States to abandon a newborn infant. But since the Safe Haven for Newborn Infants Act was passed in Arizona in August 2001, it is now legal for Arizona parents of an unharmed newborn less than 72 hours old to permanently give up their baby, no questions asked. Newborns may be left with staff members in hospitals, at designated houses of worship, or with on-duty firefighters or emergency medical technicians. How does legal abandonment protect children? In the year 2000 in Arizona, 18 babies were abandoned in Arizona, 9 of whom died. In the first 2 years since the Safe Haven legislation was passed, 10 infants were abandoned (of which 2 died), and 5 infants were delivered to a safe haven.[81] When parents unprepared to parent can easily give up their baby to a family ready for parenthood, that may save the infant's life and remove it from an environment where it would be statistically at higher risk for child maltreatment. Unfortunately, Safe Haven legislation has not been passed in every state, so it is not available throughout the country.

Fostering is the third type of parental abdication used by other cultures (typically for older children, past the age of weaning) that is not readily available to most Americans (except in the case of involuntary placement after a child is mistreated). Sometimes children are sent to live with other family members, such as grandparents, when parents cannot (or will not) care for their children. But families who cannot adequately care for their children often have little recourse but to continue on, despite mounting stress.

Social isolation is another risk factor common to many parents in the United States who mistreat their children, but this may be partly due to the fact that individuals maltreated as children often avoid relationships with others out of fear of being hurt or judged by them.[82] They often receive little or no help from their families and have few friends to turn to.[83] Mothers who maltreat may feel trapped in their apartments with several small, demanding children (who are close in age), with no one to help them or intervene when they are overwhelmed. Because parents in the United States (especially single parents) are increasingly isolated, and others in the community are either unaware of family violence or reluctant to intervene, our nation's response to child maltreatment has been described as "an ambulance service at the bottom of the cliff."[84]

Child maltreatment in the United States is often linked to unrealistic expectations for the behavior of small children. For example, abuse often follows accidents in toilet training.[85] Parents may feel ashamed or frustrated if their child isn't toilet trained by a particular age (they may believe that it reflects badly on them, or feel pressured because the child cannot be accepted into preschool until he or she is trained), or they may simply become angry when the child soils something of value. When parents view their children's failure to comply as evidence of willful resistance, rather than as normal behavior for their stage of development, abuse may be the outcome.

Finally, the culture-wide acceptance of corporal punishment in the United States places our children at higher risk for maltreatment. Although we have rules that violence toward children perpetrated by strangers, teachers, coaches, or other adults is unacceptable, we have different rules for families. The American family is, paradoxically, the most physically violent group of people our children are likely to encounter in their lives, as well as their primary source of love and care.[86] Many of our children learn from the very beginning that love and violence are close companions.

Although most parents do not maltreat their children even in the worst of circumstances, we have seen that the failure of some to parent adequately may be attributed in part to several factors such as temperament, life history, acute or chronic stressors, and cultural practices, alone or in combination. Another risk factor more commonly linked to maltreatment in Western industrial societies is the presence of a step-parent in the home.

WICKED stepmothers and cruel, lustful, stepfathers are the villains of countless Cinderella-type folktales across many cultures.[87] In Chapter 8, we saw that young children are at higher risk of being killed by step- than biological parents in the United States and Canada. Is the pattern similar for nonfatal child abuse?

Martin Daly and Margo Wilson analyzed 99 cases of child abuse that were reported and substantiated in a Canadian city of over 400,000 people (Hamilton-Wentworth) over a 12-month period in the early 1980s.[88] They noted whether or not the abused child resided with a single biological parent, two biological parents, one biological parent and one step-parent, or other types of substitute caregivers (grandparents, for example). To get an idea how many cases of abuse would be expected to occur in each type of family, 1,200 households in the area were called, and the ages, sexes, and genetic relatedness of the residents were documented. Every telephone interviewee was asked for his or her postal code, a procedure that allowed for a rough assessment of the family's income according to address. By estimating how many families of each type—single biological parent, two biological parents, or one biological parent and one step-parent—lived in Hamilton-Wentworth, Daly and Wilson could predict about how many cases of abuse would be expected for each type of family.

The youngest children, up to the age of 5, understandably were at the highest risk for abuse in all three types of families, because very young children both require constant care and are easier to physically harm than older children. Overtaxed parents may not be able to leave a very young child long enough to calm themselves down, and when they strike out, are more likely to inflict serious damage. In addition, very young children cannot report their own victimization. If they are not attending daycare or preschool, where other adults might notice the evidence of abuse, the maltreatment is easily concealed.

When Daly and Wilson analyzed the rate of abuse of children of preschool age or younger by type of family, the results were astonishing. Children residing with one biological and one step-parent were 40 times more likely to be abused than children living with two biological parents, despite the fact that income was equivalent in two-parent biological and blended families, and two parents were (at least, theoretically) available to share parenting duties in both types of families. Daly and Wilson concluded that "stepparenthood remains the single most powerful risk factor for child abuse that has yet been identified."[89]

The key risk factors for abuse by step-parents differ from those for biological parents. For example, there is no clear link between an early history of abuse or neglect and abusive behavior by step-parents. Maltreatment by step-parents is clearly selective; studies have shown that parents who abuse their stepchildren typically spare their own biological children who reside in the same home.[90] A stepfather thus is far more likely to physically abuse children from his wife's previous marriage than the child he and his wife have conceived together. Other risk factors such as low income and high stress cannot explain the huge differences between two-parent blended and biological families, whose incomes in this study were equivalent. The presence of a step-parent in the home can be the only explanation for these findings.

In the case of child murder, the rationale for ending a child's life is different for step-parents and biological parents.[91] In a Canadian study, homicides of children under the age of 5 often reflected a parent's hopelessness about his or her ability to continue to care for the children. Biological fathers killed their children (and sometimes their entire family, including themselves) when they believed that their wives were going to leave them, or when they felt overwhelmed and unable to provide for their families. In these instances, fathers typically killed their children as painlessly as possible. Biological mothers who killed children (other than newborn infants) were usually depressed and felt unable to care for their children.[92] Mothers also did not intentionally inflict pain, and many committed suicide after killing their children.

Stepfathers were 60 times more likely than biological parents to kill children, and homicides by stepfathers usually were committed in a burst of rage (the child wouldn't stop crying), out of hostility to or resentment of a particular child, or in the context of "discipline."[93] Eighty-two percent of children killed by stepfathers (compared to less than half that rate for genetic fathers) were beaten to death—the final incident in a prolonged history of abuse of a particular child. Finally, stepfathers rarely committed suicide after killing a stepchild. A biological parent murders a child in sorrow, but a stepfather murders a child in rage.

If the absence of a genetic relationship between parents and children places children at higher risk for maltreatment, how do we explain that adopted children (who are genetically related to neither parent) are not more likely to be maltreated than children residing with two biological parents? The puzzle is solved by noticing the important differences between adoptive and blended families. First, adoptive parents actively pursue parenting. Because adoption is both expensive and psychologically draining, people who see it through do so because they desperately want a child and typically have not been able to conceive one of their own. Second, once a couple adopts a child, it belongs equally to both of them. Third, an adopted child does not blame either parent for breaking up his family, and thus easily attaches to both of them. Fourth, adoptive parents are carefully screened, and a loving, relatively stress-free home with high-functioning parents typically is found for the adoptee. And finally, adoptive families are wealthier and suffer fewer stressors than average families.

For step-parents, unlike adoptive parents with their active pursuit of parenting, parental investment in stepchildren is simply the price they are expected to pay in order to remarry.[94] Some of the hostility in blended families stems from the behavior of stepchildren, who may be indifferent to or antagonistic toward their step-parents. Step-parents are often told, in no uncertain terms, "You can't tell me what to do—you aren't my father/mother." Sometimes children intentionally cause trouble in their newly blended families, because they want their biological parents to reconcile. So in addition to wicked step-parents, there are also intentionally disruptive stepchildren.

Daly and Wilson suggest that the heightened risk for abuse in blended families is best understood in the context of evolutionary theory. Because raising children requires a huge investment of time and parental resources, parents should selectively invest in those children for whom they will receive the greatest evolutionary payoff—those capable of sending the parents' genes into the next generation. But these issues seem less compelling in preindustrial societies, in which fostering of nongenetic children is common. Foster parents in these cultures actively pursue parenting, and foster children invariably make some form of valuable contribution to their household, rather than just consuming resources like American children.

Step-parents in Western societies have all the disadvantages of being parents but none of the advantages. When a step-parent is asked to parent a stepchild, therefore, the job may be difficult, or even harrowing. Maltreatment certainly is not inevitable in blended families, and most children in blended families are adequately cared for. But because we are not inclined to offer a huge parental investment to nonkin (and because a child in Western societies is expensive to raise and offers no immediate payback for its care), there is simply more resentment and hostility when we are expected to do so. Resentment may be highest, and therefore the risk of abuse greatest, when children are very young and the effort required for their care is great.

UNDER what circumstances would evolutionary theory predict the neglect or abuse of offspring? Parental-investment theory does predict severe neglect or abandonment of infants (viewed as a failure to "invest" in offspring) when circumstances are unfavorable for raising young.[95] For example, a mother who is very young, or in less than optimal physical condition, places herself (and thus her baby) at high risk when she invests resources she can ill afford; it might be in her "best" interest, as far as her long-term lifetime reproductive success is concerned, to withdraw care from a healthy infant that she is likely to lose anyway (because of her poor condition or lack of resources), so that she can be better prepared to invest in the next one. But although parental-investment theory predicts neglect or even abandonment of offspring under conditions unfavorable for rearing young (and instances of neglect or abandonment are not unusual in many species of mammals, including humans, under these circumstances), it is exceedingly rare for nonhuman primate mothers in the wild to severely neglect or abandon their offspring, regardless of their own physical condition or that of their infant.

The primatologist Susan Perry tells a remarkable story about a brown capuchin mother named Abby who never abandoned her infant, Omni, born with an umbilical hernia.[96] Normal capuchin in-

White-faced capuchins *(Cebus capucinus)*; photo by Katherine C. MacKinnon

fants are able to cling to their mothers unsupported, so that their mother's quadrupedal locomotion is unhampered. But Omni was unable to hang on by himself. Abby clutched Omni to her chest and walked on two legs instead of four. She curled her tail around Omni to protect him while she fed. Once when Abby used both hands to climb a tree, Omni fell a few inches; Abby retrieved him and managed to scamper up by "squishing him between herself and the tree." For the next 3 days until Omni died, Abby continued to care for him. She helped him nurse, protected him, and held him with one hand as she maneuvered through the trees, impeding her own locomotion and undoubtedly elevating her risk of falling. As Omni weakened, he no longer could cling to Abby. Whenever Abby inadvertently dropped Omni, she instantly retrieved him. Abby continued to carry Omni even after he was no longer moving and his hands and feet were stiffly clenched. Nonhuman primate mothers such as Abby often have been observed to care for seriously impaired infants that cannot survive, and may carry recently deceased infants for days, at increased risk to their own safety.[97]

Is there anything in evolutionary theory that might predict the abuse of young? Abusive rhesus monkey mothers simultaneously abused their babies *and* provided for their basic needs. These babies received too much of their mothers' attention, rather than too little. Alternating attentiveness with abuse makes no sense, evolutionarily or otherwise.[98] The conclusion must be that the physical abuse of young is both pathological and maladaptive.

ANNE SAVAGE, a primatologist actively involved in the conservation of the cottontop tamarin, writes that more than a third of the current captive population of cottontops lack the appropriate social skills to rear their offspring successfully.[99] Savage believes that the hand-rearing of infant cottontops by humans is responsible for this discouraging statistic, because it prevents youngsters from having the social experiences necessary for competent adult parenting. The rate of infant survival is higher for wild than captive tamarins, despite the abundance of food and absence of predators in captivity, because wild tamarins have lent a hand (or a back) in the care of younger siblings.[100] Parent-training programs designed to supply missing experiences, impart crucial information, and provide support for parents can improve parenting in species as different as cottontop tamarins, rhesus macaques, gorillas, and humans.

We have seen that an important part of the preparation for parenting is designing a living environment that meets an individual's needs for space, comfort, and company. Housing gorilla mothers in normal family groups and providing sufficient space for them to perform their customary behaviors are key ingredients for normal parenting in this species. But when a nonhuman primate mother has been raised by humans, the provision of an adequate environment may not be enough. Observing an experienced, competent mother care for her offspring allows inexperienced mothers to emulate parenting experts of their own species. Role models for competent mothering have been used successfully in several species of monkeys and apes.

Because infant primates raised by humans often grow up to be inadequate parents, programs have been created for hand-rearing infant primates (whose mothers have either died or are incompetent) to enhance their performance as parents later on. An example of this approach is the Responsive Care Program for chimpanzees at the Yerkes Regional Primate Center, designed by Kim Bard. An intimate knowledge of the normal behavior of chimpanzees, gleaned from field studies in their natural habitat, was the foundation for this program's design.

Bard's goal is to rear chimpanzees who will parent competently as adults.[101] She emphasizes that the best care for any chimpanzee is that offered by its biological mother, and a key component of her program is that human caregivers attempt to model the type of behaviors performed by normal chimpanzee mothers with their infants. For example, caretakers respond to an infant's behavior, rather than initiating interactions with or attempting to stimulate it. Perhaps most important, infant chimpanzees interact with others of their kind—peers or other individuals of various ages—every day. And since hands-on experience is crucial for female chimpanzees to become competent mothers, hand-raised youngsters are given many opportunities to handle young infants. In this way, orphaned chimpanzees acquire the necessary skills for interacting with others as they grow up. Raising chimpanzees who will one day be competent parents requires that they be properly socialized by other chimpanzees and their human caretakers to "fit" into normal chimpanzee society.

Just as chimpanzees need certain key experiences and a proper living environment to parent adequately, so do humans. When human parents are socially isolated, subjected to high stress, have experienced inadequate or abusive parenting, or face full responsibility for parenting before they themselves are fully grown, there is a greater likelihood that their parenting behavior will be impaired. What type of training can be provided for at-risk human parents?

Because social isolation is an enormous risk factor for inadequate parenting, an essential element of effective parenting programs is that older, experienced, parents serve as role models for younger parents who lack social support. One such program has been created in Kansas City, Missouri, by Lynn Blinn Pike of the University of Missouri-Columbia.[102] Called Mentor Moms, this program was designed to pair mature mothers with young pregnant women between the ages of 13 and 22. Experienced mothers educate their younger charges about infant care, encourage them in their quest to finish high school, and advise them about how to avoid another pregnancy. The mentors remain in contact with the young mothers even after their babies are born, continuing to advise, encourage, and support them. Despite the high stress that is a fact of life for many young mothers, having a mentor mom means that they do not face their problems and responsibilities alone.

Three years after the program's inception, the group of young women with mentors was compared to a control group of similar young women without them. The mentored group had a lower risk of depression and social isolation than the control group, and a reduced risk for child abuse.[103] In addition, they breastfed their babies longer and utilized hospital emergency rooms less frequently.

It wasn't simply that the mentored mothers were better educated about childcare; rather, it appeared that the regular contact between mentors and inexperienced mothers increased the chances that new mothers would be receptive to the information given to them. Young mothers with a mentor to lean on were less discouraged, more hopeful, and better able to make use of the advice offered to them—if not this week, then the next—than those without mentors.

Unlike nonhuman primates, inexperienced human parents can take classes, read books, join groups that offer parent-child activities or parenting education, or ask a competent relative or friend for support or advice. Adults maltreated as children can seek psychotherapy before (or after) having children of their own. Humans can use their large, complex brains and their capacity for language to acquire the knowledge needed to parent effectively, and to motivate themselves to change their behavior.

CHAPTER 11

How Much Do Parents Matter?

I WAS the invisible one," said a client who learned as a child to entertain himself; his wife complains that he is distant and uninvolved with her.

"I was afraid whenever Dad was home," said a client who is still afraid to express her feelings, especially to her husband.

"We never talked back to our parents," said a couple with little ability to resolve conflict.

"My mother did everything around the house and my dad was basically uninvolved with housework or raising us kids," said a client whose wife complains that she has raised their children by herself while he devoted himself to his career.

"My dad was very passive; I never respected him," said a woman whose boyfriends have been controlling and domineering.

"My mom never stepped in when my dad was beating me," said a man who has been unable to develop a trusting, intimate relationship with a woman.

"I babysat my younger brothers while my parents went out every weekend," said a woman who has decided not to have children.

From the way my clients describe their families while they were growing up, it is difficult to believe that parents have little effect on how their children turn out. But exactly how much influence do parents have?

In 1924 the first behavioral psychologist, John Watson, wrote the following affirmation of the power of parents: "Give me a dozen healthy infants, well-formed, and my own specified world to bring them up in and I'll guarantee to take any one at random and train him to become any type of specialist I might select—doctor, lawyer, artist, merchant-chief, and, yes, even beggar-man and thief, regardless of his talents, penchants, tendencies, abilities, vocations, and race of his ancestors."[1]

Is it true that parents can mold their children into whatever they want them to be, regardless of talent or inclination? By simply inhabiting the same home, do parents transfer their traits to their children so that they become miniature versions of their parents? When one looks at enduring traits such as intelligence (as measured by IQ), or personality characteristics such as extraversion, sociability, impulsiveness, and moodiness, just to name a few, the answer is a resounding no.

Although the influence of family environment on adult personality is small (in the middle-class, adequately functioning households in which these phenomena have been studied), parents do influence their children's personalities in another, very important way—via their genes. Although no one has demonstrated that single genes control specific behaviors or characteristics, it has been shown that arrays of genes do influence behavior. Many genes may influence the same behavior, and different behaviors may be influenced by the same gene. Studies of identical twins (whose genes are identical) reared by different families show that the personalities of identical twins are more similar to each other than to the family members who raised them. Conversely, the personalities of adopted children reared in the same home do not resemble those of their adoptive family. The behavioral geneticist David Rowe asserts that "individuals who share genes are alike in personality regardless of how they are reared, whereas rearing environment induces little or no personality resemblance."[2]

Behavioral geneticists report that up to 50 percent of the variation in IQ, and a smaller but significant proportion of the variance of many personality traits, can be attributed to genetic make-up.[3] Yet the influence of environment on IQ is also clear, as is demonstrated by a study of 20 French infants abandoned by parents of low socioeconomic status and adopted by upper-middle-class parents.[4] All 20 infants had biological siblings who remained with and were raised by their biological mother in an impoverished environment. When the adoptees and their biological siblings were tested in middle childhood, the average IQ of the adoptees was 14 points higher.

Heredity also may increase the chances (but does not guarantee) that one will suffer from a serious mental illness (such as schizophrenia or mood disorder), become an alcoholic, or engage in criminal behavior. For example, children with a genetic predisposition for schizophrenia (other biological family members have the disease) who are adopted into dysfunctional families are at higher risk of developing a serious mental illness than those adopted into higher functioning families.[5] The findings are similar for adopted children whose biological parents have a history of criminal behavior: when they are adopted into low-functioning homes, about 40 percent commit petty crimes as adults. When they are adopted into high-functioning families, however, only 12 percent were later involved in petty crime.[6] Although behaviors or traits are influenced by genes, it is clear they are not determined by them.

That personality and IQ are influenced by our genes is no surprise to most parents, who can sometimes spot differences between their children from the moment of birth, if not in utero. My older daughter, for example, was an angel in the womb. Never inclined to turn somersaults in the middle of the night, she kicked politely for short periods predictably throughout the day. A placid baby, she has matured into a laid-back adolescent. My younger daughter, a gymnast in utero, kicked harder and more frequently than our older daughter, throughout the day and night, with no respect for sleep or any other maternal activity. An on-the-go baby, she gave up her daily nap at the same time as our older daughter, to my considerable consternation. She remains in perpetual motion today, and is better described as intense and persistent than easy-going. Most parents quickly learn that "equal" treatment does not produce an equal outcome among children, and that individual differences in personality and temperament must be accepted and respected.

It is not the belief of most behavioral geneticists, however, that nature inevitably trumps nurture. In fact, they carefully explain that most of the traits that they study are influenced as much if not more by environmental factors than by genes. If it isn't the shared family environment that influences the development of many personality traits, what "environment" are we talking about?

B̲ECAUSE children in the same family typically are not treated exactly the same way by their parents (for example, the behaviors of children with very different temperaments trigger different parental responses), some aspects of the family environment are better described as nonshared than shared. Perhaps it is the differences in the way parents behave with each child that most crucially affect developmental outcome. For example, differential parental treatment according to birth order could conceivably produce consistent differences in personality if certain predictable personality traits were linked with birth order. Despite the popular idea that parents treat their oldest child differently from their youngest (reflected by a voluminous research literature on birth order as well as a large number of popular books on the subject), scholarly reviews of the research on birth order conclude that it has little or no consistent effect on personality development.[7] What researchers have found is that although parents consistently describe personality differences among their own children that they attribute to birth order, these patterns are most apparent within the family of origin, but disappear in other contexts.[8] Birth-order effects, therefore, may best describe behavior within one's family rather than enduring personality traits.

Other examples of nonshared environment that might influence developmental outcome include differential treatment of boys and girls (either by individual families or culture-wide) and accidents (or chronic illness) experienced by some, but not all, children in a family. A parent's debilitating illness, such as clinical depression, may affect each child differently, depending on his or her temperament and stage of development, and on the availability of other sources of emotional support (such as friends, relatives, coaches, or teachers). Even a child's perception that he or she is treated differently than her siblings, despite a lack of objective evidence, could significantly affect psychological development.[9]

Experience with peers is another type of nonshared environmental influence, which is more important during some developmental stages than others. We have seen that when primate mothers refocus their attention on a new baby, older youngsters often turn to their peers for company. Juvenile and adolescent human and nonhuman primates spend much of their time with companions of the same age.

How crucial are experiences with peers in the formation of personality traits that will endure throughout adulthood? Judith Rich Harris, author of *The Nurture Assumption,* suggests that virtually all of the variation in personality development not accounted for by genes can be attributed to experiences and relationships with peers.[10] Although Harris convincingly argues that family members (parents and siblings) have little effect on the development of a child's personality, her case for the profound influence of peers on personality development, although intriguing, is not bolstered by data. Her reasoning is that if it is not parents that influence personality development, then it must be peers.

Harris's goal is "to dissuade you of the notion that a child's personality—what used to be called 'character'—is shaped or modified by the child's parents."[11] Although Harris allows that parents influence how their children behave at home, she emphasizes that they have little effect on their children's behavior in the world outside the home. From Harris's perspective, if a child does not respond exactly as her parents would, that is evidence of the limited influence of family. But what of the abused child, now an adult, who is not abusive with her own children? Despite the fact that she was raised with violence, her bright, open mind and her nurturing husband have helped her avoid abusing her children: she was able to undo the lessons learned from her parents about childrearing. Does that mean that her parents had no influence on her development? Children learn from their parents, but not only from their parents, and are capable of changing their attitudes and behavior throughout their lives.

A poignant story from Harris's own childhood sets the stage for the development of her adamant belief that peers matter more than parents in the development of a child's personality.[12] Harris described herself as a loud, gregarious, outgoing, and self-confident youngster. Although her mother wanted her to be ladylike and wear frilly dresses, Harris was true to the tomboy within and rejected her parents' attempts to feminize her. When she moved to "a snooty" suburb in the Northeast in the fourth grade, she did not fit in with the other girls, who were interested in sylish hair and pretty clothes. Never accepted by her peer group in the 4 years that she lived there, Harris reveals that she became introverted and insecure—that her personality was permanently changed by her experience with her peers, in contrast to her resilience in the face of her parents' efforts to encourage ladylike behavior—and she never again regained the confident fearlessness of her early childhood. She thanks her peers for rejecting her, however, because if they hadn't, she believes she would have turned out like them.

But Harris's story could be interpreted differently. Perhaps because her parents loved and accepted her, she could be herself with them despite their efforts to make her "a little lady." With her peers, however, not fitting in meant rejection. If she had truly been socialized by her peers, she would have given up her tomboy ways, worn the uniform of her peer group, and more than likely been accepted by them. But her character was strong enough to resist peer pressure. She remained true to herself, just as she had done with her parents. That she responded to rejection by her peers with withdrawal and intro-version in that context is understandable; most of us avoid others who treat us cruelly, regardless of the strength of our relationships with our families. But did Harris truly become less confident, or even insecure, as the result of this experience? Perhaps. But how can we explain her fearlessness as she took on the entire fields of socialization and developmental psychology, and her meticulous efforts to re-fute the life work of her peers? Inhibition, shyness, insecurity, and a lack of self-confidence are not the traits that come to mind in de-scribing the woman that Harris is today.

That we behave similarly to other members of a group we have chosen to join does not imply that the group determines our behav-ior, nor does it negate the importance of family. Teenagers in the same peer group are, without question, behaviorally similar. But is that because the group influences the adolescent, or because the teenager selects the group in which he or she fits best? Socialization researchers agree that "a child with antisocial inclinations may be far more likely to fall into a similarly inclined peer group, than an anti-social peer group is to corrupt a well behaved youngster."[13]

Perhaps a secure relationship with our parents actually facilitates integration into our peer group, which then further influences our psychological growth and development. Research with children re-veals that relationships with parents influence the child's choice of a peer group and the influence of its members. Not only are parents ef-fective at steering their children toward some peer groups and away from others, but the susceptibility of adolescents to the influence of their peers is affected by the nature of their relationship with their parents.[14] Parents who are both demanding and responsive ("author-itative") have adolescents who are less swayed by peer pressure to perform antisocial behaviors (such as using drugs), but are more af-fected by peer pressure to engage in positive behaviors (such as doing well in school).[15] But when parents are harsh or coercive with their children, they may set in motion a chain of events including aggressive behavior and school problems, which in turn may influence the selection of an antisocial peer group by their children.[16]

Rather than choosing between peers and parents as the crucial influences on a youngster's personality, it is more plausible for us to consider the idea that children are influenced in an idiosyncratic way by a variety of experiences or relationships throughout their childhood. This concept, embraced by socialization scientists and behavioral geneticists alike, suggests that children inhabit their own micro-environments: each reacts according to his own temperament, genetic make-up, and life history to environmental events and stressors, treatment by parents and siblings, and experiences with peers, teachers, and others in the community.[17] Although the idea of micro-environments makes a lot of sense, it is difficult to study the complex phenomenon of individual differences in a laboratory setting. This type of single-case study usually is the domain of clinical psychologists, whose focus typically is on recovery rather than research.

Clinical psychologists certainly find evidence of differential parental treatment of children, although differences may not be systematic, consistent, or predictable. In some families the oldest child is favored, but in most families it is the youngest who receives the greatest share of parental love and attention.[18] Boys are preferred in some families, girls in others. Some parents may be thrilled with high academic performance, others with musical or athletic ability. Conversely, a child who lacks talent, or reminds his mother of his absentee father or of characteristics of herself that she dislikes, may be less favored. Children with difficult temperaments (highly irritable, shy, or fearful) are likely to receive less favorable treatment from their parents. In some families a disabled child garners a greater share of parental attention, while in others such a child may be neglected. Harris derides idiosyncratic effects on children as post hoc and unprovable. But just because we cannot consistently predict differential treatment of children by parents on any of these dimensions doesn't mean it does not occur, with harmful results for individual children.

The nature of personality is only one of many developmental outcomes that could be considered in evaluating the influence of parents on their children. What about the effect of parents on a child's sense of well-being, self-esteem, or self-acceptance? Alan Sroufe and his colleagues have followed children's development from infancy to adulthood. They found that from an early age, the nature of parent-child relationships sets the stage for the developmental outcome in many areas, including school success or failure, social competence, and psychopathology.[19] Parents may not influence their children's personality or what they want to be when they grow up, but they may affect their confidence, the likelihood that they will achieve their goals, how they cope with adversity, and even whether or not they like themselves.

THE concept of the good-enough mother, first introduced by the psychoanalyst Donald Woods Winnicott, suggests that parents do not need to be perfect—merely good enough—for their children to grow up healthy and happy.[20] Good-enough parenting will not produce parental clones, but then that isn't the goal of most parents. In fact, many parents coach their children on how to be different from them in an attempt to help them avoid the mistakes they made during their own youth. Parents are unlikely to succeed if their goal is to produce a child who is either just like them or, in contrast, the exact opposite. When parents expose their children to the experiences they need for a balanced life and accept them for who they are, the prognosis for a positive outcome is good.

First and foremost, parents must provide for a child's basic needs. Shelter, nutritious food, clothing, and medical care increase the chances of a child's survival and differentiate a physically healthy child from a neglected one. Basic emotional needs must be met too. We have seen that all primates benefit from considerable parental contact early in life and from the consistent availability of parents while they are growing up. Physical contact is a source of warmth and affection and makes primate young feel loved and safe.

In *Your Child's Self Esteem*, a classic in the parenting literature, Dorothy Corkville Briggs describes parents as a mirror in which a child sees his or her reflection.[21] If what children usually see in their parent's eyes is acceptance, respect, and affection, the outcome is different than when what children see is contempt, disappointment, or disapproval. When parents are developmentally prepared to parent (they are adults, financially able to support a child, eager for the role of parent, and have some support for childrearing), the reflection their child sees is positive more often than not. A teenaged parent, by contrast, who may be unprepared for childrearing, is less likely to consistently offer a positive reflection.

Enough love is a relative thing. In a family whose parents are equally standoffish with each child, none will feel that they were slighted. If, however, only the youngest is showered with affection and attention, older children will feel dismissed, and a lifelong sibling rivalry or resentment of their parents may be the result. Researchers have found that siblings who feel that they have received equivalent treatment from their parents, in terms of affection and control, have less conflict with their brothers and sisters than when they believe that one sibling has received a greater share of the parental goodies.[22] It is easier for nonhuman primates than humans to avoid favoring one offspring over another because the birth spacing characteristic of each nonhuman species ensures that one offspring is developmentally ready to function independently by the time the next arrives.

Behavioral geneticists point out the importance of differentiating parent-to-child from child-to-parent effects: the question is does negative parental behavior produce a difficult child, or does a difficult child elicit negative parental behavior? Certainly both types of effects occur in every family. But even if a child with a difficult temperament provokes his parents to behave negatively toward him, that does not mean that his parents' behavior to him has no effect on his development, or that he "deserves" whatever treatment he receives. Researchers have found that when parents respond harshly to difficult children, their kids are more likely to have behavior problems as adolescents.[23] When parents are able to execute firm, restrictive control with children who are difficult or hard to manage, their children are less likely to exhibit behavior problems or disorders.[24] Children with difficult temperaments may be in even greater need of loving, involved parents than more easy-going youngsters.

We have seen that nonhuman primate mothers are always in close proximity to their infants. Although infants are encouraged in their attempts at independence, nonhuman primate mothers retrieve their youngsters when they are harassed by others in the living group or threatened by a predator. Human children are dependent on their parents even longer than nonhuman primate offspring. They benefit from the consistent availability and watchful eyes of their parents throughout adolescence.

Unlike group-living nonhuman primates, who learn about the relationships between males and females by observing others in their community, human children's first lessons about how men and women relate come from observing their parents. Children notice when one parent dominates the other, one parent beats the other, and conflict is repetitive, unresolved, or simply ignored. Children can't help learning from their parents, regardless of whether the lessons are intentional or helpful. Sometimes children grow up and choose a spouse much like a problematic or poorly functioning parent, perhaps to have another opportunity to resolve a childhood dilemma. At other times, a spouse may be chosen who appears to be the opposite of the offending parent, which provides relief in one area, but may cause problems in another. For example, choosing a passive or disengaged husband as an antidote for a controlling or aggressive father may be disappointing in the long term, when the wife discovers that the absence of aggressive control does not make up for a lack of interaction or initiative. Searching for a spouse who is "not Dad" or "not Mom" greatly reduces our choices in life. Children growing up with parents who respect each other have a better chance of choosing life partners who will do the same.

Just as the gorilla family charges to the rescue when a youngster is perceived to be in danger, human parents must also be aware when their children are threatened. Since threats to their children are not always obvious, parents need to be available and ready to intervene. Parents must set limits on what their children can or cannot do based on their developmental stage and personality. Parents must be willing to dole out responsibility as children become ready to handle it, offer appropriate discipline when it is called for, intervene when changes in a child's behavior suggest that a serious problem is developing, and make sure that they have adequate social support so that they do not lean heavily on their children to help them with their problems, or treat them as partners in parenting younger family members.

THE basic principles of primate parenting—nurturance, physical care, emotional care, discipline (or setting an example for appropriate behavior), protection, and separation (parents focusing attention on a new infant or on themselves as older children become more capable of caring for themselves)—apply to good-enough parenting in all primates, including humans. It is clear that youngsters are pretty resilient and parents do not have to be perfect to achieve an acceptable outcome. The experience of abuse or neglect severely impacts primate youngsters, but even in such extreme circumstances, a poor outcome is not a foregone conclusion. Primate parents without experience (or with traumatic early histories) can improve their parenting skills with education, training, and reliable social support.

We have seen that in nonhuman primates behaviors pass from one generation to the next (whether or not they are skillful or problematic), and that maternal style influences the mothering of the next generation. Human parents who were reasonably contented children similarly may display a parental style similar to that of their parents. But unlike nonhuman primates, adult humans who suffered poor parenting as children often decide to do things differently with their own children, to "make up for" their own negative childhood experiences. Someone with overly strict parents may become too permissive, while a parent who remembers what happened to her as a result of being permitted to run free may compensate by overprotecting her children. Extremes of parental behavior are equally problematic, and it is these extremes in behavior that most differentiate humans from other primate parents.

Parents are not the sole influence on how their offspring turn out, but they do matter. Very good parents may be able to help a child saddled with a difficult temperament or a serious disability be all that he or she can be. But the legacy of neglectful or abusive parenting is vigilant behavior that interferes with trust and the development of loving relationships with others. We don't need to constantly provide enrichment experiences to do a good-enough job with our children, so we can relax about providing educationally stimulating experiences or signing our children up for a relentless schedule of lessons and activities. If we can offer the basics of primate parenting, stay out of their way, and accept the final result with pride and delight, our children have a good chance of becoming the best they can be.

Who's Who among Non-Human Primates

The six main groups of living primates include (1) Malagasy lemurs; pictured are the sifaka (1A) and the aye-aye (1B); (2) galagos, pottos, and lorises; pictured is the slender loris; (3) tarsiers; (4) New World Monkeys; pictured is the titi monkey; (5) Old World Monkeys; pictured is the black and white colobus; (6) apes and humans; pictured are bonobos and humans. Illustration by Laurel Morley.

Prosimians

Prosimians live in Asia, Africa, and on the island of Madagascar. Species in this group include lorises, pottos, bush babies, and lemurs. Of all nonhuman primates, prosimians are both the least like us and the most distantly related to us. It has been about 50 million years since we shared a common ancestor.

Prosimians are in some ways more similar to other mammals than to anthropoid primates. They have wet noses like dogs and cats and rely on their sense of smell more than the visually oriented monkeys and apes. Their brains are smaller and less complex than those of the anthropoid primates. Most mammals are active at night and so are most prosimians, while virtually all monkeys, apes, and humans are most active during the day. Although some prosimians, such as ring-tailed lemurs, are gregarious, most are solitary like other mammals. But even though prosimians are less like humans than monkeys or apes, their forward-facing large eyes and long slender fingers finished with nails instead of claws are dead giveaways that these species are primates.

Tarsiers

Classified somewhere in between prosimians and monkeys is a small group of primates called tarsiers. A tarsier's most striking feature is its huge eyes, each of which is larger than its entire brain.[1] Tarsiers used to be thought of as prosimians, but because they share characteristics with both prosimians and monkeys, many taxonomists now see them as intermediate between the two. Little is known about the behavior of these creatures in the wild and they are rarely displayed in zoos.

Monkeys

New World Monkeys	Old World Monkeys
Marmosets	Macaques
Tamarins	Baboons
Owl monkeys	Mandrills
Titi monkeys	Mangabeys
Capuchins	Talapoin monkeys
Squirrel monkeys	Patas monkeys
Saki monkeys	Vervets
Uakaris	Guenons
Howlers	Colobus monkeys
Spider monkeys	Leaf monkeys
Woolly monkeys	Langurs
Muriquis	Proboscis monkeys

Monkeys are classified into two groups, depending on where they live and the shape of their noses. New World monkeys include almost 80 species of flat-nosed monkeys that live in the tropics of Central and South America. Around 90 species of round-nosed monkeys live in Asia and Africa and are called Old World monkeys.

New World monkeys include the diminutive marmosets and tamarins, family-oriented titi monkeys, nocturnal owl monkeys, manic squirrel monkeys, clever capuchins, leaping sakis, red-faced uakaris, acrobatic spider monkeys, languid howlers, furry woolly monkeys, and the egalitarian muriquis. New World monkeys range in size from quarter-pound pygmy marmosets to 25-pound woolly spider monkeys (often referred to as muriquis, the name given to them by the local indigenous people). Some, such as capuchins, are opportunistic, omnivorous feeders, while others, such as howlers, gorge themselves on leaves and spend their days munching, resting, and defecating. Some New World monkeys prefer fruit, but others diligently hunt for insects or small animals. Some have prehensile tails, which function as an extra arm or leg when the monkey is hanging from or swinging through trees. New World monkeys spend virtually all of their time in trees.

Many New World monkeys live in two-parent nuclear families. All titi and owl monkeys, many saki monkeys, and most marmosets and tamarins are believed to be monogamous. A few species, such as saddleback tamarins, may be polyandrous. Most of the rest live either in harems or in multimale multifemale groups. Mating structure varies with habitat in some species. For example, common marmosets may be polyandrous, polygynous, or members of multimale multifemale groups.

Old World monkeys are often larger than New World monkeys, and range in weight from the 2-pound dwarf guenon to the 80-plus-pound olive baboon. Both cheek-pouch monkeys (macaques, baboons, mangabeys, patas, vervets, and guenons), and leaf-eating monkeys (colobus, langurs, snub-nosed, and proboscis) belong to this group, and all Old World monkeys are active during the day. Old World monkeys vary enormously in appearance, presenting a striking array of colors, patterns, sizes, and unusual physical features.

Male Old World monkeys are significantly larger than females (sometimes even twice their size), and are often equipped with huge canine teeth with which they both intimidate and impress males and females in their living group, as well as fend off predators. Large males may be showy in other ways as well. For example, male mandrills sport bright red-and-blue-striped snouts and rumps, in contrast with females, who are often small, brown, and drab.

Old World monkeys make their living in a variety of ways. Some, such as the douc langur, spend all of their time in trees, and others, such as the hamadryas baboon, live on the ground. Some, such as the black and white colobus monkey, eat only leaves, while others are omnivorous and search for fruit, other plant materials, or animal prey. Old World monkeys live in a wider variety of habitats than New World monkeys, which are essentially restricted to tropical forests. Some Old World monkeys live in arid environments in which food is scarce and water may be hard to find at certain times of year (vervets, patas monkeys, and hamadryas baboons), while others live in lush, tropical, or other forest habitats where food and water are more plentiful (guenons, colobus, douc langurs, and proboscis monkeys). Macaques inhabit the most diverse habitats and climates of any primate other than man. They thrive in arid and tropical environments, in the temperate mountains of Japan (where they are called snow monkeys), and the rhesus macaques of India have even learned to live the urban life, coexisting side by side with humans.

Most Old World monkeys live in single-parent families headed by mothers that are embedded in larger communities. Langurs, drills, and guenons often live in polygynous families, while red colobus, macaques, mandrills, baboons, mangabeys, and vervets belong to communities in which there are no permanent pair bonds between males and females. Monogamy is rare among Old World monkeys.

Apes

Lesser Apes	Great Apes
Gibbons	Orangutans
Siamangs	Gorillas
	Chimpanzees
	Bonobos

Apes and humans are lumped together in the superfamily Hominoidea, which includes 11 species of lesser apes (gibbons and siamangs), 4 species of great apes (orangutans, gorillas, chimpanzees, and bonobos), and, of course, only 1 living species of human, *Homo sapiens*. Apes are easily distinguished from monkeys by their lack of tails, their generally larger size, broader chests, greater tendency to stand and walk upright, and the increased size and complexity of their brains.[2] Because of their large size, apes hang from branches rather than scamper across them, and are acrobats in the trees. They use their long arms to swing from branch to branch, and except for a few species of New World monkeys are the only primates to do so.

Gibbons are small, lithe, apes with serene faces. Long arms with hooklike fingers allow gibbons to swing elegantly and effortlessly through the trees. All known species of gibbons live in the rainforests of southeast Asia, are primarily fruit eaters, and are monogamous. Mated pairs stay together for many years, and as in most monogamous species males and females are about the same size. Pairs defend their territories against intrusion by other gibbon families by singing vocal duets to advertise their territorial boundaries. Their mesmerizing great calls reverberate in a mournful wail throughout the forest and have been described as "one of the wonders of the primate world."[3] Siamangs are closely related to gibbons but are larger and stockier. They live only in Sumatra and on the Malay peninsula and feed mostly on leaves. Like gibbons, siamangs are monogamous.

The four species of great apes (orangutans, gorillas, chimpanzees, and bonobos) are a very diverse group and are genetically more like humans than monkeys or prosimians. The life histories of great apes and humans are similar; females in both groups endure 8- or 9- month pregnancies and care for dependent infants for a relatively longer time than other primates. Great apes are also long-lived like humans; in captivity, apes may live more than 50 years.

Orangutans are quite different from the other three species of great apes. Orangutans are large, agile creatures with bright orange hair and extremely powerful arms for propelling themselves through the forest. They live only in Sumatra and Borneo, in rainforests or swamp forest, and prefer to eat fruit. Males are much larger than females, and the fatty pads on their cheeks signal to females that they are sexually mature. In contrast with all other monkeys and apes, orangutans are solitary.

Gorillas are the largest of all nonhuman primates and are found only in Africa. Far from the image of King Kong, gorillas are gentle creatures who spend their days feeding, resting, and traveling. They select a primarily vegetarian diet, but occasionally feast on juicy invertebrate prey, such as snails, grubs, termites, and ants. Mountain gorillas live in montane and bamboo forests in the Congo, Uganda, and Rwanda, at elevations up to 13,000 feet. Eastern and western lowland gorillas live at lower elevations in primary rainforests, bamboo forests, and marshes, from Nigeria to Zaire. Youngsters often play in trees, but the large size of adult gorillas keeps their feet on the ground most of the time.

Chimpanzees are among the most intelligent of the apes and possess a mercurial disposition. These quick-witted, volatile creatures are capable of many of the endearing and appalling behaviors characteristic of human beings. For example, although chimpanzee females are devoted and loving mothers, at least two wild females are known to have murdered several infants of other females. And though adult males from the same community are closely bonded with one another, groups of males silently patrol the borders of their home range to ambush, and sometimes murder, chimpanzees from other communities.[4]

Chimpanzees live only in Africa, in rainforests, woodland savannah, or grassland habitats. They are omnivores, and though the majority of their diet consists of fruit and leaves, they relish invertebrate and vertebrate prey. Males often join forces to hunt relatively large mammalian prey, such as red colobus monkeys, and they are the only nonhuman primates to do so. Chimpanzees live in multimale multifemale societies, and both males and females have multiple sex partners when females are sexually receptive. Chimpanzee communities may contain up to 100 individuals, but usually are smaller. Their societies are called fission-fusion, because a large community typically breaks up into smaller groups during the day, or over longer periods, in order to engage in desired activities.

Bonobos used to be called pygmy chimpanzees but are no longer, because they are not significantly smaller than chimpanzees. More lithe and slender than chimpanzees, bonobos often stand and walk upright. Bonobos live in tropical lowland rainforests in Zaire and eat fruit, plants, invertebrates, and small mammals. Unlike chimpanzees, they do not hunt for meat. Like chimpanzees, bonobos live in large multimale multifemale fission-fusion communities and mate promiscuously. The bonobo's claim to fame is that it is the most sexual of all nonhuman primates, perhaps even surpassing humans in frequency of sexual behavior.

Notes

Prologue

1. F. Aboitz, "Does bigger mean better? Evolutionary determinants of brain size and structure," *Brain, Behavior, and Evolution* 47 (1996): 225–247.

1. Learning to Parent

1. Charles Snowdon, "Infant care in cooperatively breeding species," in Peter Slater, Jay Rosenblatt, Charles Snowdon, and Manfred Milinski, eds., *Advances in the Study of Behavior*, vol. 25 (San Diego: Academic Press, 1996), pp. 643–689.
2. Charles Snowdon and Stephen Suomi, "Paternal behavior in primates," in H. Fitzgerald, J. Mullins, and P. Gages, eds., *Child Nurturance: Studies of Development in New World Primates*, vol. 3 (New York: Plenum Press, 1982), pp. 63–108.

2. The Primate Recipe for Mothering

1. Frans De Waal, *Good Natured* (Cambridge: Harvard University Press, 1996), p. 6.
2. Karen Strier, personal communication.
3. P. C. Lee, "Ecological constraints on the social development of vervet monkeys," *Behaviour* 91 (1984): 245–262; M. D. Hauser, "Do vervet monkey infants cry wolf?" *Animal Behaviour* 45 (1993): 1242–1244.

4. Lynn Fairbanks and M. T. McGuire, "Maternal condition and the quality of maternal care in vervet monkeys," *Behaviour* 132 (1995): 733–754.

5. Rose Weitz, *The Sociology of Health, Illness, and Health Care: A Critical Approach* (Belmont, CA: Thomson Wadsworth, 2004), p. 108.

6. World Health Organization, *World Health Report* (Geneva: World Health Organization, 1998).

7. Weitz, *The Sociology of Health, Illness, and Health Care*, p. 108.

8. Jeanne Altmann, "Adolescent pregnancies in non-human primates: An ecological and developmental perspective," in Jane Lancaster and Beatrix Hamburg, eds., *School-Age Pregnancy and Parenthood* (New York: Aldine De Gruyter, 1986), pp. 247–262.

9. Dian Fossey, *Gorillas in the Mist* (Boston: Houghton Mifflin, 1983), p. 75.

10. C. E. G. Tutin and P. R. McGinnis, "Chimpanzee reproduction in the wild," in C. E. Graham, ed., *Reproductive Biology of the Great Apes* (New York: Academic Press, 1981), pp. 239–264; A. H. Harcourt, Dian Fossey, K. J. Stewart, and D. P. Watts, "Reproduction in wild gorillas and some comparisons with chimpanzees," *Journal of Reproduction and Fertility* Supplement 28 (1980): 59–70; Altmann, "Adolescent pregnancies in non-human primates," pp. 247–262.

11. Melvin Konner and Marjorie Shostak, "Adolescent pregnancy and child bearing: an anthropological perspective," in Jane Lancaster and Beatrix Hamburg, eds., *School-Age Pregnancy and Parenthood* (New York: Aldine De Gruyter, 1986), pp. 325–346.

12. Altmann, "Adolescent pregnancies in non-human primates," pp. 247–262.

13. Lorna Johnson, Andrew Petto, and Prabhat Sehgal, "Factors in the rejection and survival of captive cotton top tamarins *(Saguinus oedipus)*," *American Journal of Primatology* 25 (1991): 91–102; Sarah Blaffer Hrdy, "Natural born mothers," *Natural History* 104, no. 12 (1995): 30–42.

14. Joan Silk, Susan Alberts, and Jeanne Altmann, "Social bonds of female baboons enhance infant survival," *Science* 302 (Nov. 14, 2003): 1231–1234.

15. Robert Hinde and Yvette Spencer-Booth, "The effect of social companions on mother-infant relationships in rhesus monkeys," in D.

Morris, ed., *Primate Ethology* (London: Weidenfeld and Nicolson, 1967), pp. 267–286.

16. D. Horenstein, "The dynamics and treatment of child abuse: can primate research provide the answers?" *Journal of Clinical Psychology* 33 (1977): 563–565; Jill Korbin, "The cross cultural context of child abuse and neglect," in C. Henry Kempe and Ray Helfer, eds., *The Battered Child*, 3rd ed. (Chicago: University of Chicago Press, 1980), pp. 21–35; Jill Korbin, *Child Abuse and Neglect: Cross Cultural Perspectives* (Berkeley: University of California Press, 1981); Nancy Nicolson, "Maternal behavior in human and nonhuman primates," in J. D. Loy and C. B. Peters, eds., *Understanding Behavior: What Primate Studies Tell Us about Human Behavior* (New York: Oxford University Press, 1991), pp. 17–50.

17. M. H. Klaus and J. H. Kennell, *Maternal-Infant Bonding* (St. Louis: Mosby, 1976), pp. 1–15.

18. Christopher Coe, "Psychobiology of maternal behavior in nonhuman primates," in N. A. Krasnegor and R. S. Bridges, eds., *Mammalian Parenting* (Oxford: Oxford University Press, 1990), pp. 157–183.

19. Wladyslaw Sluckin, "Human mother-to-infant bonds," in W. Sluckin and M. Herbert, eds., *Parental Behaviour* (Oxford: Basil Blackwell, 1986), pp. 208–227; Stella Chess and A. Thomas, "Infant bonding: mystique and reality," *American Journal of Orthopsychiatry* 52 (1982): 213–222.

20. Sluckin, "Human mother-to-infant bonds," pp. 208–227.

21. Robert Hinde, Thelma Rowell, and Yvette Spencer-Booth, "Behaviour of socially living rhesus monkeys in their first six months," *Proceedings of the Zoological Society of London* 143 (1964): 609–649; Robert Hinde and Yvette Spencer-Booth, "The behaviour of socially living rhesus monkeys in their first two and a half years," *Animal Behavior* 15 (1967): 169–196.

22. Hinde, Rowell, and Spencer-Booth, "Behaviour of socially living rhesus monkeys in their first six months," pp. 609–649; Hinde and Spencer-Booth, "The behaviour of socially living rhesus monkeys in their first two and a half years," pp. 169–196.

23. G. Berkson, "Social responses of animals to infants with defects," in M. Levine and L. Rosenblum, eds., *The Effect of the Infant on Its Caregiver* (New York: Wiley, 1974), pp. 233–249; Karyl Swartz and Leon-

ard Rosenblum, "The social context of parental behavior: a perspective on primate socialization," in D. Gubernick and P. H. Klopfer, eds., *Parental Care in Mammals* (New York: Plenum Press, 1981), pp. 417–455; Jane Goodall, *The Chimpanzees of Gombe: Patterns of Behavior* (Cambridge: The Belknap Press of Harvard University Press, 1986), p. 383; Nicolson, "Maternal behavior in human and nonhuman primates," pp. 17–50.

24. Harry Harlow and Margaret Harlow, "The affectional systems," in A. M. Schrier, H. F. Harlow, and F. Stollnitz, eds., *Behavior of Nonhuman Primates*, vol. 2 (New York: Academic Press, 1965), pp. 287–334.

25. Harry Harlow and R. R. Zimmerman, "Affectional responses in the infant monkey," *Science* 130 (1959): 421.

26. M. D. S. Ainsworth, "The development of infant-mother attachment," in B. M. Caldwell and H. N. Ricciuti, eds., *Review of Child Development Research*, vol. 3 (Chicago: University of Chicago Press, 1973), pp. 54–55; M. D. S. Ainsworth, S. M. Bell, and D. J. Stayton, "Infant-mother attachment and social development: socialisation as a product of reciprocal responsiveness to signals," in M. P. M. Richards, ed., *The Integration of a Child into a Social World* (Cambridge: Cambridge University Press, 1974), pp. 99–135.

27. J. D. Higley and Stephen Suomi, "Parental behaviour in nonhuman primates," in Wladyslaw Sluckin and Martin Herbert, eds., *Parental Behaviour* (Oxford: Basil Blackwell, 1986), pp. 160–161; John Bowlby, *Attachment and Loss*, vol. 1: *Attachment* (London: Hogarth Press, 1969), p. 253.

28. Higley and Suomi, "Parental behaviour in nonhuman primates," pp. 160–161.

29. Leanne Nash, personal communication.

30. John Bowlby, "The making and breaking of affectional bonds: 1. Aetiology and psychopathology in the light of attachment theory," *British Journal of Psychiatry* 130 (1977): 203.

31. Fossey, *Gorillas in the Mist*, p. 72.

32. Goodall, *The Chimpanzees of Gombe*, pp. 368–372; Lynn Fairbanks, "Individual differences in maternal style," *Advances in the Study of Behavior* 25 (1996): 579–611.

33. Lynn Fairbanks, personal communication.

34. Lynn Fairbanks, "Individual differences in maternal style," *Advances in the Study of Behavior* 25 (1996): 579–611.

35. Carol Berman, "Consistency in maternal behavior within families of free-ranging rhesus monkeys: an extension of the concept of maternal style," *American Journal of Primatology* 22 (1990): 159–169.

36. Lee, "Ecological constraints on the social development of vervet monkeys," pp. 245–262; M. D. Hauser and Lynn Fairbanks, "Mother-offspring conflict in vervet monkeys: variation in response to ecological conditions," *Animal Behaviour* 36 (1988): 802–813; P. C. Lee, P. Majluf, and I. J. Gordon, "Growth, weaning, and maternal investment from a comparative perspective," *Journal of Zoology* (London) 225 (1991): 99–114.

37. Hauser and Fairbanks, "Mother-offspring conflict in vervet monkeys," pp. 802–813; Nicolson, "Maternal behavior in human and nonhuman primates," pp. 17–50.

38. Lynn Fairbanks, "Vervet monkey grandmothers: effects on mother-infant relationships," *Behaviour* 104 (1988): 176–188.

39. Lynn Fairbanks and M. T. McGuire, "Mother-infant relationships in vervet monkeys: response to new adult males," *International Journal of Primatology* 8 (1987): 351–366.

40. Jeanne Altmann, *Baboon Mothers and Infants* (Cambridge: Harvard University Press, 1980), pp. 130–136.

41. Lynn Fairbanks, "Early experience and cross-generational continuity of mother-infant contact in vervet monkeys," *Developmental Psychobiology* 22 (1989): 669–681.

42. Berman, "Consistency in maternal behavior within families of free-ranging rhesus monkeys," pp. 159–169.

43. Jerome Kagan and N. Snidman, "Temperamental factors in human development," *American Psychologist* 46 (1991): 856–862; Jerome Kagan, "How we become who we are: reflections on the mystery of the human personality," *Family Therapy Networker* 22, no. 5 (1998): 52–63.

44. Lynn Fairbanks and M. T. McGuire, "Long-term effects of early mothering behavior on the responsiveness to the environment in vervet monkeys," *Developmental Psychobiology* 21 (1988): 711–724; Fairbanks, "Individual differences in maternal style," pp. 579–611.

45. Lynn Fairbanks and M. T. McGuire, "Maternal protectiveness and re-

sponse to the unfamiliar in vervet monkeys," *American Journal of Primatology* 30 (1993): 119–129.

46. Lee, "Ecological constraints on the social development of vervet monkeys," pp. 245–262; Hauser, "Do vervet monkey infants cry wolf?" pp. 1242–1244; Fairbanks, "Individual differences in maternal style," pp. 579–611.

47. R. I. M. Dunbar, "Demography and reproduction," in B. Smuts, D. Cheney, R. Seyfarth, R. Wrangham, and T. Struhsaker, eds., *Primate Societies* (Chicago: University of Chicago Press, 1987), pp. 240–249.

48. Robert Hinde, *Biological Bases of Human Social Behaviour* (New York: McGraw-Hill, 1974), pp. 200—203; Fairbanks, "Individual differences in maternal style," p. 574.

49. Hinde, *Biological Bases of Human Social Behaviour,* pp. 229–230; Altmann, *Baboon Mothers and Infants,* pp. 136–167.

50. Coe, "Psychobiology of maternal behavior in nonhuman primates," pp. 157–183.

51. Nancy Nicolson, "Infants, mothers, and other females," in B. Smuts, D. Cheney, R. Seyfarth, R. Wrangham, and T. Struhsaker, eds., *Primate Societies* (Chicago: University of Chicago Press, 1987), pp. 330–342.

52. De Waal, *Good Natured,* the caption from the eighth picture in the section "Cognition and Empathy," which follows p. 88.

53. Nicolson, "Maternal behavior in human and nonhuman primates," pp. 17–50.

54. Carol Berman, "Variation in mother-infant relationships: traditional and nontraditional factors," in M. Small, ed., *Female Primates: Studies by Women Primatologists* (New York: Alan Liss, 1984), pp. 17–36.

55. Robert LeVine, "Parental goals: a cross-cultural view," *Teachers College Record* 76 (1974): 226–239.

56. Meredith Small, *Our Babies, Ourselves* (New York: Anchor Books, 1998), pp. 102–107.

57. Higley and Suomi, "Parental behaviour in nonhuman primates," p. 167.

58. Galdikas, *Reflections of Eden,* p. 140.

59. Goodall, *The Chimpanzees of Gombe,* p. 383.

60. R. B. Lee, *The !Kung San* (Cambridge: Cambridge University Press, 1979), p. 1.

61. Ibid., p. 310.
62. M. J. Konner and C. Worthman, "Nursing frequency, gonadal function, and birth spacing among !Kung hunter-gatherers," *Science* 207 (1980): 788–791.
63. Sarah Blaffer Hrdy, *Mother Nature* (New York: Pantheon Books, 1999), pp. 199–201.
64. Gabrielle Palmer, *The Politics of Breastfeeding* (London: Pandora Press, 1988), pp. 20–23.
65. Ibid., pp. 82–83.
66. Linda Blum, *At the Breast: Ideologies of Breastfeeding and Motherhood in the Contemporary United States* (Boston: Beacon Press, 1999), p. 43.
67. Marilyn Yalom, *A History of the Breast* (New York: Ballantine Books, 1997), p. 142.
68. Ibid., p. 141; *New York Times Magazine*, July 27, 1975.
69. Small, *Our Babies, Ourselves*, p. 204.
70. Yalom, *A History of the Breast*, p. 141.
71. Ibid.
72. Small, *Our Babies, Ourselves*, pp. 193–195.
73. Emma Ross, "Mother's milk prevents obesity?" *Arizona Republic*, July 16, 1999.
74. Ruth Lawrence, *A Review of the Medical Benefits and Contraindications to Breastfeeding in the United States*, Maternal and Child Health Technical Information Bulletin (Arlington, VA: National Center for Education and Maternal and Child Health, 1997); Jeanne Raisler, Cheryl Alexander, and Patricia O'Campto, "Breast-feeding and infant illness: a dose-response relationship?" *American Journal of Public Health* 89 (1999): 25–30.
75. F. F. Schacter, M. L. Fuches, P. Bijur, and R. K. Stone, "Cosleeping and sleep problems in Hispanic-American urban young children," *Pediatrics* 84 (1989): 522–530.
76. Small, *Our Babies, Ourselves*, p. 112.
77. Ibid., p. 122.
78. Ibid., p. 175.
79. S. M. Bell and M. D. S. Ainsworth, "Infant crying and maternal responsiveness," *Child Development* 43 (1972): 1171–1190.
80. Small, *Our Babies, Ourselves*, pp. 153–155.

81. U. A. Hunziker and R. G. Barr, "Increased carrying reduces infant crying: a randomized controlled trial," *Pediatrics* 77 (1986): 641–648.

82. Betsy Lozoff and Gary Brittenham, "Infant care: cache or carry," *Behavioral Pediatrics* 95 (1979): 478–483; Melvin Konner, "Maternal care, infant behavior, and development among the !Kung," in R. B. Lee and I. DeVore, eds., *Kalahari Hunter-Gatherers: Studies of the !Kung San and Their Neighbors* (Cambridge: Harvard University Press, 1976), pp. 218–245.

83. Lozoff and Brittenham, "Infant care: cache or carry," pp. 478–483.

3. The Diversity of Primate Fathering

1. Devra Kleiman and J. R. Malcolm, "The evolution of male parental investment in mammals," in D. J. Gubernick and P. H. Klopfer, eds., *Parental Care in Mammals* (New York: Plenum Press, 1981), pp. 347–388.

2. Jonathan Bloom-Feshbach, "Historical perspectives on the father's role," in Michael Lamb, ed., *The Role of the Father in Child Development,* 2nd ed. (New York: John Wiley and Sons, 1981), pp. 71–112; Meredith Small, *Our Babies, Ourselves* (New York: Anchor Books, 1998), p. 31.

3. Sarah Blaffer Hrdy, Charles Janson, and Carel van Schaik, "Infanticide: let's not throw out the baby with the bath water," *Evolutionary Anthropology* 3 (1995): 151–154.

4. Sarah Blaffer Hrdy, *Mother Nature* (New York: Pantheon Books, 1999), p. 414.

5. D. P. Watts, "Infanticide in mountain gorillas. New cases and a review of evidence," *Ethology* 81 (1989): 1–18; Carolyn Crockett and R. Sekulic, "Infanticide in red howler monkeys *(Alouatta seniculus),*" in G. Hausfater and S. B. Hrdy, eds., *Infanticide: Comparative and Evolutionary Perspectives* (New York: Aldine, 1984), pp. 173–192; Hrdy, Janson, and van Schaik, "Infanticide: let's not throw out the baby with the bath water," pp. 151–154.

6. Carola Borries, Kristin Launhardt, Cornelia Epplen, Jörg Epplen, and Paul Winkler, "Males as infant protectors in Hanuman langurs *(Presbytis entellus)* living in multimale groups—defence pattern, pa-

ternity, and sexual behavior," *Behavioral Ecology and Sociobiology* 46 (1999): 350–356.

7. John Early and John Peters, *The Xilixana Yanomami of the Amazon* (Gainesville, FL: The University Press of Florida, 2000), pp. 27–28.

8. Kim Hill and Magdalena Hurtado, "Hunter-gatherers of the new world," *American Scientist,* Sept.-Oct. (1990): 437–443; Kim Hill and Magdalena Hurtado, *Áche life History: The Ecology and Demography of a Foraging People* (Hawthorne, NY: Aldine de Gruyter, 1996), pp. 435–439.

9. Martin Daly and Margo Wilson, "Abuse and neglect of children in evolutionary perspective," in R. D. Alexander and D. W. Tinkle, eds., *Natural Selection and Social Behavior: Recent Research and New Theory* (New York: Chiron Press, 1981), pp. 405–416; Martin Daly and Margo Wilson, "Stepparenthood and the evolved psychology of discriminative parental solicitude," in S. Parmigiani and F. S. von Saal, eds., *Infanticide and Parental Care* (London: Harwood Press), pp. 121–134.

10. Hrdy, *Mother Nature,* p. 244.

11. Kleiman and Malcolm, "The evolution of male parental investment in mammals," pp. 347–388; Mary Maxwell Katz and Melvin Konner, "The role of the father: an anthropological perspective," in Michael Lamb, ed., *The Role of the Father in Child Development,* 2nd ed. (New York: Wiley, 1981), pp. 155–186.

12. Barry Hewlett, "Husband-wife reciprocity and the father-infant relationship among Aka pygmies," in Barry S. Hewlett, ed., *Father-Child Relations: Cultural and Biosocial Contexts* (New York: Aldine de Gruyter, 1992), pp. 153–176.

13. Frank Marlowe, "Paternal investment and the human mating system," *Behavioural Processes* 51 (2000): 45–61.

14. D. M. Taub and P. Mehlman, "Primate paternalistic investment: a cross-species view," in J. D. Loy and C. B. Peters, eds., *Understanding Behavior: What Primate Studies Tell Us about Human Behavior* (New York: Oxford University Press, 1991), pp. 51–89; Michael Lamb, Joseph Pleck, Eric Charnov, and James Levine, "A biosocial perspective on paternal behavior and involvement," in Jane Lancaster, Jeanne Altmann, A. S. Rossi, and L. R. Sherrod, eds., *Parenting across the Life Span* (New York: Aldine de Gruyter, 1987), pp. 111–142.

15. Lamb et al., "A biosocial perspective on paternal behavior and involvement," pp. 111–142.

16. Patricia Whitten, "Infants and adult males," in Barbara Smuts, Dorothy Cheney, Robert Seyfarth, Richard Wrangham, and Thomas Struhsaker, eds., *Primate Societies* (Chicago: University of Chicago Press, 1987), pp. 343–357.

17. Patricia Wright, "Biparental care in *Aotus trivirgatus* and *Callicebus molloch*," in Meredith Small, ed., *Female Primates: Studies by Women Primatologists* (New York: Alan R. Liss, 1984), pp. 59–75.

18. Ibid., p. 63.

19. Warren Kinzey and M. Becker, "Activity patterns of the masked titi monkey, *Callicebus personatus*," *Primates* 24 (1983): 337–343.

20. Hewlett, "Husband-wife reciprocity," pp. 153–176.

21. Ibid.

22. Ibid.

23. Graeme Russell, "Primary caregiving fathers," in Michael Lamb, ed., *Parenting and Child Development in "Nontraditional" Families* (Mahwah, NJ: Lawrence Erlbaum, 1999), pp. 57–82.

24. Ibid.

25. Ibid.

26. Whitten, "Infants and adult males," pp. 343–357.

27. Ibid.; Joseph Pleck, "Paternal involvement: levels, sources and consequences," in Michael Lamb, ed., *The Role of the Father in Child Development*, 3rd ed. (New York: Wiley, 1997), pp. 66–103; Michael Lamb, "Fathers and child development: an introductory overview," in Lamb, ed., *The Role of the Father in Child Development*, 3rd ed., pp. 1–18.

28. Katz and Konner, "The role of the father," pp. 155–186.

29. Joseph Pleck, *Husbands' and Wives' Paid Work, Family Work, and Adjustment* (Wellesley: Wellesley College Center for Research on Women Working Papers, 1982).

30. T. W. Ransom and B. S. Ransom, "Adult male-infant relations among baboons *(Papio anubis)*," *Folia Primatologica* 16 (1971): 179–195. Jeanne Altmann, *Baboon Mothers and Infants* (Cambridge: Harvard University Press, 1980), pp. 109–115.

31. Altmann, *Baboon Mothers and Infants*, pp. 112–115.

32. Ibid., p. 206.

33. Ransom and Ransom, "Adult male-infant relations among baboons," pp. 179–175; Jeanne Altmann, "Infant independence in yellow baboons," in G. M. Burghardt and M. Bekoff, eds., *The Development of Behavior: Comparative and Evolutionary Aspects* (New York: Garland STPM Press, 1978), pp. 253–277.

34. Jason Buchan, Susan Alberts, Joan Silk, and Jeanne Altmann, "True paternal care in a multi-male primate society," *Nature* 425 (Sept. 2003): 179–181.

35. Ryne Palombit, Robert Seyfarth, and Dorothy Cheney, "The adaptive value of 'friendships' to female baboons: experimental and observational evidence," *Animal Behaviour* 54 (1997): 599–614.

36. Carolyn Crockett, personal communication.

37. Katz and Konner, "The role of the father," pp. 155–186.

38. Borries et al., "Males as infant protectors in Hanuman langurs," pp. 350–356.

39. Frank Du Mond, "The squirrel monkey in a seminatural environment," in L. A. Rosenblum and R. W. Cooper, eds., *The Squirrel Monkey* (New York: Academic Press, 1968), pp. 115–123.

40. Lamb et al., "A biosocial perspective on paternal behavior and involvement," pp. 111–142.

41. Michael Lamb, "Father-infant and mother-infant interactions in the first year of life," *Child Development* 48 (1977): 167–181.

42. Michael Yogman, "Games fathers and mothers play with their infants," *Infant Mental Health Journal* 2 (1981): 241–248; T. G. Power and Ross Parke, "Toward a taxonomy of father-infant and mother-infant play patterns," paper presented to the Society for Research in Child Development, San Francisco, March 1979.

43. M. Kotelchuck, "The infant's relationship to the father: experimental evidence," in Michael Lamb, ed., *The Role of the Father in Child Development*, 1st ed. (New York: Wiley, 1976), pp. 329–344.

44. Michael Lamb, "Interactions between eight-month-old children and their fathers and mothers," in Michael Lamb, ed., *The Role of the Father in Child Development*, 1st ed. (New York: Wiley, 1976), pp. 307–327.

45. Ross Parke and Stephen Suomi, "Adult male-infant relationships: human and nonhuman primate evidence," in Klaus Immelmann, George Barlow, Lewis Petrinovich, and Mary Main, eds., *Behavioral*

Development: The Bielefeld Interdisciplinary Project (Cambridge: Cambridge University Press, 1980), pp. 700–725.

46. Lamb et al., "A biosocial perspective on paternal behavior and involvement," pp. 111–142; Graeme Russell, *The Changing Role of Fathers* (St. Lucia, Queensland: University of Queensland Press, 1983), pp. 27–41; Ross Parke and Barbara Tinsely, "The father's role in infancy: determinants of involvement in caregiving and play," in Michael Lamb, ed., *The Role of the Father in Child Development,* 2nd ed. (New York: John Wiley & Sons, 1981), pp. 429–457.

47. Russell, *The Changing Role of Fathers,* pp. 27–41.

48. Lamb et al., "A biosocial perspective on paternal behavior and involvement," pp. 111–142.

49. Jay Belsky, "Mother-infant interaction: a naturalistic observational study," *Developmental Psychology* 15 (1979): 601–607; Lamb, "Father-infant and mother-infant interactions in the first year of life," pp. 167–181; Kotelchuck, "The infant's relationship to the father," pp. 329–344.

50. Lamb, "Interactions between eight-month-old children and their fathers and mothers," pp. 307–327.

51. Ross Parke, S. E. O'Leary, and S. West, "Mother-father-newborn interaction: effects of maternal medication, labor, and sex of infant," *Proceedings of the 80th Annual Convention of the American Psychological Association* (1972): 85–86. This was cited in Ross Parke and Barbara Tinsley, "The father's role in infancy," in M. E. Lamb, *The Role of the Father in Child Development,* 2nd ed. (New York: John Wiley and Sons, 1981), pp. 430–432.

52. A. M. Frodi, Michael Lamb, L. A. Leavitt, W. L. Donovan, C. Neff, and D. Sherry, "Fathers' and mothers' responses to the faces and cries of normal and premature infants," *Developmental Psychology* 14 (1978): 490–498.

53. Michael Lamb, "The development of father-infant relationships," in Michael Lamb, ed., *The Role of the Father in Child Development,* 2nd ed. (New York: Wiley, 1981), pp. 459–488.

54. B. Geiger, *Fathers as Primary Caregivers* (Westport, CT: Greenwood, 1996), p. 9.

55. Tiffany Field, "Interaction behaviors of primary versus secondary caretaker fathers," *Developmental Psychology* 14 (1978): 183–184;

Barbara Risman, *Gender Vertigo: American Families in Transition* (New Haven: Yale University Press, 1998), p. 110; L. D. Hall, A. J. Walter, and A. C. Acock, "Gender and family work in one-parent households," *Journal of Marriage and the Family* 57 (1995): 685–692.

56. Lamb, "The development of father-infant relationships," pp. 459–488.

57. D. M. Taub, and P. Mehlman, "Primate paternalistic investment: a cross-species view," in J. D. Loy and C. B. Peters, eds., *Understanding Behavior: What Primate Studies Tell Us about Human Behavior* (New York: Oxford University Press, 1991), pp. 51–89; Katz and Konner, "The role of the father," pp. 155–186.

58. S. H. Henderson and R. P. Dalton, "Parent-child relationships in simple-step, complex-step, and nondivorced families," paper presented at the biennial meeting of the Society for Research in Child Development, Indianapolis, April 1995; E. Mavis Hetherington and Sandra Henderson, "Fathers in stepfamilies," in Michael Lamb, ed., *The Role of the Father in Child Development*, 3rd ed. (New York: Wiley, 1997), pp. 212–226.

59. Carel van Schaik and Andreas Paul, "Male care in primates: does it ever reflect paternity?" *Evolutionary Anthropology* (1997): 152–157.

60. Taub and Mehlman, "Primate paternalistic investment: a cross-species view," pp. 51–89.

61. D. M. Taub, "Male caretaking behavior among wild Barbary macaques *(Macaca sylvanus),*" in D. M. Taub, ed., *Primate Paternalism* (New York: Van Nostrand Reinhold, 1984), pp. 20–55.

62. J. M. Deag and J. M. Crook, "Social behaviour and 'agonistic buffering' in the wild Barbary macaque *Macaca sylvanus L.*," *Folia Primatologica* 15 (1971): 183–200; F. D. Burton, "The integration of biology and behavior in the socialization of *Macaca sylvana* of Gibraltar," in F. E. Poirier, ed., *Primate Socialization* (New York: Random House, 1972), pp. 26–62.

63. Nelly Ménard, Franziska von Segesser, Wolfgang Scheffrahn, Jennifer Pastorini, Dominique Vallet, Gaci Belkacem, Robert Martin, and Annie Gautier-Hion, "Is male-infant caretaking related to paternity and/ or mating activities in wild Barbary macaques *(Macaca sylvanus)?*" *Life Sciences* 324 (2001): 6.

64. Jane Lancaster and Hillard Kaplan, "Parenting other men's children: costs, benefits, and consequences," in Lee Cronk, Napoleon Chagnon,

and William Irons, eds., *Adaptation and Human Behavior: An Anthropological Perspective* (New York: Aldine de Gruyter, 2000), pp. 179–202.

65. Jonathan Bloom-Feshbach, "Historical perspectives on the father's role," pp. 71–112.

66. Donald Lindburg, "The rhesus monkey in northern India: an ecological and behavioral study," in L. A. Rosenblum, ed., *Primate Behavior*, vol. 2 (New York: Academic Press, 1971), p. 88.

67. S. H. Vessey and D. B. Meikle, "Free-living rhesus monkeys: adult male interactions with infants and juveniles," in D. B. Taub, ed., *Primate Paternalism* (New York: Van Nostrand Reinhold, 1984), pp. 113–126.

68. Thelma Rowell, Robert Hinde, and Yvette Spencer-Booth, "Aunt-infant interaction in captive rhesus monkeys," *Journal of Animal Behavior* 12 (1964): 219–226; Thelma Rowell, "Contrasting adult male roles in different species of nonhuman primates," *Archives of Sexual Behavior* 3 (1974): 143–149; Yvette Spencer-Booth, "The behavior of group companions towards rhesus monkey infants," *Animal Behavior* 16 (1968): 541–557.

69. Vessey and Meikle, "Free-living rhesus monkeys," pp. 113–126.

70. William Redican, "Adult male-infant interactions in nonhuman primates," in Michael Lamb, ed., *The Role of the Father in Child Development*, 1st ed. (New York: John Wiley & Sons, 1976), pp. 345–385; William Redican and Gary Mitchell, "Play between adult male and infant rhesus monkeys," *American Zoologist* 14 (1974): 295–302.

71. Stephen Suomi, "Adult male-infant interactions among monkeys living in nuclear families," *Child Development* 48 (1977): 1255–1265; Stephen Suomi, "Differential development of various social relationships by rhesus monkey infants," in M. Lewis and L. A. Rosenblum, eds., *The Child and Its Family* (New York: Plenum Press, 1979), pp. 219–244.

72. Stephen Suomi, C. D. Eisele, S. A. Grady, and R. L. Tripp, "Social preferences of monkeys reared in an enriched laboratory environment," *Child Development* 44 (1973): 451–460.

73. Arlie Hochschild, "Understanding the future of fatherhood: the 'daddy hierarchy' and beyond," in M. C. P. van Dongen, G. A. B. Frinking, and M. J. G. Jacobs, eds., *Changing Fatherhood: An Interdisciplinary Perspective* (Amsterdam: Thesis, 1995), pp. 219–230.

74. Michael Lamb, "Fathers and child development: an introductory overview," in Michael Lamb, ed., *The Role of the Father in Child Development*, 3rd ed. (New York: Wiley, 1997), pp. 1–18.

75. Katz and Konner, "The role of the father," pp. 155–186.

76. C. Alcorta, "Paternal behavior and group competition," *Behavior Science Research*, 17 (1982): 3–23.

77. Barry Hewlett, "Demography and childcare in preindustrial societies," *Journal of Anthropological Research*, 47, no. 1 (1991): 1–38; Hewlett, "Husband-wife reciprocity," pp. 153–176.; Karen Endicott, "Fathering in an egalitarian society," in Barry Hewlett, ed., *Father-Child Relations: Cultural and Biosocial Contexts* (New York: Aldine de Gruyter, 1992), pp. 281–295; P. Bion Griffin and Marcus Griffin, "Fathers and childcare among the Cagayan Agta," in Hewlett, ed., *Father-Child Relations: Cultural and Biosocial Contexts,* pp. 297–320.

78. Katz and Konner, "The role of the father," pp. 155–186.

79. Bloom-Feshbach, "Historical perspectives on the father's role," pp. 71–112.

80. U.S. Bureau of the Census, *Statistical Abstract of the United States* (Washington, DC, 2002), table 570, p. 373.

81. Arlie Hochschild, *The Second Shift* (New York: Avon Books, 1989), pp.1–10; Alexander Szalai, *The Use of Time: Daily Activities of Urban and Suburban Populations in Twelve Countries* (The Hague: Mouton, 1972), pp. 254–257.

82. Gisela Epple, "Parental behavior in *Saguinus fuscicollis* spp. *(Callitrichidae)*," *Folia Primatologica* 24 (1975): 221–238.

83. Charles Snowdon and Stephen Suomi, "Paternal behavior in primates," in H. Fitzgerald, J. Mullins and P. Gages, eds., *Child Nurturance: Studies of Development in New World Primates,* vol. 3 (New York: Plenum Press, 1982), pp. 63–108.

84. Ross Parke and Stephen Suomi, "Adult male-infant relationships: human and nonhuman primate evidence," in Klaus Immelmann, George W. Barlow, Lewis Petrinovich, and Mary Main, eds., *Behavioral Development: The Bielefeld Interdisciplinary Project* (Cambridge: Cambridge University Press, 1980), pp. 700–725; Katz and Konner, "The role of the father," pp. 155–186; C. S. Lewis, "The role of the father in the human family," in W. Sluckin and M. Herbert, eds., *Parental Behaviour* (Oxford: Basil Blackwell, 1986), pp. 228–259.

85. T. S. Weisener, "Socialization for parenthood in sibling caretaking societies," in Jane Lancaster, Jeanne Altmann, A. S. Rossi, and L. R. Sherrod, eds., *Parenting across the Life Span* (New York: Aldine de Gruyter, 1987), pp. 237–270.

86. J. Manion, "A study of fathers and infant caretaking," *Birth and the Family Journal* 4 (1977): 174–179.

87. P. R. Zelazo, M. Kotelchuck, L. Barber, and J. David, "Fathers and sons: an experimental facilitation of attachment behaviors," paper presented to the Society for Research in Child Development, New Orleans, March 1977.

88. J. Lind, "Observations after delivery of communications between mother-infant-father," paper presented at the International Congress of Pediatrics, Buenos Aires, 1974.

89. Monica Davis, "The baby brigade," *Arizona Republic,* Sept. 6, 1998, p. EV5.

90. Lamb, "Fathers and child development," pp. 1–18.

91. Ibid.

92. W. P. O'Hare, *KIDS COUNT Data Book* (New York: Annie Casie Foundation, 1995), p. 5.

93. Joseph Pleck, *Working Wives / Working Husbands* (Beverly Hills: SAGE Publications, 1985), pp. 77–82; Lamb, "Fathers and child development," pp. 77–82.

94. Michael Lamb, "The development of father-infant relationships," in Michael Lamb, ed., *The Role of the Father in Child Development,* 3rd ed. (New York: Wiley, 1997), pp. 104–120.

95. L. Haas, *Equal Parenthood and Social Policy* (Albany: State University of New York Press, 1992), pp. 77–80.

96. Lamb et al., "A biosocial perspective on paternal behavior and involvement," pp. 111–142.

97. Lamb, "Fathers and child development," pp. 1–18.

4. The Babysitters' Club

1. Jane Goodall, "Mother-offspring relationships in chimpanzees," in D. Morris, ed., *Primate Ethology* (London: Weidenfeld and Nicolson, 1967), pp. 305–307.

2. Sarah Blaffer Hrdy, *Mother Nature* (New York: Pantheon Books, 1999), pp. 90–92.

3. J. C. Mitani and D. Watts, "The evolution of non-maternal caretaking among anthropoid primates: do helpers help?" *Behavioral Ecology and Sociobiology* 40 (1997): 213–220.

4. A. Chamove, Harry Harlow, and Gary Mitchell, "Sex differences in the infant-directed behavior of preadolescent rhesus monkeys," *Child Development* 38 (1967): 329–335.

5. Sarah Blaffer Hrdy, "Care and exploitation of nonhuman primate infants by conspecifics other than the mother," *Advances in the Study of Behavior* 1 (1976): 123–125.

6. Hillard Kaplan, "The evolution of the human life course," in K. Wachter and C. Finch, eds., *Between Zeus and the Salmon: The Biodemography of Longevity* (Washington, DC: National Academy Press, 1997), pp. 175–211.

7. Jane Lancaster, "Play-mothering: the relations between juvenile females and young infants among free-ranging vervet monkeys *(Cercopithecus aethiops)*," *Folia Primatologica* 15 (1971): 161–182.

8. Ibid.

9. Hrdy, *Mother Nature,* pp. 446–449.

10. Hrdy, "Care and exploitation of nonhuman primate infants," pp. 143–148; Hrdy, *Mother Nature,* pp. 446–449.

11. W. D. Hamilton, "The genetical evolution of social behavior," *Journal of Theoretical Biology* 7 (1964): 17–18.

12. Sarah Blaffer Hrdy, *The Langurs of Abu: Female and Male Strategies of Reproduction* (Cambridge: Harvard University Press, 1977), p. 12.

13. Hrdy, *Mother Nature,* p. 271.

14. Ibid., p. 162.

15. Mitani and Watts, "The evolution of non-maternal caretaking among anthropoid primates," pp. 213–220.

16. Ibid.

17. Charles Snowdon and Stephen Suomi, "Paternal behavior in primates," in H. Fitzgerald, J. Mullins, and P. Gages, eds., *Child Nurturance: Studies of Development in New World Primates,* vol. 3 (New York: Plenum Press, 1982), pp. 63–108.

18. W. C. McGrew, "Parental division of infant care taking varies with

family composition in cotton-top tamarins, *Animal Behaviour* 36 (1988): 285–286.

19. Eluned Price, "The costs of infant carrying in captive cotton-top tamarins," *American Journal of Primatology* 26 (1992): 23–33.

20. S. Sanchez, F. Peleaz, C. Gil-Burmann, and W. Kaumanns, "Costs of infant-carrying in cotton-top tamarins *(Saguinus oedipus),*" *American Journal of Primatology* 48 (1999): 99–112.

21. Eluned Price, "Competition to carry infants in captive families of cotton-top tamarins *(Saguinus oedipus),*" *Behaviour* 118 (1991): 66–88.

22. Gilda Morelli and Edward Tronick, "Male care among Efé foragers and Lese farmers," in Barry Hewlett, ed., *Father-Child Relations: Cultural and Biosocial Contexts* (New York: Aldine de Gruyter, 1992), pp. 231–261.

23. Edward Tronick, Gilda Morelli, and S. Winn, "Multiple caretaking of Efe (Pygmy) infants," *American Anthropologist* 89, no. 1 (1987): 96–106.

24. Ibid.

25. Barry Hewlett, "Demography and childcare in preindustrial societies," *Journal of Anthropological Research* 47, no. 1 (1991): 1–38.

26. Ibid.

27. Marc Bekoff, "Mammalian sibling interactions: genes, facilitative environments, and the coefficient of familiarity," in D. J. Gubernick and Peter Klopfer, eds., *Parental Care in Mammals* (New York: Plenum Publishing, 1981), pp. 307–346.

28. D. S. Sade, "Some aspects of parent-offspring and sibling relations in a group of rhesus monkeys, with a discussion of grooming," *American Journal of Physical Anthropology* 23 (1965): 1–18.

29. Carol Berman, "The effects of being orphaned: a detailed case study of an infant rhesus," in Robert Hinde, ed., *Primate Social Relationships: An Integrated Approach* (Oxford: Blackwell, 1983), pp. 79–81.

30. Jane Goodall, *The Chimpanzees of Gombe: Patterns of Behavior* (Cambridge: The Belknap Press of Harvard University Press, 1986), pp. 101–104.

31. J. Partch, "The socializing role of postreproductive rhesus macaque females," paper presented at the 47th annual meeting of the American Association of Physical Anthropologists, Toronto, 1978, cited in Sarah Blaffer Hrdy, "'Nepotists' and 'altruists': the behavior of old females

among macaques and langur monkeys," in P. Amos and S. Harrell, eds., *Other Ways of Growing Old* (Stanford: Stanford University Press, 1981), p. 64.

32. Lynn Fairbanks and M. T. McGuire, "Age, reproductive value, and dominance-related behavior in vervet monkey females: cross-generational influences on social relationships and reproduction," *Animal Behaviour* 34 (1986): 1710–1721.

33. Hrdy, *Mother Nature*, p. 277.

34. George Williams, "Pleiotrophy, natural selection, and the evolution of senescence," *Evolution* 11 (1957): 398–411.

35. Hamilton, "The genetical evolution of social behavior," pp. 17–52; Hrdy, "'Nepotists' and 'altruists': the behavior of old females among macaques and langur monkeys," pp. 59–76.

36. Hrdy, *Mother Nature*, pp. 284–286.

37. Kristen Hawkes, J. F. O'Connell, and Nicholas Blurton-Jones, "Hadza women's time allocation, offspring provisioning, and the evolution of long post-menopausal life spans," *Current Anthropology* 36 (1997): 551–577.

38. U.S. Bureau of the Census, "QT-P18. Marital status by sex, unmarried-partner households, and grandparents as caregivers: 2000," retrieved on 4/4/2005 from http://factfinder.census.gov/servelet/QT Table?_bm=y&.geo_id=D&-qr_nameDEC2000_SF4_U_QTP18&-ds_name=D&-_lang=en.

39. Jeanne Altmann, *Baboon Mothers and Infants* (Cambridge: Harvard University Press, 1980), p. 37; Carol Berman, "Early agonistic experience and rank acquisition among free-ranging infant rhesus monkeys," *International Journal of Primatology* 1 (1980): 153–169.

40. James McKenna, "Parental supplements and surrogates among primates: cross-species and cross cultural comparisons," in Jane Lancaster, Jeanne Altmann, A. S. Rossi, and L. R. Sherrod, eds., *Parenting across the Life Span* (New York: Aldine de Gruyter, 1987), pp. 143–184.

41. Hrdy, "Care and exploitation of nonhuman primate infants," p. 127.

42. Ibid., p. 126.

43. U.S. Bureau of the Census, *Statistical Abstract of the United States* (Washington, DC, 2002), table 571, p. 373.

44. "Indicators," *Time*, April 17, 2000, p. 16.

45. "Quality childcare; what does it look like?" *Arizona Republic,* Sept. 19, 1999, pp. B4–B5.

46. Pierrette Hondagneu-Sotelo, *Doméstica: Immigrant Workers Cleaning and Caring in the Shadows of Affluence* (Berkeley: University of California Press, 2001), pp. 35–38.

47. U.S. Bureau of the Census, 2000, "TABLE 2: Earnings by detailed occupation: 1999," retrieved on 4/4/2005 from http://www.census.gov/hhes/income/earnings/Call2usfemale.html.

48. Office of Inspector General, Department of Health and Human Services, "State's child care certificate systems: an early assessment of vulnerabilities and barriers," Publication OEI-05-97-00320, Feb. 1998, p. 1.

49. John Love, Linda Harrison, Abraham Sagi-Schwartz, Marinus van Ijzendoorn, Christine Ross, Judy Ungerer, Helen Raikes, Christy Brady-Smith, Kimberly Boller, Jeanne Brooks-Gunn, Jill Constantine, Ellen Kisker, Ellen Eliason, Diane Paulsell, and Rachel Chazan-Cohen, "Child care quality matters: how conclusions may vary with context," *Child Development* 74, no. 4 (2003): 1021–1033.

50. Ibid.; NICHD Early Child Care Research Network, "Does amount of time spent in child care predict socioemotional adjustment during the transition to kindergarten?" *Child Development* 74, no. 4 (2003): 976–1005.

51. Jane Lancaster, "Play-mothering: the relations between juvenile females and young infants among free-ranging vervet monkeys *(Cercopithecus aethiops),*" *Folia Primatologica* 15 (1971): 161–182.

5. Weaning Wars

1. Jane Goodall, *In the Shadow of Man* (Boston: Houghton Mifflin, 1971), pp. 101–103.

2. Goodall, *In the Shadow of Man,* p. 235.

3. Robert Trivers, "Parent-offspring conflict," *American Zoologist* 14 (1974): 249–264.

4. Robert Trivers, "Parental investment and sexual selection," in B. Campbell, ed., *Sexual Selection and the Descent of Man, 1871–1971* (Chicago: Aldine, 1972), pp. 136–179.

5. Harry Harlow and Margaret Harlow, "The affectional systems," in

A. M. Schrier, H. F. Harlow, and F. Stollnitz, eds., *Behavior of Non-human Primates*, vol. 2 (New York: Academic Press, 1965), pp. 287–334.

6. Nancy Nicolson, "Infants, mothers, and other females," in B. Smuts, D. Cheney, R. Seyfarth, R. Wrangham, and T. Struhsaker, eds., *Primate Societies* (Chicago: University of Chicago Press, 1987), pp. 330–342; Nancy Nicolson, "Maternal behavior in human and nonhuman primates," in J. D. Loy and C. B. Peters, eds., *Understanding Behavior: What Primate Studies Tell Us about Human Behavior* (New York: Oxford University Press, 1991), pp. 17–50.

7. Nicolson, "Infants, mothers, and other females," pp. 330–342.

8. Karen Strier, *Faces in the Forest* (New York: Oxford University Press, 1992), p. 85.

9. Nicolson, "Infants, mothers, and other females," pp. 330–342; Carol Berman, K. L. R. Rasmussen, and Stephen Suomi, "Responses of free-ranging rhesus monkeys to a natural form of social separation. I. Parallels with mother-infant separation in captivity," *Child Development* 65 (1994): 1038–1041.

10. Jane Goodall, "Mother-offspring relationships in chimpanzees," in D. Morris, ed., *Primate Ethology* (London: Weidenfeld and Nicolson, 1967), p. 313.

11. Frans De Waal, *Good Natured* (Cambridge: Harvard University Press, 1996), p. 187.

12. Barry Hewlett, "Demography and childcare in preindustrial societies," *Journal of Anthropological Research* 47, no. 1 (1991): 1–38.

13. Robert LeVine and Barbara LeVine, "Nyansongo: a Gusii community in Kenya," in Beatrice Whiting, ed., *Six Cultures: Studies of Child Rearing* (New York: John Wiley and Sons, 1963), pp. 149–151.

14. Hewlett, "Demography and childcare in preindustrial societies," pp. 1–38.

15. Beatrice Whiting, ed., *Six Cultures: Studies of Child Rearing* (New York: John Wiley and Sons, 1963), p. 149.

16. Thomas Maretzki and Hatsumi Maretzki, "Taira: an Okinawan village," in Beatrice Whiting, ed., *Six Cultures: Studies of Child Rearing* (New York: John Wiley and Sons, 1963), p. 474.

17. William Nydegger and Corinne Nydegger, "Tarong: an Ilocos barrio in the Philippines," in Beatrice Whiting, ed., *Six Cultures: Studies of*

Child Rearing (New York: John Wiley and Sons, 1963), pp. 828–829; K. Romney and R. Romney, "The Mixtecans of Juxtlahuaca, Mexico," in Beatrice Whiting, ed., *Six Cultures: Studies of Child Rearing* (New York: John Wiley and Sons, 1963), p. 648.

18. M. Shostak, "A !Kung woman's memories of childhood," in R. Lee and I. DeVore, eds., *Kalahari Hunter-Gatherers* (Cambridge: Harvard University Press, 1976), pp. 251–253.

19. Nicolson, "Infants, mothers, and other females," pp. 330–342.

20. Jeanne Altmann, *Baboon Mothers and Infants* (Cambridge: Harvard University Press, 1980), pp. 149–167.

21. Nicolson, "Maternal behavior in human and nonhuman primates," pp. 17–50.

22. R. B. Lee, *The !Kung San* (Cambridge: Cambridge University Press, 1979), pp. 310–312.

23. Meredith Small, *Our Babies, Ourselves* (New York: Anchor Books, 1998), p. 89.

24. Betsy Lozoff and Gary Brittenham, "Infant care: cache or carry," *Behavioral Pediatrics* 95 (1979): 478–483.

25. Birute Galdikas, *Reflections of Eden: My Years with the Orangutans of Borneo* (Boston: Little, Brown, 1995), pp. 117–118.

26. C. B. Clark, "A preliminary report on weaning among chimpanzees of the Gombe National Park, Tanzania," in S. Chavalier, S. Kolnikoff and F. E. Poirier, eds., *Primate Biosocial Development* (New York: Garland, 1977), pp. 235–260.

27. Dian Fossey, *Gorillas in the Mist* (Boston: Houghton Mifflin, 1983), pp. 176–177.

28. Small, *Our Babies, Ourselves*, p. 112.

29. Ibid., p. 113.

30. Jane Goodall, *The Chimpanzees of Gombe: Patterns of Behavior* (Cambridge: The Belknap Press of Harvard University Press, 1986), p. 546.

31. M. W. DeVries and M. R DeVries, "Cultural relativity of toilet training readiness: a perspective from East Africa," *Pediatrics* 60 (1977): 170–179.

32. Ibid.

33. Leigh Minturn and John Hitchcock, "The Rājpūts of Khalapur, India," in Beatrice Whiting, ed., *Six Cultures: Studies of Child Rearing* (New York: John Wiley and Sons, 1963), p. 315.

34. LeVine and LeVine, "Nyansongo: a Gusii community in Kenya," p. 146.

35. DeVries and DeVries, "Cultural relativity of toilet training readiness: a perspective from East Africa," pp. 170–179.

36. S. H. Fraiberg, *The Magic Years* (New York: Scribner's Sons, 1959), p. 91.

37. Nydegger and Nydegger, "Tarong: an Ilocos barrio in the Philippines," pp. 827.

38. Lynn Fairbanks and M. E. Pereira, "Dimensions for future research," in M. E. Pereira and Lynn Fairbanks, eds., *Juvenile Primates: Life History, Development, and Behavior* (New York: Oxford University Press, 1993), pp. 359–366.

39. Carol Berman, personal communication.

40. Goodall, *The Chimpanzees of Gombe,* pp. 129–130.

41. Berman, Rasmussen, and Suomi, "Responses of free-ranging rhesus monkeys to a natural form of social separation," pp. 1038–1041.

42. Karen Strier, *Faces in the Forest,* 2nd ed. (Cambridge: Harvard University Press, 1999), p. 85.

43. Robert Sussman, "Socialization, social structure, and ecology of two sympatric species of *Lemur*," in C. Skolnikoff and F. E. Poirier, eds., *Primate Bio-Social Development: Biological, Social, and Ecological Determinants* (New York: Garland Publishing, 1977), pp. 515–528.

44. J. J. Sacks, J. D. Smith, K. M. Kaplan, D. A. Lambert, R. W. Sattin, and R. K. Sikes, "The epidemiology of injuries in Atlanta daycare centers," *Journal of the American Medical Association* 262 (1989): 1641–1645.

45. Nicholas Blurton-Jones, "The lives of hunter-gatherer children: effects of parental behavior and parental reproductive strategy," in M. E. Pereira and L. A. Fairbanks, eds., *Juvenile Primates: Life History, Development, and Behavior* (New York: Oxford University Press, 1993), pp. 309–326.

46. Carol Berman and E. Kapsalis, "Development of kin bias among rhesus monkeys: maternal transmission or individual learning," *Animal Behaviour* 58 (1999): 883–894.

47. Lynn Fairbanks, personal communication.

48. F. Furstenberg, Jr., J. Eccles, G. Elder, Jr., T. Cook, and A. Sameroff, *Managing to Make It* (Chicago: University of Chicago Press, 1997), p. 25.

49. Carol Berman, "Immature siblings and mother-infant relationships

among free-ranging rhesus monkeys on Cayo Santiago," *Animal Behaviour* 44 (1992): 247–258.

50. Lynn Fairbanks, "Reciprocal benefits of allomothering for female vervet monkeys," *Animal Behaviour* 40 (1990): 553–562.

51. Fossey, *Gorillas in the Mist*, p. 178.

52. Nicolson, "Infants, mothers and other females," pp. 330–342; Nicolson, "Maternal behavior in human and nonhuman primates," pp. 17–50.

53. Judy Dunn and Carol Kendrick, "The arrival of a sibling: changes in patterns of interaction between mother and first-born child," *Journal of Child Psychology and Psychiatry* 21 (1980): 119–132.

54. M. K. Taylor and K. L. Kogan, "Effects of birth of a sibling on mother-child interaction," *Child Psychiatry and Human Development* 4 (1973): 53–58.

55. Goodall, *The Chimpanzees of Gombe*, p. 76.

56. Sarah Blaffer Hrdy, *Mother Nature* (New York: Pantheon Books, 1999), p. 276.

57. Carol Berman, K. L. R. Rasmussen, and Stephen Suomi, "Reproductive consequences of maternal care patterns during estrus among free-ranging rhesus monkeys," *Behavioral Ecology and Sociobiology* 32 (1993): 391–399.

58. Hrdy, *Mother Nature*, pp. 342–343.

59. Ibid., pp. 321–350

60. Sam Clark, Elizabeth Colson, James Lee, and Thayer Scudder, "Ten thousand Tonga: a longitudinal anthropological study from Southern Zambia, 1956–1991," *Population Studies* 49 (1995): 91–109.

61. Lee Cronk, "Parental favoritism toward daughters," *American Scientist* 81 (1993): 272–279.

62. Dorothy Corkville Briggs, *Your Child's Self-Esteem* (Garden City, NY: Doubleday, 1975), p. 129.

63. Harry Harlow and Margaret Harlow, "The affectional systems," in A. M. Schrier, H. F. Harlow, and F. Stollnitz, eds., *Behavior of Nonhuman Primates*, vol. 2 (New York: Academic Press, 1965), pp. 287–334.

64. M. D. S. Ainsworth and S. M. Bell, "Mother-infant interaction and the development of competence," in K. J. Connally and J. S. Bruner, eds., *The Growth of Competence* (New York: Academic Press, 1974),

pp. 97–118; Jerome Kagan and H. A. Moss, *Birth to Maturity: A Study in Psychological Development* (New York: Wiley, 1962), p. 212.

6. The Quiet Years

1. Lynn Fairbanks, personal communication.
2. Charles Janson and Carel van Schaik, "Ecological risk aversion in juvenile primates: slow and steady wins the race," in M. E. Pereira and L. A. Fairbanks, eds., *Juvenile Primates: Life History, Development, and Behavior* (New York: Oxford University Press, 1993), pp. 57–74.
3. C. M. Worthman, "Biocultural interactions in human development," in M. E. Pereira and L. A. Fairbanks, eds., *Juvenile Primates: Life History, Development, and Behavior* (New York: Oxford University Press, 1993), pp. 339–358.
4. M. E. Pereira and Lynn Fairbanks, "What are juvenile primates all about?" in M. E. Pereira and L. A. Fairbanks, eds., *Juvenile Primates: Life History, Development, and Behavior* (New York: Oxford University Press, 1993), pp. 3–12.
5. Ibid.
6. Dorothy Cheney and Robert Seyfarth, *How Monkeys See the World: Inside the Mind of Another Species* (Chicago: University of Chicago Press, 1990), p. 253.
7. Leanne Nash, "Juveniles in nongregarious primates," in M. E. Pereira and Lynn Fairbanks, eds., *Juvenile Primates: Life History, Development, and Behavior* (New York: Oxford University Press, 1993), pp. 119–137.
8. Nicholas Blurton-Jones, "The lives of hunter-gatherer children: effects of parental behavior and parental reproductive strategy," in M. E. Pereira and Lynn Fairbanks, eds., *Juvenile Primates: Life History, Development, and Behavior* (New York: Oxford University Press, 1993), pp. 309–326.
9. Janson and van Schaik, "Ecological risk aversion in juvenile primates," pp. 57–74.
10. Eleanor Maccoby, *Social Development: Psychological Growth and the Parent-Child Relationship* (New York: Harcourt, Brace, Jovanovich, 1980), pp. 212–217; Worthman, "Biocultural interactions in human development," pp. 339–358.

11. Stephen Suomi, "Sibling relationships in nonhuman primates," in M. E. Lamb and B. Sutton-Smith, eds., *Sibling Relationships: Their Nature and Significance across the Lifespan* (Hillsdale, NJ: Lawrence Erlbaum Associates, 1982), pp. 329–356; P. C. Lee, "Sibships: cooperation and competition among immature vervet monkeys," *Primates* 28 (1987): 47–59; A. E. Pusey, "Behavioural changes at adolescence in chimpanzees," *Behaviour* 115 (1990): 203–246.

12. R. Fagen, *Animal Play Behavior* (New York: Oxford University Press, 1981), p. 371.

13. Alice Schlegel and Herbert Barry, *Adolescence: An Anthropological Inquiry* (New York: The Free Press, 1991), p. 45.

14. Marc Bekoff, "Mammalian sibling interactions: genes, facilitative environments, and the coefficient of familiarity," in D. J. Gubernick and Peter H. Klopfer, eds., *Parental Care in Mammals* (New York: Plenum Publishing Corp., 1981), pp. 307–346.

15. Cheney and Seyfarth, *How Monkeys See the World*, p. 76.

16. Lee, "Sibships: cooperation and competition among immature vervet monkeys," pp. 47–59.

17. Frans De Waal, *Good Natured* (Cambridge: Harvard University Press, 1996), pp. 49–50.

18. Lynn Fairbanks, "Juvenile vervet monkeys: establishing relationships and practicing skills for the future," in M. E. Pereira and L. A. Fairbanks, eds., *Juvenile Primates: Life History, Development, and Behavior* (New York: Oxford University Press, 1993), pp. 211–227.

19. L. S. Rajpurohit and Volker Sommer, "Juvenile male emigration from natal one-male troops in Hanuman langers," in M. E. Pereira and L. A. Fairbanks, eds., *Juvenile Primates: Life History, Development, and Behavior* (New York: Oxford University Press, 1993), pp. 86–103.

20. C. M. Crockett and T. R. Pope, "Consequences of sex differences in dispersal for juvenile red howler monkeys," in M. E. Pereira and L. A. Fairbanks, eds., *Juvenile Primates: Life History, Development, and Behavior* (New York: Oxford University Press, 1993), pp. 104–118.

21. Brenda Bryant, "Sibling relationships in middle childhood," in M. E. Lamb and B. Sutton-Smith, eds., *Sibling Relationships: Their Nature and Significance across the Lifespan* (Hillsdale, New Jersey: Lawrence Erlbaum Associates, 1982), pp. 87–121; H. G. Ross and J. J. Milgram,

"Important variables in sibling relationships: a qualitative study," in M. E. Lamb and B. Sutton-Smith, eds., *Sibling Relationships: Their Nature and Significance across the Lifespan* (Hillsdale, New Jersey: Lawrence Erlbaum Associates, 1982), pp. 225–249.

22. Bryant, "Sibling relationships in middle childhood," pp. 87–121.

23. Sarah Blaffer Hrdy, *Mother Nature* (New York: Pantheon Books, 1999), p. 321.

24. Ibid., pp. 318–350.

25. Lynn Fairbanks and M. T. McGuire, "Relationships of vervet mothers with sons and daughters from one to three years of age," *Animal Behavior* 33 (1985): 40–50.

26. Ann Minnett, Deborah Vandell, and John Santrock, "The effects of sibling status on sibling interaction: influence of birth order, age spacing, sex of child, and sex of sibling," *Child Development* 54 (1983): 1064–1072.

27. Lee, "Sibships: cooperation and competition among immature vervet monkeys," pp. 47–59.

28. S. Gouzoules, H. Gouzoules, and P. Marler, "Rhesus monkey (*Macaca mulatta*) screams: representational signaling in the recruitment of agonistic aid," *Animal Behavior* 32 (1984): 182–193.

29. Jane Goodall, *The Chimpanzees of Gombe: Patterns of Behavior* (Cambridge: The Belknap Press of Harvard University Press, 1986), p. 328; A. H. Harcourt and K. J. Stewart, "The influence of help on contests of dominance rank in primates: hints from gorillas," *Animal Behavior* 35 (1987): 182–190.

30. Jeanne Altmann, "Adolescent pregnancies in non-human primates: an ecological and developmental perspective," in Jane Lancaster and Beatrix Hamburg, eds., *School-Age Pregnancy and Parenthood,* (New York: Aldine De Gruyter, 1986), pp. 247–262.

31. D. P. Watts and A. E. Pusey, "Behavior of juvenile and adolescent great apes," in M. E. Pereira and L. A. Fairbanks, eds., *Juvenile Primates: Life History, Development, and Behavior* (New York: Oxford University Press, 1993), pp. 148–167.

32. Ron Taffel, "Discovering our children," *The Family Therapy Networker* 23, no. 5 (1999): 24–35.

33. Ibid.

34. Dian Fossey, *Gorillas in the Mist* (Boston: Houghton Mifflin, 1983), p. 89.

35. Carol Berman, personal communication.

36. J. R. Walters and R. M. Seyfarth, "Conflict and cooperation," in B. Smuts, D. Cheney, R. Seyfarth, R. Wrangham, and T. Struhsaker, eds., *Primate Societies* (Chicago: University of Chicago Press, 1987), pp. 306–317.

37. B. Chapais and C. Gauthier, "Early agonistic experience and onset of matrilineal rank acquisition in Japanese macaques," in M. E. Pereira and L. A. Fairbanks, eds., *Juvenile Primates: Life History, Development, and Behavior* (New York: Oxford University Press, 1993), pp. 245–258.

38. Walters and Seyfarth, "Conflict and cooperation," pp. 306–317.

39. Lynn Fairbanks, "Juvenile vervet monkeys: establishing relationships and practicing skills for the future," pp. 211–227.

40. Jane Goodall, *In the Shadow of Man* (Boston: Houghton Mifflin, 1971), pp. 112–117.

41. Blurton-Jones, "The lives of hunter-gatherer children," pp. 309–326.

42. Ibid.

43. Ibid.

44. Ibid.

45. J. C. Caldwell, "Toward a restatement of demographic transition theory," *Population Development Review* 2 (1976): 321–366.

46. R. Mace, "Evolutionary ecology of human life history," *Animal Behaviour* 59 (2000): 1–10.

7. Emptying the Nest

1. J. J. Arnett, "Emerging adulthood: a theory of development from the late teens through the twenties," *American Psychologist* 55 (2000): 469–480.

2. Alice Schlegel and Herbert Barry, *Adolescence: An Anthropological Inquiry* (New York: The Free Press, 1991), pp. 18–20.

3. J. R. Walters and R. M. Seyfarth, "Conflict and cooperation," in B. Smuts, D. Cheney, R. Seyfarth, R. Wrangham, and T. Struhsaker, eds., *Primate Societies* (Chicago: University of Chicago Press, 1987), pp. 306–317.

4. Schlegel and Barry, *Adolescence: An Anthropological Inquiry*, pp. 33–35.
5. J. M. Tanner, M. E. Wilson, and C. G. Rudman, "Pubertal growth spurt in the female rhesus monkey: relation to menarche and skeletal maturation," *American Journal of Human Biology* 2 (1990): 101–106.
6. Jane Goodall, *In the Shadow of Man* (Boston: Houghton Mifflin, 1971), pp. 83–84.
7. Meredith Small, *Female Choices: Sexual Behavior of Female Primates* (Ithaca: Cornell University Press, 1993), pp. 122–126.
8. Schlegel and Barry, *Adolescence: An Anthropological Inquiry*, p. 13.
9. Ibid., pp. 107–132.
10. Ibid.
11. M. D. Resnick, P. S. Bearman, R. W. Blum, K. E. Bauman, K. M. Harris, J. Jones, J. Tabor, T. Beuhring, R. E. Sieving, M. Shew, M. Ireland, L. H. Bearinger, and J. R. Udry, "Protecting adolescents from harm," *Journal of the American Medical Association* 278 (1997): 823–832.
12. W. J. Demarest, "Incest avoidance among human and nonhuman primates," in S. Chevalier-Skolnikoff and F. E. Poirier, eds., *Primate Bio-Social Development* (New York: Garland Publishing Co. 1977), pp. 323–342.
13. J. Shepher, "Mate selection among second-generation kibbutz adolescents," *Archives of Sexual Research* 1 (1971): 293–307.
14. Jane Goodall, *The Chimpanzees of Gombe: Patterns of Behavior* (Cambridge: The Belknap Press of Harvard University Press, 1986), pp. 466–470.
15. Small, *Female Choices: Sexual Behavior of Female Primates*, pp. 166–172.
16. Ibid.
17. Stephen Suomi, "Sibling relationships in nonhuman primates," in M. E. Lamb and B. Sutton-Smith, eds., *Sibling Relationships: Their Nature and Significance across the Lifespan* (Hillsdale, NJ: Lawrence Erlbaum Associates, 1982), pp. 329–356; Schlegel and Barry, *Adolescence: An Anthropological Inquiry*, pp. 20–25.
18. Suomi, "Sibling relationships in nonhuman primates," pp. 329–356.
19. Schlegel and Barry, *Adolescence: An Anthropological Inquiry*, pp. 20–25, 182–183.
20. D. E. Brown, *Human Universals* (Philadelphia: Temple University Press, 1991), pp. 118–129.

21. Carol Berman, personal communication.

22. Ibid.

23. Schlegel and Barry, *Adolescence: An Anthropological Inquiry*, pp. 193–196.

24. A. C. Petersen, N. Leffert, B. Graham, J. Alwin, and S. Ding, "Promoting mental health during the transition into adolescence," in John Schulenberg, Jennifer Maggs, and Klaus Hurrelmann, eds., *Health Risks and Developmental Transitions during Adolescence* (New York: Cambridge University Press, 1997), pp. 471–497.

25. Goodall, *The Chimpanzees of Gombe*, p. 366.

26. Birute Galdikas, *Reflections of Eden: My Years with the Orangutans of Borneo* (Boston: Little, Brown, 1995), p. 351.

27. Dian Fossey, *Gorillas in the Mist* (Boston: Houghton Mifflin, 1983), pp. 198–200.

28. Schlegel and Barry, *Adolescence: An Anthropological Inquiry*, pp. 65–66.

29. Ibid., p. 45.

30. Ibid., pp. 134–138.

31. Urie Bronfenbrenner, *Two Worlds of Childhood: U.S. and U.S.S.R.* (New York: Simon and Schuster, 1970), p. 102.

32. Jim Moore, "Inbreeding and outbreeding in primates: what's wrong with the dispersing sex?" in N. W. Thornhill, ed., *The Natural History of Inbreeding and Outbreeding* (Chicago: University of Chicago Press, 1993), pp. 392–426; A. E. Pusey and C. Packer, "Dispersal and philopatry," in B. Smuts, D. Cheney, R. Seyfarth, R. Wrangham, and T. Struhsaker, eds., *Primate Societies* (Chicago: University of Chicago Press, 1987), pp. 250–266.

33. Devra Kleiman, "Parent-offspring conflict and sibling competition in a monogamous primate," *American Naturalist* 114 (1979): 753–759.

34. Donna Leighton, "Gibbons: territoriality and monogamy," in B. Smuts, D. Cheney, R. Seyfarth, R. Wrangham, and T. Struhsaker, eds., *Primate Societies* (Chicago: University of Chicago Press, 1987), pp. 135–145.

35. Carolyn Crockett, "Family feuds," *Natural History* August (1984): 28–35.

36. Carolyn Crockett, personal communication.

37. Crockett, "Family feuds," pp. 28–35; Carolyn Crockett and T. R. Pope,

"Consequences of sex differences in dispersal for juvenile red howler monkeys," in B. Smuts, D. Cheney, R. Seyfarth, R. Wrangham, and T. Struhsaker, eds., *Primate Societies* (Chicago: University of Chicago Press, 1987), pp. 104–118.

38. R. Mace, "Evolutionary ecology of human life history," *Animal Behaviour* 59 (2000): 1–10.

39. J. J. Arnett, "Learning to stand alone: the contemporary American transition to adulthood in cultural historical context," *Human Development* 41 (1998): 295–315.

40. Ibid.

41. J. J. Arnett, "Reckless behavior in adolescence: a developmental perspective," *Developmental Review* 12 (1992): 339–373.

42. D. L. Murphy, J. C. Wright, M. S. Buchsbaum, A. Nichols, J. L. Costa, and R. J. Wyatt, "Platelet and plasma amine oxidase activity in 680 normals: sex and age differences and stability over time," *Biochemical Medicine* 16 (1976): 254–265.

43. Arnett, "Reckless behavior in adolescence," pp. 339–373.

44. Ibid.; M. Zelnik and J. P. Kantner, "Sexual activity, contraceptive use, and pregnancy among metropolitan-area teenagers, 1971–1979," *Family Planning Perspectives* 12 (1980): 230; Ceci Connolly, "Survey: teens putting off sex," *Arizona Republic,* Dec. 11, 2004, p. A5.

45. Arnett, "Reckless behavior in adolescence," pp. 339–373.

46. Ibid., p. 349.

47. Resnick et al., "Protecting adolescents from harm," pp. 823–832.

48. Ibid.

8. Parenting with Partners

1. D. E. Brown, *Human Universals* (Philadelphia: Temple University Press, 1991), p. 136.

2. Sarah Blaffer Hrdy, "Heat loss: the absence of estrus reflects a change in sexual strategy," *Science* 83, no. 11 (1983): 73–78.

3. Charles Snowdon and Stephen Suomi, "Paternal behavior in primates," in H. Fitzgerald, J. Mullins, and P. Gages, eds., *Child Nurturance: Studies of Development in New World Primates,* vol. 3 (New York: Plenum Press, 1982), pp. 63–108; Robert LeVine, Suzanne Dixon, Sarah LeVine, Amy Richman, P. H. Leiderman, Constance

Keefer, and T. Berry Brazelton, *Child Care and Culture: Lessons from Africa* (Cambridge: Cambridge University Press, 1994), p. 64.

4. Peggy Stack, "Why do people practice polygamy?" *Salt Lake Tribune*, Sept. 20, 1998, p. A1.

5. Sarah Blaffer Hrdy, *Mother Nature* (New York: Pantheon Books, 1999), p. 32.

6. Sarah Blaffer Hrdy, *The Langurs of Abu: Female and Male Strategies of Reproduction* (Cambridge: Harvard University Press, 1977), p. 165.

7. Ibid., p. 237.

8. J. T. Peterson, *The Ecology of Social Boundaries: Agta Foragers of the Philippines* (Urbana: University of Illinois Press, 1978), p. 16.

9. P. Bion Griffin and Marcus Griffin, "Fathers and childcare among the Cagayan Agta," in Barry Hewlett, ed., *Father-Child Relations: Cultural and Biosocial Contexts* (New York: Aldine de Gruyter, 1992), pp. 297–320.

10. Ibid.

11. M. J. Goodman, A. Estioko-Griffin, P. B. Griffin, and J. S. Grove, "Menarche, pregnancy, birth spacing, and menopause among the Agta women foragers of Cagayan Province, Luzon, the Philippines," *Annals of Human Biology* 12, no. 2 (1985): 169–177.

12. Griffin and Griffin, "Fathers and childcare among the Cagayan Agta," pp. 297–320.

13. Ibid.

14. Ibid.

15. Barry Hewlett, "Demography and childcare in preindustrial societies," *Journal of Anthropological Research*, 47, no. 1 (1991): 1–38.

16. Griffin and Griffin, "Fathers and childcare among the Cagayan Agta," pp. 297–320.

17. Ibid.

18. Dian Fossey, "Infanticide in mountain gorillas (*Gorilla gorilla beringei*) with comparative notes on chimpanzees," in Glenn Hausfater and Sarah Blaffer Hrdy, eds., *Infanticide* (New York: Aldine, 1984), p. 222.

19. LeVine et al., *Child Care and Culture*, p. 109.

20. Ibid., p. 64.

21. Robert LeVine and Barbara LeVine, "Nyansango: a Gusii community

in Kenya," in Beatrice Whiting, ed., *Six Cultures* (New York: John Wiley and Sons, 1963), p. 153.

22. Ibid., p. 138.

23. John Dougherty, "Bound by fear: polygamy in Arizona," *New Times,* March 13–19, 2003, pp. 16–30.

24. Irwin Altmann and Joseph Ginat, *Polygamous Families in Contemporary Society* (Cambridge: Cambridge University Press, 1996), pp. 366–377.

25. Hrdy, *Mother Nature,* p. 251.

26. John Dougherty, "Bound by fear," pp. 16–30.

27. Tom Zoellner, "Polygamy on the dole," *Salt Lake Tribune,* June 28, 1998, p. A1.

28. Maxine Hanks, "Polygamous wives need help to escape," *Salt Lake Tribune,* June 7, 1998., p. AA5.

29. D. M. Taub and P. Mehlman, "Primate paternalistic investment: a cross-species view," in J. D. Loy and C. B. Peters, eds., *Understanding Behavior: What Primate Studies Tell Us about Human Behavior* (New York: Oxford University Press, 1991), pp. 51–89.

30. Eduardo Gallardo, "Divorce is law in Chile at last," *Los Angeles Times,* Nov. 19, 2004, p. A18.

31. Snowdon and Suomi, "Paternal behavior in primates," pp. 63–108; Donna Leighton, "Gibbons: territoriality and monogamy," in B. Smuts, D. Cheney, R. Seyfarth, R. Wrangham, and T. Struhsaker, eds., *Primate Societies* (Chicago: University of Chicago Press, 1987), pp. 135–145.

32. Jeanne Altmann, *Baboon Mothers and Infants* (Cambridge: Harvard University Press, 1980), p. 6.

33. Barbara Risman, *Gender Vertigo: American Families in Transition* (New Haven: Yale University Press, 1998), p. 72.

34. Leighton, "Gibbons: territoriality and monogamy," pp. 135–145.

35. Richard Wrangham, "Evolution of social structure," in B. Smuts, D. Cheney, R. Seyfarth, R. Wrangham, and T. Struhsaker, eds., *Primate Societies* (Chicago: University of Chicago Press, 1987), pp. 282–296; Carel van Schaik and Robin Dunbar, "The evolution of monogamy in large primates: a new hypothesis and some crucial tests," *Behaviour* 115 (1990): 30–59; Ulrich Reichard and Volker Sommer, "Group en-

counters in white-handed gibbons *(Hylobates lar)*: agonism, affiliation, and the concept of infanticide," *Behaviour* 134 (1997): 1135–1174; Carel van Schaik and Peter Kappeler, "Infanticide risk and the evolution of male-female association in primates," *Proceedings of the Royal Society of London* B 264: (1997): 1687–1694; Ryne Palombit, "Infanticide and the evolution of pair bonds in nonhuman primates," *Evolutionary Anthropology* 7 (1999): 117–129; Volker Sommer, "The holy wars about infanticide. Which side are you on? And why?" in Carel van Schaik and Charles Janson, eds., *Infanticide by Males and Its Implications* (Cambridge: Cambridge University Press, 2000), pp. 9–26.

36. Van Schaik and Dunbar, "The evolution of monogamy in large primates," pp. 30–59.

37. L. Leland, T. T. Struhsaker, and T. Butynski, "Infanticide by adult males in three primate species of Kibale Forest, Uganda," in Glenn Hausfater and Sarah Blaffer Hrdy, eds., *Infanticide: Comparative and Evolutionary Perspectives* (New York: Aldine Publishing Co., 1984), pp. 151–172.

38. Van Schaik and Dunbar, "The evolution of monogamy in large primates," pp. 30–59; J. C. Mitani, "Territoriality and monogamy among agile gibbons *(Hylobates agilis)*," *Behavioral Ecology and Sociobiology* 20 (1987): 265–269.

39. Martin Daly and Margo Wilson, "A sociobiological analysis of human infanticide," in G. Hausfater and S. B. Hrdy, eds., *Infanticide* (New York: Aldine de Gruyter, 1984), pp. 487–502; Martin Daly and Margo Wilson, *Homicide* (New York: Aldine De Gruyter, 1988), pp. 45–46; G. P. Murdock and D. R. White, "Standard cross-cultural sample," *Ethnology* 8 (1969): 329–369.

40. Daly and Wilson, *Homicide,* p. 47.

41. Ibid., p. 92, fig. 4.11.

42. Taub and Mehlman, "Primate paternalistic investment," pp. 51–89; Michael Lamb, Joseph Pleck, Eric Charnov, and James Levine, "A biosocial perspective on paternal behavior and involvement," in J. B. Lancaster, J. Altmann, A. S. Rossi, and L. R. Sherrod, eds., *Parenting Across the Life Span* (New York: Aldine de Gruyter, 1987), pp. 111–142; Melvin Konner and Mary Maxwell Katz, "The role of the father in child development: the anthropological perspective," in Michael

Lamb, ed., *The Role of the Father in Child Development*, 2nd. ed. (New York: Wiley, 1981), pp. 155–186.

43. Monique Borgerhoff-Mulder, "The demographic transition—are we any closer to an evolutionary explanation?" *Trends in Ecology and Evolution* 13 (1998): 255–296.

44. Hewlett, "Demography and childcare in preindustrial societies," pp. 1–38.

45. Borgerhoff-Mulder, "The demographic transition," pp. 255–296.

46. Arlie Hochschild, *The Second Shift* (New York: Avon Books, 1989), p. 4.

47. Pepper Schwartz, *Peer Marriage: How Love between Equals Really Works* (New York: Free Press, 1994), pp. 3–6; Barbara Risman, *Gender Vertigo* (New Haven: Yale University Press, 1998), p. 97.

48. Karen Endicott, "Fathering in an egalitarian society," in Barry Hewlett, ed., *Father-Child Relations: Cultural and Biosocial Contexts,* (New York: Aldine de Gruyter, 1992), pp. 281–295.

49. Ibid., p. 285.

50. Snowdon and Suomi, "Paternal behavior in primates," pp. 63–108.

51. Ibid.

52. Anne Goldizen, "Facultative polyandry and the role of infant-carrying in wild saddle-back tamarins *(Saguinus fuscicollis),*" *Behavioral Ecology and Sociobiology* 20 (1987): 99–109.

53. W. C. McGrew, "Parental division of infant care taking varies with family composition in cotton-top tamarins," *Animal Behaviour* 36 (1988): 285–286.

54. Anne Savage, L. H. Giraldo, and Charles Snowdon, "Demography, group composition, and dispersal in wild cotton-top tamarin (*Saguinus oedipus*) groups," *American Journal of Primatology* 38 (1996): 85–100; Lorna Johnson, Andrew Petto, and Prabhat Sehgal, "Factors in the rejection and survival of captive cotton top tamarins *(Saguinus oedipus),*" *American Journal of Primatology* 25 (1991): 91–102.

55. David Popenoe, J. B. Elshtain, and D. B. Blankenhorn, *Promises to Keep: Decline and Renewal of Marriage in America* (Lanham, MD: Bowman and Litchfield, 1996), p. 75; E. Mavis Hetherington, "What matters? What does not?" *American Psychologist* 53, no. 2 (1998): 167–184.

56. C. Bachrach, "Children in families: characteristics of biological, step-, and adopted children," *Journal of Marriage and the Family* 45 (1983): 171–179; E. Mavis Hetherington and Sandra Henderson, "Fathers in stepfamilies," in Michael Lamb, ed., *The Role of the Father in Child Development,* 3rd ed. (New York: Wiley, 1997), pp. 212–226.

57. Hewlett, "Demography and childcare in preindustrial societies," pp. 1–38.

58. Martin Daly and Margo Wilson, "Stepparenthood and the evolved psychology of discriminative parental solicitude," in S. Parmigiani and F. S. von Saal, eds., *Infanticide and Parental Care* (London: Harwood Press, 1994), pp. 121–134.

59. Mark Flinn, "Paternal care in a Caribbean village," in Barry Hewlett, ed., *Father-Child Relations: Cultural and Biosocial Contexts* (New York: Aldine de Gruyter, 1992), pp. 57–84.

60. N. Zill, "Long-term effects of parental divorce on parent-child relationships, adjustment, and achievement in young adulthood," *Journal of Family Psychology* 7 (1993): 91–103; N. Zill, "Behavior, achievement, and health problems among children in stepfamilies," in E. M. Hetherington and J. Arasteh, eds., *Impact of Divorce, Single Parenting, and Stepparenting on Children* (Hillsdale, NJ: Erlbaum, 1988), pp. 325–368; Hetherington and Henderson, "Fathers in stepfamilies," pp. 212–226.

61. G. S. Becker, E. M. Landes, and R. T. Michael, "An economic analysis of marital instability," *Journal of Political Economy* 85 (1977): 1141–1187.

62. Jane Lancaster and Hillard Kaplan, "Parenting other men's children: costs, benefits, and consequences," in Lee Cronk, Napoleon Chagnon, and William Irons, eds., *Adaptation and Human Behavior: An Anthropological Perspective* (New York: Aldine de Gruyter, 2000), pp. 179–202.

63. Stephen Emlen, "The evolutionary study of human family systems," *Social Science Information* 36 (1997): 563–589.

64. L. Duberman, "Demographic consequences of infanticide in man," *Annual Review of Ecology and Systematics* 6 (1975): 107–137; Martin Daly and Margo Wilson, "Abuse and neglect of children in evolutionary perspective," in R. D. Alexander and D. W. Tinkle, eds., *Natural*

Selection and Social Behavior: Recent Research and New Theory (New York: Chiron Press, 1981), pp. 405–416.

65. S. H. Henderson and R. P. Dalton, "Parent-child relationships in sim-ple-step, complex-step, and nondivorced families," paper presented at the biennial meeting of the Society for Research in Child Develop-ment, Indianapolis, April 1995.

66. Hetherington and Henderson, "Fathers in stepfamilies," pp. 212–226.

67. E. Mavis Hetherington, "Coping with family transitions: winners, los-ers, and survivors," *Child Development* 60 (1989): 1–14; Hetherington and Henderson, "Fathers in stepfamilies," pp. 212–226.

68. Lu Yuan and Sam Mitchell, "Land of the Walking Marriage," *Natural History* 11 (2000): 58–64.

69. Hewlett, "Demography and childcare in preindustrial societies," pp. 1–38.

70. Ibid.

71. Hrdy, *Mother Nature*, pp. 266–271.

9. Parenting Solo

1. Karen Strier, *Faces in the Forest*, 2nd ed. (Cambridge: Harvard Univer-sity Press, 1999), pp. xxviii–xxix.

2. D. E. Brown, *Human Universals* (Philadelphia: Temple University Press, 1991), p. 136.

3. Naomi Miller, *Single Parents by Choice: A Growing Trend in Family Life* (New York: Insight Books, 1992), p. 1.

4. Martha De Acosta, "Single mothers in the USA: unsupported workers and mothers," in Simon Duncan and Rosalind Edwards, eds., *Single Mothers in an International Context: Mothers or Workers* (London: UCL Press, 1997), pp. 81–113; Simon Duncan and Rosalind Edwards, "Single mothers in Britain: unsupported workers or mothers?" in Duncan and Edwards, eds., *Single Mothers in an International Con-text*, pp. 45–79; Ito Peng, "Single mothers in Japan: unsupported mothers who work," in Duncan and Edwards, eds., *Single Mothers in an International Context*, pp. 115–147; Marilyn McHugh and Jane Millar, "Single mothers in Australia: supporting mothers to seek work," in Duncan and Edwards, eds., *Single Mothers in an Interna-*

tional Context, pp. 149–178; Nadine Lefaucheur and Claude Martin, "Single mothers in France: supported mothers and workers," in Duncan and Edwards, eds., *Single Mothers in an International Context*, pp. 217–239; Martina Klett-Davies, "Single mothers in Germany: supported mothers who work," in Duncan and Edwards, eds., *Single Mothers in an International Context*, pp. 179–215; Eithne McLaughlin and Paula Rodgers, "Single mothers in the Republic of Ireland: mothers not workers," in Duncan and Edwards, eds., *Single Mothers in an International Context*, pp. 9–43.

5.   E. Mavis Hetherington, "Should we stay together for the sake of the children?" in E. Mavis Hetherington, ed., *Coping with Divorce, Single Parenting, and Remarriage: A Risk and Resiliency Perspective* (Mahwah, NJ: Lawrence Erlbaum Associates, 1999), pp. 93–116.

6.   Duncan and Edwards, "Single mothers in Britain," pp. 45–79; Kris Kissman and JoAnn Allen, *Single Parent Families* (Newbury Park, CA: Sage Publications, 1997), p. 2.

7.   Peng, "Single mothers in Japan, pp. 115–147; U.S. Bureau of the Census, *Statistical Abstract of the United States* (Washington, DC, 2002), table 51, p. 49; Lefaucheur and Martin, "Single mothers in France," pp. 217–239; De Acosta, "Single mothers in the USA," pp. 81–113; McHugh and Millar, "Single mothers in Australia," pp. 149–178; Duncan and Edwards, "Single mothers in Britain," pp. 45–79.

8.   Kissman and Allen, *Single Parent Families*, pp. 41–43.

9.   Klett-Davies, "Single mothers in Germany," pp. 179–215. De Acosta, "Single mothers in the USA," pp. 81–113.

10. Birute Galdikas, "Orangutan diet, range, and activity at Tanjung Puting, Central Borneo," *International Journal of Primatology* 9 (1988): 1–35; Carel van Schaik and Jan van Hooff, "Toward an understanding of the orangutan's social system," in W. C. McGrew, L. F. Marchant, and T. Nishida, eds., *Great Ape Societies* (Cambridge: Cambridge University Press, 1996), pp. 3–15.

11. Birute Galdikas, *Reflections of Eden: My Years with the Orangutans of Borneo* (Boston: Little, Brown, 1995), p. 141.

12. Ibid., p. 240.

13. Ibid.

14. Galdikas, "Orangutan diet, range, and activity," pp. 1–35; van Shaik

and van Hooff, "Toward an understanding of the orangutan's social system," pp. 3–15.

15. Strier, *Faces in the Forest*, 2nd ed.

16. Ibid., pp. 3–5.

17. Karen Strier, *Faces in the Forest*, 1st ed. (New York: Oxford University Press, 1992), pp. 74–81.

18. Strier, *Faces in the Forest*, 2nd ed., p. 73.

19. Ibid.

20. Karen Strier, personal communication, 2000.

21. Strier, *Faces in the Forest*, 2nd ed., p. 85.

22. Amy Parrish, "Sex and food control in the 'uncommon chimpanzee': how bonobo females overcome a phylogenetic legacy of male dominance," *Ethology and Sociobiology* 15 (1994): 157–179.

23. Takayoshi Kano, "Social behavior of wild pygmy chimpanzees *(Pan paniscus)* of Wamba: a preliminary report," *Journal of Human Evolution* 9 (1980): 243–260.

24. Ibid.; Takayoshi Kano, "The bonobos' peaceable kingdom," *Natural History* 99, no. 11 (1990): 62–70.

25. Kano, "Social behavior of wild pygmy chimpanzees," pp. 243–260; T. Furuichi, "Social interactions and the life history of female *Pan paniscus* in Wamba, Zaire," *International Journal of Primatology* 10 (1989): 173–197.

26. Kano, "The bonobos' peaceable kingdom," pp. 62–70.

27. Furuichi, "Social interactions and the life history of female *Pan paniscus* in Wamba, Zaire," pp. 173–197; G. Idani, "Social relationships between immigrant and resident bonobo (*Pan paniscus*) females at Wamba," *Folia Primatologica* 57 (1991): 83–95.

28. Idani, "Social relationships between immigrant and resident bonobo *(Pan paniscus)* females," pp. 83–95.

29. Furuichi, "Social interactions and the life history of female *Pan paniscus* in Wamba, Zaire," pp. 173–197; Idani, "Social relationships between immigrant and resident bonobo *(Pan paniscus)* females," pp. 83–95.

30. Furuichi, "Social interactions and the life history of female *Pan paniscus* in Wamba, Zaire," pp. 173–197; Parrish, "Sex and food control in the 'uncommon chimpanzee,'" pp. 157–179.

31. Richard Wrangham, "Sex differences in chimpanzee dispersion," in D. A. Hamburg and E. R. McCown, eds., *The Great Apes* (Menlo Park, CA: Benjamin/Cumming, 1979), pp. 481–489.

32. Kano, "Social behavior of wild pygmy chimpanzees," pp. 243–260; Kano, "The bonobos' peaceable kingdom," pp. 62–70.

33. Kano, "The bonobos' peaceable kingdom," pp. 62–70.

34. Ibid.

35. Takayoshi Kano, personal communication.

36. Ibid.

37. Furuichi, "Social interactions and the life history of female *Pan paniscus* in Wamba, Zaire," pp. 173–197.

38. Takayoshi Kano, "Male rank order and copulation rate in a unit-group of bonobos at Wamba, Zaire," in W. C. McGrew, L. F. Marchant, and T. Nishida, eds., *Great Ape Societies* (Cambridge: Cambridge University Press, 1996), pp. 135–155.

39. Miller, *Single Parents by Choice,* pp. 21–47.

40. Barry Hewlett, "Demography and childcare in preindustrial societies," *Journal of Anthropological Research,* 47, no. 1 (1991): 1–38.

41. R. B. Lee, *The !Kung San* (Cambridge: Cambridge University Press, 1979), pp. 54–67, 451–439.

42. Kim Hill and Magdalena Hurtado, *Áche Life History: The Ecology and Demography of a Foraging People* (Hawthorne, NY: Aldine de Gruyter, 1996), pp. 434–439.

43. Sara McLanahan, "Father absence and the welfare of children," in E. Mavis Hetherington, ed., *Coping with Divorce, Single Parenting, and Remarriage: A Risk and Resiliency Perspective* (Mahwah, NJ: Lawrence Erlbaum Associates, 1999), pp. 117–147; Sara McLanahan and Julien Teitler, "The consequences of father absence," in M. E. Lamb, ed., *Parenting and Child Development in "Nontraditional" Families* (Mahwah, NJ: Lawrence Erlbaum Associates, 1999), pp. 83–102.

44. E. Mavis Hetherington, Margaret Bridges, and Glendessa Insabella, "What matters? What does not? Five perspectives on the association between marital transitions and children's adjustment," *American Psychologist* 53 (1998): 167–184.

45. McLanahan, "Father absence and the welfare of children," pp. 117–147.

46. H. Z. Reinhertz, R. M. Giaaconia, A. M. C. Hauf, M. S. Wasserman,

and A. B. Silverman, "Major depression in the transition to adulthood: Risks and impairments," *Journal of Abnormal Psychology* 108 (1999): 500–510.

47. Ibid.; A. Bifulco, T. Harris, and G. Brown, "Mourning or early inadequate care? Reexamining the relationship of maternal loss in childhood with adult depression and anxiety," *Developmental Psychopathology* 4 (1992): 433–449.

48. Irwin Sandler, Tim Ayers, Sharlene Wolchik, Jenn-Yun Tein, Oi-Man Kwok, Rachel Haine, Joan Twohey-Jacobs, Jesse Suter, Kirk Lin, Sarah Padgett-Jones, and Janelle Weyer, "The family bereavement program: efficacy evaluation of a theory-based prevention program for parentally bereaved children and adolescents," *Journal of Consulting and Clinical Psychology* 71, no. 3 (2003): 587–600.

49. U.S. Bureau of the Census, *Statistical Abstract of the United States* (Washington, DC, 2002), table 68, p. 60, table 75, p. 64; Rebekah Coley and P. Lindsay Chase-Lansdale, "Adolescent pregnancy and parenthood," *American Psychologist* 53 (1998): 152–156.

50. U.S. Bureau of the Census, *Statistical Abstract of the United States,* table 68, p. 60, table 75, p. 64.

51. E. M. Foster and S. D. Hoffman, "Nonmarital childbearing in the 1980's: assessing the importance of women 25 and older," *Planning Perspectives* 28 (1996): 117–119.

52. Kissman and Allen, *Single Parent Families,* pp. vii, 9–11.

53. Ibid., p. 98.

54. Ibid., pp. 102–104.

55. J. Brooks-Gunn and P. L. Chase-Lansdale, "Adolescent parenthood," in M. H. Bornstein, ed., *Handbook of Parenting,* vol. 3: *Status and Social Conditions of Parenting* (Mahwah, NJ: Erlbaum, 1995), pp. 113–149.

56. F. F. Furstenberg Jr., J. Brooks-Gunn, and S. P. Morgan, *Adolescent Mothers in Later Life* (New York: Cambridge University Press, 1987), pp. 190–219.

57. R. M. Goerge, and B. J. Lee, "Abuse and neglect of the children," in R. A. Maynard, ed., *Kids Having Kids: Economic Costs and Social Consequences of Teen Pregnancy* (Washington, DC: Urban Institute Press, 1997), pp. 205–230.

58. Martha Zaslow, M. Robin Dion, Donna Morrison, Nancy Weinfeld,

John Ogawa, and Patton Tabors, "Protective factors in the development of preschool-age children of young mothers receiving welfare," in E. Mavis Hetherington, ed., *Coping with Divorce, Single Parenting and Remarriage: A Risk and Resiliency Perspective*, (Mahwah, NJ: Lawrence Erlbaum Associates, 1999), pp. 193–223.

59. V. C. McLoyd, "The impact of economic hardship on black families and children: psychological distress, parenting, and socioemotional development," *Child Development* 61 (1990): 311–346; Zaslow et.al., "Protective factors in the development of preschool-age children of young mothers receiving welfare," pp. 193–223.

60. Karen Endicott, "Fathering in an egalitarian society," in Barry Hewlett, ed., *Father-Child Relations: Cultural and Biosocial Contexts* (New York: Aldine de Gruyter, 1992), p. 283.

61. A. Magdalena Hurtado and Kim Hill, "Paternal effect on offspring survivorship among Aché and Hiwi hunter-gatherers: implications for modeling pair-bond stability," in Barry Hewlett, ed., *Father-Child Relations: Cultural and Biosocial Contexts* (New York: Aldine de Gruyter, 1992), pp. 31–55.

62. Hetherington et al., "What matters? What does not?" pp. 167–184.

63. Ibid. Hetherington, "Should we stay together for the sake of the children?" pp. 93–116.

64. E. Mavis Hetherington, "Coping with family transitions: winners, losers, and survivors," *Child Development* 60 (1989): 1–14; Hetherington et al., "What matters? What does not?" pp. 167–184.

65. Hetherington et al., "What matters? What does not?" pp. 167–184; Hetherington, "Should we stay together for the sake of the children?" pp. 93–116.

66. Ibid.

67. Hetherington et al., "What matters? What does not?" pp. 167–184.

68. McLanahan and Teitler, "The consequences of father absence," pp. 83–102.

69. Sanford Braver, Ira M. Ellman, and William Fabricius, "Relocation of children after divorce and children's best interests: new evidence and legal considerations," *Journal of Family Psychology* 17, no. 2 (2003): 206–219.

70. McLanahan, "Father absence and the welfare of children," pp. 117–147.

71. P. R. Amato and B. Keith, "Parental divorce and adult well-being: a meta-analysis," *Journal of Marriage and the Family* 53 (1991): 43–58; P. R. Amato, L. S. Loomis, and A. Booth, "Parental divorce, marital conflict, and offspring well-being during early adulthood," *Social Forces* 73 (1995): 895–915.

72. Hetherington, "Should we stay together for the sake of the children?" pp. 93–116.

73. Hetherington et al., "What matters? What does not?" pp. 167–184; Hetherington, "Should we stay together for the sake of the children?" pp. 93–116.

74. P. R. Amato and A. Booth, *A Generation at Risk: Growing Up in an Era of Family Upheaval* (Cambridge: Harvard University Press, 1997), pp. 218–220; P. R. Amato, "The consequences of divorce for adults and children," *Journal of Marriage and the Family* 62 (2000): 1269–1287.

75. Amato et al., "Parental divorce, marital conflict, and offspring well-being during early adulthood," pp. 895–915.

76. Hetherington et al., "What matters? What does not?" pp. 167–184.

77. Ibid.

78. Ibid.; Hetherington, "Should we stay together for the sake of the children?" pp. 93–116.

79. Hetherington et al., "What matters? What does not?" pp. 167–184; Hetherington, "Should we stay together for the sake of the children?" pp. 93–116.

80. Lillie Weiss and Sharlene Wolchik, "New beginnings: an empirically-based intervention program for divorced mothers to help their children adjust to divorce," in J. M. Briesmeister and C. E. Schaefer, eds., *Handbook of Parent Training: Parents as Co-Therapists for Children's Behavior Problems* (New York: John Wiley & Sons, 1998), pp. 445–478.

81. Geoffrey Greif, *Single Fathers* (Lexington, MA: Lexington Books, 1988), p. 3; U.S. Bureau of the Census, *Statistical Abstract of the United States*, table 51, p. 49.

82. U.S. Bureau of the Census, *Statistical Abstract of the United States,* table 51, p. 49.

83. Greif, *Single Fathers,* pp. 27–49.

84. Amato and Keith, "Parental divorce and adult well-being," pp. 43–58; Hetherington et al., "What matters? What does not?" pp. 167–184.

85. Hetherington et al., "What matters? What does not?" pp. 167–184.

86. E. Thompson, Sara McLanahan, and R. B. Curtin, "Family structure, gender, and parental socialization," *Journal of Marriage and the Family* 54, no. 2 (1992): 368–378; L. D. Hall, A. J. Walter, and A. C. Acock, "Gender and family work in one-parent households," *Journal of Marriage and the Family* 57 (1995): 685–692; Barbara Risman, *Gender Vertigo: American Families in Transition* (New Haven: Yale University Press, 1998), pp. 49–52.

87. U.S. Bureau of the Census, *Statistical Abstract of the United States,* table 654, p. 434.

88. Risman, *Gender Vertigo,* p. 52.

89. Alice S. Rossi, "Parenthood in transition: from lineage to child to self-orientation," in Jane Lancaster, Jeanne Altmann, A. Rossi, and L. Sherrod, eds., *Parenting across the Life Span* (Hawthorne, NY: Aldine, 1987), pp. 54–56; Greif, *Single Fathers,* pp. 1–6; Kissman and Allen, *Single Parent Families,* p. 111.

90. Greif, *Single Fathers,* pp. 53–55; Hetherington et al., "What matters? What does not?" pp. 167–184.

91. Hetherington et al., "What matters? What does not?" pp. 167–184.

92. Greif, *Single Fathers,* pp. 82–85; Hetherington et al., "What matters? What does not?" pp. 167–184.

93. Hetherington et al., "What matters? What does not?" pp. 167–184.

94. V. C. McLoyd, "Socioecomonic disadvantage and child development," *American Psychologist* 53 (1998): 185–204; McLanahan, "Father absence and the welfare of children," pp. 117–147.

95. McLanahan, "Father absence and the welfare of children," pp. 117–147.

96. Ibid.

97. H. B. Biller and J. L. Kimpton, "The father and the school-aged child," in Michael Lamb, ed., *The Role of the Father in Child Development,* 3rd ed. (New York: Wiley, 1997), pp. 143–161; David Popenoe, J. B. Elshtain, and D. B. Blankenhorn, *Promises to Keep: Decline and Renewal of Marriage in America* (Lanham, MD: Bowman and Litchfield, 1996), p. 261.

98. Michael Lamb, "Fathers and child development: An introductory overview," in Michael Lamb, ed., *The Role of the Father in Child Development,* 3rd ed. (New York: Wiley, 1997), pp. 1–18; Louise Silverstein

and Carl Auerbach, "Deconstructing the essential father," *American Psychologist* 54 (1999): 397–407.

10. The Dark Side of Parenting

1. William Mason, "Words, deeds, and motivations: comment on Maestripieri and Carroll," *Psychological Bulletin* 123 (1998): 231–233.
2. National Center for Child Abuse and Neglect, "Child maltreatment 2001: summary of key findings," Washington, DC: *National Clearinghouse on Child Abuse and Neglect Information*, retrieved on Feb. 20, 2004, from www.calib.com/nccanch/.
3. Hendrika Cantwell, "Child Neglect," in C. Henry Kempe and Ray Helfer, eds., *The Battered Child*, 3rd ed. (Chicago: University of Chicago Press, 1980), pp. 183–197; James Weston, "The pathology of child abuse and neglect," in Kempe and Helfer, eds., *The Battered Child*, pp. 241–271.
4. Ruth Kempe, Christy Cutler, and Janet Dean, "The infant with failure to thrive," in C. Henry Kempe and Ray Helfer, eds., *The Battered Child*, 3rd ed. (Chicago: University of Chicago Press, 1980), pp. 147–162.
5. R. L. Burgess and R. D. Conger, "Family interactions in neglectful and normal families," *Child Development* 49 (1978): 1163–1173; M. F. Erickson and B. J. Egeland, "Child neglect," in J. Briere, L. Berliner, J. Bulkley, C. Jenny, and T. Reid, eds., *The APSAC Handbook on Child Maltreatment* (Thousand Oaks, CA: Sage, 1996), pp. 4–20.
6. Sarah Blaffer Hrdy, *Mother Nature* (New York: Pantheon Books, 1999), pp. 288–308.
7. M. Dickemann, "Demographic consequences of infanticide in man," *Annual Review of Ecology and Systematics* 6 (1975): 107–137; Martin Daly and Margo Wilson, "Evolutionary social psychology and family homicide," *Science* 242 (1988): 519–524.
8. Richard Lee, *The !Kung San* (Cambridge: Cambridge University Press, 1979), pp. 317–320, 451.
9. Hrdy, *Mother Nature*, pp. 318–320.
10. Jill Korbin, "Introduction," in Jill Korbin, ed., *Child Abuse and Neglect: Cross Cultural Perspectives* (Berkeley: University of California Press, 1981), pp. 1–12.
11. Orna Johnson, "The socioeconomic context of child abuse and ne-

glect in native South American horticultural communities," in Jill Korbin, ed., *Child Abuse and Neglect: Cross Cultural Perspectives,* (Berkeley: University of California Press, 1981), pp. 56–70.

12.   Jill Korbin, "The cross cultural context of child abuse and neglect," in C. Henry Kempe and Ray Helfer, eds., *The Battered Child,* 3rd ed. (Chicago: University of Chicago Press, 1980), pp. 21–35.

13.   C. H. Kempe, F. N. Silverman, B. F. Steele, W. Droegemueller, and H. K. Silver, "The battered-child syndrome," *Journal of the American Medical Association* 181 (1962): 105–112.

14.   Murray Straus, *Beating the Devil out of Them: Corporal Punishment in American Families* (New York: Lexington Books, 1994), p. 4.

15.   Murray Straus and J. H. Stewart, "Corporal punishment by American parents: national data on prevalence, chronicity, severity, and duration, in relation to child and family characteristics," *Clinical Child and Family Psychology Review,* 2 (1999): 55–70.

16.   S. H. Bitensky, "Spare the rod, embrace our humanity: toward a new legal regime prohibiting corporal punishment of children," *University of Michigan Journal of Law Reform,* 31 (1998): 353–474; EPOCH-USA, "Legal reforms: corporal punishment of children in the family," retrieved on June 30, 2001, from http://www.stophitting.com/legalReform.php.

17.   Elizabeth Gershoff, "Corporal punishment by parents and associated child behaviors and experiences: a meta-analytic and theoretical review," *Psychological Bulletin* 128, no. 4 (2002): 539–579, p. 553.

18.   P. D. Coontz and J. A. Martin, "Understanding violent mothers and fathers: assessing explanations offered by mothers and fathers of their use of control punishment," in G. T. Hotaling, D. Finkelhor, J. T. Kirkpatrick, and M. A. Straus, eds., *Family Abuse and Its Consequences: New Directions in Research* (Newbury Park, CA: Sage, 1988), pp. 77–90; D. G. Gil, *Violence against Children: Physical Abuse in the United States* (Cambridge: Harvard University Press, 1973), pp. 30–31.

19.   National Center for Injury Prevention and Control, "Child maltreatment: fact sheet," retrieved on 4/17/2005 from http://www.cdc.gov/ncipc/factsheets/cmfacts. html.

20.   C. S. Widom and Michael Maxfield, "Motivation and child maltreatment," in D. J. Hanson, ed., *An Update on the "Cycle of Violence"* (Washington, DC: National Institute of Justice Research in Brief, 2000), pp. 1–8.

21. Ibid.

22. V. Felitti, R. Anda, D. Nordenberg, D. Williamson, A. Spitz, and V. Edwards, "Relationship of childhood abuse and household dysfunction to many of the leading causes of death in adults," *American Journal of Preventive Medicine* 14, no. 4 (1998): 245–258.

23. Ibid.

24. Hrdy, *Mother Nature,* pp. 178–179.

25. Gerald Ruppenthal, Gary Arling, Harry Harlow, Gene Sackett, and Stephen Suomi, "A 10-year perspective of motherless-mother monkey behavior," *Journal of Abnormal Psychology* 85 (1976): 341–349.

26. Harry Harlow, Margaret Harlow, R. O. Dodsworth, and Gary Arling, "Maternal behavior of rhesus monkeys deprived of mothering and peer associations in infancy," *Proceedings of the American Philosophical Society* 110 (1966): 58–66; Ruppenthal et al., "A 10-year perspective of motherless-mother monkey behavior," pp. 341–349.

27. Ruppenthal et al., "A 10-year perspective of motherless-mother monkey behavior," pp. 341–349.

28. Harlow et al., "Maternal behavior of rhesus monkeys deprived of mothering and peer associations in infancy," pp. 58–66; Ruppenthal et al., "A 10-year perspective of motherless-mother monkey behavior," pp. 341–349.

29. Stephen Suomi and Christopher Ripp, "A history of motherless monkey mothering at the University of Wisconsin Primate Laboratory," in M. Reite and N. G. Caine, eds., *Child Abuse: The Nonhuman Primate Data* (New York: Alan R. Liss, 1983), pp. 49–78.

30. Ruppenthal et al., "A 10-year perspective of motherless-mother monkey behavior," pp. 341–349; Suomi and Ripp, "A history of motherless monkey mothering," pp. 49–78.

31. Ibid.

32. Suomi and Ripp, "A history of motherless monkey mothering," pp. 49–78; Gary Arling and Harry Harlow, "Effects of social deprivation on maternal behavior," *Journal of Comparative and Physiological Psychology* 64 (1967): 371–377; Gary Mitchell, Gary Arling, and G. W. Moller, "Long-term effects of maternal punishment on the behavior of monkeys," *Psychonomic Science* 8 (1967): 209–210.

33. Mariko Hiraiwa, "Maternal and alloparental care in a troop of free-ranging Japanese monkeys," *Primates* 22 (1981): 309–329.

34. Brandt Steele, "Psychodynamic factors in child abuse," in C. Henry Kempe and Ray Helfer, eds., *The Battered Child*, 3rd ed. (Chicago: University of Chicago Press, 1980), pp. 49–85.

35. Harold Martin, "The consequences of being abused and neglected: how the child fares," in C. Henry Kempe and Ray Helfer, eds., *The Battered Child*, 3rd ed. (Chicago: University of Chicago Press, 1980), pp. 347–365.

36. Steele, "Psychodynamic factors in child abuse," pp. 49–85; Kempe et al., "The battered-child syndrome," pp. 105–112; Brandt Steele and C. Pollock, "A psychiatric study of parents who abuse infants and small children," in C. Henry Kempe and Ray Helfer, eds., *The Battered Child* (Chicago: University of Chicago Press, 1968), pp. 89–133.

37. Ray Helfer, "Developmental deficits which limit interpersonal skills," in C. Henry Kempe and Ray Helfer, eds., *The Battered Child*, 3rd ed. (Chicago: University of Chicago Press, 1980), pp. 36–48.

38. M. G. Morris and R. W. Gould, "Role reversal: a concept in dealing with the neglected/battered child syndrome," in *The Neglected-Battered Child Syndrome* (New York: Child Welfare League of America, 1963), pp. 29–49.

39. Steele, "Psychodynamic factors in child abuse," pp. 49–85.

40. Dario Maestripieri and Kelly Carrol, "Behavioral and environmental correlates of infant abuse in group-living pigtail macaques," *Infant Behavior and Development* 4 (1998): 603–612; Dario Maestripieri, "Parenting styles of abusive mothers in group living macaques," *Animal Behaviour* 55 (1998): 1–11; Dario Maestripieri and Kelly Carroll, "Risk factors for infant abuse and neglect in group-living monkeys," *Psychological Science* 9 (1998): 143–145.

41. Maestripieri, "Parenting styles of abusive mothers in group living macaques," pp. 1–11; Maestripieri and Carroll, "Behavioral and environmental correlates of infant abuse," pp. 603–612.

42. Maestripieri and Carroll, "Behavioral and environmental correlates of infant abuse," pp. 603–612.

43. A. Troisi and F. R. D'Amato, "Ambivalence in monkey mothering: infant abuse combined with maternal possessiveness," *Journal of Nervous and Mental Disease* 172 (1984): 105–108.

44. Ibid.; Lynn Fairbanks, "Individual differences in maternal style," *Advances in the Study of Behavior* 25 (1996): 579–611; Maestripieri,

"Parenting styles of abusive mothers in group living macaques," pp. 1–11; Dario Maestripieri and Kelly Carroll, "Child abuse and neglect: usefulness of the animal data," *Psychological Bulletin* 123 (1998): 211–223.

45. A. Troisi and F. R. D'Amato, "Mechanisms of primate infant abuse: the maternal anxiety hypothesis." in S. Parmigiani and F. vom Saal, eds., *Infanticide and Parental Care* (London: Harwood, 1994), pp. 199–210.

46. Ibid.

47. Maestripieri, "Parenting styles of abusive mothers in group living macaques," pp. 1–11.

48. Maestripieri and Carroll, "Risk factors for infant abuse and neglect in group-living monkeys," pp. 143–145.

49. Ibid.

50. Mastripieri, "Parenting styles of abusive mothers in group living macaques," pp. 1–11; Maestripieri and Carroll, "Child abuse and neglect: usefulness of the animal data," 211–223.

51. Maestripieri, "Parenting styles of abusive mothers in group living macaques," pp. 1–11; Maestripieri and Carroll, "Risk factors for infant abuse and neglect in group-living monkeys," pp. 143–145; Maestripieri and Carroll, "Child abuse and neglect: usefulness of the animal data," 211–223.

52. C. Heim, D. J. Newport, S. Heit, Y. P. Graham, M. Wilcox, R. Bonsall, A. H. Miller, and C. B. Nemeroff, "Pituitary-adrenal and autonomic responses to stress in women after sexual and physical abuse in childhood," *Journal of the American Medical Association* 284 (2000): 592–597.

53. J. Kaufman and E. Zigler, "Do abused children become abusive parents?" *American Journal of Orthopsychiatry* 57 (1987): 186–192; C. S. Widom, "The cycle of violence," *Science* 244 (1989): 160–166.

54. B. Egeland, D. Jacobvitz, and K. Papatola, "Intergenerational continuity of abuse," in R. Gelles and J. Lancaster, eds., *Child Abuse and Neglect: Biosocial Dimensions* (Chicago: Aldine, 1987), pp. 255–276; Jay Belsky, "Etiology of child maltreatment: a developmental-ecological analysis," *Psychological Bulletin* 114 (1993): 413–434.

55. R. Kirchshofer, "Gorillazucht in zoologischen garten und forschungsstationen," *Der Zoologischer Garten* 38 (1970): 73–96.

56. R. D. Nadler, "Child abuse: evidence from nonhuman primates," *Developmental Psychobiology* 13 (1980): 507–512.

57. Terry Maple and Amye Warren-Luebecker, "Pongid parenting," in M. Reite and N. G. Caine, eds., *Child Abuse: The Nonhuman Primate Data* (New York: Alan R. Liss, 1983), pp. 119–137; Nadler, "Child abuse: evidence from nonhuman primates," pp. 507–512; Robert Hinde and Yvette Spencer-Booth, "The effect of social companions on mother-infant relationships in rhesus monkeys," in D. Morris, ed., *Primate Ethology* (London: Weidenfeld and Nicolson, 1967), pp. 267–286.

58. Robin Malinosky-Rummell and David Hansen, "Long term consequences of child abuse and neglect," *Psychological Bulletin* 114 (1993): 68–79.

59. L. H. Pelton, "The role of material factors in child abuse and neglect," in G. B. Melton and F. D. Barry, eds., *Protecting Children from Abuse and Neglect: Foundations for a New Strategy* (New York: Guilford Press, 1994), pp. 131–181.

60. Martin Daly and Margo Wilson, "Evolutionary social psychology and family homicide," pp. 519–524; S. J. Zuravin, "The ecology of child abuse and neglect: review of the literature and presentation of data," *Violence and Victims* 4 (1989): 101–120.

61. Martin Daly and Margo Wilson, "Abuse and neglect of children in evolutionary perspective," in R. D. Alexander and D. W. Tinkle, eds., *Natural Selection and Social Behavior: Recent Research and New Theory* (New York: Chiron Press, 1981), pp. 405–416.

62. L. Rabasca, "Bill promotes collaboration between child welfare and substance-abuse agencies," *Monitor on Psychology* 31 (2000): 11.

63. Rebecca Black and Joseph Mayer, "Parents with special problems: alcohol and opiate addiction," in C. Henry Kempe and Ray Helfer, eds., *The Battered Child,* 3rd ed. (Chicago: University of Chicago Press, 1980), pp. 104–112.

64. J. Erwin, "Primate infant abuse: communication and conflict," in M. Reite and N. G. Caine, eds., *Child Abuse: The Nonhuman Primate Data* (New York: Alan R. Liss, 1983), pp. 79–102.

65. Ibid.

66. N. G. Caine and M. Reite, "Infant abuse in captive pigtailed macaques: relevance to human child abuse," in M. Reite and N. G. Caine, eds., *Child Abuse: The Nonhuman Primate Data* (New York: Alan R.

Liss, 1983), pp. 19–27; Tiffany Field, "Child abuse in monkeys and humans: a comparative perspective," in Reite and Caine, eds., *Child Abuse,* pp. 151–174.

67. James Ritchie and Jane Ritchie, "Child rearing and child abuse: the Polynesian context," in Jill E. Korbin, ed., *Child Abuse and Neglect: Cross Cultural Perspectives* (Berkeley: University of California Press, 1981), pp. 186–204.

68. Ibid.

69. D. M. Fergusson, J. Fleming, and D. P. O"Neill, *Child Abuse in New Zealand* (Wellington: Government Printer, 1972), cited in Ritchie and Ritchie, "Child rearing and child abuse," P. 194.

70. Ritchie and Ritchie, "Child rearing and child abuse," pp. 186–204.

71. Ibid., p. 197.

72. L. L. Langness, "Child abuse and cultural values: the case of New Guinea," in Jill Korbin, ed., *Child Abuse and Neglect: Cross Cultural Perspectives* (Berkeley: University of California Press, 1981), pp. 13–34.

73. Sarah LeVine and Robert LeVine, "Child abuse and neglect in sub-Saharan Africa," in Jill Korbin, ed., *Child Abuse and Neglect: Cross Cultural Perspectives* (Berkeley: University of California Press, 1981), pp. 35–55.

74. Johnson, "The socioeconomic context of child abuse and neglect in native South American horticultural communities," pp. 56–70.

75. Jill Korbin, "Child maltreatment in cross-cultural perspective: vulnerable children and circumstances," in R. Gelles and J. Lancaster, eds., *Child Abuse and Neglect: Biosocial Dimensions* (New York: Aldine, 1987), pp. 31–55; Johnson, "The socioeconomic context of child abuse and neglect in native South American horticultural communities," pp. 56–70; Martin Daly and Margo Wilson, *Homicide* (New York: Aldine De Gruyter, 1988), pp. 43–59; William Friedrich and B. A. Boriskin, "The role of the child in abuse: a review of the literature," *American Journal of Orthopsychiatry* 46, no. 4 (1976): 580–590; Belsky, "Etiology of child maltreatment," pp. 413–434.

76. Korbin, *Child Abuse and Neglect,* pp. 14, 64, 128–129.

77. Langness, "Child abuse and cultural values: the case of New Guinea," pp. 13–34.

78. Korbin, "Child maltreatment in cross-cultural perspective," pp. 31–55.

79. Robert Emery and Lisa Laumann-Billings, "An overview of the na-

ture, causes, and consequences of abusive family relationships," *American Psychologist* 53 (1998): 121–135.

80. Ibid.

81. Division of Children, Youth, and Families, *Child Welfare Reporting Requirements: Arizona Child Protective Services Semi-annual Report* (Phoenix: Arizona Department of Economic Security, 2001, 2002, 2003).

82. N. A. Polansky, J. M. Gaudin, P. W. Ammons, and K. B. Davis, "The psychological etiology of the neglectful mother," *Child Abuse and Neglect* 12 (1985): 265–275.

83. N. A. Polansky, M. A. Chalmers, E. Buttenwieser, and D. P. Williams, *Damaged Parents* (Chicago: University of Chicago Press, 1981), pp. 86–96; M. A. Disbrow, A. Doerr, and C. Caulfield, "Measuring the components of parents' potential for child abuse and neglect," *International Journal of Child Abuse and Neglect* 1 (1977): 279–296.

84. Richard Gelles, "Child abuse as psychopathology: a sociological critique and reformulation," *American Journal of Orthopsychiatry* 43 (1973): 611–621.

85. Field, "Child abuse in monkeys and humans," pp. 151–174.

86. Murray Straus, "Stress and child abuse," in C. Henry Kempe and Ray Helfer, eds., *The Battered Child*, 3rd ed. (Chicago: University of Chicago Press, 1980), pp. 86–103.

87. Martin Daly and Margo Wilson, "Risk of maltreatment of children living with stepparents," in R. Gelles and J. Lancaster, eds., *Child Abuse and Neglect: Biosocial Dimensions* (New York: Aldine, 1987), pp. 215–232.

88. Martin Daly and Margo Wilson, "Child abuse and other risks of not living with both parents," *Ethology and Sociobiology* 6 (1985): 197–210.

89. Daly and Wilson, *Homicide*, pp. 87–88.

90. J. L. Lightcap, J. A. Kurland, and R. L. Burgess, "Child abuse: a test of some predictions derived from evolutionary theory," *Ethology and Sociobiology* 3 (1982): 61–67; Daly and Wilson, "Child abuse and other risks of not living with both parents," pp. 197–210.

91. Martin Daly and Margo Wilson, "Some differential attributes of lethal assaults on small children by stepfathers versus genetic fathers," *Ethology and Sociobiology* 15 (1994): 207–217.

92. Daly and Wilson, *Homicide*, p. 78.

93. Daly and Wilson, "Some differential attributes of lethal assaults on small children by stepfathers versus genetic fathers," pp. 207–217.

94. Daly and Wilson, "Risk of maltreatment of children living with stepparents," pp. 215–232.

95. Robert Trivers, "Parental investment and sexual selection," in B. Campbell, ed., *Sexual Selection and the Descent of Man, 1871–1971* (Chicago: Aldine, 1972), pp. 136–179; Robert Trivers, "Parent-offspring conflict," *American Zoologist* 14 (1974): 249–264.

96. Susan Perry, personal communication.

97. G. Berkson, "Social responses of animals to infants with defects," in M. Levine and L. Rosenblum, eds., *The Effect of the Infant on Its Caregiver* (New York: Wiley, 1974), pp. 233–249.

98. Sarah Blaffer Hrdy, "When the bough breaks," *The Sciences* 24 (1984): 45–50; Maestripieri and Carroll, "Child abuse and neglect: usefulness of the animal data," 211–223.

99. Anne Savage, "The cotton-top tamarin (*Saguinus oedipus*)," in *The AZA SSP Master Plan* (Providence, RI: Roger Williams Park Zoo, 1995), p. 12.

100. Anne Savage, L. H. Giraldo, and Charles Snowdon, "Demography, group composition, and dispersal in wild cotton-top tamarin (*Saguinus oedipus*) groups," *American Journal of Primatology* 38 (1996): 85–100.

101. Kim Bard, "Responsive care: behavioral interventions for nursery reared chimpanzees," in Virginia Landau, ed., *The 1996 Chimpanzoo Conference* (Ridgefield CT: The Jane Goodall Institute, 1996), pp. 3–5.

102. Karen Uhlenhuth, "Mentors help young moms build better lives," *Arizona Republic*, Jan. 25, 2000, p. E3.

103. Ibid.

11. How Much Do Parents Matter?

1. J. B. Watson, *Behaviorism* (New York: Norton, 1924), p. 104.

2. David Rowe, *The Limits of Family Influence* (New York: Guilford Press, 1994), p. 64.

3. Robert Plomin, *Nature and Nurture* (Belmont, CA: Brooks/Cole Publishing Co., 1990), pp. 70-97.

4. M. Schiff, M. Duyme, A. Dumaret, and S. Tomkiewitz, "How much

could we boost scholastic achievement and IQ scores? A direct answer from a French adoption study," *Cognition* 12 (1982): 165–196.

5. P. Tienari, L. C. Wynne, J. Moring, I. Lahti, M. Naarala, A. Sorri, K. E. Wahlberg, O. Saarento, M. Seitma, M. Kaleva, and K. Lasky, "The Finnish adoptive family study of schizophrenia: implications for family research," *British Journal of Psychiatry* 23, suppl. no. 164 (1994): pp. 20–26.

6. M. Bohman, "Predispositions to criminality: Swedish adoption studies in retrospect," in G. R. Bock and J. A. Goode, eds., *Genetics of Criminal and Antisocial Behavior*, vol. 194, Ciba Foundation Symposium (Chichester, Eng.: Wiley, 1996), pp. 99–114.

7. Judith Dunn and Robert Plomin, *Separate Lives: Why Siblings Are So Different* (New York: Basic Books, 1990), p. 85; C. Ernst and J. Angst, *Birth Order: Its Influence on Personality* (Berlin: Springer-Verlag, 1983), pp. 283–284.

8. Ernst and Angst, *Birth Order*, pp. 283–284.

9. Shirley McGuire and Judith Dunn, "Nonshared environment in middle childhood," in John DeFries, Robert Plomin, and David Fulker, eds., *Nature and Nurture during Middle Childhood* (Cambridge, MA: Blackwell, 1994), pp. 201–213.

10. Judith Rich Harris, *The Nurture Assumption* (New York: The Free Press, 1998), pp. 168–217.

11. Ibid., p. xv.

12. Ibid., pp. 146–147.

13. W. Andrew Collins, Eleanor Maccoby, Laurence Steinberg, E. Mavis Hetherington, and Marc Bornstein, "Contemporary research on parenting: the case for nature and nurture," *American Psychologist* 55 (2000): p. 227.

14. Collins et al. "Contemporary research on parenting," pp. 218–232; R. Parke and N. P. Bhavnagri, "Parents as managers of children's peer relationships," in D. Belle, ed., *Children's Social Networks and Social Support* (New York: Wiley, 1989), pp. 241–259.

15. Collins et al., "Contemporary research on parenting," pp. 218–232; N. Mounts and L. Steinberg, "An ecological analysis of peer influence on adolescent grade point average and drug use," *Developmental Psychology* 31 (1995): 915–922.

16. B. DeBaryshe, G. Patterson, and D. Capaldi, "A performance model for academic achievement in early adolescent boys," *Developmen-*

tal Psychology 29 (1993): 795–804; T. Dishion, G. Patterson, M. Stoolmiller, and M. Skinner, "Family, school, and behavioral antecedents to early adolescent involvement with antisocial peers," *Developmental Psychology* 27 (1991): 172–180.

17. Eleanor Maccoby and J. A. Martin, "Socialization in the context of the family: parent-child interaction," in E. Mavis Hetherington, ed., *Handbook of Child Psychology: Socialization, Personality, and Social Development*, vol. 4, 4th ed. (New York: Wiley, 1983), pp. 59–76.

18. Frank Sulloway, *Born to Rebel: Birth Order, Family Dynamics, and Creative Lives* (New York: Pantheon, 1996), pp. 64–65; Harris, *The Nurture Assumption*, p. 45.

19. Beth Azar, "How do parents matter? Let us count the ways," *Monitor on Psychology* 31 (2000): 62–68.

20. Donald Woods Winnicott, "Transitional objects and transitional phenomena," *International Journal of Psychoanalysis* 34 (1953): 89–97.

21. Dorothy Corkville Briggs, *Your Child's Self-Esteem* (Garden City, NY: Doubleday & Co., 1975), pp. 9–45.

22. G. Brody, Z. Stoneman, and M. Burke, "Child temperaments, maternal differential behavior, and sibling relationships," *Developmental Psychology* 23 (1987): 354–362.

23. J. Bates, G. Pettit, and K. Dodge, "Family and child factors in stability and change in children's aggressiveness in elementary school," in J. McCord, ed., *Coercion and Punishment in Long-term Perspectives* (New York: Cambridge University Press, 1995), pp. 124–138.

24. J. Bates, G. Pettit, K. Dodge, and B. Ridge, "Interaction of temperamental resistance to control and restrictive parenting in the development of externalizing behavior," *Developmental Psychology* 34 (1998): 982–995.

Who's Who among Nonhuman Primates

1. Noel Rowe, *The Pictorial Guide to the Living Primates* (East Hampton, NY: Pogonias Press, 1996), p. 52.

2. Ibid., p. 207.

3. Ibid.

4. Jane Goodall, *The Chimpanzees of Gombe: Patterns of Behavior* (Cambridge: The Belknap Press of Harvard University Press, 1986), pp. 503–522.

Acknowledgments

When I was taking a power walk through my neighborhood about 10 years ago, my head suddenly filled with thoughts about human and nonhuman primate parents. I hurried home, eager to get my ideas on paper, so that I could discuss them with my husband, Andrew Smith, Professor of Conservation Biology at Arizona State University. He encouraged me to undertake this project, and as he as done throughout our marriage, provided support, advice, and helpful feedback along the way. He reviewed every chapter, correcting my simplistic notions about the ecology of social behavior. Without his continued encouragement, I might not have completed this project.

Two men read an early version of the manuscript and offered helpful criticism. My neighbor and friend John Alcock, Professor of Life Sciences at Arizona State University, helped me understand the difference between proximate and ultimate factors in evolution. My colleague and friend clinical psychologist Victor Nahmias, reviewed the clinical issues and case histories in the book, giving me useful suggestions about dynamics and interpretation. My friend Rose Weitz, Professor of Sociology and Women's Studies at Arizona State University, read the final manuscript and enlightened me about the many ways society influences parenting.

Other colleagues and friends critiqued parts of the manuscript. James E. King, a primatologist and Professor of Psychology at the University of Arizona, offered feedback about my descriptions of primates and primate behavior. The anthropologist Leanne Nash critiqued the chapters on mothers, toddlers, juveniles, and adolescents. The primatolologists Lynn Fairbanks and Carol Berman, and my friend developmental psychologist Martha

Zaslow, read the chapter on mothers and gave me feedback on my interpretation of their research. The child therapist Lyn Krahulec reviewed the chapter about toddlers. The school psychologist Melissa Denton critiqued Chapter 7 on adolescents. The cultural anthropologist Barry Hewlett reviewed the chapter on parenting partnerships.

My editor at Harvard University Press, Elizabeth Knoll, provided much help and encouragement. She helped me slim down the manuscript to a readable length, and her suggestions concerning the book's organization were very helpful.

I want to thank all of the primatologists who generously responded to my request for interviews: Carol Berman, Carolyn Crockett, Lynn Fairbanks, Takayoshi Kano, Devra Kleiman, and Karen Strier. Carol Berman, Carolyn Crockett, Lynn Fairbanks, Susan Perry, and Karen Strier all reviewed the text pertaining to their research and to the anecdotes they shared with me.

I am especially grateful to my clients, whose stories have helped me to understand the connections between human and nonhuman primate parenting. I also thank my children, Rachel and Justine, not only for what they have taught me about parenting, but for the patience they have had with me over the last 7 years while I wrote this book. And last I acknowledge my cottontops, with whom I lived for almost 30 years, for what they taught me about parenting, and for the pleasure of their company.

Index